WORKING CHEF'S COOKBOOK
FOR NATURAL WHOLE FOODS

WORKING CHEF'S COOKBOOK FOR NATURAL WHOLE FOODS

Jackson F. Blackman

Central Vermont Publishers • Morrisville, Vermont

TO THE READER: This is presented as a modern adaptation of written accounts of ancient Oriental medicine, which has, for thousands of years, provided the guiding principles of acupuncture and other successful therapies. The author and publisher assume no responsibility for improper application or interpretation of the simple ideas expressed here, and this book is not intended as a substitute for consulting your physician.

Published by
Central Vermont Publishers
P.O. Box 700
Morrisville, Vermont 05661

Typeset by
Equinox Publishing Company
R.R.2, Box 1522
Plainfield, Vermont 05667

Printed and bound in the United States of America.

First Printing, First Edition

Library of Congress Catalog Card Number: 88-063694

ISBN 0-9621747-6-9

To my sons, Andy, Brad, and Jack. This is written for them. Hopefully they will move to it, each at his own speed.

This book is for thinking people, without whom it would be of no value.

ACKNOWLEDGMENTS

For their many days of consultation and active interest in the formulation of this work, I must pay tribute to: Blake R. Gould, Director of North Star—Health Care for the Whole Person, a leading authority in nutrition and meal planning for individuals and high-volume institutions—in his twenty years of experience, he has helped thousands of people recover from illness and maintain optimum health and vitality; Chris Quilty, past Executive Chef for the Marriott-Raddison, and presently Chef-Instructor and Assistant Program Director of the New England Culinary Institute and International Food Service Consultant; and Andy Blackman, a chef at a prestigious three-star restaurant in New York. Both Chris and Andy are graduates of the Culinary Institute of America, one of the world's foremost chefs' schools, which has trained more Culinary Olympic Medal winners than any other institution.

To those also, without whose help and inspiration this book would not have been written: Richard and Sharon Bernard; Judy Brown; Christine Chaumeny; Dr. Hakim M. Chishti; Leslie Colket; Goretti Cotovio; Lora Gould; Robin Hopps; Janice Jamail, Director of the Macrobiotic Center of Texas; Edward and Pamela Kentish; Chris Kilham; Elly Lee of Equinox Publishing Company; Amy Mattinat; Mary Naccour; Holly Pedrini; Tim Sestrick; Kym Stevens; Sharon Brown Steimle, whose tenacity for typing and editing was overwhelming; Richard Sultani; Linda Wright; Richard Wright; and all those who answered one question after another.

Institutional Acknowledgments: Center for Science in the Public Interest; The Monroe Institute; National Restaurant Association; National American Produce Association, Ocean Spray Cranberries, Tsuki Publishing House, United Fresh Fruit and Vegetable Association.

TABLE OF CONTENTS

FOREWORD

This book is an effort to fill a long-felt gap for those professional and private persons who are being introduced to the preparation of natural whole food and balanced menus, both for themselves and for others. As society's acceptance of the necessity of eating natural whole foods is slow to come, so is the availability of serious natural whole food cookbooks such as this one.

I myself am an example. I spent the first fifty-five years of my life eating the typical modern American diet, and found myself coming apart, physically, mentally, and emotionally. My mainstay was soft drinks, meat, dairy products, sandwiches, and sweets, all fast and convenient—for I had so many more important things to do than take care of my body and mind. Since I ate out much of the time, I consumed whatever food was available, causing accelerated use and thus the early exhaustion of my organs and general well-being. Fortunately, I discovered natural whole foods and was able to begin repairing the damage.

One of my sons is a successful chef in New York City, and has said to me, "Dad, I can tantalize and titillate their taste buds in a seven-course dinner, but before it's over, they feel bad. After dinner, and the next morning, they'll have a hangover without even the benefit of alcohol, and I don't feel good about that, and certainly wouldn't eat it myself." Diet-related physical and mental deterioration have become a silent and not-so-silent concern to an ever-increasing number of people.

Recent dramatic statements in the media made by the American Heart Association, American Cancer Society, the U.S. Congressional Select Committee on Nutrition, and leading cardiologists have brought tremendous new awareness to the relationship between diet and health. Most newspapers, magazines, and talk shows repeatedly support this change of attitude. Thus, the level of awareness of the value of eating natural whole foods is slowly but surely increasing.

The public's food tastes are changing to include such foods as "French Nouveau"; "California cuisine"; "lite" beer (with little or no alcohol); dairy, bread, meat products, etc., with fewer additives and less processing; and more whole foods. Labels, too, advertise, "No additives, No Preservatives." It may be noted that this new trend emphasizes less fat, animal food, sugar, and salt.

What began twenty years ago as a fad movement has begun to be embraced by many respected and conservative national medical authorities. A full-fledged demand for natural whole foods has emerged as the means to avoid heart disease, cancer, and other serious health problems. Every segment of the public is demanding restaurants, cafeterias, fast food chains, hospitals, and hotels that provide a choice of conscious health selections on the menu.

THE HEIGHT OF STUPIDITY

Recently a friend of mine told me a very personal and moving story. His, mother had just been rushed to an intensive care unit in a regional hospital with a heart attack, after leading what appeared to be a reasonably healthy life. For her first dinner in the hospital she was offered a choice of hamburger, ham steak, or macaroni and cheese! (These items all fall within the categories of food that the

American Heart Association recommends avoiding or reducing, since they are high in cholesterol, in order to reduce the risks of heart attack.[1])

Her son, my friend, immediately went to his mother's doctor and asked him to order a health-promoting diet for his mother, or at least one that was not health-destroying. The doctor, who himself ate natural whole foods and in fact often recommended them to his patients, became embarrassed. He agreed that my friend's mother's diet had not been healthy, but humbly added that if he were to try to correct the quality of the hospital food, "Many people would become very unhappy," and he inferred that damage might be done to his standing in that community.

Patients have the right to not eat what is put in front of them, if they are aware of the danger. But many people aren't aware, and end up eating the food that will help them get another heart attack!

Who would think that a hospital would serve food that is not good for you?

Perhaps, with books such as this, people like my friend and the doctor will soon no longer be in the minority.

I claim no originality for this book, have invented none of it, discovered none of it, but have simply written what has been taught and proven over a period of time. In this book, an attempt has been made to present the material in a manner that is understandable to those who prepare food for the most serious of purposes.

Likening a book such as this to the ocean, which seems to spread forever, it is hoped some will meet the challenge of its deepest depths, while others will venture varying distances from the shore that is shallow enough for children to wade in.

J.F.B.
April, 1989

INTRODUCTION

"By observing myself I know about others and their diseases. By observing external symptoms one gathers knowledge about internal disturbances."
The Yellow Emperor's
Classic of Internal Medicine

The information in this book is presented as a modern, personal adaptation of what I believe are the synthesized philosophies or dietary guidelines of the following:

•The traditional ancient books of Ayurvedic medicine of India (still used to this day);

•The Hippocratic physicians of ancient Greece;

•A translation of *The Yellow Emperor's Classic of Internal Medicine*, referred to as the *Su Wen*, written 2,000–3,000 B.C. (parts of which still dominate the theory of most Chinese doctors today);

•The principles of Macrobiotics;

•The Surgeon General of the United States;

•The American Cancer Society;

•The American Heart Association;

•The U.S. Department of Agriculture;

•The U.S. Senate Select Committee on Nutrition;

•The National Institute of Health;

•Leading cardiologists and physicians of today.

Inasmuch as there is no perfect diet for all people at all times, this book offers a basis of information, both as a reference book and as a story book, and encourages our freedom of choice to develop an understanding of ourselves, our needs, and the needs of others.

We must be free to find our own selves: to discover both our general needs, and what foods we need to eat to keep ourselves healthy. This involves becoming aware of the day-to-day effects of food on the body.

Natural whole foods, when properly prepared and eaten, help protect us from the plague of degenerative diseases and various malaises recently sweeping over the western world, often through its high-tech, highly processed foods.

CONSTITUTION–CONDITION–DISCHARGE

We were born into the world with our personal *constitution*—that is, our personal state of health at birth that has been determined by the health of:

•Parents;

•Grandparents;

•Great-grandparents;

•Previous ancestors.

This we can't do much about.

What we can do something about is our *condition*, which is a person's recent or present state of health, rather than his or her inherited state of health.

Discharge includes all physical and psychological conditions and behavior that can be seen as a discharge of energy or matter from the body. The quality of the discharge depends on the quality of the physical nourishment.

Examples of unhealthy discharge are: obesity and pimples; excess mucus; kidney stones and gallstones; tumors; hardening of the arteries; negative feelings and thoughts; anti-social acts.

Examples of healthy discharge are: pink tongue and clean breath; clear, lustrous skin; strong, flexible body movement; normal elimination; joy, enthusiasm, creativity, and courage; socially constructive acts.

We do have the choice. We can improve our condition and the state of our discharge, primarily by our selection of:

• the food we eat;

•the quality of that food;

•the manner and style in which it is cooked.

Other overlooked factors are the need to eat slowly and chew well, allowing for maximum assimilation of nutrients throughout the body; and the need to eat at a time when there is no stress.

When hard-to-digest food is put into the stomach, much less combined with liquids that dilute digestive juices, or iced liquids that retard digestion—or eaten with animal products, which increase the rate of putrefaction in the stomach—trouble begins. There is an overburdening of the stomach, liver, kidneys, and intestines, and the quality of food that is then absorbed into the blood stream and distributed over the whole body leaves its stamp of decay on growing cells and body tissues. Healthy cells can ward off unhealthy influences, as long as they are healthy—but if, over a period of time, they are continually exposed to harmful or noxious residue, then weakness will overcome them. The cells and tissues then tend to become rotten, because of the food and chemicals they absorb. These weakened cells can become the breeding ground for degenerative diseases such as AIDS, arthritis, or infectious diseases like the common cold and systemic yeast infections.

Human beings, unlike their cells, do have the right of intelligent selection of what they eat in order to establish healthy maintenance and growth of the bodies, physically, mentally, morally, and emotionally. With so much unhealthy (but unfortunately tempting) food available, for some people, a concerted effort must be made to discriminatingly select what is good for them and reject what is not good for them. The act of selecting the food you eat for a specific purpose other than entertaining the taste buds is a relatively new thought to many.

Again and again, all over the world, from archaeological studies and written history since the beginning of man, we have been confronted with the fact that generation after generation of strong, whole-grain–eating people heavily contribute to making strong families and societies, countries, and nations. As people turn to meat, refined sugar, white flour, and processed foods, the decline (in future generations) always occurs. You are what you eat—as a person, a family, a society, and a country.

If you are of the twentieth century, live in the "First World," (as opposed to the Third World), and come from what is known as the Western Civilization, overwhelming evidence shows that you have a greater opportunity and chance for developing any one of a number of degenerative diseases. The conventional American diet that you have been eating since you were a baby probably assures that you are, at this very moment, destroying—among other things—your arteries.

Often, people vibrating with health, who have no reason to see a doctor and probably think that their diet is adequate, or even healthy—are, unbeknownst to them, actually in the early, silent, hidden stages of disease.

Over a million Americans die each year from heart disease and stroke (more than seventeen times the number who died in Vietnam over a ten-year period).

"When Peter Sellers died at fifty-four, the hospital spokesman said he died of, 'natural causes.' But there is nothing 'natural' about dying of heart disease at fifty-four. Heart muscle and blood vessels are meant to last longer than that. Heart disease is treacherous, and most often kills without warning. Fifty-four percent of deaths from heart failure come this way. Every year 400,000 people die without knowing what hit them. No warning twinges of angina give them a chance to take any steps against heart disease. Paul Lynde, famous for his quick wit on 'Hollywood Squares,' didn't show up for a party. He was found dead of a heart attack at home. Congressman William Steiger of Wisconsin was felled in the same way. But, though sudden heart attack is common enough, it is no more 'natural' than death by gunshot or car accident."[1]

The attitude of many is, "Meat and potatoes followed by a good cup of hot coffee is man's food, and no one can tell me any differently. Look at me—I'm healthy." Degenerative diseases or conditions today, such as arteriosclerosis, arthritis, cancer, diabetes, gout, hypertension, heart disease, poor memory, cataracts, glaucoma, cirrhosis of the liver, senility, psychotic, violent, and antisocial behavior, etc., can result in large part from the steady ingestion of toxic and poisonous foods. Today, more than one of every two adults suffers from some form of degenerative disease, to the list of which can be added hearing loss, tooth decay, poor eyesight, and obesity.

Thus a diet of meat, refined and chemically treated white flour and sugar, eggs, refined salt, deep-fried foods, alcohol, coffee, chemicalized cigarettes, artificial colorings and flavorings, not to mention recreational drugs, is a very dangerous way to live. It's no wonder so many Americans who lead extremely active lives one day suddenly drop, or are confronted with the brute reality of their personal killer disease, which they have been developing and fine-tuning for years.

If this describes you or your customers, this book in general will help you, and specifically, the "Daily Use" section of the *Food Effects Chart* on page 23.

It is only common sense (which isn't very common) that natural whole foods cause natural behavior and condition in the body; unnatural food causes unnatural behavior and condition in the body.

RESEARCH SHOWS AMERICAN DIET KILLS

The National Cancer Institute, in a long-term study with the U.S. Department of Agriculture, found that, of those studied, on a typical day:

• Less than half ate garden vegetables other than potatoes or a salad;

• All were eating less than $1/3$ of the required fiber;

• More than 75% were not eating fruits and vegetables;

• More than 40% were eating meat that had been cured with salt and nitrites, or had been smoked or pickled;

• More than 80% were not eating whole grains of any sort.

The study said that this diet is estimated to contribute to about 35% of all cancer deaths.[2]

The National Restaurant Association's extensive study entitled "Consumer Attitude and Behavior Study" (September 1986) stated that, "Americans are increasingly concerned about their health and nutrition, along with a marked increase in the consumption of 'healthy' foods. Over half claim that they are on a diet or have been on one in the last year."

They have also found the public divided: 47% weight- and health-conscious consumers, 38% traditional consumers, 4% uncommitted. 65 to 68% are restricting salt, sugar, and foods with high cholesterol and fat, and 50% are restricting additives. In addition, 67% of consumers are including high fiber, whole grains, rice, and pasta in their diets, and 68% are including calcium.[3]

Despite many good intentions, it is a fact that both the management and the staff of most commercial kitchens are not knowledgeable about, nor trained in, natural and whole food cooking. Too often, the results of their attempts at "natural cooking" are disappointing and unpalatable.

WORKING CHEF'S COOKBOOK FOR NATURAL WHOLE FOODS offers a complete and authoritative guide for the professional and non-professional chef to add to his or her skills a background on whole and natural foods cooking, as well as over 365 delicious, tested recipes for the commercial or home kitchen. They include whole grain breads, entrees and main dishes, sauces, and desserts . . . a complete cuisine.

Over 45,000,000 meals are served daily in non-residential kitchens in the United States, featuring primarily processed, frozen, canned, or precooked food, usually with an array of artificial additives and pesticides that add up to over five pounds per consumer annually.

In the following pages, we draw on the best of ethnic cooking from the world over by using natural and regional flavors. This gives an endless choice of dishes that have been made for thousands of years without benefit of modern dietary techniques and knowledge. While some of the recipes in this book include "transitional" foods (such as chicken and fish, as well as vegetables from the nightshade family), none of them contains dairy products, eggs, refined sugar, or processed grains.

The primary reason for using natural whole foods is to achieve and maintain health and well-being with foods that taste good. Although the recipes in this book are meant to be appetizing to all the senses, it is not our intention to include the preparation of foods that appeal only to taste or have only entertainment value.

This book is meant ultimately to prepare the cook or chef for the development of instinct and intuition in the preparation of natural whole food.

This process supports the natural maintenance and growth of healthy body cells and tissues of the consumer.

"The best illustration is the case of man being his own physician, for nature is like that—physician and patient at once."
Aristotle

PART I.
Information, Philosophy, Technique

1. HEALTHY AND UNHEALTHY FOODS

DEFINITIONS

For the purpose of this book, these foods are defined as follows:

Natural Foods. Those foods that have not been processed or subjected to synthetic chemical additives or preservatives during or after being harvested are *natural foods*. Foods are often treated with artificial coloring or preservatives to overcome shipping conditions, to preserve them for extended periods of time in refrigerated warehouses, and to give them a longer shelf life in the store; though they may originally have been healthy, they are not considered natural foods.

Organic Foods. *Organic foods* are those crops that are grown naturally, without any chemical fertilizers or toxic additives or pesticides used in the soil or on the plants during or after growing. Natural additives, such as humus, natural compost, manure, stone dust, etc., may be added to improve the soil.

Whole Foods. Those unprocessed foods that are whole and still contain the life force that is lost during processing, such as brown rice, barley, beans, nuts, seeds, fresh fruit, and vegetables, are *whole foods*. Whole foods may include some minimally processed foods, such as grains, of which only the outer hull or shell has been removed when ground, for example, into whole wheat flour.

Processed Foods. Food that has been bottled, canned, condensed, ground, flaked, frozen, homogenized, pasteurized, irradiated, juiced, shredded, texturized, etc., constitutes *processed food*. Processing, by and large, diminishes the natural life force and nutritional value. (Skilled natural foods cooking, however, enhances these life-giving qualities.)

Various groups have their own definitions of these terms for their own reasons and/or convenience. Since there may be only a limited number of choices available in the marketplace, one must make the best choices that one can.

> *"Most illnesses arise solely from long continued errors of diet and regimen."*
> Avicenna

MALFUNCTION OF ORGANS

Most leading scientists and naturalists, including Albert Einstein and Charles Darwin, agree: Man's composition, internal and external, is designed for eating fruits, grains, and other high-fiber, high-carbohydrate vegetables.

The human body is a natural thing, and is not made for the continuous consumption of unnatural products. The natural state of the body is to be healthy. The effects of the food we eat (good and bad) accumulate over a period of time, and heavily influence what we are. When we continually bombard our bodies with unnatural substances and refined products, we become sick, the aging process of our vital organs accelerates, existing cells become weak and decay, and the new cells grow in an unhealthy manner.

Weak cells make weak organs. Eating refined sugar overstimulates and weakens the pancreas, perhaps causing hypoglycemia, and maybe eventually diabetes. Eating eggs and cheese surrounds the ovaries and womb with fatty sludge, causing cysts and perhaps tumors.

It has been said that after age twenty-six, the body begins to age and slowly die. Inasmuch as we spend most of our responsible lives beyond that age, it may be in our best interest to preserve what we have for as long as possible. As we age:

• Lean tissue (muscle) begins to turn to fat;

• Flexibility of the spine and joints decreases;

• The physical body slows in its ability to bend and adapt to everyday actions;

• Stomach and intestinal muscles and digestive juices slow, and we are unable to eat all the foods we used to eat;

• Food moves more slowly through the digestive tract, and distension of the stomach develops and constipation occurs;

• Blood flows more slowly;

• The nutritional value of foods we eat is absorbed into the body at a slower rate, and the body gets less food value for the food consumed;

• Animal fat tends to build up around the organs and clogs the body.

TODAY'S DIET

Foods that have been refined to produce a long shelf life, as well as treated with an endless set of chemical additives and preservatives, are directly related to cell decay and degenerative disease. Human beings, when consuming unnatural foods, subject themselves to accelerated physical and mental decay. Our modern-day, fast-track, over-stimulated, instant-gratification lifestyles are reflected in the food most available to us. The continuous consumption of minimally nutritious processed foods leaves the body with less than nothing after it has expended the energy to digest the food.

Osteoporosis

Over a number of decades, several studies have been made about third-world women who have many children, and who breast-feed them year after year. Without benefit of large amounts of meat and dairy products, these women have a relatively low intake of, and a high output of, calcium—yet osteoporosis is virtually unheard of in these areas. These studies seem to show that the osteoporosis so prevalent in primarily affluent, progressive societies may be caused not by calcium deficiency, as is so often claimed, but by the consumption of rich foods (for example, too much protein, coffee, sugar, alcohol, fruit juice, etc.) that ultimately cause the deficiency.

> The Environmental Defense Fund studied the breast milk of 1,400 women in 46 states. The study found widespread contamination of breast milk with pesticides. The levels of contamination were twice as high in meat and dairy consuming women as in vegetarians. Because pesticides are concentrated in animal foods, the study advised, "Women who expect to breastfeed their babies to avoid meat, some kinds of fish, and high-fat dairy products."
> The McDougall Plan, John A. McDougall, M.D.[1]

Animal Foods

In the last few decades, animal foods (meat, eggs, and dairy products) have become the mainstay of most meals—but, in the long run, they are an inefficient energy source. Animal foods, as mentioned, require extended exertion of the organs to process the food for energy. Vegetable foods require much less work to obtain the same amount of energy.

An excess of animal products—the over-consumption of eggs, for example—can also contribute to stroke and heart attack by lining the blood vessels with cholesterol plaque.

Animal foods quickly create an unclean and sluggish intestinal condition and, if consumed at all, should be eaten in small servings, only once or twice a week. Animal foods lack cellulose fiber, which is found only in vegetable foods, and is essential for the health of the intestines, the major organ that allows our bodies to manufacture the fuel and cause the regeneration by which we live.

To convert animal protein into energy, the body must break down a complex molecule containing nitrogen and other elements, as opposed to the simple, clean-burning carbohydrates of vegetable foods.

Nitrogen and other excess components of animal protein must be excreted in large amounts through the kidneys, contributing to the overtaxing and decay of the other vital organs, and thus to other parts of the body. The continual bombardment of the kidneys with excessive wastes from animal metabolism leaves a residue in the blood system that can have toxic effects throughout the body.

But there is another choice the consumer can make—and that is to select food based on its capability of producing more energy than is required to digest it: natural whole food.

Although a natural whole food diet is not necessarily limited to grains, beans, and vegetables, care should be taken when preparing and eating animal products as part of this diet. If animal products are consumed, they should be totally organic, which precludes the use of most of what is found in the market today.

Many people choose to be vegetarians for health reasons, and others for moral, social, or spiritual reasons. Whatever the reason, all dietary needs of the vegetarian can be met by making a careful study of the principles of natural whole food diet.

ANTINUTRIENT, NONNUTRIENT, AND POISONOUS FOODS

Food starvation and its effects are obvious. Nutrient starvation, caused by the consumption of antinutrients, is not quite as obvious, but is far more insidious. Nutrient-deprived organs will eventually malfunction. The deprivation can result from a number of different causes, three of which are:

•Antinutrient food consumption;

•Nonnutrient food consumption;

•Poisonous food consumption.

Antinutrient foods are those that accelerate the leaching out of essential vitamins, minerals, and enzymes that are existing in the body at the time of consumption. For example, the excessive protein intake from eating large portions of meat or chicken, common in the average American diet, draws calcium out of the bones,

helping to cause osteoporosis.

Nonnutrient foods are those that have been processed to such a state that there are minimal or no nutrients left in them, as contrasted to their natural state. Examples in this category include highly refined white sugar, flour, and rice, all of which lack their natural proportions of minerals, vitamins, and other nutritional elements.

Poisonous foods come in three categories:

•Those that do not cause or help the body's cells to regenerate in a healthy manner, or that kill the body's cells, such as those foods in the Nightshade family;

•Those containing artificial colorings, flavorings, life-extenders, pesticides, etc.;

•Those animal foods that have been so treated with antibiotics that antibiotic-resistant bacteria, such as salmonella, begin to thrive.

"Illness comes through the mouth."
Ancient Oriental Saying

DIET-INDUCED CRIME

A simplistic view makes the analogy of the human body as a car. A car needs gas, oil, grease, and a number of other fluids to function. If one is neglected or omitted, something will fail or cause parts to need replacement. Using low-quality fuels and fluids, and not maintaining the car's engine, will make it so that it cannot perform well, either short- or long-term. This treatment will reduce the designed performance and the car's lifetime.

The human body is very similar, in that it also needs fuel for energy. Bad fuel—food—translates into low performance and short lifespan. Good fuel—food—produces maximum performance and long natural life.

There is no doubt that the extreme foods under "Avoid" on the *Food Effects Chart* (see pg. 23)—such as animal foods, sugars, stimulants, and chemical-laced foods—tend to cause imbalance in the body. This imbalance affects the brain and the actions it causes, which become more pronounced in the extreme.

The treatment with controlled diet changes of patients in mental institutions and inmates in penal institutions has had marked success throughout history. As Dr. Hakim Chishti wrote in the *Book of Sufi Healing*, criminal behavior results from the failure to exercise proper control over the appetites of the body.

"As the common diet moves further away from the soil, so too society becomes more dislocated and diffused."
Socrates

In the last few decades many formalized studies about food-induced emotional reactions (FIER) have been done, and programs have been successfully established in penal institutions. The following has been found:

•The mother's health during pregnancy contributes to whether or not the unborn child will have antisocial behavior patterns.

•Food-created, biochemical-based internal stress is a factor in the etiology of crime.

•Marginal nutrition, blood sugar imbalance, and severe hypoglycemic conditions are believed by some scientists to be associated with aggressive and anti-social behavior.

•Sociopaths, who had displayed consistently antisocial behavior, had high levels of elements such as calcium, cadmium, lead, and iron, and low levels of copper, zinc, lithium, and cobalt.

•Prescribed dietary changes with nutritional supplements have much the same effect on health as doctor-prescribed medicine.

•Preliminary results show that 80% of those who have undergone treatment programs report long-term improvement.

•Studies of 6,000 inmates in sugar-reduction programs in ten juvenile correctional centers across the United States have found decreased incidences of as-saults, fights, suicide attempts, and insubordination.

•One common denominator is the significant imbalance in brain chemistry of those who do commit crimes and those who do not.

•Of 129 delinquents in custody, only 13, when tested, had blood sugar levels within the normal limits.

•Marital and domestic (wife and child beating) violence, as well as accidental aggression (car and hunting accidents), have been linked to diet and low blood sugar levels.

•Some objections to these tests and programs have been raised by the American Medical Association and lobbyists for the sugar industry.

"Man is the first species of living being, in our biosphere that has acquired the power to wreck the biosphere and in it wrecking himself."
Anonymous

PESTICIDES

The recent North American "cheap food" mentality has sacrificed quality for low cost and quantity. Farmers are forced by competition, in part from corporate agriculture and lower-cost imports, to use methods that create maximum production without regard for possible health risks or damage to the environment.

Today, conventionally processed food usually involves methods that:

•Degrade soil structure with the use of highly soluble fertilizers, thereby causing erosion, and reducing nutritional values in and/or adding artificial characteristics to the farm product;

•Depend on toxic materials to control weeds, pests, and diseases, causing environmental contamination and health hazards.

•Use enormous amounts of petroleum resources and require huge farm debt loads;

•Artificially enhance the appearance,

color, texture, and flavor as well as help the food withstand long storage times and transportation conditions;

• Employ fertilizers containing nitrite, a known carcinogen.

Of the 35,000 different pest control materials now available, many are known to have adverse long-term effects, such as cancer, birth defects, Alzheimer's disease, and various other degenerative diseases.

Despite the fourfold increase in pesticide use in twenty years, annual crop pest losses have actually increased. Natural enemies are wiped out and pests quickly become immune, requiring more toxic products to control them.

Local feed stores are sometimes adamant about not selling grains and soybeans for human consumption, because they have been treated with so many toxic or unhealthy chemicals. These products are meant only for animals—but one way or the other they end up being consumed by people.

> A new environmental controversy is brewing over pesticides. According to a draft report by the National Academy of Sciences, many grains, vegetables and fruits in the American diet absorb residues from pesticides that, over time, may cause cancer or neurological damage, especially in children. The report will criticize the Environmental Protection Agency for lax regulation. The E.P.A., hampered by budget cuts and a backlog of hundreds of pesticide chemicals to evaluate, is an easy target. Congress will likely boost the E.P.A. budget and direct the Agency to streamline its procedures. But the real test will come when lawmakers have to face the problem of who will pay for replacing many of the toxic pesticides with nontoxic pest controls.
>
> *U.S. News and World Report*
> April, 1987

Flies In The Egyptian Desert

One time, at the end of the day as the sun was going down and a hush came over the village in the shadow of the pyramids of Giza, I sat with a Bedouin friend as his wife and six children gathered in a circle on the floor. The dinner was a grand ar-

ray of dishes prepared by his wife, and hordes of flies also gathered for the feast that smelled so good. My host, Fadlallah, noticing my body-language objection to the flies, jumped up and began profusely and continuously spraying the whole banquet with a can of bug repellent, missing nothing. In utter shock and surprise, I committed one more social *faux pas* by loudly announcing he should stop immediately. My host, becoming much abashed, said, "It's okay, it's poison to kill the flies; that is what they do in all the better meat stores [in lieu of refrigeration]." I explained that if it was a poison for flies, it was also a poison for people. It made sense to him and he stopped using the spray. He said, "I never thought of that"—as, indeed, such connections have not been intuitively obvious in some of our culture either.

Once again, there *is* an alternative, although still at this point in the minority: the principle of organic agriculture, used successfully by some farms, is that a healthy plant grows from healthy soil completely free of chemical pesticides, and is more resistant to pests and diseases.

> *"Man is made to be free; because, once thrown into the world, he is responsible for everything he does."*
> Jean-Paul Sartre

COMMON ADDITIVES

The "advanced" techniques of infiltrating our food supply with thousands of standard manufacturing components, most with no food value, are used routinely.

Here is a list of some common foods and composite, generic lists of the additives that are included on most of their packaging labels:

Baking Powder: Calcium aluminum phosphate, sodium aluminum phosphate.

Bread, White: Wheat flour, corn syrup, partially hydrogenated animal and vegetable shortening (partially hydrogenated soybean, cottonseed, lard, beef fat), yeast. Contains 2% or less of each of the following: salt, dough conditioners (azodicarbonamide, potassium bromate, monocalcium phosphate, calcium sulfate, aluminum sulfate, polysorbate 60, potassium iodate), whey, soy flour, calcium propinate (a preservative), corn starch, mono and diglycerides, nonfat dry milk, buttermilk, malted barley flour, niacin, reduced iron, thiamine mononitrate, riboflavin.

NOTE: The American baking industry uses 16 million pounds of chemicals annually.

Butter Spread: Vegetable mono and diglycerides, potassium sorbate, calcium disodium, EDTA (a preservative), carotene (coloring).

Cereal, Breakfast—"high nutrition" brand: Corn flour, sugar, oat flour, salt, rice flour, coconut oil, brown sugar, sodium ascorbate (a Vitamin C source), vitamin E acetate, reduced iron, niacinamide (one of the B Vitamins), Yellow 5, margarine [partially hydrogenated soybean oil, liquid soybean oil, cottonseed oil, cultured skim milk and skim milk, mono and diglycerides, lecithin, sodium benzoate (a preservative), artificial flavor, BETA carotene, vitamin A palmitate], Yellow 6, pyridoxine hydrochloride, riboflavin, thiamine mononitrate, vitamin A palmitate, folic acid, vitamin D ,and vitamin B-12.

Cereal, Breakfast–children's "sweetened" brand: Rice, sugar, hydrogenated coconut and/or palm kernel oil, cocoa, corn syrup, salt, caramel coloring and artificial flavoring (vitamins and minerals added).

Ice Cream, Vanilla: Milkfat and nonfat milk, corn sweetener, whey, sugar, stabilizer (contains lecithin, guar gum, mono and diglycerides, polysorbate 80, and carrageenan), natural and artificial flavor, artificial color (contains FD&C Yellow #5).

Instant Mashed Potatoes: Dehydrated potatoes, partially hydrogenated vegetable oil (may contain one or more of the following oils: coconut, cottonseed, palm, palm kernel, safflower, soybean oil), corn syrup solids, salt, potassium casemate, mono and diglycerides, sugar, dipotassium phosphate, malto dextrin-distilled propylene, glycol, monostearate, sodium silicoaluminate, carrageenan sodium acid pyrophosphate, natural flavor, artificial flavor, sodium bisulfite, artificial color, citric acid and BHA to preserve quality.

Half and Half: Sodium citrate (as a stabilizer), sugar, disodium phosphate.

Chocolate Milk: Sugar, whey, corn syrup solids, cocoa processed with alkalai, partially hydrogenated vegetable oil, nonfat dry milk, salt, sodium casseinate, cellulose gum, dipotassium phosphate, mono and diglycerides, artificial flavor.

Citrus Punch: Water, sugar, corn syrup, concentrated orange, tangerine and lime juice, citric acid, starch, cottonseed oil, algin, sodium citrate, ascorbic acid, natural flavor, calcium phosphate, Yellow #5, carotene, vitamin B-1, sorbic acid as a preservative, color added.

Coffee Creamer, Non-dairy: Corn syrup solids, partially hydrogenated coconut oil and/or soybean oil, sodium casseinate, dipotassium phosphate, mono and diglycerides, sodium silicoaluminate, artificial flavor and color.

Coffee and Decaffeinated Coffee, Instant: Methylene chloride.

Macaroni and Cheese: Enriched macaroni, cheese sauce mix, whey, dehydrated cheese (granular cheddar, milk, cheese culture, salt, enzymes), whey protein concentrate, skim milk, buttermilk, sodium tripolyphosphate, sodium phosphate, citric acid, Yellow 5 (color), artificial color, lactic acid.

Margarine: Liquid corn oil, partially hydrogenaed corn oil, water, salt, whey, vegetable mono and diglycerides and Lecithin (emulsifiers), sodium benzoate (0.1%) as a preservative, artificially flavored and colored (carotene), vitamin A palmitate and vitamin D-2 added.

Peanut Butter: Roasted peanuts with sugar, hardened vegetable oil (to prevent separation), salt, molasses, mono and diglycerides (to improve creaminess).

Potato Chips: BHT (butylated hydroxanisole), high-cholesterol oil, and salt.

Processed Cheese: Skim milk, cheese, water, American cheese, Swiss cheese, sodium citrate, cream, whey, salt, enzyme-modified cheese, citric acid, grau gum, sorbic acid (preservative), beta carotene (color in colored cheese), acetic acid.

Processed Meats: Salt, sugar, dextrose, corn syrup solids, sodium erythorbate, sodium nitrate, sodium nitrite, sodium phosphate, modified food starch, MSG, caramel coloring, nonfat dry milk, hydrolyzed vegetable protein and flavor, cereal, citric acid and propyl callate.

Produce, Fresh: Chemical dyes are used on some fruits and vegetables. Pesticides are applied before and after harvesting. Fungicides and fumigants are used after harvesting, such as thiabendazole (used as a medicine for worming sheep), prothophenylphenyl, diphenyl, and other bacteria-sprouting inhibitors.Waxing (an embalming process that cannot be washed off with equipment or materials found in most kitchens), is commonly used to extend the shelf life of, and for cosmetic improvement of, apples, avocados, bell peppers, cantaloupes, cucumbers, eggplant, grapefruit, lemons, limes, pineapples, pumpkins, rutabagas, squash, sweet potatoes, tomatoes, and turnips. Six FDA-approved waxes for eighteen fruits and vegetables contain shellac. Also used are polyethylene, and materials found in car, floor, and furniture wax. Fungicides are often mixed in with the waxes. Some fruits and vegetables, harvested before they are ripe, and before shipping and holding, are gassed with ethylene to produce a ripe-looking color and texture. Other innovations include the development of carrots without points, so they won't puncture plastic bags, and bruise-resistant vegetables.

Salt, Table: Sodium silico aluminate, yellow prussate of soda, potassium iodide, sodium bicarbonate, dextrose (sugar derivative).

Snack Crackers: Whole wheat flour, enriched flour, lard, partially hydrogenated soy bean oil, hydrogenated cottonseed oil, sugar, salt, high fructose corn syrup, malted barley flour, oleoresins (vegetable colors), annato extract (vegetable colors), TBHQ and citric acid, acid pyrophosphate, monocalcium phosphate.

Soft Drinks: Phosphoric acid, Yellow #6, quinine, saccharine, heptyl paraben, BVO (bromated vegetable oil), caffeine, phosphates, sodium benzoate.

Tea, Iced: Citric acid (provides tartness), instant tea, maltodextrin, sodium saccharine, natural lemon flavor.

Whipping Cream: Cream, mono and diglycerides, sodium alginate and polysorbate 80 added.

"Tell me what you eat and I will tell you what you are."
Brillat-Savarin

EGGS

Egg yolks contain one of the highest concentrations of cholesterol of all foods, as well as high amounts of fat and protein. Most large egg-producers increase egg production in an artificially controlled environment with similar additives as mentioned under Meat (see below).

Furthermore, raw or undercooked eggs—even sanitized, solid Grade A eggs—may contain the salmonella bacteria that has been found throughout the country and elsewhere.

"I fancy it must be the quality of animal food eaten by the English which renders their character insusceptible of civilization. I suspect it is in their kitchens and not in their churches that their reformation must be worked."
Thomas Jefferson
Letter to Mrs. John (Abigail) Adams
September 25, 1785

MEAT

Long ago, in medieval times, the regular diet of most of our ancestors was grains, beans, vegetables, and fruit, and on certain days, for seasonal or political reasons, a "carnival" was proclaimed. The Latin derivative for "carnival" means *you may eat meat*, and thus, according to our modern American diet, every day is a "carnival" day.

Additives, Preservatives, Pesticides

Most meat found in the marketplace today contains a high degree of toxic materials such as:

• Pesticides—the highest percentage is from feed that is used by the agro-industry to increase crop yield per acre;

• Steroids, hormones, stimulants, tranquilizers, and antibiotics, etc., given directly to the animal.

Processed meats, such as hot dogs, salami, liverwurst, bologna, sausage, knockwurst, and kielbasa, often contain, in addition to the above, chemicals needed for coloring and flavor enhancing, and spoilage retardants; they also contain a higher amount of saturated fat than unprocessed meats do.

Antibiotics, used to control microorganisms that interfere with animal growth, are commonly used to compensate for dirty, crowded, and heavily contaminated feedlots in meat, egg, and milk production. The continuous use of antibiotics increases the prevalence of antibiotic-resistant bacteria and microorganisms, thus requiring the use of more and stronger antibiotics. *Arsenic* is widely used as a growth stimulant by hog farmers and poultry producers. *DES* (diethylstilbestrol), a synthetic hormone given to livestock as a growth stimulant, has a direct relationship to human cancer. *Sodium Nitrate and Sodium Nitrite*, according to retired FDA Commissioner Dr. Carl C. Edwards, can be poisonous to small children, can deform features of developing fetuses, are harmful to aging persons, and also are known to cause cancer.

Most chemicals and additives are cumulatively collected during the lifetime of the animal. The maximum concentration is present when it is slaughtered. These chemicals cannot be washed or cooked out of the meat and are unknowingly and cumulatively ingested and spread throughout the body of the consumer.

"While we ourselves are the living graves of murdered animals, how can we expect any ideal conditions on the earth?"
Leo Tolstoy

Human Digestion

Not only is the human body not designed for effective handling of these additives, it is not designed for the digestion of meat. Meat-eating animals have sharp claws and long, sharp teeth or beaks designed for handling, ripping, or killing their prey. The human has only saliva containing amylase, for the sole purpose of digesting complex carbohydrates found in plant food.

Meat-eating animals have short intestines for their size, which allows for the quick elimination of putrefying bacteria from decomposing flesh. The human intestine is some twenty feet long at maturity, allowing for the slower, easier, and more complete digestion of plant food. When meat is eaten and enters this long tract, fermentation begins, resulting in putrefaction as it continues through the digestive system. During this slow process, some of the meat's rotted residue will enter the blood stream, tissues, cells, and brain.

Dr. Irving Fisher of Yale University made extensive tests of athletes, faculty, and staff, and clearly found that non-meat eaters had nearly twice the stamina of meat eaters.

Many sports world records have been set by vegetarians. Murray Rose, a three-time Olympic gold medal winner, eats no meat. A vegetarian British swimmer set a world record for swimming the English Channel. A. Anderson of Austria has set world records in weight lifting. Johnny Weissmuller, the swimmer, set over fifty-five world records, and ate no meat.

"Truly man is king of beasts, for his brutality exceeds them. We live by the death of others. We are the burial place. I have, since an early age, abjured the use of meat and the time will come when men will look upon the murder of animals as they now look upon the murder of men."
Leonardo da Vinci

DAIRY PRODUCTS

"Because dairy products and meat have so many similarities in their micronutrient content, dairy foods can be thought of as 'liquid meat.'" (*The McDougall Plan*, John A. McDougall, M.D.)

Human milk is designed to meet the needs of human infants. Cow's milk is designed to meet the needs of young cows. Humans, for some reason or other, are the only mammals to consume milk after weaning. In the initial stages of life, for humans and many animals, natural milk drinking is advantageous because of its high content of fat, protein, and cholesterol (containing no fiber). Their young, growing bodies need and accept this type of food because their digestion hasn't yet developed to accept or assimilate fiber. The mature digestive systems of both cows and humans are designed to handle fiber.

Like meat, milk is a rich food, far richer than the body is designed to readily digest or assimilate, and tends to cause various symptoms such as lactose intolerance, diarrhea, gas, stomach cramps, as well as low blood calcium levels caused by phosphate levels in cow's milk. Other effects are asthma, skin rashes, acne, constipation, intestinal obstruction, stomach distension, runny nose, irritability, headache, excessive mucus, etc.

The use of chemical additives is now generally accepted for a number of dairy products. These products also contain chemicals given directly to the cows to promote increased milk production, and the lifetime accumulation of pesticides, etc., used to accelerate feed production. The consumption of dairy products can speed up the human aging process by overtaxing the organs, and exposes the consumer to chemicals that cannot be removed by pasteurization.

With the consumption rate of ice cream at 700,000,000 gallons annually (an estimated $2.8 billion in 1987), the average American consumes 32 pints a year. In addition to emulsifiers, expanders, sugar, oil, and body agents, ice cream may also include:

• Ethyl acetate, used to give a pineapple flavor (and also used as a cleaner of textiles and leather goods). Its highly toxic vapors have been known to cause cirrhosis of the liver, and lung and heart damage.

• Diethylene glycol, used as an egg substitute and emulsifier (and in antifreeze and paint removers).

• Benzyl acetate, used for strawberry flavor (and as a nitrate solvent).

• Butyraldehyde, used as a nut flavoring (and in making rubber cement).

Even the natural ice cream, which contains none of these additives, is damaging to health because of the sugar, cold temperature, excess protein, and fat.

NOTE: Ice-temperature foods or liquids consumed with meals and put into a warm (98.6° F) stomach have a weakening effect on the digestive functions. Thus, serving iced drinks with the meal, or adding iced desserts to an already full stomach, inhibits normal digestion.

"Things sweet to taste prove in digestion, sour."
Shakespeare

SUGAR

Sugar, sometimes known as a narcotic, is produced by a multi-level chemical processing of the juice of sugar cane or beets, removing all fiber, protein, minerals and other nutrients, except sucrose.

Because sugar is a rapidly burning fuel, it can create a low blood sugar condition that results in a depressed physical and emotional state after a brief rush of energy. Sugar temporarily stimulates most of the digestive organs, tends to inflame the liver, and alters the balance of brain chemicals. It therefore brings accelerated fatigue and rapid aging of the vital organs, and often ends up as fatty deposits in the liver, heart, or blood vessels. Another effect can be the onset of depression, physical discomfort, and anxiety. Regular consumption of sugar is also known to deplete the body's calcium, B vitamins, and other minerals.

A 12-ounce can of Pepsi has ten teaspoons of sugar dissolved in artificially flavored seltzer water. In fact, soda is the largest single source of sugar in the American diet. We get ten times more sugar from a can of soda than from a candy bar.[2] Per capita consumption of soft drinks in the United States is 40 gallons annually.

A compulsive eater, when anxious or depressed, usually turns to pies, cakes, cookies, and candy, using the sugar as an "upper" or a "downer." Sweets at bedtime have often been used for aiding in getting to sleep. Few people can write their own prescription for Desipramine or Valium, but they can get sugar. Many people, when feeling nervous and upset, just take a candy bar or other form of sugar, which, though it may help psychologically in the short run, is in the long run actually causing the organs live in the fast lane.

The state of our health today may be imagined in observing that 126 pounds of refined or processed sugar was consumed per capita in the United States in 1976, as contrasted with 40 pounds in 1840.

Artificial sweeteners (saccharin, aspartame, etc.) have their own set of disadvantages. Some sweeteners are carcinogenic, others have been reported to have immediate physical side effects such as dizziness.

There are healthier alternatives available. Rice syrup and barley malt, both sugars, are absorbed into the body's system far more slowly, causing a lower rate of what is termed the energy rush and the resulting overstimulation of the organs.

Types of sugar commonly used:
- Brown sugar
- Corn syrup
- Corn syrup solids
- Dextrose
- High-fructose corn syrup
- Fructose
- Glucose
- Honey
- Lactose
- Maltodextrines
- Maple syrup
- Molasses
- Refined white sugar
- Sorghum
- Sucrose
- Turbinado (raw) sugar

Common types of artificial sweeteners:
- Acesulfame K (Sunette), 200 times sweeter than sugar
- Sorbitol
- Mannitol
- Saccharin
- Aspartame (Equal™, Nutrasweet™)

"He that eat till he is sick must fast till he is well."
English Proverb

UNHEALTHY NATURAL FOODS

Pure, natural whole foods are not necessarily synonymous with healthy foods. Unlike animals, as man has become civilized, he has lost some of his discretionary instincts in selecting the food he eats. Even some natural foods should not be eaten continuously, and others minimally

or not at all, such as:

- Spinach, swiss chard, and beet greens—these are high in oxalic acid, interfere with the calcium metabolism, and can contribute to the formation of kidney stones, gallstones, and calcium deposits;

- Avocado, coconut, and Brazil and cashew nuts—these have a high oil content;

- Cottonseed and palm oil—these are high in polyunsaturated fats;

- White rice and most white flours;

- Refined sugars (sucrose, fructose);

- Fruit juices and tropical fruits, consumed in excess, as in the standard American diet;

- Drugs, often of vegetable origin, used indiscriminately;

- Alcohol, in excess;

- Commercial chemicalized herb teas;

- Eggplant, tomatoes, peppers, potatoes. These are of the nightshade family (see below).

The sophisticated human being has lost his inborn instincts and intuitive judgmental powers to select healthy food. Wild animals, on the other hand, seem to manage quite well.

"None for me. I appreciate the potato only as a protection against famine."
Brillat-Savarin

The Nightshade Family

The nightshade family includes eggplant, tomatoes, potatoes, peppers of all kinds (except black and white peppercorns), belladonna, mandrake, henbane, and tobacco. Their active ingredients are concentrated alkaloids and, like meat, they are richly endowed with nitrogen. Rather than being cell and tissue builders, they have traditionally been known to be stimulants, hallucinogens, medicines, and poisons. Alkaloids may also affect the calcium balance, drawing calcium out of the body and facilitating osteoporosis. Among the better-known alkaloids are caffeine, opium, morphine, heroin, nicotine, belladonna, and theobromine (found in chocolate).

The nightshade family of plants has been used for many centuries. The Borgias, the notorious ruling family of 15th and 16th century Italy, used them successfully as poisons for hundreds of years, to kill their enemies in a discreet fashion.

The "deadly nightshade" plants cause reduced body secretions, decreased digestive function, increased heart rate, and are supportive of arthritis, bursitis, lower back pain, and gout. Over-consumption of alkaloids can cause high blood pressure, restlessness, confusion, and hallucinations. Death can result from respiratory failure in extreme cases.

Common examples of nightshade food combining are:

- Fish and chips;
- Meat and potatoes;
- Pizza with cheese and tomato sauce;
- Meat with ketchup.

These combinations, while "balanced," are not health supporting, especially when consumed regularly. They are found on the extreme ends of the *Food Effects Chart* (see pg. 23), and can contribute to the physical and mental imbalances detailed there.

"There is no safe level of radiation exposure."
Dr. Karl Z. Morgan
Director of Health Physics Dept.
Oak Ridge National Laboratory (for 29 years)

RADIATION: MICROWAVED AND IRRADIATED FOODS, AND NUCLEAR CONTAMINATION

Microwaves

It is generally accepted that high-frequency radiation, such as in X-rays, can cause fatal illness, cancer, and genetic damage causing birth defects. When these rays penetrate human tissue, they can tear apart cells and turn atoms into charged particles called ions, and thus this process is known as ionizing radiation.

Most scientists agree that ionizing radiation has a cumulative effect, no matter how small the dose. Furthermore, it is recognized that non-ionizing radiation, produced by microwave ovens, has the same harmful cumulative effect to the human body of the oven operator.

The interim nature of acceptable microwave-radiation-level standards is fraught with uncertainties, and seems unlikely to be resolved soon.

A recent article in the *New England Journal of Medicine*,[3] points out the dangers of microwave ovens:

> "MICROWAVE OVENS: AN UNEXPECTED DANGER
> Leaking microwave ovens, it's been discovered, can heat the aluminized plastic adhesive strip of a transdermal nitroglycerine patch enough to burn the patient wearing it. In one case, a patient sitting near the oven began to experience warmth in the patch area. Before he could pull off the patch, he sustained a second-degree burn. The oven was subsequently found to have a microwave leak."

Reasons for not using microwave ovens:

- Microwave ovens have been in widespread use for about twelve years and as they age, malfunction—with subsequent inadvertent microwave exposure—has the increasing potential of being a serious problem.

- Pulsating sensations from excessive amounts of microwave energy, felt when standing near an oven, may be noticed when:

    —the oven is first turned on;

    —during its operation;

    —as it is turned off and the door is opened.

- Cataracts and testicular damage are known and proven microwave health risks.

- Animal studies of exposure to low-level microwave energy show:

—changes in the immune system function;

—altered behavior;

—changes in the permeability of the brain to molecules carried in the blood;

—damage to chromosomes;

—development of cancer.

•If it has these effects on animals, imagine what it does to the natural nutrient value the body needs when it is used to reheat food, much less cook it.

•Microwave oven—injury presents a new type of heat injury unlike any other burn. It selectively heats tissue with a high water and fat content, doing little apparent damage to the skin, as would occur in a second-degree burn.

"For a man seldom thinks with more earnestness of anything than he does his dinner."
Samuel Johnson

Irradiation

A relatively recent form of preserving food is with radiation. Irradiation processing consists of exposing the food for one to two minutes with doses of 100,000 to 3,000,000 times that of a chest X-ray, which kills the bacteria.

In 1984, Margaret Heckler, Secretary of Health and Human Services, declared that irradiated foods are "not completely safe."

The National Institute of Nutrition in India selected fifteen children suffering from severe protein/calorie malnutrition and fed them a diet of irradiated food. Before the scheduled completion of the study, multiple chromosomes and other blood abnormalities were found in their blood samples, and the study was called to a halt. A gradual reversal of the blood condition was noted with the withdrawal of the irradiated food. [4]

Food irradiation effects are as follows:

•Vitamins A, B-1, B-2, B-6, C, E, and K are depleted or destroyed. The amino acids tryptophan, crysteine, phenylalanine, and methionine are broken down.

•Food may become contaminated after irradiation, without any warning smell.

•New chemicals have been found in the food, known as Unique Radiolytic Products (URPS), that have never been tested.

•Chemicals are usually added to counteract the undesirable changes in texture, color, odor and flavor created by the irradiation process.

In 1979, Dr. Josef Barna of the Hungarian Academy of Sciences published a review of 1,223 food irradiation studies done between 1925 and 1979. He found 1,414 negative effects of irradiation, including: higher death rate among test animals, lower fertility rates, slower growth, and gene mutation. Dr. Barna found only 185 positive effects.

According to a study done by Soviet scientists, A. E. Ivanov and A. I. Levina, studies on the effects of eating irradiated foods have shown many negative side effects, including a decrease in the number of offspring of experimental animals, and disturbances in metabolism. The authors also reported the results of their own test with 120 male rats, each fed one of three levels of irradiated food. They found that a significant number of rats, especially those fed food with higher levels of radiation, developed abnormalities of the testes.

". . . indicated that the use of fetal X-rays—at the time in wide use throughout the industrialized world and the U S . in particular—was significantly affecting childhood mortality rates. In other words, [Dr. Alice Stewart, Epidemiologist at Oxford University, 1956] was telling physicians that they were killing their patients. While the medical community reacted with horror and denial, much of Stewart's findings were eventually incorporated into medical practice, although she was never given credit for the reforms."
Greenpeace Magazine

Nuclear Contamination

In 1986, a grave nuclear accident occurred at Chernobyl in the Soviet Union, which released unprecedented amounts of radioactive elements into our atmosphere. While we cannot attempt to address in this book the technology or political ramifications of nuclear fusion and fission, we can discuss the health effects of nuclear radiation apart from these other issues.

Manmade nuclear byproducts are not the only culprit: naturally occurring elements in the earth, such as strontium, cesium, and iodine, become radioactive, dangerous, and life-threatening.

We are exposed daily to radiation of many kinds and sources, in our air, food and water, in addition to that caused by Chernobyl and other nuclear accidents and tests. *We are receiving a cumulative amount, be it in small doses over a long period of time, or in short-term massive doses. This exposure increases our chances of developing a series of degenerative diseases, often taking years to reveal themselves.*

Dr. Robert Gibson, of the National Cancer Institute, said that an adult male has from 3–6 times the chances of developing leukemia if he receives 41 diagnostic X-rays to any part of his body.

According to the *McNeil-Lehrer Report*, April 29, 1986, strontium, cesium, and iodine isotopes were the principal forms of radiation we would receive from Chernobyl, and we are exposed to these naturally occurring isotopes in smaller amounts daily.

According to scientists at McGill University, sodium alginate will reduce from 50-80% of strontium (Sr-90) absorbed into bone tissue. Sodium alginate is a natural substance found in sea vegetables, especially kelp and agar-agar. Sodium alginate is also found in sunflower seeds and under the skins of apples. Pectin helps eliminate effects of several forms of radiation, including Sr-90.

The Atomic Energy Commission, now known as Nuclear Regulatory Commission (NRC), said that the maximum protection against exposure to Sr-90 requires 2 tablespoons of sodium alginate daily, and for larger doses, 2 tablespoons four times a day.

Radioactive iodine absorbs readily when there is a deficiency of iodine in the body. Radioactive iodine causes thyroid cancer and is found most highly concentrated in milk. According to Dr. Russell Morgan, Chief Radiologist at Johns Hopkins University, 1 mg. of iodine for children and 5 mg. for adults will reduce radioactive iodine accumulated in the thyroid by about 80%.

Iodine should be consumed daily. Good sources of iodine are:

- kelp;
- other sea vegetables;
- turnip greens;
- onions;
- watercress;
- artichokes;
- seafoods.

Cesium and other radioactive isotopes entering the body may be thwarted by foods containing calcium and magnesium, which can be found in:

- sea vegetables;
- dark leafy greens;
- parsley;
- sesame seeds;
- almonds, seeds, and nuts;
- soy beans and other beans.

An incredible account of the ability of natural foods consumption creating an immunity to nuclear destruction is related by Tatsuichiro Akizuki, M.D. Dr. Akizuki was Director of the Department of Internal Medicine at St. Francis's Hospital, located in Nagasaki, near the center of the blast at the time of the world's first plutonium atomic bombing on August 9, 1945. The following material is excerpted from his book, *Documentary of A-Bombed Nagasaki*, published by the Nagasaki Printing Co., Inc., (2-14 Gotoo-machi, Nagasaki City, Japan).

"On August 9, 1945, the atomic bomb was dropped on Nagasaki. Lethal atomic radiation spread over the razed city. For many it was an agonizing death. For a few it was a miracle. Not one co-worker in the hospital suffered or died from radiation. The hospital was located only one mile from the center of the blast. My assistant and I helped many victims who suffered the effects of the bomb. In the hospital there was a large stock of miso and tamari. We also kept plenty of rice and wakame (seaweed used for soup stock or in miso soup). I had fed my co-workers brown rice and miso soup for some time before the bombing. None of them suffered from atomic radiation. I believe this is because they had been eating miso soup . . . .

"On the tenth of August at 8 a.m., the Uragami Hospital was still burning. It was truly a miracle that there was not a single death in this hospital. I took up again the treatment of the maladies at 9 a.m., praying to God as I could not be-lieve what happened. The supply of medicine was low. The hospital attendants prepared as usual a meal consisting of brown rice, miso soup with Hokkaido pumpkin and wakame, two times per day, at 11 a.m. and 5 p.m . . . ."

"An ounce of prevention is worth a pound of cure."
Benjamin Franklin

2. GETTING STARTED

"To punish in pillories or on pinning stools, brewers, bakers, butchers and cooks for these be the men on earth who do the most harm to the poor people, who buy piece meal. They poison them secretly and often."
William Langland, 14th Century English Poet

ECONOMIC ADVANTAGES

The economic advantages of using natural whole foods are as follows:

•Lower food costs are achieved by buying unprocessed foods, which have a long shelf life, and upon rehydration will from double to quadruple in size and weight as they absorb water. Examples are:

—One pound of garbanzo beans costs $1.00 and will serve six. One pound of red meat may cost $5.00 and serve only two.

—Grains, the basis of a natural whole foods diet, cost roughly 60¢ per pound, and one large serving will cost 11¢, as compared to meat.

—A two-ounce bag of potato chips costs about 68¢, while two ounces of sunflower seeds cost only 15¢ and are high in nutrient value; roasted in tamari they would cost another 2¢.

•Lower storage facility costs, due to lower refrigeration costs and preferably no freezing requirement, as freezing is a form of processing that reduces the "life force" in the food; with the elimination of butter, cream, cheese, and milk, which tend to go bad even with refrigeration, most natural foods will keep indefinitely without refrigeration. The refrigeration space is primarily for fresh produce, since processing is held to a minimum. Most condiments do not have to be refrigerated after opening, and onions, rutabagas and squash do not have to be refrigerated. Dehydrated foods also require no refrigeration.

•Longer shelf life of dehydrated foods allows for larger quantity purchasing, reducing inventory and ordering requirements.

•Packaging of whole grains, beans, and fresh vegetables packaging have far less solid waste cost (which has become a serious concern nationwide) per portion served than customary packaging.

•Pre-soaking most hydrates reduces energy costs.

•Setting menus according to peak harvesting seasons should have the advantage of higher quality and lower price. In-season, locally grown vegetables, fruit, and other products—which taste better and are of higher quality—cost less.

MANAGEMENT AND CONSUMER ADVANTAGES

Preparing and serving natural whole foods go hand in hand with the financial as well as the health concerns of the present and future.

Advantages for Management

•Fewer employees are required.

•Less money is tied up in inventory.

•A substantial part of the labor force needs to be minimally trained; fewer highly skilled employees are needed.

•Less formal culinary training in the traditional cuisine is needed.

•These foods are substantially adaptable to more steaming.

•There is opportunity for more flexible menus.

•The food holds well.

•There is less deep frying and no major grease disposal.

•Less (hood) filter cleaning is required; it is less costly to keep the kitchen clean.

•Far less undesirable exhaust and emissions are produced.

•There are fewer sanitation problems because of minimal, if any, animal products used (see *Bacteria Poisoning Chart* pg. 47).

•There is less solid waste.

•Less use of strong chemical cleaners, and less washing of pots and pans, is required because of no animal fat ingredients.

•Smaller storage area is required.

•Uniform product codes (UPC's) are applicable.

Advantages for Consumers

•Natural whole foods contain:

–Fewer calories;

–Natural flavors and enhancements;

–Richer natural flavors without fats and excessive salt;

–Fewer pesticides and chemical additives;

–Greater appeal to foreign consumers;

–Easily identifiable ingredients and nutritional details;

–Fat, salt, and sugar substitutes that are non-chemical.

•Customer nutritional concerns are being addressed.

•Produce retains color and flavor better during preparation.

•Natural whole foods:

–Appeal to (but are not limited to) those who want lower fat and cholesterol, less salt, and more produce and white meat;

–Are more digestible for older customers;

–Provide greater opportunity for new food preparation concepts;

–Fit well with take-out and/or delivery; flexibility of concept of menu and service; self-service options; and attractive displays.

"It's better to keep a friend than a diet."
Herman Aihara

BLENDING INTO EXISTING MENU

With moderation and balance, let your diet and menu change gently and naturally. Be honest, not hard and overbearing. Don't rush to upset the present equilibrium. Initially, keep all your existing menus and slowly add new items, a few at a time. As they become satisfactory, slowly decrease and finally eliminate, over a period of time, those items that are no longer for you or for your house.

Getting started is simple and straightforward, and can be accomplished in a flexible manner.

Phase 1. Start by including once or twice a week:

•Fresh house-made soup—for example, vegetable, beans, tamari, or miso;

•Whole grain breads or rolls;

•Sandwiches with whole grain bread and no animal products (see Sandwiches, pg. 251);

•Whole grains in any of a number of dishes;

•Cakes, pies, and desserts with whole grain flour, and no dairy products or refined sugar;

•Fresh fruit selections and more vegetable selections.

Phase 2. As time goes on, further suggested menu items may include:

•Scrambled tofu (see Tempeh Bacon, pg. 206) as an alternative to scrambled eggs;

•A dish that resembles beef tips with mushrooms and gravy, but made with seitan (see recipe, pg. 178), rather than with beef;

•Stroganoff using seitan instead of beef;

•Pizza, using soy cheese as an alternative to high-sodium and -cholesterol mozzarella cheese;

•Dishes containing barley, oatmeal, or soy milk instead of animal milk.

In general:

•Feature locally-grown, in-season, organic fruits and vegetables.

•Reduce the use of animal products, including eggs and dairy products.

•Reduce the use of anything white: flour, sugar , salt, etc.

"The word HAL (Anglosaxon) is the derivitive of the English words HAPPY, HEALTH, HOLY, WHOLE."

RELATING TO THE PUBLIC

No. 1: Communicate that these are natural whole foods and contain *no*:

•animal products;

•refined sugar or added salt;

•cholesterol or polyunsaturated fats.

Indicate this on menu boards, table tents, on a special card in the menu, or by having serving personnel mention it.

No. 2: Monitor public acceptance and demand by noting remarks made by customers and by tracking:

•food selection and quantity consumed (plate waste);

•the number of second helpings requested;

•the number of repeat requests.

No. 3: Front-of-house employees should taste each item, learn in detail how it is selected and prepared, learn the cooking method and how it is balanced with other foods.

No. 4: When dessert time comes, ask, for example, "Would you like to try a natural whole food homemade apple pie, made with no refined sugar or animal products?"

A friend of mine tells me that a few years ago at the University of Maine, at the request of some of the students, a natural whole food facility was opened, in addition to the already established facility serving typical institutional fare. By the end of the first semester, the new eating establishment was serving the majority of the university population. This happened not through peer pressure, but by the natural selection of the consumers.

So much of institutional food today—because of how it was cooked or handled before eating—has become tasteless, and needs to be doctored up with salt, sugar, or fat. Selecting natural whole foods that are innately tasty and succulent, fitting with the season and complementary to the existing menu, should assure the success of the transition to a healthy diet that will build and maintain greater health and general well-being.

Making natural whole foods appealing to the jaded American palate is really quite simple, and can be done in a number of ways. With the development of the chef's skills in the methods of preparation, suitable combining of foods, appropriate use of herbs, spices, condiments, and fresh vegetables and fruits, a whole new menu can be formed for a complete meal.

When good, healthy food is served, the consumer is filled with a good, healthy, satisfied feeling. Thankful is the chef or restaurateur whose customers leave with a positive feeling about the food, and who want to come again and again because they associate this good feeling with dining there.

"If doctors of today will not become the nutritionist of tomorrow, the nutritionists of today will become the doctors of tomorrow."
Thomas Edison

3. MEAL DESIGN

"The greatest of all professions...the chef or cook...who holds in the palm of the hand the quality, happiness and future of today's and coming generations."

Anonymous

There are two basic types of whole food meals—conventional and medicinal—and we will deal only with the conventional. Medicinal meals are usually prepared by those who are well versed in using appropriate foods as medicine for some specific illness.

Each ideal conventional meal should include whole grain or whole grain products, including wheat, buckwheat, corn, brown rice, barley, or millet. The other two meals should include whole grains, whole grain breads, or whole grain noodles, such as whole wheat or buckwheat. Vegetables should be included in every meal, and leafy green and root vegetables each at least once a day, along with a choice of round or other vegetables once a day.

Include miso soup once a day, and bean or bean products once a day except for children or nursing mothers, who tend to need more. Once a day also for condiments, sea vegetables, and pickles (served at the end of the meal for digestion). Included also are options of a beverage and white-fleshed meat a few times a week, although these are not highly recommended.

The conventional meal is more flavorful and more sensuous than the medicinal, with more salt or salt condiments, oil, nuts or nut butter, fruits, sweets, sauces, herbs, and spices. Select foods that are grown in your geographic area, the closer the better. Generally speaking, those in the northern United States and southern Canada are in the same temperate zone as northern Europe, China, and Russia, Australia and the southern parts of South America. Organically grown products are preferable, as are natural products that are not processed and don't have toxic residue or changes caused by chemical or high-heat treatment.

"The willpower and discipline for using proper nourishment, exercise, and self-awareness is not easy."

Elson M. Haas, M.D.

BEGINNER'S GUIDE

The *Beginner's Guide* is not meant to be the final goal for eating "right." It is only a guide in the first step, and the most important one, for those on the typical Western diet. It is one of the first steps in changing the diet away from consuming most animal foods.

The *Food Effects Chart* (see pg. 23) is a guide to balanced natural food meals, as are the *Meal Planning Charts* (see pp. 30–31).

BEGINNER'S GUIDE

EAT MORE OF OR EMPHASIZE:		EAT LESS OF OR ELIMINATE:
–fresh fruits & vegetables, organically grown if available –raw fruits and vegetables –frozen when fresh not available –dried fruit in moderation –raw fermented vegetables (home-made sauerkraut, pickles, etc.)	**FRUITS AND VEGETABLES**	–canned fruits & vegetables, especially with added salt or sugar –overcooked fruits and vegetables –sulfured dried fruits –fried & french-fried vegetables –potato chips, corn chips, etc.
–brown rice –millet –barley –buckwheat –whole oats, old-fashioned rolled oats –wheat & rye kernels –quinoa –cracked whole grains (bulgur and cracked wheat) –whole grain flours, freshly ground –whole grain breads without preservatives, homemade if possible	**GRAINS**	–white flour, bleached & unbleached –white rice –white bread, rolls, pastries, cookies, crackers, cakes, etc. –white pasta –dry cereals (highly processed) –wheat germ (highly processed)
–cooked peas and beans, all kinds –bean sprouts –tofu (soybean curd) –miso (should not be boiled) –soy flour and soy grits	**BEANS**	–raw dry beans (except string beans) unless sprouted –texturized soy protein, texturized vegetable protein (TVP) & products made from them
–whole raw nuts & seeds, unsalted –nut and seed butters –roasted, peanuts, natural peanut butter –sprouted seeds	**NUTS AND SEEDS**	–salted, roasted nuts –dry-roasted nuts –raw peanuts –commercial homogenized and sugared peanut butter
–unrefined cold-pressed oils, not heated to high temperatures (such as corn, olive, sesame) –butter (not desirable, but better than margarine)	**FATS AND OILS (in moderation)**	–colorless and odorless processed oils –margarine and lard –vegetable shortening (Crisco™, etc.) –fat from meat and fowl
–live-culture yogurt & buttermilk –natural cheeses	**DAIRY PRODUCTS (in moderation)**	–pasteurized homogenized milk –instant powdered milk –evaporated or condensed milk –processed cheese, sour cream –cheese spread & cheese food –dairy products of all types
–fish, especially smaller and white-fleshed varieties, from unpolluted waters – organically raised meat & poultry –organic fertile eggs	**MEAT, FISH, AND EGGS (in moderation)**	–beef, pork, veal, lamb, poultry, eggs, and all meats –meat with nitrates or nitrites (such as ham, bacon, corned beef, bologna) –processed meat (such as hot dogs, luncheon meat, turkey loaf, etc.) –canned fish –fried chicken or fish

(Continued on next page.)

BEGINNER'S GUIDE continued

EAT MORE OF OR EMPHASIZE:		EAT LESS OF OR ELIMINATE:
—barley malt syrup and rice syrup —100% real maple syrup —raw unfiltered honey, comb honey —blackstrap molasses	SWEETS (in moderation)	—can and beet sugars (white, brown, raw, turbinado) —corn syrup, corn sweetener —fructose, glucose, sucrose, dextrose, sorbitol, etc. —artificial sweeteners —foods with added sugar (ice cream, cold cereals, candy, most processed food)
—fruit & vegetable juices, fresh and unpasteurized if available —spring or distilled water —herb teas —grain beverages (Cafix™, Postum™, etc.)	BEVERAGES	—drink mixes —juice drinks —soft drinks and diet sodas —tap water —coffee, tea, decaffeinated coffee, chocolate drinks —alcoholic beverages
—rock salt or sea salt containing trace minerals —kelp, dulse, & other seaweeds —fresh, pure herbs & spices —carob —apple cider vinegar	OTHER	—refined (white) salt, sea or mined —MSG —chocolate, cocoa —white distilled vinegar

FOOD/HEALTH BENEFIT OUTLINE

Whole Grains:

1. Offer high-quality, long-lasting energy without the damaging side effects of the usual energy sources, such as sweets, coffee, alcohol, etc., which cause vitamin and mineral depletion, emotional instability and depression, and liver damage (by upsetting the sugar metabolism of the pancreas and liver, as well as weakening the functions of digestion and excretion; this contributes to obesity and an excess of fatty buildup around the heart and other internal organs).

2. Provide a high-quality protein (together with beans and legumes) without the detrimental effects of using animal products.

3. Supply fiber and roughage for natural cleanliness, health, and muscle tone of the digestive tract.

Beans, Legumes, and Soy Products:

1. Provide sufficient high-quality protein without the harmful side effects of animal products, which cause excess fat and buildup of cholesterol, including the overworking of the liver and kidneys. Other side effects of excess animal protein include: contributing to heart disease and stroke; lack of fiber, which causes a weakened digestive system; and contributing to the cause of various forms of cancer.

2. Supply fiber and roughage, as described under whole grains.

3. Provide a significant source of calcium.

4. Provide a source of high-quality oils that are easily digested and are beneficial in small quantities.

Vegetables:

1. Provide fiber and roughage as described above.

2. Contain the entire range of vitamins (except B-12, which is found in the following vegetable foods: miso, tamari, correctly-made tempeh, and sea vegetables; and in animal foods).

3. Strongly counteract the negative effects of devitalized, refined, and processed foods, and clean the body of unwanted wastes such as fats and toxins.

Seeds, Nuts, Nut Butters, and Oils:

1. Contain no cholesterol, in contrast to all animal products such as butter, cheese, lard, milk, eggs, etc.

2. Contain high-quality, generally unsaturated oils for easy digestion.

3. In the case of nuts, nut butters, and seeds, have a high degree of protein and calcium.

Sauces and Condiments:

Woven into the fabric of natural whole foods cooking are the threads of the five basic tastes, which naturally appeal to the consumer, and gratify the basic stimulation of the five major organs, according to the philosophy of Oriental medicine. Sauces and condiments are one easy way to bring forth these five basic taste characteristics. At least three should be included in each meal, either in the food, or in the sauces and condiments.

1. Sweet: stimulates the spleen, pancreas and stomach, and the heart; found in barley malt or rice syrup, which give gentle stimulation to the internal organs, as opposed to the overstimulation caused by refined sugars.

2. Sour: stimulates the liver. Found in lemons, limes, some apples, vinegar, cranberries, sauerkraut, pickles.

3. Pungent: stimulates the respiratory system. Mostly found in onions, garlic, daikon, ginger, mustard, horseradish, watercress, raw cabbage, and some other greens.

4. Salty: stimulates the kidneys; found in natural salt, sea salt, shoyu, tamari, pickles, sea vegetables, etc.

5. Bitter: stimulates the heart; found in grain coffee, parsley, mustard greens, dandelions, chickory, etc.

Beverages:

Can provide not only fluid, some vitamins, minerals, and enzymes, but also, depending on their ingredients and taste, satisfy one's nutritional need for contractive or expansive stimulation at the time.

White Meat:

Provides protein and, for some people, is more easily assimilated than red meat; is lighter, with less fat and cholesterol, than darker meats, making it easier to digest. It is a good choice for anyone making the transition away from dark, red meats and eggs.

Whole Fresh Fruits:

1. Provide fiber and roughage.

2. Contain vitamins and minerals.

3. Provide quick energy and the pleasure of sweetness without the harmful side effects of refined or artificial sweeteners.

Sweeteners:

Barley malt and rice syrup are assimilated into the body's system more slowly than other sugars, and are less taxing to the pancreas and other organs. Honey, maple syrup, and molasses, although almost as intensely sweet as other, less desirable sweeteners (cane sugar, fructose, corn syrup, etc.), are less addictive and upsetting to body chemistry.

"The fate of the nation has depended on the good or bad digestion of a prime minister."

Voltaire

FOOD EFFECTS CHART

The *Food Effects Chart* is used by selecting evenly from the Contractive and Expansive sides of the chart, as well as for the specific needs of the consumer. The center vertical line acts as a fulcrum. To maintain balance, select foods evenly from both sides of the fulcrum in like pairs, such as items listed under "Daily Use" or "Transitional."

For example, under "Daily Use," if you select grains, then simply select another complementary item listed under "Daily Use" from the other side of the fulcrum line, such as a vegetable. If beans are also used, again go to the other side of the line and select another vegetable, or some fruit, etc. Another example is balancing white-fleshed fish or fowl with a potato, both from the "Transitional" column, and from each side of the fulcrum line. On occasion (the less often the better), white meat may be added; preferably in 3- or 4-ounce portions rather than the customary 8 ounces, and balanced by the "Transitional" column on the other side of the fulcrum. NOTE: a health-supportive diet contains minimal or no animal products.

Physical and emotional side effects can be developed through many years of a particular food consumption style, depending in whole or in part on the types and quantities of food consumed—thus the term "contributing to or tending towards." Inasmuch as everyone is different, so too are the effects. While one person may be unaffected by emotional characteristics, some of the physical characteristics may be slowly but surely maturing. After all, gallstones don't grow overnight, and often muscle and joint stiffness can develop over such a long period of time, and in such small amounts, that it initially isn't a problem, or grows to become accepted and is tolerated. After a while, the stiffness becomes intolerable or unacceptable, and thus becomes classified as a problem. During the transitional time while you are adjusting your diet, the ailment or condition may be stopped from further development or may partially or totally regress—as a result of the correct natural whole foods diet.

This chart is not intended to be a rigid prescription or a straitjacket regimen. It provides tools that can be used for creating greater health and happiness. As with any tool, practice, time, and insight of its use will bring greater skill and better results.

Descending order of preference for eating food following the chart (for improved digestion and assimilation) is as follows:

Contractive Daily Use

Expansive Daily Use

Contractive Transitional

Expansive Transitional

Contractive Avoid

Expansive Avoid

Definitions:

Expansive: creating in the body and mind the effects of expansion; for example, dilation of blood vessels or broadening one's point of view.

Contractive: creating in the body and mind the effects of contraction; for example, tightening of blood vessels or focusing one's point of view.

See the next page for *Food Effects Chart*.

"Those who rebel against the basic rules of the universe sever their own roots and ruin their true selves . . . the two principles in nature (expansion and contraction) and the four seasons are the beginning and the end of everything and they are also the cause of life and death. Those who disobey the laws of the universe will give rise to calamities and visitations while those who follow the laws of the universe remain free from dangerous illness."
The Yellow Emperor's Classic
of Internal Medicine
U. of California Press, 1966

FOOD EFFECTS CHART

CONTRACTIVE

AVOID OR REDUCE	TRANSITIONAL	DAILY USE
Red meat	Shellfish	Sea salt
Processed meat	White-fleshed fish:	Whole grains:
Cheese	flounder	whole grain products,
Artificial cheese	halibut	bread, pasta
Eggs	herring	Dried beans and peas
Dark-fleshed fish:	Butter	Bean Products:
bluefish	Yogurt	tempeh, tofu, miso,
salmon	Egg whites	tamari
swordfish	Organic poultry	Beverages from
tuna	and rabbit	roasted grains, roots,
Caviar		or stems
Refined salt		Flavoring herbs and
		spices from roots,
		stems, or bark

CONTRIBUTING TO OR TENDING TOWARDS

PHYSICAL

DAILY USE	AVOID OR REDUCE
Strength	Hardness
Body warmth	Rigidity, Arthritis
Physical vitality	Congestion
Strong red blood cells	Hyperactivity
Contractive muscular power	Hardening of the arteries
Strong respiration and digestion	Gallstones
	Kidney stones
	Tight muscles
	Stiff joints
	Tumors, etc.

EMOTIONAL

DAILY USE	AVOID OR REDUCE
Assertiveness	Arrogance
Confidence	Aggressiveness
Willpower	Hostility
Enthusiasm	Anger
Good memory	Obsession
Perseverance	Criticism
Joy	Extreme individualism
Decisiveness, etc.	Foolhardiness
	Carelessness

EXPANSIVE

DAILY USE	TRANSITIONAL	AVOID OR REDUCE
Leafy greens	Tropical fruits:	Alcohol
Root vegetables	citrus, dates, figs	Oleomargarine
Round vegetables	Tropical nuts:	Artificial sweeteners:
Sea vegetables	Brazil, cashews,	saccharine, sucrose,
Temperate-climate	coconut	aspartame, dextrose
nuts and fruits	Asparagus, beets	Refined sugars:
Barley malt	Tomatoes, peppers	molasses, fructose,
Rice syrup	Eggplant	corn syrup, white,
Beverages from	Maple syrup	brown, date,
leaves or blossoms	Tropical spices:	turbinado
Flavoring herbs and	cayenne, nutmeg,	Honey, glucose
spices from leaves,	clove, etc.	Tea, coffee
bulbs, or rhizomes	Leavening agents:	Chocolate
(parsley, oregano,	yeast, baking soda	Ice cream, candy
garlic, ginger)	and powder	Soft drinks

CONTRIBUTING TO OR TENDING TOWARDS

PHYSICAL

DAILY USE	AVOID OR REDUCE
Flexible joints	Fatigue
Strong nervous system	Underactivity
Muscle tone	Flabbiness
Deep and restful sleep	Degeneration of tissue function
Alertness and sensitivity	Frigidity
Expansive muscular power	Impotence
Stimulates enzymes, hormones, and digestive juices	Sterility, etc.
	Fluid retention or swelling

EMOTIONAL

DAILY USE	AVOID OR REDUCE
Sensitivity	Fear, worry
Openness	Depression
Flexibility	Insecurity
Imagination	Lack of focus
Adaptability	Sadness
Planning ability	Loneliness
Tolerance	Paranoia
Cooperativeness	Frustration
Caution	Indecision

SEASONAL CHANGES IN DIET

The following lists indicate the types of food and cooking methods that are best used in spring, summer, fall, and winter. Many people have already been eating this way for generations, or experienced it in childhood.

The lists have been drawn up according to two basic practices: using locally grown and in-season foods as much as possible, and preparing the food according to the seasonal needs of the body (known in Oriental medicine as the five transformations).

Using the lists mainly involves understanding the transition of food from peak season to peak season, and which to eat from one season to the next. Vegetables and fruits are changed according to harvesting times or changes in the seasons. The listings also support the body's seasonal changes; in the summer we want to be cooled, and in the winter we want to be warmed by the food we eat. Winter foods hold a lot of heat from the long cooking time, and oil is the catalyst for the body to absorb the heat. Thus, in the winter we tend to naturally eat more baked goods, hearty stews, fried food, etc. Conversely, in the summer we want to support coolness and naturally tend to eat less warming and more cooling foods, like salads, raw or minimally cooked foods, less oil, salt, and dried beans.

To eat warming winter foods in the sum- mer, or cooling summer foods in the winter, is a contradiction that can cause considerable discomfort.

"Each patient carries his own doctor inside of him."
Albert Schweitzer

SPRING (Change)

- Less baking and sauteeing.
- Shorter cooking time for vegetables, more boiling and steaming and raw salads.
- Less oil, nuts, nut butter, salt, salty condiments, and flour products.
- Increase green vegetables, decrease grains, root vegetables and squash.

SUMMER (Peak)

- Least cooking time, with less baking, oils, nuts, beans, salt, flours, grains.
- More boiling and steaming, vegetables, grain salads (tabouli) and whole grain pasta salads, raw vegetables.
- Most vegetables grown aboveground.
- Fruits: fresh, seasonal, cooked or raw, with or without agar-agar.
- Most tofu, excellent for cooling, and as a replacement for beans.
- More noodles, barley, and long-grain brown rice, bulgur.

FALL (Change)

- Less boiling, steaming, and raw foods.
- More cooking.
- More grains, especially millet and rice, and more round vegetables.
- More nuts, seeds, nut butters, oil, salt.

WINTER (Peak)

- Longest cooking time with more frying, baking, and boiling.
- Stews, with root vegetables and tempeh, tofu, or seitan ("wheat meat").
- More grains in general, especially short-grain brown rice, sweet rice, oats, and buckwheat, whole wheat berries.
- Largest amounts of oils, nuts, seeds, nut butters.
- Stronger seasoning with salt, miso, tamari, and salty condiments.
- More beans, especially in hearty soups and baked.

See the following pages for *Seasonal Menu Suggestions.*

SEASONAL MENU SUGGESTIONS

3 Main Meals		SPRING 1	2	3
	Soup	Cauliflower Puree	Celery Soup, Cream of	Miso Soup with Fresh Greens
	Condiment	Chopped Parsley	Chopped Fresh Mint	Scallions, Chopped
	Salad	Pasta Salad	Lebanese Salad	Tabouli
	Salad Dressing	(in salad)	Lebanese Dressing	(in salad)
50%	**Whole grains**	Brown Rice & Wheat	Bulgur, Tarragon	Couscous
10%	**Beans**	Pinto Beans with Caraway & Cumin	Great Northern	Lentil Pate
30%	**Green Veg.**	Cabbage Singapore	Greens (Kale), Steamed	Cabbage, Chinese
	Root Veg.	Carrots Vichy	(in condiment)	Carrots, Mint-Glazed
	Other Veg.	Celery	Cucumbers	Squash
	Sea Veg.	(in beans)	(in beans)	(in dessert)
10%	**Oil**	(in sauce)	(olive oil in grain)	(in salad)
	Sauces	Brown Sauce, Basic	Onion–Tamari Sauce	Tahini–Tofu Sauce
	Condiment	Gomasio	Daikon and Tamari	Sunflower Seeds, Tamari–Garlic
	Pickle	(in salad)		Tamari Pickles
	Dessert	Baked Pears	New Year's Pudding	Apple Kanten
	Topping	Roasted Walnuts	Roasted Almonds	Roasted Hazelnuts
	Beverage			

[NOTE: Recipes for all dishes can be found in Part II of this book.]

SEASONAL MENU SUGGESTIONS			
3 Main Meals	**SUMMER**		
	1	2	3
Soup	Miso Soup, Korean	Barley Soup & Greens	Squash, Summer, Puree
Condiment	Chopped Parsley	Scallions, Chopped	Chopped Parsley
Salad	Pasta Salad	Tofu Salad on Lettuce	Brown Rice Salad & Tofu
Salad Dressing	(in salad)	Tahini, White Miso & Mustard	Tofu Salad Dressing
50% **Whole grains**	Barley	Noodles, Cool Tamari Broth, Scallions	Corn on the Cob
10% **Beans**	Lima Beans	Great Northern	Hummus
30% **Green Veg.**	Zucchini	Broccoli	Bok Choy
Root Veg.	Daikon	Squash, Summer (yellow), Spiced	Rutabaga
Other Veg.	Cauliflower	Cucumbers	Celery
Sea Veg.	(in dessert)	(in beans)	(in soup)
10% **Oil**			
Sauces	Tahini Dip, Basic	Tofu–Tamari Sauce	Mushroom Sauce, Basic
Condiment	Ginger Pickles	Chopped Parsley	Pumpkin Seeds, Tamari-Roasted
Pickle		Tamari Pickles (using cabbage)	
Dessert	Apple Kanten	Peaches, Sliced	Ambrosia
Topping	Tofu Supreme Icing		
Beverage			

[NOTE: Recipes for all dishes can be found in Part II of this book.]

SEASONAL MENU SUGGESTIONS

3 Main Meals		FALL		
		1	2	3
	Soup	Squash Puree	Carrot Puree with Miso	Onion Soup
	Condiment	Chopped Parsley	Chopped Fresh Mint	Chopped Cilantro
	Salad	Brown Rice Salad, Italian	Grated Root Salad	Pressed Salt Pickles
	Salad Dressing	Tofu Dressing	Olive Oil & Vinegar	
50%	**Whole grains**	Millet	Rice, Brown & Red Lentils	Wheat
10%	**Beans**	Lentils (Brown or Green)	Garbanzo (Hummus)	Garbanzos & Greens
30%	**Green Veg.**	Chinese Cabbage Greens	Steamed Greens	Brussels Sprouts
	Root Veg.	Parsnips	Turnips, Boiled, & Sea Veg.	Rutabaga
	Other Veg.	Cauliflower	Squash, Winter (butternut)	Beans, Green—Ginger
	Sea Veg.	(in beans)	(in root veg.)	(in beans)
10%	**Oil**	(in beans)	(in salad dressing)	(in beans)
	Sauces	Curry Sauce	Mushroom Sauce, Basic, with Tamari	Onion—Tamari Sauce
	Condiment	Pumpkin Seeds, Tamari-Roasted	Tofu, Marinated	Chutney
	Pickle	Tamari Pickles (using cabbage)	Salt Pickles	(in salad)
	Dessert	Hot Apple Pie	Flan	Couscous Cake
	Topping	Tofu Supreme Icing	Maple—Tahini Glaze	Caramel Sauce, Mock
	Beverage			

[NOTE: Recipes for all dishes can be found in Part II of this book.]

SEASONAL MENU SUGGESTIONS

3 Main Meals		1	WINTER 2	3
	Soup	Lentil Soup, Greek	Vegetable Soup, Basic	Squash, Winter Puree
	Condiment	Chopped Scallion	Chopped Parsley	Chopped Celery Greens
	Salad	Root Vegetable, Grated	Root Vegetable on Lettuce	Alfalfa Sprouts
	Salad Dressing	(in salad)	(in salad)	Tahini
50%	Whole grains	Rice, Sweet & Roasted Walnuts	Buckwheat & Onions	Cauliflower & Millet, Mashed with olive oil
10%	Beans	Adzuki Beans & Squash	Navy Beans (Baked Beans)	Garbanzos & Greens
30%	Green Veg.	Broccoli	Steamed Greens & Watercress	Cabbage, Chinese, & Lentils
	Root Veg.	Turnips, boiled	Beets	Rutabaga
	Other Veg.	Cauliflower	Squash, Winter ("Calbaza")	Peas & Mushrooms
	Sea Veg.	(in soup)	(in soup)	
10%	Oil	(in soup)	(in beans)	(in beans)
	Sauces	Miso–Tahini Sauce, Basic	Tahini Sauce, Basic, with Tamari	Mustard–Tahini Sauce
	Condiment	Nori Strips, Crushed	Carrot–Walnut Pate	Gomasio
	Pickle	Tamari Pickle	Pickle, Basic Brine	Pickle, Basic Brine
	Dessert	Apple Crisp	Baked Pears	Rice Pudding
	Topping	Tofu Supreme Icing	Walnuts, Roasted & Chopped, & Raisins	Hazelnuts, Roasted & Chopped
	Beverage			

[NOTE: Recipes for all dishes can be found in Part II of this book.]

"Keep away from dainty foods while we eat the healthful foods in moderation."

Galen

THE MEAL PLANNING CHARTS

Two *Meal Planning Charts* follow. The first is more for beginners, and lists the categories and some common food selection alternatives that allow for easy planning of a complete, wholesome menu for one meal, or the entire day. The type of food is listed on the left-hand side of the page, followed by the percentage suggested. The three columns for breakfast, lunch, and dinner can easily be filled in advance by the executive chef or whoever is responsible for establishing the menu. This can be done according to consumer demand, and what is in stock, or the schedules of order and delivery.

As each food item is selected, it should be cross-checked with the *Food Effects Chart* (pg. 23) to obtain balance for each meal.

The second chart allows more space for planning, but assumes familiarity with the food categories. Both charts have been designed for reproduction for the executive chef's convenience.

NOTE: Percentages can vary as much as 20%, and are not applicable to some people.

To maintain interest in the meal, at least three of the five basic tastes may be included:

Sweet: brown rice, whole wheat bread, some root vegetables, fruit, barley malt, rice syrup.

Sour: lemon, lime, some apples, vinegar, cranberry, pickles, sauerkraut.

Pungent: onions, garlic, daikon, ginger, mustard, horseradish, watercress, cilantro.

Salty: natural salt, shoyu, tamari, pickles, sea vegetables.

Bitter: grain coffee, parsley, greens, mustard, dandelions, chickory.

MEAL PLANNING CHART

	DAILY %	BREAKFAST	LUNCH	SUPPER
WHOLE GRAINS: barley, brown rice, buckwheat, corn, couscous, millet, rye, whole wheat. Whole grain products: bread, pasta, oatmeal, etc.	50%			
BEANS: adzuki, lima, turtle, garbanzo, great northern, kidney, lentil, mung, navy, pinto, soy, split pea, etc.	10%			
LEAFY GREENS: brussels sprouts, Chinese cabbage, cabbage, cilantro, endive, greens, lettuce, parsley, watercress, etc.	30%			
ROOT VEGETABLES: burdock, carrots, daikon, onions, parsnip, radishes, rutabaga, turnips, etc.				
OTHER VEGETABLES: artichokes, broccoli, cauliflower, celery, cucumbers, green beans, mushrooms, peas, squash, etc.				
SEA VEGETABLES: agar-agar, arame, dulse, Irish moss, hiziki, kelp, nori, wakame, etc.				
WHITE MEATS: fish, shellfish, rabbit, chicken, etc.	10%			
SEEDS & NUTS: almonds, filberts, pecans, pine nuts, walnuts; sesame, sunflower, and pumpkin seeds, etc.				
FRUITS: apples, berries, peaches, pears, plums, prunes, etc.				
SAUCES: tamari, miso, tahini, etc.				
CONDIMENTS: daikon, ginger, gomasio, pickles, purees, sauces, etc.				
SWEETENERS: barley malt, maple syrup, rice syrup				
BEVERAGES: teas from twigs, barks, leaves, blossoms; or juice				
OILS: olive, corn, sesame, soybean, safflower, etc.				

MEAL PLANNING CHART			
	Soup			
	Condiment			
	Salad			
	Salad Dressing			
50%	Whole grains			
10%	Beans			
30%	Green Veg.			
	Root Veg.			
	Other Veg.			
	Sea Veg.			
10%	Oil			
	Sauces			
	Condiment			
	Pickle			
	Dessert			
	Topping			
	Beverage			

4. DIRECTED DIETS FOR SPECIFIC OCCASIONS

"There is no love sincerer than the love of food."
George Bernard Shaw

Traditional cooking for special occasions has been practiced around the world for centuries. Following are suggestions and recommendations for six different social occasions.

At the end of each occasion description you will find a set of suggested menus for both winter and summer (Happy Occasions has two sets of menus). *The blank column is for your use.*

BUSINESS MEETINGS OR STUDENT EXAMINATIONS

Designed for:

•Clarity, sharpness, and subtlety;

•Ability to focus, be persuasive, and hold your own in meeting unexpected challenges;

•Perception and strength;

•Shrewdness in getting the upper hand.

Useful:

•Whole grains for high-quality energy: brown rice, barley, buckwheat, and millet are preferred to breads and noodles;

•Salt, slightly more than usual, and a pickle or salty condiment;

•Root vegetables, leafy greens in equal parts;

•Seasonings, slightly more than usual;

•A little white-fleshed fish or shellfish.

Avoid:

•Oils, nuts, and nut butters, which are hard to digest when maximum energy is needed for the challenge;

•Fruits, sweets, and alcohol have a euphoric effect, undermining strength, self-awareness, and self-interest;

•Beans, which repair tissue and muscle, are hard to digest, and thus do not serve any immediate purpose.

HAPPY OCCASIONS

Designed for:

•Extremes in taste, using the five basic tastes (NOTE: With elegant tastes, be careful not to overwhelm the tastebuds);

•Extremes in texture: soft and creamy, crisp and rough, chewy, etc.;

•Elegant but simple tastes and presentations;

•Richness and expansiveness: using more oil and salt;

•Unusual ethnic cuisine.

Useful:

•Two soups: hearty bean or lentil, carrot and miso and clear broth with tamari, tofu, ginger, and scallions;

•Two leafy greens, such as watercress and radish salad, steamed kale with tofu, tahini-based Hollandaise sauce;

•Three whole-grain dishes: vegetable sushi, pasta salad with oil and vinegar dressing, and plain rice balls rolled in gomasio;

•Variety of bread and dips;

•Choice of sauces with heavy use of herbs and spices;

•Condiments: nuts, seeds, pickles, chutney, jams, nut butters;

•Festive beverages with herbs, spices or fruits, natural alcoholic beverages with no preservatives or sugar, organic wines;

•Dips and sauces with blanched vegetables.

RELAXING EVENINGS
Designed for:

- Refreshing, enlivening, and relaxing;
- Nourishing lightly (not providing the major nourishment of the day, which ideally is to be taken at breakfast and lunch).

Useful:

- Broth soups;
- Whole grains;
- A variety of vegetables.

Avoid:

- Heavy foods;
- Large quantities;
- Beans;
- Animal foods.

ROMANCE

Much has been written in most traditional societies about aphrodisiacs. Shakespeare's Macbeth refers to alcohol as provoking desire and "undoing the point." Sexual energy is an expression of physical and emotional vitality; therefore, eating to increase sexual stimulation or satisfaction means eating a more balanced, natural diet, not overeating sexually stimulating foods.

To this end, some of the characteristics seen here are also listed under "Business Meetings" or "Sports."

Designed for:

- Strengthening foods that will equally relax and excite.

Useful:

- Grains, greens;
- Root vegetables;
- Salt, a little more than usual;
- Sweets, little;
- Oil, little;
- Hot spices, pepper, garlic, ginger, little.

Avoid:

- Cucumbers;
- Tofu;
- Salt and sweets in abundance;
- Alcohol.

In some cultural traditions, the following are felt to be sexually stimulating:

Food: Artichokes, asparagus, avocado, buckwheat, burdock, carrots, celery, fish/shellfish, kola nuts, olives, onion family, pistachios, pumpkin seeds, sesame seeds.

Luscious Fruit: Bananas, fresh figs, mango, papaya, peaches (fresh), pears (ripe).

Beverages & Spices: Black tea, cayenne pepper, clove, garlic, ginseng, licorice, mustard, nutmeg, pepper, peppermint, rosemary, saffron, thyme, vanilla, wild mint.

SOMBER TIMES
Designed for:

- Basically plain foods, strong and simple;
- Providing food that is plain and that will sustain at a time of emotional instability.

Useful:

- Strong miso soup or stew with root vegetables and beans;
- Hot spice, little;
- Grains: brown rice with adzuki beans;
- Greens and root vegetables parboiled;
- Moderate use of salt, oil, and sweets;
- Strong bean dishes;
- Noodle casserole with root vegetables.

Avoid:

- Sauces, spices, sweets;
- Excess garnishes;
- Rich and elaborate presentation.

SPORTS

Designed for:

•Strong muscular energy for both short bursts and continuous exertion;

•Keen, rapid, accurate observation abilities with minimum reaction times.

For two weeks before the sports event is to take place, a training diet of the following will be helpful:

•Whole grains—60% twice a day;

•Beans—15% twice a day;

•Vegetables, equal amounts of root and leafy—23% twice a day;

•Other—2%.

Avoid:

•Animal products that will overburden the internal organs such as the liver, kidneys, and heart;

•Coffee, alcohol, excessive fruit juices;

•Sweets and white flour products, which tend to weaken energy and dull the acuteness of the nervous system (reaction time).

In the last meal before the event, use:

•Whole grain—30%;

•Equal amounts of greens and root vegetables—50%;

•White flesh—10%;

•Whole fruit, cooked or raw—10%;

Immediately before the sports event (about 15-30 minutes) have:

•Strong miso soup or tamari broth;

•Followed by whole fruit, cooked or raw, or fresh juice.

See the following pages for suggested menus.

		WINTER	SUMMER	
BUSINESS MEETINGS AND STUDENT EXAMINATIONS				
	Soup	Barley Soup With Kelp	Noodle Broth with Tamari	
	Condiment	Parsley	Scallions	
	Salad			
	Salad Dressing			
50%	Whole grains	Buckwheat	Millet	
10%	Beans			
30%	Green Veg.	Broccoli	Greens (Kale), Steamed	
	Root Veg.	Rutabaga	Carrots, Mint-Glazed	
	Other Veg.	Squash, Winter (butternut)	Bok Choy	
	Sea Veg.	(in soup)	(in soup)	
10%	Oil			
	Sauces	Savory Root Sauce	Mushroom Sauce, Basic	
	Condiment	Daikon	Scallions, Miso	
	Pickle			
	Dessert			
	Topping			
	Beverage	Fennel Tea	Fennel Tea	

[NOTE: Recipes for all dishes can be found in Part II of this book.]

		HAPPY OCCASIONS		
		WINTER	**SUMMER**	
	Soup	Lentil Soup, Basic	Carrot Aspic	
	Condiment	Diced Cilantro	Scallions	
	Salad	Lebanese	Tabouli	
	Salad Dressing	Lebanese	(in salad)	
50%	**Whole grains**	Rice and Wheat	Brown Rice Salad, Italian	
10%	**Beans**	Garbanzo (Hummus)	Lima Beans	
30%	**Green Veg.**	Greens (Kale), Steamed	Broccoli	
	Root Veg.	Turnips, Boiled	Carrot	
	Other Veg.	Squash, Winter (buttercup)	Onions, Pearl, Glazed	
	Sea Veg.	(in soup and beans)	(in beans)	
10%	**Oil**	(in bean)	(in salad)	
	Sauces	Tahini	Mushroom Sauce, Basic, on Broccoli	
	Condiment	Sunflower Seeds, Tamari–Garlic	Breads and Dips, Chutney	
	Pickle	Pressed Salt Pickles	Pickles, Basic Brine	
	Dessert	Spice Cake	Kanten	
	Topping	Tofu Supreme Icing and Chopped Nuts		
	Beverage	Barley Tea	Sparkling Water & Grape Jc. w/ Lemon	

[NOTE: Recipes for all dishes can be found in Part II of this book.]

HAPPY OCCASIONS

		WINTER	*SUMMER*	
	Soup	Fish Soup	Broccoli Soup, Cream of	
	Condiment	Chopped Parsley	Celery Leaves	
	Salad	Pressed Salt Pickles	Wheat Berry Salad	
	Salad Dressing		Verte Dressing	
50%	**Whole grains**	Rice Balls	Tabouli	
10%	**Beans**	Navy Beans With Maple Syrup	Tofu Cubes with Ginger and Tamari	
30%	**Green Veg.**	Greens Sauteed with Olive Oil & Garlic	Steamed Broccoli and Other Greens	
	Root Veg.	Daikon	Beets	
	Other Veg.	Potato, Sweet, Baked	Corn on the Cob	
	Sea Veg.	Nori Strips	(in soup)	
10%	**Oil**	(in green vegetable)	(in Tabouli)	
	Sauces	Miso–Tahini Sauce, Basic		
	Condiment	Pumpkin Seeds, Tamari-Roasted	Bread and Chutney	
	Pickle	Ginger Pickles	Tamari Pickles	
	Dessert	Rice Pudding	Watermelon Balls with Chopped Mint	
	Topping	Diced Roasted Filberts		
	Beverage	Licorice–Cinnamon Tea	Fennel Tea	

[NOTE: Recipes for all dishes can be found in Part II of this book.]

RELAXING EVENING			
	WINTER	**SUMMER**	
Soup	Miso	Miso Soup (white)	
Condiment	Cilantro	Parsley	
Salad			
Salad Dressing			
50% **Whole grains**	Millet	Quinoa and Saffron	
10% **Beans**			
30% **Green Veg.**	Green Beans	Cabbage, Chinese	
Root Veg.	Beets	Rutabaga	
Other Veg.	Squash	Corn	
Sea Veg.			
10% **Oil**			
Sauces	Mushroom		
Condiment			
Pickle			
Dessert			
Topping			
Beverage			

[NOTE: Recipes for all dishes can be found in Part II of this book.]

		WINTER	SUMMER	
	ROMANCE			
	Soup			
	Condiment	Olives	Olives	
	Salad			
	Salad Dressing			
50%	Whole grains	Basmati Rice With Nutmeg	Quinoa with Saffron	
10%	Beans			
30%	Green Veg.	Artichokes	Bok Choy	
	Root Veg.	Daikon	Carrot	
	Other Veg.			
	Sea Veg.			
10%	Oil			
	Sauces	Cinnamon Sauce, Sweet	Ginger–Tamari Sauce	
	Condiment	Chutney	Chutney	
	Pickle	Root Vegetable	Root Vegetable	
	Dessert			
	Topping			
	Beverage	Fennel Tea	Jasmine Tea	
	Other	Shrimp	Lobster	

[NOTE: Recipes for all dishes can be found in Part II of this book.]

		WINTER	SUMMER	
	SOMBER TIMES			
	Soup	Miso Soup	Broccoli Soup, Cream of, with Miso	
	Condiment			
	Salad			
	Salad Dressing			
50%	Whole grains	Brown Rice	Noodles	
10%	Beans	Adzuki	Garbanzo	
30%	Green Veg.	Peas	Cabbage, Boiled, with Caraway	
	Root Veg.	Rutabaga	Parsnips	
	Other Veg.	Celery	Corn	
	Sea Veg.			
10%	Oil			
	Sauces			
	Condiment			
	Pickle			
	Dessert	Baked Apple	Sliced Peaches	
	Topping			
	Beverage	Kukicha Tea	Kukicha Tea	

[NOTE: Recipes for all dishes can be found in Part II of this book.]

		WINTER	**SUMMER**	
	SPORTS (2 WEEK)			
	Soup	Carrot Puree	Miso Broth with Nori	
	Condiment		Parsley	
	Salad			
	Salad Dressing			
50%	**Whole grains**	Oats	Barley	
10%	**Beans**	Garbanzo	Great Northern	
30%	**Green Veg.**	Cabbage, Chinese	Bok Choy	
	Root Veg.	Carrots	Parsnips	
	Other Veg.			
	Sea Veg.	(kelp in beans)	(kelp in beans)	
10%	**Oil**		(olive oil in beans)	
	Sauces	Tahini Sauce		
	Condiment	Chutney	Nori Strips	
	Pickle			
	Dessert	Wonderful Wheat	Apple Kanten	
	Topping	Tofu Supreme Icing	Tofu Supreme Icing	
	Beverage			

[NOTE: Recipes for all dishes can be found in Part II of this book.]

	SPORTS (Last Meal)		
	WINTER	**SUMMER**	
	Soup			
	Condiment			
	Salad			
	Salad Dressing			
30%	**Whole grains**	Buckwheat	Millet	
10%	**Beans**			
25%	**Green Veg.**	Broccoli	Kale	
25%	**Root Veg.**	Carrots	Parsnips	
	Other Veg.			
	Sea Veg.			
10%	**Oil**			
	Sauces			
	Condiment			
	Pickle			
	Dessert	Baked Apple	Fruit Cocktail	
	Topping			
	Beverage			
10%	**Other**	Broiled Fish	Boiled Shrimp	

[NOTE: Recipes for all dishes can be found in Part II of this book.]

5. PHILOSOPHY, PRACTICE, AND TRADITION

"If you bake bread with indifference you bake a bitter bread that feeds but half a man's hunger."
Kahlil Gibran

The chef or cook of natural whole foods must keep in mind three major considerations:

•Moderation and balance, along with common sense and freedom of choice, can be used for the betterment of ourselves and those we cook for.

•It is important that the chef choose food and methods of cooking with insightful awareness, because his choice will influence the physical vitality, feeling, thinking, and actions of his customers.

•Inasmuch as there is no perfect food for any individual, we must be free to choose according to our needs, as they change from day to day and from season to season.

LIFE FORCE

2,500 years ago Pythagoras said, "Only living and fresh foods can enable man to apprehend the truth." Eating food containing life force (known in Sanskrit as *prana*) to sustain life is the prime reason for eating. Whole grains, beans, vegetables, and fruits, when first picked, are alive with the maximum life force that will give the most life to consumers and most positively affect their lives. The quality of a person's physical, mental, emotional, and moral status is directly related to the selection, quality, and quantity of the food and the life force in it.

The soil a vegetable is grown in, how long ago it was picked, how long it has been stored and under what conditions, how it has been cooked, when it is eaten after cooking, not to mention the number of times it has been reheated or the length of time it is stored in the refrigerator, are all factors that determine its food value. Eating dead food, where the life force has been diminished or depleted by commercial processing, chemical additives, repeated reheating, or storage for many days after cooking, is not conducive to the growth and support of healthy cells or tissues. Obviously, it is preferable to reduce the time between picking, cooking, serving, and eating to maintain the optimal food value.

EXISTING EATING HABITS—CULTURE VERSUS INSTINCT

When food consumption habits are being formed, more often than not the guiding force is convenience (and ignorance), not good health. Meat and milk consumption are habits that grow from childhood, generation after generation—but out of cultural tradition, not from sensible concern about health. After they have become a habit, they are looked upon as good. A meat-eating society will often take affront when it is suggested that the body is designed for consuming foods other than meat to obtain the same or better nutritional results.

As a society we usually don't eat according to principles that promote the best possible health. The forces and influences of our culture don't always have our individual interests at heart. We are told to eat—or fed, or given the choice of eating—food that is convenient, fast, was on sale, is what our friends or peers eat, etc. Often, the typical American diet is designed to fill our stomachs for a relatively long time, because the food is not readily digestible. Many foods are designed primarily to titillate our taste buds.

Yet, hasn't almost everyone eaten a

nourishing home-cooked meal and had that feeling right then and there that it was *good and good for you*? And still, hours after a healthy meal of food that is easily digestible and maintains the growth of body cells, the positive feeling is sustained because the body and mind are performing well.

To have that feeling requires proper preparation and balancing of good-quality food, for preparing food is the greatest of all arts.

Transformation Of Food Into Cells And Tissues

Cooking is a work of beauty, both for satisfying the senses and creating, maintaining, and uplifting life itself. It is also the first step in digestion, a transformation of the raw materials of nature into a form that becomes blood and tissue, capable of maintaining the human mind, body, and spirit. As a chef, the condition of your health and the vitality of your mind and body determine the essence of a successful kitchen. When you are personally strong and creative, you prepare your food exceptionally. The most important ingredient in food preparation is being your best self.

> *"Food is the chief of all things. It is therefore said to be medicine for all diseases of the body."*
> Taittitiva Upanishad

FOOD PREPARATION

Some basic guidelines in food preparation are:

•Maintain cleanliness and order, not only in the kitchen layout, but in the chef, too; have everything in its place, and keep a focused, clear mind while cooking.

•Select foods with the most life-giving energy and cook them according to the season and the occasion, considering where they come from, if they have been treated, and how old they are.

•Balance the food to be consumed using the *Food Effects Chart* on pg. 23.

•Develop and use intuitive knowledge about seasonal foods, color selection, cooking methods, flavorings, heat applications, etc., to best enhance the goodness and life force of the food.

•Make a plan for your work and allow time to complete it.

•Look upon yourself with gratitude and honor, as a conductor or channel of the basic energies of the world. The quality of your channelling saturates the food as you plan and execute your calling.

•The chef's thoughts, mental status, and vibrations are transmitted into the food being prepared.

•If the non-health-supporting habits and tastes of management prevail, it is preferable to leave your job, rather than sacrifice your philosophies or principles of food preparation, as long as you have a realistic set of values.

TRADITIONS: BRAHMIN, SUFI, WESTERN

Traditional and ritual cultural elements, like ethnic foods, are near and dear all over the world.

In the Zen Buddhist tradition, the kitchen is regarded as the altar of the house. In the Brahmin tradition, things are only slightly different. "The wife carefully prepares food after bathing, putting on clean clothes and readying herself to approach the kitchen with serenity and devotion. Only she can perform the ritual of preparing food. Her motions are carried out with studied grace, and her mind is kept focused and calm through the repetition of special mantras. Though she never tastes the food until it is blessed, dedicated to the ennobling spirit, and until she has fed those for whom she has prepared it, she remains closely attuned to its changing properties and seldom fails to add the right seasonings or the proper amount of heat at the precisely correct moment to create a delicious and healthful dish." [1]

Not unlike the homemaker, the skilled professional chef is inured by habit and necessity, following rituals deeply instilled over many years.

Historically, and even today, in Sufi schools, the cooks have priority and sit with the *skeik* (leader, wiseman) more than anyone else does.

In Sufi tradition, it is believed that as time goes on, higher levels of subtle understanding occur (something that is comprehended by the most famous non-Sufi chefs). Other philosophical guidelines are:

• Everything relates.

• As the chef is inspired, so is the food.

• A state of harmony exists in the kitchen that prepares good food.

• Tradition and common sense, not an esoteric secret, make good food.

• Keys to success are the outward effort and the inward effort.

• The quality of the food improves as its preparer's awareness grows.

• Acquire the subtlety to "see" with all your senses all that is in plain sight.

• The preparer of food needs to be the observer and the participant. The next step is to be the observer, the participant, and, at the same time, that which is being observed.

In Western tradition, many chefs come to work in street clothes, and, through an unspoken ritual, prepare for the day. Donning fresh, clean whites before the mirror, he or she adjusts the coat, and adds the apron, carefully folding it. The scarf is carefully folded and knotted, just so, sometimes even with a stick pin. The toque blanc is added, tilted in just the correct manner. Now the chef is ready. The ritual continues, each as the needs have been forged. After the chef enters the kitchen, the scene varies from chef to chef. One may go directly to the coffee, another to the walk-in to stir the imagination, another to the office for the specific requirements of the day. Some meet with the other cooks or chefs who will receive absolution, directions for the day, or instructions, both personal and professional.

The leader has arrived. The ship now has its captain, all know what they are supposed to do; calm, peace, and order reign, and each can go forward with intelligence and the best interlocking innate intuitiveness. Woe be unto those who rattle the system!

DEVELOPMENT

Within certain limits, the food you eat affects the quietness of your mind. Let your diet change gently and naturally; be honest with yourself. Don't force changes: to try to give up a food too soon only makes you focus on it all the more. The point is to let go of thoughts as well as the food. To keep the thoughts of a certain type of food and not eat it is upsetting.

Some foods make you more agitated and stimulated, so it's hard to sit still. Your sensitivity to such foods will change. As you come to feel lighter, for example, red meats will seem too heavy.

Slowly your diet will shift away from red meats, cheese, and eggs, toward poultry and fish, and finally, perhaps, to just grains, beans, vegetables, seeds, nuts, and fruits.

EXPERIENCE, EXPERIENCE, AND EXPERIENCE

Considering all the elements of preparing food—including acquisition, storage, seasonal and color selection, cutting, method of cooking, application of heat, combining basic foods and flavorings, plate preparation, garnishing, proper use of vegetable trimmings (not to mention cooking for an express purpose)—it is no wonder it is said that food preparation is the greatest of all arts and the most important of all sciences. And no wonder the beginner's mental computer tends to break down in the face of such involved decision making. Thus, the chef must rely on tradition and the painstaking development of his or her intimate intuition, usually created by thought, feeling, trial tasting, and, hopefully, only a few errors. Recognize your mistakes and develop your intuition by learning from your mistakes.

6. CHARTS AND LISTS

BACTERIA POISONING CHART

BACTERIA	SYMPTOMS	FOODS COMMONLY INVOLVED	USUAL INCUBATION TIME AFTER CONSUMED	USUAL DURATION OF POISONING
Botulism	Begins with dizziness; headache; dry skin, throat & mouth; stomach & intestinal problems; constipation. Ends with muscle weakness, paralysis, respiratory failure, double vision, and sometimes death	Canned meat, meat products, low-acid vegetables	3 hours–8 days	1–20 days
Perfringens	Mild abdominal pain, diarrhea	Meat, stuffing, gravies	8–22 hours	1–2 days
Salmonellosis (Salmonellae)	Vomiting, abdominal pain, diarrhea, fever, sometimes chills & headache	Eggs, cracked eggs, meat poultry	6–48 hours	2–7 days
Staphylococcus (Staph)	Nausea, vomiting, abdominal cramps, diarrhea, headache, sweating, low temperature	Meat, poultry, cream sauces, custards, dairy products	3–12 hours	1–2 days
Trichinosis	Muscle pain, fever, stomach or intestinal pain, sometimes death	Uncooked pork or wild game	3–28 days	Up to months
Vibrio Papahaemolyticus	Severe stomach pain, nausea, vomiting, diarrhea, chills, headache	Fish, seafood, cooked or uncooked	12–24 hours	1–2 days

DESCENDING ORDER OF PREFERENCE CHART

(The degree of desirability is high at the beginning of each list, and descends to the least desirable; the last one is generally discouraged altogether.)

BEVERAGES
Spring, well, or mineral water
Broths or teas from fresh vegetables, roots, stems, bark, herbs, spices
Carbonated mineral water
Decaffeinated tea or coffee
Tea or coffee
Hot chocolate
Soft drinks
Milk
Alcohol

LEAVENING
Fermented grains (such as rice or wheat)
Sourdough
Yeast
Baking Powder without Sodium Aluminum Phosphate
Baking powder
Baking soda

MEAT
White-fleshed fish
Shellfish
Rabbit
Chicken, white meat (free-roaming, hand-cleaned)
Meat of beef, pork, mutton, etc.
Processed meats

OILS
Cold-pressed oils (such as olive, corn, sesame)
Sunflower
Safflower, Peanut
Soy
Cottonseed, Palm
Highly processed, odorless oil

PASTA
Buckwheat, gray (Soba)
Whole wheat, tan (Udon)
Durum, yellow
Semolina, yellow or white
Ramen
White flour

PICKLES
Naturally fermented (salt)
Preserved in vinegar
Preserved in sugar

STARCHES FOR THICKENING
Kuzu
Arrowroot
Rice flour, whole wheat pastry flour, tapioca
Cornstarch

SWEETENERS
Fresh fruit
Barley malt
Rice syrup
Fruit juices
Dried or pureed fruit
Maple syrup
Honey and corn syrup
Artificial sweeteners
Molasses
Date sugar
Brown sugar
Turbinado
Refined white sugar

VEGETABLES AND FRUITS
Locally grown and in-season
Locally grown
Fresh but grown in same climate zone
Frozen
Fresh but grown in another climate zone
Canned

VINEGAR
Whole grain (for example, rice)
Apple cider
Wine
Distilled white

KITCHEN UTENSILS
Wood/bamboo
Stainless steel
Aluminum
Plastic

POTS AND PANS
Cast iron
Glass, porcelain
Baked pottery, Stoneware*
Stainless steel
Aluminum†
Plastic-covered aluminum, non-stick ware

COOKING FUELS
Wood
Coal
Gas
Electric
Microwave

*Red ceramics are lead-based and should be avoided.
†Aluminum, a soft material, causes milk products to turn gray, may contribute to Alzheimer's Disease. Tomato eats it or pits it and lemon juice turns it green.

EQUIVALENCY & SUBSTITUTION CHART
(Space is provided for you to add your own.)

1 Tbs. kuzu = 2 Tbs. arrowroot
1 Tbs. arrowroot = 2 Tbs. cornstarch
1 Tbs. arrowroot = 3 Tbs. flour
1 Tbs. cornstarch = 1 Tbs. tapioca
1 Tbs. cornstarch = 2 Tbs. unbleached or
whole wheat pastry flour
1 Tbs. flour = 1 Tbs. quick-cooking
tapioca
2 bars kanten = 4 Tbs. agar-agar flakes
1 Tbs. agar-agar pdr. = gels 1 qt. apple cider/jc.
butter or margarine = same amt. corn oil + $\frac{1}{2}$
tsp. salt per cup

=

=

=

sm. garlic cl. minced = $\frac{1}{4}$ tsp.
med. garlic cl. minced = $\frac{1}{2}$ tsp.
lg. garlic cl. minced = $\frac{3}{4}$–1 tsp.

=

=

$\frac{3}{4}$ cup sugar, white = 2 cups apple juice
" = $1\frac{1}{2}$ cups barley malt
" = 1 cup apple butter
" = 2 cups rice syrup
" = $\frac{1}{2}$ cup maple syrup

=

=

#4 scoop = 8 oz. / 1 cup
#8 scoop = 4 oz. / $\frac{1}{2}$ cup
#12 scoop = 2.66 oz. / $\frac{1}{4}$+ cup
#20 scoop = 1.6 oz. / $\frac{1}{4}$- cup

1 tsp. dry mustard = 1 Tbs. prepared mustard
1 tsp. tamari = $\frac{1}{4}$ tsp. salt
1 tsp. lemon juice = $\frac{1}{2}$ tsp. vinegar
2 cups water = 1 lb.
1 inch vanilla bean = 1 tsp. vanilla extract
$\frac{1}{2}$ lb. tofu = 1 cup tofu
5 cups batter = 9 × 13" pan or 12-hole
$2\frac{1}{4}$" muffin pan
$\frac{1}{4}$ lb. tofu = 1 egg (in baking)
1 Tbs. arrowroot = $\frac{1}{4}$ cup tofu (in baking)
1 tsp. miso = $\frac{1}{2}$ tsp. salt

=

EQUIVALENCY, METRIC PACKAGE

1 tsp. dry measure	=	4 grams	1 lb. 14 oz. (lg. can)	=	850 grams
1 tsp. liquid measure	=	5 grams	2 pounds	=	900 grams
1 ounce	=	28.35 grams	3 pounds	=	$\frac{1}{4}$ kilograms
3.57 ounces	=	100 grams	1 microgram	=	1/1,000,000 gram
$\frac{1}{4}$ pound (4 oz.)	=	113 grams	1,000 micrograms	=	1 milligram
$\frac{1}{2}$ pound (8 oz.)	=	225 grams	1 milligram	=	1/1,000 gram
$\frac{3}{4}$ pound (12 oz.)	=	340 grams	1,000 milligrams	=	1 gram
15 ounces	=	425 grams	100 milliliters	=	1 deciliter (dl)
1 pound (16 oz.)	=	450 grams	10 deciliters	=	1 liter (l)
$1\frac{1}{2}$ pounds	=	675 grams	1,000 grams	=	1 kilogram (kg)

EQUIVALENCY, COMMON LIQUID AND DRY

Liquid Measure

1 teaspoon	=	$^1/_3$ tablespoon	=		=	5 milliliters
3 teaspoons	=	1 tablespoon	=		=	15 milliliters
2 tablespoons	=	$^1/_8$ cup	=	1 fluid ounce	=	30 milliliters
4 tablespoons	=	$^1/_4$ cup	=	2 fluid ounces	=	59 milliliters
$5^1/_3$ tablespoons	=	$^1/_3$ cup	=		=	79 milliliters
8 tablespoons	=	$^1/_2$ cup	=	4 fluid ounces	=	118.4 milliliters
16 tablespoons	=	1 cup	=	8 fluid ounces	=	.2366 liters
		2 cups	=	1 pint	=	.4732 liters
		4 cups	=	1 quart	=	.9463 liters

Dry Measure

1 ounce	=		=	28.35 grams
3.57 ounces	=		=	100 grams
16 ounces	=	1 pound	=	.45 kilograms
2.2 pounds	=		=	1 kilogram
2 pints	=	1 quart		
4 quarts	=	1 gallon		
2 gallons	=	1 peck		
4 pecks	=	1 bushel		

METRIC CONVERSION

teaspoons	×	5	=	milliliters
tablespoons	×	15	=	milliliters
fluid ounces	×	30	=	milliliters
cups	×	0.24	=	liters
pints	×	0.47	=	liters
quarts	×	0.94	=	liters
ounces (by wght.)	×	28	=	grams
pounds	×	0.45	=	kilograms

EQUIVALENCY, LIQUID OZ.

1 ounce	=	$^1/_8$ cup + 2 Tbs.
2 ounces	=	$^1/_4$ cup
3 ounces	=	$^1/_4$ cup + 2 Tbs.
4 ounces	=	$^1/_2$ cup
5 ounces	=	$^1/_2$ cup + 2 Tbs.
6 ounces	=	$^3/_4$ cup
7 ounces	=	1 cup less 2 Tbs.
8 ounces	=	1 cup
16 ounces	=	1 pint
32 ounces	=	1 quart
128 ounces	=	1 gallon

EQUIVALENCY, METRIC

$^1/_8$ tsp.	=	.5 milliliters (ml.)
$^1/_4$ tsp.	=	1.5 milliliters
$^1/_2$ tsp.	=	3 milliliters
$^3/_4$ tsp.	=	4 milliliters
1 tsp.	=	5 milliliters
1 Tbs.	=	15 milliliters
2 Tbs. (1 oz. liquid)	=	30 milliliters
$^1/_4$ cup	=	60 milliliters
$^1/_3$ cup	=	85 milliliters
$^1/_2$ cup	=	125 milliliters
$^2/_3$ cup	=	170 milliliters
$^3/_4$ cup	=	180 milliliters
1 cup	=	240 milliliters
2 cups	=	480 milliliters
3 cups	=	720 milliliters
4 cups	=	960 milliliters

EQUIVALENCY, MEASUREMENT

tsp.	=	teaspoon
Tbs.	=	tablespoon
speck	=	less than $^1/_8$ tsp.
pinch	=	appx. $^1/_8$ tsp.
60 drops	=	1 tsp.

3 tsp.	=	1 Tbs.
$^1/_3$ Tbs.	=	1 tsp.
$^1/_2$ Tbs.	=	$1^1/_2$ tsp.
$^1/_2$ of 3 Tbs.	=	1 Tbs. + $1^1/_2$ tsp.
$^1/_3$ of 5 Tbs.	=	1 Tbs. + 2 tsp.
$^1/_2$ of 5 Tbs.	=	2 Tbs. + $1^1/_2$ tsp.
$^1/_3$ of 7 Tbs.	=	2 Tbs. + 1 tsp.
$^1/_2$ of 7 Tbs.	=	3 Tbs. + $1^1/_2$ tsp.

$^1/_8$ cup	=	2 Tbs.
$^1/_4$ cup	=	4 Tbs.
$^1/_3$ cup	=	5 Tbs. + 1 tsp.
$^1/_2$ cup	=	8 Tbs.
$^2/_3$ cup	=	10 Tbs. + 2 tsp.
$^3/_4$ cup	=	12 Tbs.

$^7/_8$ cup	=	1 cup less 2 Tbs.
1 cup	=	16 Tbs.

$^1/_3$ of $^1/_4$ cup	=	1 Tbs. + 1 tsp.
$^1/_3$ of $^1/_3$ cup	=	1 Tbs. + $2^1/_4$ tsp.
$^1/_3$ of $^1/_2$ cup	=	2 Tbs. + 2 tsp.
$^1/_3$ of $^2/_3$ cup	=	3 Tbs. + $1^1/_4$ tsp.
$^1/_3$ of $^3/_4$ cup	=	$^1/_4$ cup

$^1/_2$ of $^1/_4$ cup	=	$^1/_8$ cup or 2 Tbs.
$^1/_2$ of $^1/_3$ cup	=	2 Tbs. + 2 tsp.
$^1/_2$ of $^1/_2$ cup	=	$^1/_4$ cup
$^1/_2$ of $^2/_3$ cup	=	$^1/_3$ cup
$^1/_2$ of $^3/_4$ cup	=	6 Tbs.

1 gill	=	$^1/_2$ cup
1 pint	=	2 cups
1 quart	=	2 pints / 4 cups
1 gallon	=	4 quarts
1 peck	=	8 quarts (dry)
1 bushel	=	4 pecks (dry)

EQUIVALENCY, METRIC LIQUID

1 fl oz	=	29.573 mL	1 gal	=	3.785 L	1 L	=	1.057 qt
2 fl oz	=	59.15 mL	2 gal	=	7.57 L	2 L	=	2.11 qt
3 fl oz	=	88.72 mL	3 gal	=	11.36 L	3 L	=	3.17 qt
4 fl oz	=	118.30 mL	4 gal	=	15.14 L	4 L	=	4.23 qt
5 fl oz	=	147.87 mL	5 gal	=	18.93 L	5 L	=	5.28 qt
6 fl oz	=	177.44 mL	6 gal	=	22.71 L	6 L	=	6.34 qt
7 fl oz	=	207.02 mL	7 gal	=	26.50 L	7 L	=	7.40 qt
8 fl oz	=	236.59 mL	8 gal	=	30.28 L	8 L	=	8.45 qt
9 fl oz	=	266.16 mL	9 gal	=	34.07 L	9 L	=	9.51 qt
10 fl oz	=	295.73 mL	10 gal	=	37.85 L	10 L	=	10.57 qt

1 qt	=	0.946 L	1 mL	=	0.034 fl oz	1 L	=	0.26 cup
2 qt	=	1.89 L	2 mL	=	0.07 fl oz	2 L	=	0.53 cup
3 qt	=	2.84 L	3 mL	=	0.10 fl oz	3 L	=	0.79 cup
4 qt	=	3.79 L	4 mL	=	0.14 fl oz	4 L	=	1.06 cups
5 qt	=	4.73 L	5 mL	=	0.17 fl oz	5 L	=	1.32 cups
6 qt	=	5.68 L	6 mL	=	0.20 fl oz	6 L	=	1.59 cups
7 qt	=	6.62 L	7 mL	=	0.24 fl oz	7 L	=	1.85 cups
8 qt	=	7.57 L	8 mL	=	0.27 fl oz	8 L	=	2.11 cups
9 qt	=	8.52 L	9 mL	=	0.30 fl oz	9 L	=	2.38 cups
10 qt	=	9.46 L	10 mL	=	0.34 fl oz	10 L	=	2.64 cups

FLAVOR COMBINATIONS, EXCEPTIONALLY COMPATIBLE
(Space is provided for you to add your own.)

GENERAL FLAVORS

Celery ↔ Tarragon
Cinnamon ↔ Garlic
Cumin ↔ Coriander
Lemon ↔ Coriander
Lemon ↔ Ginger
Ginger ↔ Tamari
Maple ↔ Mustard
Maple ↔ Tamari
Mint ↔ Tahini
Saffron ↔ Tarragon
Salt ↔ Sweetener
Fennel ↔ Cumin, caraway
Legumes ↔ Cumin, caraway
Sesame ↔ Green onions
Thyme ↔ Sage, rosemary
Cardamom ↔ Cinnamon (for pastry)

↔

↔

↔

SAUCES

Basil ↔ Oregano
Bay leaf ↔ Fennel seed
Caraway ↔ Marjoram
Celery ↔ Tarragon
Cinnamon ↔ Cilantro
Cucumber ↔ Tarragon
Garlic ↔ Parsley
Mint, olive oil ↔ Lemon juice, garlic
Mustard ↔ Tarragon
Rosemary ↔ Thyme
Miso ↔ Tahini, lemon
Tofu ↔ Tahini, mustard
White miso ↔ Mustard, lemon

↔

↔

↔

VEGETABLES AND FRUITS

Apples ↔ Fennel
Asparagus ↔ Vanilla
Berries ↔ Lemon
Cabbage ↔ Caraway
Cucumbers ↔ Tarragon
Leafy greens ↔ Brown rice vinegar, Tahini Sauce
Mushrooms ↔ Oregano
Onion ↔ Apples
Raspberries ↔ *Light* salt
Sea vegetables ↔ Mirin, lemon juice
Squash ↔ Fennel, anise seed
Squash ↔ Bulgur
Squash ↔ Whole wheat noodles
Strawberries ↔ Mint

↔

GRAINS/BEANS

Barley, whole wheat ↔ Saffron
Wheat berries, barley ↔ Mint, rice vinegar, tamari
Buckwheat ↔ Tamari, onion, garlic
Buckwheat ↔ Mushrooms
Buckwheat ↔ Olive Oil, onions
Bulgur ↔ Rice vinegar, chives, basil, oregano
Couscous ↔ Mint, cilantro
Oats ↔ Fennel, barley malt
Oats ↔ Cinnamon, clove, cardamom
Brown Rice ↔ Thyme, bay leaf, garlic, parsley, onion, tamari
Brown rice ↔ Cilantro
Brown rice ↔ Ginger, sesame seed or oil
Basmati rice ↔ Coriander, cumin, pepper, turmeric
Beans (most) ↔ Ginger, garlic
Beans (most) ↔ Cumin, coriander, turmeric, mustard
Chickpeas, lentils, mung ↔ Curry
Corn meal ↔ Italian seasonings
Millet ↔ Rosemary, cinnamon
Grains (most) ↔ Raisins, nuts, gomasio
Grains (most) ↔ Tamari, tahini

↔

GARNISH CHART

Alfalfa Sprouts	Whole.
Beets	Whole, julienned, sliced.
Carrots	Tops, sticks, curls, grated, flowers.
Celery	Tops, hearts, sticks, inner pieces.
Chives	Chopped.
Clover	Sprigs.
Corn silk	Trim dark away.
Cucumbers	Sliced, sticks, rounds, forked.
Daikon	Grated, chopped, sliced, julienned.
Dill	Chopped, sprigs.
Green onion	Chopped, whole, shredded, florets.
Green/red pepper	Rings, julienned, diced.
Honeydew melon	Balls, 1" wedges.
Lemons, limes, oranges	Slices, twists, wedges.
Lettuce	Leaves, shredded.
Marjoram	Sprigs, diced.
Mint	Sprigs, diced.
Nuts	Roasted, halved, sliced, chopped.
Olives	Whole, halved, chopped.
Paprika	Sprinkle lightly.
Parsley	Sprigs, chopped.
Pickles	Whole, sliced, chopped.
Radishes	Whole, sliced, chopped, flowers.
Rosemary	Sprigs, chopped.
Sage	Sprigs, chopped.
Savory	Sprigs, chopped.
Tarragon	Sprigs, chopped.
Thyme	Sprigs, chopped.
Watercress	Sprigs, chopped.

INGREDIENTS OF A WELL-TAUGHT CLASS

Reprinted by permission from *Restaurants U.S.A.*, Washington D.C., © February 1987

•**A personable, well-organized teacher.** Choose a chef with human relations skills as well as technical knowledge. The best teachers have a clear speaking voice, an ability to explain each step in a logical way, a knack for encouraging interaction with students and enthusiasm for their profession. A sense of humor helps, too.

•**Good recipes.** Gear the complexity of recipes to the abilities of students and make sure the ingredients are available in the supermarkets and other stores your students must use.

Also, avoid recipes requiring specialized equipment, such as a heavy-duty mixer, which students may not own. Test all recipes to make sure they work and that instructions are clear. Leave room on recipe cards or pages for students to jot down their own notes.

•**An innovative structure.** Most students want more from a cooking class than the ability to replicate specific recipes. Structure classes to broaden students' understanding of food and culinary techniques. One teacher shows students how to appreciate different combinations of color, texture and flavor by analyzing a plate of food like a bottle of wine. Another demonstrates basic approaches for preparing dishes almost entirely in advance, then finishing them just before serving.

•**Painstaking organization.** Good cooking teachers often spend much longer preparing for a class than teaching it. Use the *mise en place* method of arranging all recipe ingredients on a tray to save precious class time and lessen the risk of omitting something. Prepare finished versions of recipes that require too much time for completion in class (examples: a slow-rising bread or a stew that must simmer for hours) so students can see how they turn out.

•**Good visibility.** Resist the impulse to overbook; schedule the class for a space large enough so that all students can see each step. Remove equipment and other visual impediments. When performing a tricky operation, such as caramelizing sugar or sauteeing onions, tilt the pot to show students several different stages of the process. Consider installing a mirror over the preparation and cooking area so the students can see well from anywhere in the room.

•**Opportunities for tasting.** Tasting the end product is the natural climax of a cooking lesson; skip it, and any student will feel deprived. Beyond satisfying appetites, the tasting gives students a basis for comparing their own renditions to the teacher's version. When the number of students exceeds the amount of food, one recipe should be distributed to one part of the audience, a second recipe to another part.

INITIAL STOCKING LIST
100 MEALS PER DAY

Whole Grain and Whole Grain Products

Brown rice	100 lbs.
Barley	25 lbs.
Millet	25 lbs.
Bulgur	25 lbs.
Whole wheat pasta	25 lbs.
Whole wheat bread flour	25 lbs.
Whole wheat pastry flour	25 lbs.
Unbleached, unbromated white flour	25 lbs.

Legumes

Lentils	25 lbs.
Red lentils	25 lbs.
Garbanzos	25 lbs.
Pintos	25 lbs.
Limas	25 lbs.
Split peas	25 lbs.

Nuts and Seeds

Walnuts	25 lbs.
Filberts	15 lbs.
Almonds	15 lbs.
Sunflower seeds	15 lbs.
Pumpkin seeds	15 lbs.
Sesame seeds	25 lbs.

Sea Vegetables

Nori, kelp, dulse	1 lb. ea.

Natural Sweeteners

Barley malt	5 gal.
Maple syrup	5 gal.

Oils

Olive oil	2 gal.
Corn oil	2 gal.
Sesame oil	2 gal.
Sesame oil, dark	1 qt.
Soy oil	5 gal.

Miscellaneous

Miso	4 lbs.
Tamari	5 gal.
Tahini	5 gal.
Kukicha (twig tea)	10 lbs.
Apple juice or cider	10 gal.
Grape juice	10 gal.
Natural salt or sea salt	25 lbs.
Arrowroot powder	2 lbs.
Raisins	25 lbs.
Rice vinegar	1 gal.
Fresh fruits & vegetables	as needed

INITIAL STOCKING LIST
12 MEALS PER DAY

Whole Grains

Brown rice, barley, millet, buckwheat, bulgur, whole grain noodles	3 lbs. ea.

Legumes

Limas, garbanzos, great northerns, pintos, adzukis, lentils, red lentils, split peas	2 lbs. ea.

Sea Vegetables

Agar-agar, nori, dulse	4 oz. ea.

Seeds and Nuts

Almonds, filberts, walnuts, sesame, sunflower, pumpkin seeds	1/2 lb. ea.

Miscellaneous

Tamari, miso	1 qt. ea.
Tahini	1 lb.
Kukicha (twig tea)	1/4 lb.
Juice	2 qts.
Rice cakes	2 packs
Whole grain bread	1 loaf
Natural salt or sea salt	1 lb.
Olive, sesame, corn oils	1 qt. ea.
Arrowroot powder	1/8 lb.
Raisins	2 lb.
Rice vinegar	1 pint
Fresh fruits & vegetables	as needed

Sweeteners

Rice Syrup, barley malt, maple syrup	1 pt. ea.

INTERNATIONAL FLAVORING CHART

	Armenian	Cambodian	Chinese	Cuban	Danish	Dutch	Egyptian	Filipino	Finnish	French	German	Greek	Hungarian	Indonesian	Iranian	Iraquian	Italian	Japanese	Jewish	Korean	Lebanese	Mexican	Norwegian	Polish	Polynesian	Puerto Rican	Russian	Spanish	Swedish	Syrian	Turkish	Vietnamese
Allspice																													•			
Anise	•	•		•	•		•		•		•		•	•	•		•		•		•	•	•			•				•	•	•
Basil	•	•	•	•			•			•	•			•	•	•	•				•	•		•		•	•			•	•	•
Bay Leaf			•	•						•	•	•	•		•		•		•		•	•	•			•				•	•	•
Caraway			•	•	•	•			•	•	•	•	•	•	•		•		•		•	•	•	•		•	•	•		•	•	•
Cardamom			•							•			•	•	•		•	•	•		•					•				•	•	
Cayenne	•		•							•					•	•			•		•	•	•								•	•
Celery Seed	•	•	•	•			•	•	•	•	•	•			•	•	•	•			•	•	•			•	•			•	•	•
Chervil								•	•					•					•				•				•		•	•	•	•
Chili Pepper				•	•			•	•	•					•	•										•				•		
Chives		•	•			•							•				•		•								•					•
Cilantro		•		•	•			•	•			•			•	•		•				•			•					•	•	•
Cinnamon					•																•						•					
Clove	•	•	•	•	•	•	•		•	•	•	•	•	•	•	•			•	•	•	•	•			•		•		•	•	•
Coriander	•		•	•	•	•			•	•	•	•	•				•			•	•	•	•			•	•	•		•		
Currants	•	•	•	•		•	•					•	•		•		•		•	•	•		•			•	•	•	•	•	•	•
Curry	•		•		•	•					•		•	•	•		•		•		•					•	•	•	•	•	•	•
Dill Seed		•		•	•	•	•	•	•	•		•		•	•	•	•	•				•		•		•				•		•
Dill Weed			•	•					•	•			•	•		•	•				•								•	•	•	•
Fennel			•	•				•	•		•							•	•	•		•						•				
Garlic		•	•	•		•		•	•	•		•	•	•	•		•			•		•			•	•	•	•	•	•	•	•
Ginger	•	•	•	•	•		•	•	•	•	•	•	•	•	•	•	•	•	•	•	•	•	•	•	•	•	•	•	•	•	•	•
Mace		•	•	•	•			•		•	•	•	•		•	•	•	•	•	•	•	•			•	•	•	•	•	•	•	•
Marjoram			•		•	•		•	•	•		•			•				•	•	•	•		•					•			
Mint			•	•	•			•	•	•	•	•			•		•		•	•	•	•			•							
Mustard	•	•		•			•			•	•		•	•	•	•	•		•	•		•		•			•		•	•	•	•
Nutmeg		•		•	•			•	•	•		•		•	•		•		•	•									•			
Onion		•	•	•	•	•		•	•	•	•	•	•	•		•		•		•	•	•	•		•	•	•	•	•	•	•	•
Oregano	•		•	•			•		•		•	•		•	•	•	•	•	•	•	•	•	•	•	•	•	•	•	•	•	•
Paprika		•	•	•			•			•		•			•		•	•			•	•				•						
Parsley		•		•	•	•		•	•	•		•				•			•		•					•	•	•	•	•	•	•
Pepper, black	•	•	•	•	•	•	•		•	•				•	•	•	•	•		•	•	•	•		•	•	•	•	•	•	•	•
Pepper, white		•	•	•	•		•		•	•	•	•	•	•	•	•	•		•		•	•	•		•	•	•	•	•	•	•	•
Poppy Seed		•	•		•		•	•	•	•		•	•		•								•			•	•					•
Rosemary							•	•		•			•		•		•				•				•		•		•			
Saffron			•				•	•	•	•		•	•	•	•		•		•		•		•				•	•	•	
Sage			•				•			•			•		•	•	•		•		•		•			•	•	•	•	•	•
Savory								•	•	•				•	•							•					•	•	•	
Sesame Seed			•	•																				•		•			•	
Tarragon		•				•				•		•	•				•		•	•	•				•		•	•	•	•	
Thyme	•			•				•	•	•		•		•			•		•		•				•	•	•	•	•	•
Turmeric		•				•	•	•	•	•	•		•	•	•	•	•		•		•	•			•		•	•	•	
Sweet Rice Wine		•			•								•	•	•				•									•			
Miso		•			•												•														
Rice Vinegar		•													•	•													•
Tahini		•													•	•													•
Tamari		•													•	•													•
Lemon		•										•			•	•													•

NUTRIENT SOURCE CHART

Nutrient	Source
Vitamins	
A	Those vegetables with the highest concentration of green pigment; also carrots, pumpkin, squash, collards, kale, broccoli.
B-1	Whole grains, legumes, corn, collards, turnip greens.
B-2	Green vegetables, broccoli, legumes, oats, mushrooms.
B-3	Whole Grains, most vegetables, fruits, mushrooms.
B-6	Whole grains, cauliflower, legumes, most vegetables, leafy greens.
B-12	Miso, tamari, sea vegetables, naturally fermented pickles, traditionally-made tempeh, fish, shellfish, foods from animal origin.
C	Turnip greens, kale, crucifers (e.g., cabbage), broccoli, asparagus, fruits.
D	Fish, fish oil, sunlight.
E	Most vegetables, whole grains, vegetables oils, tahini, nuts and seeds.
K	Kelp, alfalfa, green vegetables.
Folic Acid	Leafy greens, fresh fruit, grains, dried beans.
Pantothenic Acid	Leafy greens, mushrooms, cauliflower, most fresh vegetables and fruits.
Protein	Grains, beans, miso, tamari, white flesh, tofu, tempeh, seeds, nuts, nut butters, tahini.
Minerals	
Biotin	Whole grains, cauliflower, peas, vegetables, rice bran, leafy greens.
Calcium	Leafy green vegetables, sea vegetables, broccoli, kale, tahini (very high content).
Chloride	Salt, vegetables.
Chromium	Whole grains.
Cobalt	Sea vegetables.
Copper	Whole grains, green vegetables, legumes, water from copper pipes, nuts.
Fluoride	Whole grains, vegetables, fruit, kukicha.
Iodine	Sea vegetables.
Iron	Leafy greens, wheat, legumes, corn, iron cookware, tahini, dried fruit, sea vegetables.
Magnesium	Fresh green vegetables, corn, apples, almonds, beans.
Manganese	Whole grains, green vegetables, nuts, seeds, tahini.
Molybdenum	Legumes, whole grains, dark green vegetables.
Phosphorus	Whole grains, vegetables, nuts, seeds, legumes.
Potassium	Vegetables, fruit, whole grains, prunes, raisins, cantaloupe.
Selenium	Fish, whole grains, broccoli, onions.
Sodium	Sea vegetables, artichokes, beets, celery, chard, kale, mustard greens, salt.
Sulfur	Legumes, peas, mushrooms, Brussels sprouts, cabbage.
Zinc	Whole grains, nuts, seeds.

SAMPLE RECIPE FORM

Pan size:
Cooking time:
Oven temp.:

Yield: _____
Serves: _____
Portion: _____

Yield: _____
Serves: _____
Portion: _____

RECIPE #:
TITLE:

Variations:

Pan size:
Cooking time:
Oven temp.:

Yield: _____
Serves: _____
Portion: _____

Yield: _____
Serves: _____
Portion: _____

RECIPE #:
TITLE:

Variations:

7. INGREDIENT DESCRIPTION

FRUITS

"Great eaters and great sleepers are incapable of anything else that is great."
Henry IV of France

IMPORTANT GUIDELINES FOR FRUIT PREPARATION AND COOKERY

Preparation:

• Wash or rinse in cold water, not bruising the skin.

• Peel fruit because of pesticides or waxes (except berries).

• Keep minimum time from refrigeration to cooking or serving.

Buying:

• Develop locally-grown, organic produce suppliers.

• Insist on freshness.

• Inspect deliveries.

• Buy fruit that is not bruised.

• In-season fruit has the highest nutritive and flavor value, and the lowest price.

• Out-of-season fruit has the lowest nutritive and flavor value, and the highest price.

• Avoid leaky fruit as seen through boxes.

Storing:

• Refrigerate immediately upon delivery, except those fruits needing room-temperature-ripening, as noted.

APPLES (see chart next page)

Preparing:

Peel apples because of pesticides or waxes. Organic apples do not need peeling.

Rinse in cold water.

Handle carefully to avoid bruising or puncturing the skin.

Serving:

Apples can be sliced or diced in salads, or baked, stuffed, or stewed; used in sauces, pies, tarts, cobblers, dumplings, pancakes, strudels, puddings, or cakes; in mincemeat, fresh fruit cocktails, or chutney.

Quality:

Buy firm apples; shininess is not an indication of quality.

Avoid apples that are discolored, bruised, or soft.

Buying:

Buying by the bushel (approx. 36–42 pounds net):

Apple Diameter	Number of Apples
2 1/2"	168
2 5/8"	150
2 3/4"	138
2 7/8"	125
3 "	113
3 1/8"	100
3 1/4"	88
3 1/2"	72

Grades: U.S. Extra Fancy; U.S. Fancy; U.S. 1; U.S. Utility and Combination.

APPLE CHART

VARIETY	SEASON	COLOR	FLAVOR/TEXTURE	FRESH/SALAD	PIE	SAUCE	BAKING	CANNING
Baldwin	Oct–Jan	red/yellow	mild/firm	good	very good	excellent	good	excellent
Cortland*	Oct–Jan	green/purple	mild/tender	excellent	excellent	very good	good	good
Empire	Sep–Nov	red	sweet/semi-firm	excellent	good	good	fair	fair
Gold Delicious*	Sep–May	yellow	sweet/semi-firm	excellent	very good	good	very good	very good
Granny Smith	Apr–Jul	green	tart/crisp	good	good	good	good	good
Greening, R.I.	Sep–Nov	green	slight tart/firm	poor	excellent	excellent	very good	good
Ida Red	Oct	red	slight tart/firm	good	good	very good	very good	very good
Jonathan	Sep–Jan	bright red	tart/tender	very good	very good	very good	poor	good
McIntosh	Sep–Jun	green-red	slight tart/tender	excellent	excellent	good	poor	fair
Northern Spy	Oct	red	tangy/tender	excellent	excellent	fair	very good	good
Pippin	Sep–Jun	green-red	slight tart/firm	poor	good	good	very good	good
Red Delicious	Sep–Jun	scarlet	sweet/mellow	excellent	poor	fair	poor	fair
Rome Beauty	Oct–Jun	red	slight tart/firm	good	very good	very good	excellent	very good
Stayman	Oct–Mar	red	tart/semi-firm	excellent	good	good	good	good
Winesap	Oct–Jun	red	slight tart/firm	excellent	good	good	good	good
York Imperial	Oct–Apr	green-yellow	tart/firm	fair	good	very good	good	good

*These varieties will not darken after slicing and are particularly good in salads.

Storing:

Best stored at 32° F. Apples will ripen twice as fast at 40° F.

Damage easily.

Basis:

Originated in the Stone Age, in the area that is now Austria and Switzerland. The apple was prominent in the English countryside in Medieval times, where it was used in fertility rites.

APRICOTS

Preparing:

Wash in cold water.

Serving:

Serve cold, raw, whole, baked, or glazed, use in fresh fruit cup, couscous cake and other cakes, and sauces.

Quality:

Buy tree-ripened, preferably; full golden color, plump and tender.

Avoid fruit that has a greenish color or is hard.

Buying:

Grades: U.S. 1; U.S. 2.

Packed: Lug 24 lb.

Some varieties:

Royal (orange-yellow tending to a reddish tinge)

Tilton

Blenheim

Perfection

Morpark

Riland

Storing:

Best stored at 34° F. with 90% relative humidity.

Basis:

Originated in China; brought to Persia, to the Mediterranean, then to the New World.

AVOCADOS

Preparing:

Peel; slice, dice, or mash.

Serving:

Use in salads, guacamole, spreads, and dips.

Quality:

Look for skin that is thick and the best texture.

Size and color do not relate to flavor.

Slight skin discoloration will not affect flavor.

For maximum flavor, fruit should be slightly soft and yielding to pressure.

Avoid badly bruised and mildewed fruit.

Buying:

Grades: U.S. 1; U.S. Combination; U.S. 2 or U.S. 3.

Storing:

Best stored in refrigerator. Unripened avocados keep at room temperature until ripe.

Basis:

Originated in Mexico and Central America.

BLACKBERRIES (Dewberries, Boysenberries, Loganberries, Youngberries)

Preparing:

Wash; serve cold.

Simmer only a short time to keep shape and natural integrity.

Serving:

Use in toppings, garnishes, salads, tarts, pies, and sauces.

Quality:

Blackberries should be black and bright, large and plump.

Loganberries are dark red.

Youngberries have a deep wine color.

Avoid dull colors, soft moldy berries, and decay.

Buying:

Grades for blackberries and dewberries: U.S. 1; U.S. 2

Packed: Containers are pints or quarts in flats.

Storing:

Best stored at 34° F. at 90% relative humidity. Use berries quickly; have short shelf life.

BLUEBERRIES

Preparing:

Wash berries.

Pick out leaves; small, hard, light-colored berries; and soft berries.

Serving:

Can be served fresh with soy milk over cereal, in tofu parfait, muffins, pancakes, or waffles.

Mix with other fresh fruits.

Use in cream puffs, pies, tarts, cobblers and cakes; serve as a cheesecake topping, or as icing on a cake.

Serve fresh berries with whipped topping in a clear glass and top with a strawberry for a striking color combination.

Use in puree pastry filling or icing.

Quality:

Buy plump, firm berries that are light bluish-gray in color. A few berries may be reddish in color.

Avoid soft berries and boxes with many leaves, twigs, or clusters of unripe berries, to reduce labor required.

Buying:

There are no U.S. standards.

Packed: Usually in pint containers in 12-pint flats.

Large berries cost more.

Storing:

Best stored at 34° F. with 90% relative humidity. Use quickly; have short shelf life.

Basis:

Come mostly from Maine and the Maritime Provinces of Canada.

CANTALOUPE

Preparing:

Takes 1-3 days to ripen at room temperature to make fruit softer and juicier (not sweeter).

It is ready to eat when a definite fragrance develops and a yellow tinge comes over it; it becomes slightly springy when squeezed between the palms of your hands, and bleaching appears on the side the melon rested on.

May be served immediately or refrigerated.

Remove seeds.

Serving:

Serve at room temperature.

Serve melon halves filled with blueberries or strawberries.

Use cubes or balls in fruit cup.

Flavor with lemon or vanilla.

Place on lettuce.

Use thin wedges as garnish.

Use in a beverage with floating balls.

Can be diced on lettuce with chopped filberts or pecans.

Quality:

Buy healthy-looking, with cream-colored netting over a cream-colored background, and a smooth, round depressed area at stem end.

Melon should have a fragrant aroma; giving gently indicates ripeness.

Avoid melons that are cracked, punctured, soft, or bruised.

Buying:

Grades: U.S. Fancy; U.S. 1; U.S. Commercial.

Storing:

Best stored at 50° F. with 80–85% relative humidity.

Basis:

A member of the squash family. Originally from the Orient.

CHERRIES

Preparing:

Wash and cook.

Use raw (Bing cherries).

Serving:

Use cherries in pies, cakes, tarts.

Serve stewed and spiced.

Use as a topping, in a fruit cup, or as a dessert.

Quality:

Buy firm, well-matured, well-colored, juicy fruit.

Avoid cherries that are soft, light-colored, small, dry, or bitter.

Buying:

Grades: U.S. 1; U.S. Commercial.

Packed: in 12- and 20-lb. containers.

Storing:

Best stored at 36° F. with 90% relative humidity.

Basis:

Originated in Asia.

CRANBERRIES

Preparing:

Sort, wash, and cook.

Increased cooking tends to increase bitterness.

Serving:

Use in sauces, muffins, pies, and breads.

Use in aspic, mousse, and toppings.

Quality:

Purchase bright, firm, plump berries.

Avoid berries that are dull, shriveled, and soft.

Buying:

Grades: U.S. Consumer Grade A.

Packed: in 25-lb. boxes or cartons of 12-oz. or 16-oz. packages.

Storing:

Best stored at 35–40° F. with 90% relative humidity. May be frozen.

Basis:

Originated with the American Indians, who cooked them with honey to eat with meat, and used them for medicinal purposes and dyes.

GRAPES

Preparing:

Wash and serve raw.

Serve in bunches, cut to size desired, or picked from bunches.

Garnish with small bunches.

Serving:

Serve as a dessert, in a fruit cup, in a fruit salad.

Use for color contrast.

Serve chilled or in a sauce.

Quality:

Purchase grapes with good color, fresh stems, and plump fruit.

Avoid soft, bad-colored, dried stems, and bad color where the grape meets the stem.

Color choice: Green

Yellow-green

Red

Blue-black

Buying:

Grades: U.S. Fancy; U.S. Extra No.1; U.S. 1.

Storing:

Best stored at 36° F. with relatively high humidity and maximum circulation of air.

Basis:

Originated around the Caspian Sea.

HONEYDEWS

Preparing:

Cut, remove seeds, and serve.

Serving:

Cut into halves, quarters, eighths or slivers for garnish.

Dice and serve in fruit cup or with contrasting colored fruits.

Serve blended in a frothy shake with a little water or apple juice.

Mix with cucumber in a summer salad.

Serve with avocado and tofu dressing.

Quality:

Avoid overripe melons, and those with cuts, cracks, or bruises.

The blossom end should be soft with a rounded depression on the stem end. When ripe it has a delicate aroma, creamy skin color, slightly soft blossom and feel of the seeds when shaken.

Buying:

Grades: U.S. 1; U.S. Commercial; U.S. 2.

Packed: Shipped in flats: pony—32 lbs. (6–12 melons); standard—40 lbs.(6–12 melons); jumbo—45 lbs. (6–12 melons).

Storing:

Best stored at 50° F. with 80–85% relative humidity. Unripe melons can be stored at room temperature for three days, then refrigerated.

Basis:

Originally grown in southern France and Algeria.

LEMONS

Preparing:

Wash.

Slice or squeeze.

Serving:

Use juice for flavoring.

Serve grated for flavoring or as a garnish.

Quality:

Buy fruit that is firm and heavy, with fine textured skin, in the size desired.

Avoid fruit that is soft, whitish, or with mildewed skin.

Buying:

Grades: U.S. 1; U.S. Combination; U.S. 2

Packed: 37–40-lb. containers (count from 63–235).

Storing:

Best stored at 50° F. with 80–85% relative humidity.

Basis:

A native of Asia. In 1299 the Mongolians drank lemonade; brought by returning crusaders to Europe.

PEACHES

Preparing:

Remove skins unless peaches are organic: place peaches in rolling boiling water for $1/2$ minute, and cool in cold water so that skins will come off easily.

Remove stone and stem.

Do not leave at room temperature.

Slice or dice.

Serving:

Can be baked, glazed, or stewed.

Add to pie or cake.

Puree in a blender, cooked or raw, for sauces or icing (with or without some nuts).

Serve raw in salad, with or without other fruits and nuts or raisins.

Quality:

Buy fruit that is mature, tree-ripened, yellowish colored tinged with red; plump. Taste test for sweetness.

Avoid fruit that is green (does not ripen), shriveled, or bruised.

Peaches will ripen at room temperature, some sooner than others.

Buying:

Grades: U.S. Fancy; U.S. Extra 1; U.S. 1; U.S. 2.

Packed: 38-lb. containers. Buy by size or count.

Storing:

Best stored at 34° F. with 90% relative humidity.

Basis:

Originated in China, developed in Persia and were called "Persian apples."

PEARS

Preparing:

Peel if not organic; halve and core.

Slice, dice, leave halved, or quarter.

Serving:

Serve raw for dessert with another fruit and a lemon sauce, sliced or diced.

Stew with cinnamon, bake with or without a tofu glaze, or poach in a raisin sauce.

Slice in a salad with cucumber, celery, tofu mayonnaise, and topped with roasted hazelnuts.

Quality:

Buy plump, ripe or green (which will ripen at room temperature), smooth, juicy, firm, and unbruised fruit.

Avoid misshapen, bruised fruit with dark spots or juicy skin.

Buying:

Grades: Extra Fancy; U.S. 1 Fancy; U.S. Combination; U.S. 2.

Packed: In lugs of 22–24 lbs. with undetermined count.

Varieties	Salads	Baking	Poaching	Raw
Anjou		•	•	
Bartlett	•		•	•
Bosc		•	•	
Comice		•	•	

Storing:

Best stored at 32° F. for ripe pears; unripened pears at 60–65° F. with 85–95% relative humidity.

Basis:

Originated in central Asia, then came to Europe.

PLUMS

Preparing:

Wash if organic.

If not organic, place in rolling boiling water for one minute to make skins easily removable. Remove seed.

Serving:

Serve raw or cooked, slightly seasoned.

Puree in blender to make sauce or topping for other fruits, cakes, or pie decoration, with or without a clear thickening agent.

Finely dice and serve with yogurt and granola.

With cut half up, bake with a teaspoon of cinnamon–raisin sauce topped with a walnut.

Stew, adding vanilla; use as topping with a dab of tofu topping.

Quality:

Do not ripen after harvesting.

Buy plump, clean, and fresh-looking fruit, soft enough to yield slightly to pressure.

Avoid hard, shriveled, poorly colored and flavored, very soft, or leafy fruit.

Buying:

Grades: U.S. Fancy; U.S. 1; U.S. Combination.

Packed: crates or lugs ranging from 22 to 32 lbs.

Storing:

Best stored at 36° F. with 90% relative humidity. Bruise easily from weight.

Basis:

Originated in Asia.

RASPBERRIES

Preparing:

Take from refrigerator and gently quick-soak in cold water and drain. They bruise easily and absorb water. Serve or use immediately.

Serving:

Since raspberries are one of the most perishable fruits, it is convenient to mash, sweeten, bring to a boil, and simmer a minute; the resulting sauce keeps very well.

Whole, they are an excellent addition to fruit cup.

Serve fresh with thick barley milk or cream.

Excellent flavoring for icings, glazes, parfaits, puddings, tarts, or layered in cakes before baking.

Use raspberry sauce on shortcake with tofu topping.

Quality:

Very perishable.

Buy clean, bright, plump berries with full color and fresh appearance.

Avoid berries that are dull, leaky, hard, soft, or moldy.

Buying:

No U.S. Grades.

Storing:

Best stored at 32° F. with 90% relative humidity; highly perishable.

RHUBARB

(Rhubarb is sometimes referred to as a vegetable.)

Preparing:

Dice to size desired (1–2").

Serving:

Use in strawberry–rhubarb pie filling.

Can be baked, covered.

Stew or cook with lemon.

Quality:

Buy rhubarb that is firm, fresh, crisp, and has a bright appearance; well-formed stalks, young stems with small leaves tend to be more tender and have a more delicate flavor.

Avoid stalks that are soft or flabby; large stalks tend to be tough.

Portions:

100 portions @ 3 oz. cooked—buy 19 lbs. trimmed.

Buying:

Grades: U.S. Fancy; U.S. 1; U.S. 2.

Packed: 10 5-lb. cartons per container

Western apple box—35 lbs.

Western box—5 lbs.

Storing:

Best stored at 36° F. with 90-95% relative humidity; ample air circulation.

Basis:

Originated in Tibet, coming to Europe about 300 years ago.

STRAWBERRIES

Preparing:

Quick-rinse in cold water and drain.

Remove green stems by pulling or twisting off, or cutting with a small knife.

Do not soak or wash berries without their stems, for it will drastically alter their natural flavor and texture.

Serving:

Garnish other fruits with whole berries, including stems.

Blend into tofu icing.

Use as a glaze on cake.

Cut to bite size and serve in fruit cup.

Serve plain with soy milk.

Blend cooked or raw for sauce and add water or apple juice for a cool drink.

Quality:

Very perishable.

Buy berries that are bright red (not pink or yellow), plump, fresh-looking, bright, with green caps.

Avoid berries that are moldy, very sweet, leaky, small, misshapen, or that have off-color spots or hard green areas.

Buying:

Grades: U.S. 1; U.S. Combination; U.S. 2.

Storing:

Best stored at 36° F. with 90% relative humidity; highly perishable.

Basis:

Grow wild throughout the world.

WATERMELON

Preparing:

Wash, slice, or dice.

Serving:

Serve sliced or diced.

Use as a garnish.

Serve in fresh fruit cup or as melon balls.

Blend for beverages.

Quality:

Proportionately large melons have more edible fruit than small ones. Buy large, 30 lb.-plus melons, symmetrical, fresh and attractive-looking, with velvety appearance, and yellowish on the bottom.

Avoid immature, small melons that are white on the bottom, cracked, or bruised.

Buying:

Grades: U.S. 1; U.S. Commercial; U.S. 2.

Storing:

Best stored at 50° F. with 80–85% relative humidity; keep very well.

Basis:

Found in Central America by Dr. David Livingston.

FRUIT COOKED–YIELD CHART

FRUIT	UNPREPARED LBS.†	PREPARED* CUPS	COOKED LBS.	COOKED CUPS	NOTES
Apples	1	4	1	2	when covered w/ liquid
Apricots	1	$3^1/2$	$2^3/4$	$3^1/2$	
Apricots, Dry	1	3	2.4	4	
Blackberries†	1	$2^1/2$	1	2	
Blueberries†	1	$2^1/2$	1.1	2	wet
Cantaloupe	1	$2^1/4$			
Cranberries†	1	3			
Currants	1	$3^1/4$	1.6	$3^3/4$	cooked w/ 2 cups water
Grapes	1	$1^3/4$			
Honeydew	1	$2^1/4$			
Peaches	1	$3^3/4$	1	2	
Pears	1	3	1	$2^1/4$	
Plums	1	$2^1/2$	$1^1/4$	$2^1/2$	very liquid when boiled
Prunes	1	$3^1/2$	$^1/4$	3.8	seedless
Raspberries†	1	2	1.1	$1^3/4$	
Raisins	1	3	1.6	$3^1/3$	cooked w/ $1^1/2$ cups water
Rhubarb	1	4	1.6	$3^1/2$	
Strawberries†	1	$2^1/2$	.8	1.9	
Watermelon	1	2			

*Stoned, cored, sliced, or $^3/4$"-inch diced.   †Berries are in pint quantity, not pounds.

FRUIT FLAVORING CHART

	Apples	Applesauce	Apricots	Blackberries	Blueberries	Canteloupe	Cherries	Cranberries	Currants	Honeydew	Peaches	Pears	Plums	Prunes	Raspberries	Raisins	Rhubarb	Strawberries	Watermelon
Allspice	●	●	●																
Anise	●	●	●				●	●	●			●				●			
Basil					●		●	●	●			●				●			
BayLeaf																			
Caraway																			
Cardamom	●	●																	
Cayenne						●		●			●		●			●			
Celery Seed																			
Chervil																			
Chili Pepper																			
Chives																			
Cilantro																			
Cinnamon	●	●	●																
Clove	●	●	●					●	●		●	●				●			
Coriander							●	●	●							●			
Currants	●																		
Curry																			
Dill Seed																			
Dill Weed																			
Fennel						●													
Garlic																			
Ginger	●	●	●																
Mace	●	●	●		●				●		●	●				●			
Marjoram							●	●	●		●	●				●			
Mint	●					●				●									
Mustard												●	●				●	●	●
Nutmeg	●																		
Onion							●	●	●		●	●				●			
Oregano																			
Paprika																			
Parsley																			
Pepper, black																			
Pepper, white																			
Poppy Seed						●				●									
Rosemary																			
Saffron																			
Sage																			
Savory																			
Sesame Seed																			
Tarragon						●				●				●					
Thyme																			
Turmeric																			
Barley Malt																			
Maple Syrup				●							●					●	●	●	
Cooking Sherry																●	●	●	
Miso																			
Rice vinegar																			
Tahini																			
Tamari																			
Lemon	●			●		●				●	●								

FRUIT SHIPPING CHART
(National Distribution in U.S.)

FRUIT	JAN	FEB	MAR	APR	MAY	JUN	JUL	AUG	SEP	OCT	NOV	DEC
Apples	○○○	○○○	○○○	○○○	○○○	○○○	○○○	○○○	○○○	●●●	●●●	●●●
Apricots	- - -	- - -	- - -	- - -	- - -	●●●	●●●	- - -	- - -	- - -	- - -	- - -
Avocados	○○○	○○○	●●●	- - -	●●●	●●●	●●●	●●●	●●●	○○○	○○○	○○○
Bananas	○○○	○○○	○○○	○○○	●●●	●●●	○○○	○○○	○○○	○○○	○○○	○○○
Blackberries	- - -	- - -	- - -	- - -	○○○	○○○	●●●	●●●	- - -	- - -	- - -	- - -
Blueberries	- - -	- - -	- - -	- - -	●●●	●●●	●●●	●●●	- - -	- - -	- - -	- - -
Cantaloupes	- - -	- - -	- - -	- - -	●●●	●●●	●●●	●●●	●●●	○○○	○○○	○○○
Cranberries									●●●	●●●	●●●	○○○
Figs	- - -	- - -	- - -	- - -	- - -	○○○	○○○	●●●	●●●	○○○	- - -	- - -
Grapefruit	○○○	○○○	○○○	○○○	○○○	- - -	- - -	- - -	- - -	○○○	○○○	○○○
Grapes	○○○	○○○	○○○	- - -	- - -	○○○	○○○	○○○	○○○	○○○	○○○	○○○
Honeydews	- - -	- - -	- - -	- - -	- - -	●●●	●●●	●●●	●●●	●●●	- - -	- - -
Kiwifruit	●●●	●●●	●●●	- - -	○○○	○○○	○○○	○○○	○○○	○○○	- - -	●●●
Lemons	○○○	○○○	○○○	○○○	○○○	○○○	○○○	○○○	○○○	○○○	○○○	○○○
Limes	- - -	- - -	- - -	- - -	- - -	○○○	●●●	●●●	- - -	- - -	- - -	- - -
Mangoes	- - -	- - -	- - -	○○○	○○○	○○○	○○○	○○○	- - -	- - -	- - -	- - -
Nectarines	- - -	- - -	- - -	- - -	○○○	○○○	○○○	○○○	○○○	- - -	- - -	- - -
Oranges	○○○	○○○	○○○	○○○	- - -	- - -	- - -	- - -	- - -	- - -	- - -	○○○
Papayas	- - -	- - -	- - -	○○○	○○○	○○○	- - -	- - -	- - -	○○○	○○○	- - -
Peaches	- - -	- - -	- - -	- - -	- - -	●●●	●●●	●●●	- - -	- - -	- - -	- - -
Pears	○○○	○○○	○○○	○○○	○○○	- - -	○○○	●●●	●●●	●●●	●●●	●●●
Persians	- - -	- - -	- - -	- - -	- - -	- - -	○○○	○○○	○○○	○○○	- - -	- - -
Persimmons	- - -	- - -	- - -	- - -	- - -	- - -	- - -	- - -	- - -	○○○	○○○	○○○
Pineapples	○○○	○○○	○○○	○○○	○○○	○○○	○○○	- - -	- - -	- - -	- - -	○○○
Plums	○○○	○○○	○○○	- - -	- - -	- - -	- - -	●●●	●●●	●●●	○○○	- - -
Pomegranates	- - -	- - -	- - -	- - -	- - -	- - -	- - -	- - -	○○○	○○○	○○○	- - -
Raspberries	- - -	- - -	- - -	- - -	- - -	- - -	●●●	●●●	○○○	○○○	○○○	- - -
Strawberries	○○○	○○○	○○○	○○○	●●●	●●●	●●●	○○○	○○○	○○○	○○○	○○○
Tangelos	○○○	○○○	○○○	○○○	- - -	- - -	- - -	- - -	- - -	○○○	○○○	○○○
Tangerines	○○○	○○○	○○○	- - -	- - -	- - -	- - -	- - -	- - -	○○○	○○○	○○○
Watermelons	- - -	- - -	- - -	- - -	- - -	- - -	●●●	●●●	○○○	○○○	- - -	- - -

Peak harvesting season: ●●●   Available in large volume: ○○○   Low availability: - - -

Peak harvesting seasons of locally-grown produce will vary according to temperature and region. Buy locally-grown *organic* fruit when possible.

GRAINS

See pages 156–178.

HERBS & SPICES

Definitions

Herbs. The leaves of certain temperate-climate plants used for seasoning.

Spices. Buds, fruits, flowers, barks or seeds, of usually tropical-zoned plants.

General Guidelines

• Ground herbs and spices do not keep well; generally, they have a six-month shelf life.

• Whole herbs and spices keep their flavor well and maximize shelf life; grind as needed.

• Blend your own mixtures for maximum quality and choice of flavor. Often inferior leaves are used for commercially ground mixtures.

• Crush seeds with the broad side of a knife to help release flavor; or grind in a small coffee mill.

• Average ratio: one part dry herbs to three parts fresh herbs.

• Store away from heat, light, and moisture in an airtight container.

• Herbs or spices added to a cold dish should rest two hours to allow infusion of flavor into food.

• Commercially ground herbs and spices have been known to have extenders added to them, such as bark or stems, etc.

• If food is overspiced, add more unspiced food, or serve cold.

• Use flavor to enhance, not dominate, the taste of food.

• When in doubt, use less.

• Fresh herbs can be grown in a kitchen or dining room window, for both cooking value and consumer relations.

"In general, mankind, since the improvement of cookery, eats twice as much as nature requires."

Benjamin Franklin

HERBS AND SPICES CHART

HERB/SPICE	FRESH	WHOLE	GROUND	DESCRIPTION/USE
Allspice		•		A berry of a West Indian tree of the Myrtle family with the aroma of cinnamon and nutmeg.
Anise		•	•	Sweet, licorice, aromatic flavor. Used in sweet pastry of all types, some seafoods and vegetables.
Basil	•	•	•	Mild, mint-licorice aroma; extremely versatile; minty with a hint of clove.
Bay leaf		•	•	Woody, lemon-clove perception; when leaf is tinged with green (freshest), it has the strongest flavor, which intensifies with a few minutes' cooking. Mostly used in soups, stews, and some seafood dishes and with some vegetables. Avoid ground. Generally use 1 large leaf per 10 cups of food.
Caraway		•	•	Acute and pungent flavor; very versatile. Also used in breads, cookies, stews, and dressings.
Cardamom		•	•	Ginger-like flavor. Used in pastries, pies, cookies, and fruit dishes.
Cayenne	•	•	•	Hottest of peppers; versatile for hot dishes; Mexican.
Chervil	•	•	•	Delicate, parsley-like flavor. Used in dressings, sauces, garnishes; very versatile.
Chilies	•	•	•	Range from hot to sweet. Mexican, South American, Oriental; versatile.
Chives	•	•		Mild onion flavor. Used in garnishes, sauces, and dressings.
Cilantro	•	•		Strong, pungent flavor, from coriander leaves, and like coriander; a strong flavor enhancer. Chopped stems are good in soups, stews, and beans, added 15 minutes before completion. Mince leaves for garnish or condiment.
Cinnamon		•	•	Spicy, pungent, burning, slightly bitter and woody flavor. Recommended in pastries, desserts, fruit sauces
Cloves		•	•	Hot, spicy, penetrating. Used in some soups, desserts, fruit sauces.
Coriander		•	•	Resembles a mixture of caraway, cumin, sage, and lemon-orange flavor. Used in cookies, dressings, pastries, some salads, and soups. Spanish.
Cumin		•	•	Very warm, distinctive, salty-sweet; similar to a caraway; pharmaceutical smell. Used in Oriental, Middle Eastern, Indian, and Mexican dishes. Use sparingly in exotic dishes.

HERB/SPICE	FRESH	WHOLE	GROUND	DESCRIPTION/USE
Curry			•	A distinctive, yellow blend of pungent, hot spices, including cumin, coriander, turmeric, etc.
Dill	•	•	•	Similar to caraway, but milder and sweeter. It is preferable to use dill weed rather than dill seed. Used with seafood, poultry, dips, dressings, sauces, soups, and salads.
Fennel seed		•	•	Anise-licorice flavor; used in cookies, breads, rolls, sweet pastries, stews, and apples; a member of the carrot family; good for digestion.
Five Spices (Chinese)			•	Fragrant, sweet, and pungent; a ground combination of star anise, anise, fennel, clove, and cinnamon. Use sparingly, mostly with poultry.
Garlic	•		•	Distinctive, very strong onion-like flavor; versatile; mince so that flavor may be infused into oil or liquid. Semi-crush with side of a knife to loosen skin and store in a cool, dark place, Garlic is a member of the onion family.
Garam Massala (India)			•	Rich, strong, exotic, distinctive flavor; a ground combination of equal parts of cardamom, cinnamon, clove, cumin, and black pepper.
Ginger Root (Chinese)	•		•	Pungent, sweet, spicy, penetrating; complements most sweets of all sorts, soups, dressings. A member of the rhizome family. Peel before using. Mince, grate, juice, or slice; cook and remove slices.
Gumbo File			•	A powder made from sassafras leaves; used in Creole and Cajun cooking. It offers a delicate, yet heavy flavor.
Mace		•	•	Nutmeg flavor; recommended in creamed fish, cakes, cookies, fish sauces; complements sweets.
Marjoram	•	•	•	Strong, sage-like, sweet flavor with delicate aftertaste. Used with meat, soups, stews, sauces, salads.
Mint	•	•	•	Cool, pungent taste; used with meat, fish, sauces, poultry, fruit, salads.
Mustard		•	•	Aromatic, fruity, distinctive; used in salads, sauces, and soups.
Nutmeg		•	•	Spicy, sweet, pungent, heavy, penetrating; used in desserts, stews, sauces, creamed dishes, soups.
Oregano	•	•	•	Spicy, pungent, somewhat bitter; reminiscent of marjoram and thyme; used in soups, fish, poultry, dips, and green salads.
Parsley	•	•	•	Mildly spicy, refreshing; fresh parsley is highly aromatic and goes well with garlic. May be used as condiment, garnish, in soups, stews, poultry, fish, salads.

HERB/SPICE	FRESH	WHOLE	GROUND	DESCRIPTION/USE
Pepper		•	•	Hot, penetrating; usually used with heavy foods. Comes from the berries of a climbing vine. Black pepper comes from immature berries and white pepper comes from mature berries with the hull removed.
Poppy Seed		•		Nutty flavor; used in breads, cakes, cookies, dressings, sauces, soups, and most vegetables.
Rosemary	•	•	•	Piney, peppery, pungent, and spicy, with a slightly bitter aftertaste. Fresh rosemary is very fragrant. Used with fruits, herbed breads, dressings, sauces, salads, many vegetables, and marinades.
Saffron		•	•	Exotic, sweet, spicy floral odor, earthy flavor. Used in breads, rolls, fish, chicken, sauces, cream soups, and coloring and flavoring of rice dishes. It is made from dried stigma of saffron crocus, is very expensive; a little goes a long way.
Sage	•	•	•	Aromatic, slightly woody, pungent, warm and astringent; used in fish soups, consomme, aspics, cream soups; use sparingly.
Savory	•	•	•	Aromatic, delicate sage flavor; resinous and warm. Used in salads, soups, sauces, seafoods, poultry, and rice. Winter savory is stronger than summer savory.
Sesame		•		Nutlike flavor when toasted; excellent in breads, cookies, rolls, salads, stews, and toppings.
Star Anise		•	•	Strong, distinctive, pungent flavor and odor; unlike anise, which is of the parsley family and native to the Mediterranean; star anise is of the magnolia family and is native to the Far East.
Sorrel	•	•	•	Lemon-like aroma and taste; excellent in salads, soups, and seafood.
Tarragon	•	•	•	Resembles sharp, aromatic anise flavor; slightly bitter. Used in sauces, soups, marinades, garnishes, poultry, fish, shellfish, and dressings; use sparingly.
Thyme	•	•	•	Strong, pungent, clove flavor; mint-like odor with lingering sharpness. Use sparingly in gumbo, shellfish, poultry, beans.
Turmeric	•	•	•	Aromatic, mild, warm; used in salad dressings, fish, rice dishes, and used for coloring.
Watercress	•			Pleasing, peppery, and sharp; recommended in salads, sauces, as a garnish.

LEGUMES

See pages 183–196.

MISCELLANEOUS FOOD DESCRIPTION

Arrowroot: An easily digested starch with little flavor; commonly used as a thickener for sauces, soups, and glazes. Mix into a slurry equal amounts of arrowroot and water, or a little more water; bring liquid you want thickened to a boil and slowly add arrowroot slurry, stirring until thickened. Used traditionally to remove poison from wounds made by poison arrows.

Barley malt: A thick, dark sweetener made from barley; has a rich roasted taste. It is the lowest-cost natural sweetener and is used for making desserts, baking, and sweet and sour sauces. The sweetness is mainly maltose and comes two ways:

•100% barley malt, which is less sweet;

•60% barley malt and 40% corn malt, which is sweeter.

Bok choy: *(Chin.)* Tender and delicate with a clear, light taste; a combination of cabbage and celery and requires very little cooking. Cut out white stalks and cook longer than greens. Year-round crop; winter crop is best. Very high nutritional value. Served raw in salads. Correctly spelled *baak choy* in Chinese and *shirona* in Japanese.

Brown rice vinegar: *(Oriental)* A mild and delicate vinegar made from fermented brown rice. It is not acid forming as are other vinegars.

Chinese cabbage:*(Chin.)* Tender, delicate, light taste and requires little cooking. Cut out white stalks and cook them longer than greens. A cross between Romaine and cabbage; highly nutritious.

Burdock: Long, thin, brown root of the burdock weed. A staple in Japanese diet (called *gobo*). Used traditionally in Scotland and referred to as *Butter-Bur* or *Beggars Bottoms*. Is known to be strengthening to the reproductive organs and kidneys. Often used in soup or stew or grated into a tea.

Chinese white cheese: *(Chin.)* Tofu marinated and fermented in rice wine; taste and texture of Camembert cheese. Used as flavoring for noodles or vegetables, or served as a condiment.

Daikon (die'-kun): A large, white root vegetable, similar in shape and size to a carrot, although usually larger, and with a smoother skin. Has a rich, bity taste, similar to a radish. Served with other root vegetables and is known to reduce fat around the organs and near the surface of the body. Often grated for a tea base. Japanese word is *daikon* and Chinese word is *loh baak*.

Gomasio: (goo-mas-ee-o) Has a nutty, salty flavor; used as a condiment, spread on grains and sometimes on vegetables. Considered a salt extender. Made from roasted sesame seeds and roasted sea salt. Very high in calcium. (See recipe, pg. 120.)

Kukicha: *(Jap.)* Comes from the unprocessed twigs and stems of the tea plant; no chemical dyes and very low in caffeine and tannin. Neutralizes acid and alkaline conditions of the stomach when correctly brewed. (See recipe, pg. 105.)

Kuzu: *(Jap.)* A root starch, ideal thickening agent for clear sauces or glazes. Stir with 3 parts water to 1 part kuzu into a thick sauce and add to simmering liquids;

stir until sauce becomes clear. Rich in minerals, very digestible, traditionally known as a medicinal food for the digestive system.

Maple syrup: Mild and unique flavor, excellent sweetener for pastry, desserts, and cooked fruits. The darker the color, the sweeter it is. Principally from New England and Canada.

Mirin: *(Jap.)* A naturally sweet cooking wine made from sweet rice; used for flavoring grains, beans, dressings, broths, and sauces.

Miso: *(Jap.; mee-so)* A naturally fermented paste made from soy beans, sea salt, and often with whole grains. Used mostly as a soup base, for flavoring beans, in casseroles or as a condiment base.

• Dark-colored miso is served in the winter;

• Light-colored miso is served in the summer.

Highly nutritious; when taken daily it strengthens the immune system and provides easily digested protein, valuable oils, and a trace of Vitamin B-12. (See pg. 57.)

Rice syrup: *(Jap.)* Has a gentle flavor; used in pastries, baking, or added to cooked fruit. Comes two ways:

• Clear and amber, made with 20% barley malt;

• White and opaque, made mostly from rice with additional enzymes other than barley enzymes.

Salt (including miso and tamari), when added to:

• vegetables *at the beginning of cooking*, will help keep them firm and improve the flavor;

• grains and flour *at the beginning of cooking*, makes them more digestible, flavorful, and more alkaline to the body;

• oily foods *at the beginning of cooking*, makes them more digestible;

• beans *near the end of the cooking process*, will allow the rehydration process to expand the bean, letting it cook faster and be more digestible.

Salt comes in four basic types:

• Common table salt, which has been heated, refined, and extensively processed, first by heating to 350–400°, eliminating or altering natural minerals and trace elements. To make this salt more marketable, pure white, and easy to pour in a humid atmosphere, it has usually been treated with or had added to it a bleaching process, silico-aluminate, potassium Iodide, sodium bicarbonate, yellow prussiate of soda, or dextrose (a sugar additive).

• Sea salt that has many of the same apparent characteristics of common table salt has also been processed.

• High-quality sea salt is not white, and contains most of the natural minerals.

• Mined salt, such as Real Salt™, is processed only by fine grinding, leaving the maximum quantity of minerals and trace elements.

Inasmuch as salt is essential to humans, either present in the food or added to it, and is used over the period of a lifetime, it is preferable to use the highest quality. The linguistic derivative of "salt" is *sal*. The derivative of the word "salary" is *sal*. Caesar often paid his soldiers in salt. Today, in most of the Mediterranean languages, the word for "salt" is *sal*.

Cooking with salt throughout the whole cooking process (except when cooking legumes) will allow for maximum distribution of the salt evenly through the food. Adding salt, tamari, shoyu, or soy sauce at the table creates the likely possibility of overuse and has a much harsher effect on the body, causing excess contraction or tightening of the organs, especially the liver and kidneys.

Seitan: *(say-tan; called "wheat meat")* An easily seasoned, high-protein gluten that is used as a meat substitute in almost every way. It provides most RDA protein requirements for a 167-lb. man from ⅔ of a cup of raw gluten, for less than 20¢ in material cost. Seitan is high-gluten flour, with the bran removed, and cooked in seasoned water; it is served like meat, hot or cold, in sandwiches or in soups, stews, beans, sauces, or in its own gravy. Brought by Buddhist priests from China to Japan 4,000 years ago; now used extensively in most of Asia and somewhat in Africa.

Shiitake mushrooms: *(shi-tahk-ee)* For flavoring broths and sauces. Not recommended for daily use by those in a weakened condition. They help to dissolve animal fats.

Snow peas: *(Chin.)* Tasty and tender with a short cooking time. They retain color with stir frying and steam well. *Hoh laan dow* in Chinese and *saya endo* in Japanese.

Shoyu: *(Jap.)* A dark-brown liquid soy sauce, naturally fermented for several months up to two years and made from soy beans and wheat; salty. It has a long shelf life; refrigeration is not necessary.

Soba noodles: A traditional Japanese noodle made principally of buckwheat flour.

Soy milk: *(Oriental)* Made from soy beans. There are two types:

•*American* style, which is highly processed; repeatedly heated at high temperatures and often flavored for popular tastes.

•*Oriental* style, which is minimally processed, not flavored, offers a heavy bean taste, and is highly nutritious.

Soy cheese: *(Amer.)* Made by using soy beans instead of animal milk. It comes in a number of types, the most popular of which is mozzarella.

Tahini or tahinah (sesame butter): A paste made of crushed, raw, hulled sesame seeds into a rich puree. Highly versatile in baking, sauces, dips, flavorings, and often used with vegetables. Tahini is traditional to the Mediterranean and the Middle East. It has no salt, is very high in protein and calcium, and a number of other nutrients. It has a long shelf life (tends to settle), and needs no refrigeration.

Tamari: *(Oriental)* A dark-brown liquid, rich tasting and very versatile for flavoring many things, or as a salt substitute. Tamari is made from fermented soy beans, water, and salt, a liquid byproduct of miso making.

Tempeh: *(tem-pay)* Fermented split soy beans in a solid form, sometimes with other grains added. Offers a taste and texture similar to veal or pork; used as a meat substitute, is chewy and satisfying. High in nutritive value. Keep frozen; commercially made. It originated in Indonesia.

Tofu: *(Jap.)* Soybean curd. Has a bland taste and easily absorbs flavors. Highly versatile; used in sauces, soups, dressings, icings, marinated, in baking breads or cakes, or fried. Keep refrigerated. Tofu comes two ways:.

•In a *sealed package* with a noted shelf life.

•In *bulk*; keep covered with water; keeps for six to seven days, if you change the water daily. To extend the life further, boil for five minutes in salt water, drain, and change the water daily for four more days.

Tofu can be used as a meat substitute. It is made from soy beans, cooked, pureed into a thick liquid, and left to set into a solid curd.

NOTE: Do not serve tofu raw. If tofu is to be used in salads, sauces, icings, etc., boil 1/2-lb. blocks (maximum) for five minutes in salted water, and cool before using.

Deep-fried tofu is used as an offering at Shinto shrines to the Fox Spirits in Japan.

Udon noodles: A traditional Japanese noodle made principally of whole wheat flour.

NUTS AND SEEDS

Almonds: Originated in North Africa; currently come mostly from California. Good almonds have a smooth and even shape. The skin should be intact, although shelling-process scratches may be apparent. May be eaten raw, roasted, or blanched. Refrigeration preserves quality for long shelf life.

Chestnuts: Used by the ancient Greeks and Chinese. To this day they are usually eaten roasted or boiled. Chestnuts are low in calories, fat, and protein, but higher than other nuts in starch and carbohydrates. If roasted, put a small knife point into the shell before putting in the oven. Remove shell before boiling. Shells should be a deep reddish brown and silky smooth, and are called roasting chestnuts. Dried chestnuts should be soaked overnight before cooking in a liquid.

Filberts (Hazelnuts): Named for the Goddess Phyllides, who was turned into a nut tree. The Celts used hazelnut wood for dowsing rods. Roasted, they have a rich toasty taste and are delicious on desserts.

Pecans: Used in desserts and in baking. Rich, delicate taste; high oil content. Keep refrigerated. Native to North America; the Algonquin called it *paccan* and the Cree called it *pakan*.

Walnuts: An ancient symbol of fertility, high in protein, fat, and oil. They are mostly raised in the United States with chemical fertilizers, insecticides, and fungicides. Refrigerate. A delicacy in ancient Rome and Greece.

Pumpkin Seeds (Pepitas): Highly nutritious; come mostly from Central America; contain 29% protein. They are delicious roasted, with or without tamari.

Sesame Seeds (unhulled): Roast in skillet over medium flame until they puff up and you can hear them crack. They have a delicious nutty, rich flavor. Sesame seeds are customarily used as a condiment, in baking, or toasted as a garnish. They are very nutrititious and have twice as much calcium as milk and 35% protein. Used by the Aztecs; now come mostly from the Mediterranean area, the Orient, and Central America. They were used by the ancient Egyptians, Romans, and, 5,000 years ago, by the Chinese.

Sunflower Seeds: Higher than sesame seeds in protein and phosphorus, vitamins D, E, and B Complex. They should be firm, not rubbery or too dried out. Sunflower seeds are good for condiments or baking.

OILS

Processed Oils

Processed oils have a long shelf life, minimum color, taste, and odor; they are without almost all of their nutritive value. The refining of oils usually includes hot centrifuging to remove gummy substances and lecithin which, left in natural oils, tend to smoke at high temperatures. The removal of fatty materials is done by washing with a highly alkaline caustic solution containing lye or sodium carbonate. Bleaching consists of mixing with bleaching clay or activated charcoal that has been treated with sulfuric or hydrochloric acid, then agitated in a vacuum at 120–220°. Deodorization consists of vacuum steam heating from 450–470° for ten to twelve hours, further removing odor, flavor, and color. Common antioxidents used are BHA or BHT with the common defoaming agent methyl silicone.

Natural Oils

Pressed, mechanically pressed, expeller pressed: These are unrefined oils that have not been bleached, deodorized, filtered through clay or charcoal, and still retain their maximum nutrients and life force.

Unrefined oils can be recognized by the darker than usual color, and a thick murky sediment at the bottom; there is also a distinctive odor of the product from which they have been pressed.

A dish will be characterized by the unrefined oil selected for it, which will permeate its flavor. A good example is olive oil, or corn oil used in baking, which tends to have a buttery flavor.

Keep these oils in a dark, cool place or in the refrigerator.

Cholesterol

We get cholesterol in two ways: the body can make what little it needs, and we can get it directly from foods of animal origin, such as meat, poultry, seafood, and dairy products (the latter is the undesirable way). Egg yolks and organ meats are very high in cholesterol. Although low in total fat, shrimp and lobster are fairly high in cholesterol and are therefore limited in this eating plan.

Foods of plant origin such as fruits, vegetables, grains, cereals, nuts and seeds contain no cholesterol. These foods are highly recommended.

Saturated Fats

These are fats that usually harden at room temperature; they are found in animal products and some vegetable products. They tend to raise the level of unwanted cholesterol in the blood, so they are also limited in this plan.

Saturated animal fats are found primarily in beef, veal, lamb, pork, and ham; in butter, cream, and whole milk. These foods also contain cholesterol.

Saturated vegetable fats are found in many solid and "hydrogenated" shortenings, in coconut oil, cocoa butter, palm oil, and palm kernel oil. These products are sometimes advertised as "cholesterol free," which is true; however, they are very high in saturated fat and should be avoided. These oils are often used in store-bought bakery products, candies, fried foods, and also in non-dairy milk and cream substitutes. Read labels carefully to avoid these products.

Hydrogenated Oils

These are fats and oils changed from their natural liquid form to become more solid, such as most margarines and shortenings. They may be partially or almost completely hydrogenated. Avoid completely hydrogenated oils; they resemble saturated fats. Many margarines contain partially hydrogenated oils and may be acceptable if they contain twice as much polyunsaturated as unsaturated fat.

Polyunsaturated Oils

These are oils from vegetable products such as safflower and sunflower seeds, corn, soybeans, and cottonseeds, which are usually liquid at room temperature. They help lower the level of blood cholesterol by helping the body get rid of excessive, newly formed cholesterol.

Monounsaturated Oils

These are liquid vegetable oils such as canola and olive oils. Recent evidence indicates that they may be as effective as polyunsaturated oils in decreasing blood cholesterol levels. Some scientists believe that more evidence is needed to firmly establish this, however. Keep in dark, cool place or refrigerator.

NOTE: Cotton is not considered a food by the Food and Drug Administration, so that even more toxic materials may be used against the bollweevils, etc., in making cotton oil than would be used on those plants classified as foods.

Description of Specific Oils

Corn Oil. 85% unsaturated fat. Offers a corn and buttery flavor, and competes with other food flavors. Corn oil that has been pressed from the whole kernel includes what is called corn gluten oil, usually tends to be dark red, and has a strong popcorn-like odor. Corn oil is used in salads, baking, and sauteeing; has a short shelf life.

Olive Oil. Unlike other oils, the fruit (not the nut or seed) is pressed, and no heat is required for "Extra Virgin," which has extra flavor and aroma. "Fine Virgin" and "Plain Virgin" are from later pressings and tend to be mixed or flavored with "Extra Virgin," and are progressively more acidic. Olive oil is mainly used for sauteeing, salad dressings, and pasta sauces.

Peanut Oil. 34% polyunsaturated, with slightly heavy, nutty taste. Used mostly in Oriental food preparation. It is good for stir fries, but sometimes tends to flash at high temperatures. Peanut oil keeps indefinitely without refrigeration.

Safflower Oil. Very slight nutty flavor with the highest percentage of unsaturated fats. General use: may be diluted with stronger flavored oils, salad dressings, baking, frying (does not foam).

Sesame Oil. 87% unsaturated fat with excellent stability and resistance to oxidation. Available in light and dark.
- *Light:* mild and nutty tasting, and goes well in salads, Oriental dishes, and stir fries.
- *Dark:* made from roasted seeds and has a very strong toasted, smoky flavor; commonly used in Chinese cooking. Often diluted with other oils or liquids for lesser flavor as in salad dressings.

Soybean Oil. Good stability and high resistance to oxidation. Good for salads, particularly when mixed with other flavorful oils. High smoke point if unrefined.

Sunflower Oil. 92% unsaturated; very slightly flavored. Good stability in cooking and resistance to oxidation. Used in salad oils, frying, baking, and may be diluted with other more flavorful oils. Tends to have short shelf life.

VEGETABLES

(See pages 290–336.)

SEA VEGETABLES (Sea Weeds)

General

Sea vegetables contain about twenty times more minerals than land-grown vegetables, and much more than milk. They often have the fresh aroma of the sea when cooked, and may be used for appetizers, salads, entrees, side dishes, and desserts. Millions of people eat sea vegetables unknowingly: carageenan, a sea vegetable, is used in ice cream as a thickening agent.

As sea vegetables are fairly uncommon in the typical American diet, we start with a very brief description of their past and present uses.

Sea vegetables were prized for their medicinal value by the Imperial Court of China in the sixth century B.C. They were also used by the ancient kings of Hawaii and the Maoris of New Zealand, even until World War II, when Maori troops ate them on long marches in the Middle East. All ancient cultures living near the sea used sea vegetables, including the ancient Celts, Vikings, and Romans. Today sea vegetables are sold in Canada, and in the British Isles, mainly in Wales, Scotland and Ireland. They are also sold in Japan, most Asian countries, South Africa, France, Greenland, Iceland, and Germany.

"So popular have sea vegetables become in Japan that in recent times demand has outstripped supply and some coastal waters are intensively farmed. Current production of Nori alone is a staggering 10,000,000,000 sheets a year, of which the Japanese themselves consume an average of 96 sheets a year." [1]

Sargasso, a sea vegetable, is used in Spain as a salad ingredient.

"The famous women pearl divers of Japan and Korea, who dive to considerable depths virtually naked throughout the year, until well past their seventieth birthday, are careful to consume wakame, hijiki, and nori each day. It is well-known among the Japanese people that the regular consumption of hijiki and arame will ensure a clear complexion, soft pliant skin, and thick shiny hair." [2]

General instructions:

• Wash and inspect for sea shells and salt crystals.

• If used as a side dish, soak before cooking.

Japanese Sea Vegetables

Agar-agar. A tasteless, colorless gelling agent used to make desserts called Kanten. It will not melt as readily as commercial gelatin and has no calories. Thin strips, in bars, flakes, or powder, are dissolved in boiling water; stir until dissolved. Usually used in summer desserts or aspics. One tablespoon of agar-agar powder to one quart of liquid (see Equivalency Chart, pg. 49). Make quantity adjustments depending on acidity contents; acid foods require more agar-agar than alkaline foods do. For example, the acidity of various fruits and fruit juices will weaken the agar-agar; with these a higher proportion must be used.

To check gel quality: Place 2 or 3 teaspoons in refrigerator before dissolving agar-agar in liquid to be gelled. Place a teaspoon of liquid to be tested in cold spoon and return to refrigerator for a few minutes. Then check to see:

• If all the agar-agar has dissolved;

• If desired degree of gel firmness has been reached;

– If soft, add more agar-agar;

– If too firm, add more liquid.

Agar-agar flakes require more simmering, dissolving, and stirring than powder. Sprinkle agar-agar powder evenly over liquid to be gelled and avoid coagulation of powder.

At completion of cooking test gel characteristics.

Stir in cold fruits after cooking and starting to cool, when liquid begins to turn to a heavy syrup, to prevent fruit from settling or floating.

To prepare:

• Put very light coat of tasteless oil on mold.

• After refrigerated and firm:

– Run knife blade around edge;

– Place bottom of mold in very hot water for two or three seconds;

– Place serving platter over mold, quickly invert jelly to platter;

– Refrigerate until served.

Agar-agar bonds with and eliminates radioactive elements in the body (see pg. 13).

Arame. Used for treating high blood pressure and disorders of the female reproductive system. Quickly rinse, soak for ten minutes, use soaking water in cooking the dish you are making or save for soups or stews later. Goes well with tofu and delicate-tasting vegetables.

Hiziki. From the Orient and very high in calcium. Used for enhancing beauty and adding luster and resilience to the hair. Quickly rinse twice, soak fifteen minutes; will expand to five times its original size.

Kombu. A member of the kelp family, from the Far East and the Atlantic. Kombu strengthens and detoxifies the intestines and is a traditional remedy for colitis. It is a strong flavoring agent and contains natural MSG. Good for soup stock and noodle broths. Used mostly in cooking with beans, for it tends to reduce flatulence and reduces the cooking time. Use about 2" per cup of beans. High in minerals and has the ability to soften the fiber of other foods it is cooked with.

Nori. High in vitamins A and B, and helps break down and reduce fat deposits and cholesterol. Nori is over 30% protein. Used mostly in making sushi and as a condiment. The nori sheet is drawn over a burner until it changes from a dark purple to a dark green color. Also aids digestion when served with fried foods, and for those who consume a heavy dairy diet. Originated in the Orient and the British Isles.

Wakame (Alaria). Used mostly in soups, but also delicious with sauteed onions or cooked with green vegetables. When lightly baked and crumbled, wakame makes a good condiment for brown rice. Soak for ten minutes, rinse quickly, and cut out the stem or main rib. High in calcium, iron, and B Vitamins, and has the ability to soften fibers of other vegetables and legumes.

American Sea Vegetables

Alaria. Wild taste. Presoak and simmer at least twenty minutes. Calcium rich, good in soups and stews. Grows more delicate in taste the longer it is cooked. Known to absorb and eliminate certain radioactive elements in the human digestive system. Japanese studies show that it will relieve hypertension and inhibit tumor formation.

Dry-roast in a warm oven for about an hour, until crunchy, and then store in an airtight container.

Dulse. Has a distinctive taste. Good in soups, sandwiches, and salads; chewy texture. Oven-roast for an hour or more until crisp and store in an airtight container.

May be soaked for five minutes, chopped, and used in salads.

Native to North America and Alaska, Canada and New England. Rich in iron, with abundant amounts of potassium, magnesium, iodine, and phosphorus.

Kelp. Has sweet salty taste, somewhat like kombu. Acts as tenderizer when cooked with beans. Contains one of the highest forms of natural glutamic acid (as in MSG), which acts as the tenderizing agent. Rich in calcium, potassium, iodine, and mannitol, which give it a sweet taste.

Known to absorb and eliminate certain radioactive elements in the human digestive system. Japanese studies show that kelp may relieve hypertension and inhibits tumor growth.

Good for dry roasted flakes, soups, and to add to bean cooking to make them more digestible and to reduce flatulence.

Irish Moss (Carrageenan). Pre-soak half an hour in four parts water, rinse and cook. Acts as a thickener and stabilizer. Has been widely used as a soothing remedy for ulcers. The longer you simmer, the less it tastes of the sea. High in vitamin A, iodine, and minerals.

Nori. (See *Japanese Sea Vegetables*, pg. 80). Has rich, sweet, salty, nutty flavor. Dry-roast to enhance flavor. Good dried, ground, or crushed as a comdiment (such as Gomasio, pg. 120) in soups, salads, on yellow or white vegetables, or dried and unground in sandwiches. Crumble and add to grains during cooking, or crumble and add as a garnish at serving. Crumble and add to sauteed vegetables while cooking or add to stir fries while cooking.

Reduces cholesterol deposits and inhibited arteriosclerosis in laboratory animals.

Dry nori is 35% protein and very high in B vitamins. Traditionally used on both sides of the Atlantic and Pacific Oceans.

"Unquiet meals make ill digestion."
Shakespeare

8. CULINARY DEFINITIONS AND DESCRIPTIONS

"A glutton digs his grave with his teeth."
French Proverb

The following are culinary definitions, terms, and names used in all levels of kitchens, from the five-star restaurant to the mass feeding establishment to the home kitchen.

Adjust: To fix, alter, or modify for desired flavor, thickness, to compensate for lack of continuity of materials or desired results.

A la bouquetiere: Served surrounded with a variety of vegetables in season. Usually associated with broiled meat or fish.

Ambrosia: Assorted fruits and shredded coconut.

Animal food: Food that comes from animals, such as meat, eggs, and dairy products.

Al dente: Food that has been cooked to a point of firmness, so that it is not soft and mushy.

Au naturel: Uncooked or cooked in a simple, natural way.

A point: Not overcooked, not undercooked; cooked just right.

Arrowroot: A very fine flour from the arrowroot, used as a thickening agent by mixing with water to sauce consistency and adding to what is to be thickened; also used as a glaze that finishes in a high sheen.

Aromatics: Vegetables, sea vegetables, herbs, or spices that are steamed with meat, fish, or other vegetables.

Arteriosclerosis: A disease characterized by the thickening and loss of elasticity of artery walls, due to deposits of fatty substances.

Astringent: Contracts body tissue and nerves; an example is the acid in lemons.

Atherosclerosis: A type of arteriosclerosis where the inner layer of the artery wall is made thick and irregular by deposits of fatty substances and thus decreases the internal diameter of the blood vessel.

Au/aux: *(Fr.)* With a manner or fashion of.

Aux croutons: *(Fr.)* With croutons of toasted, seasoned pieces of bread.

Aux cresson: *(Fr.)* With watercress.

Bake: To cook foods by surrounding with hot, dry air, as in an oven.

Barbecue: To cook food, which has been seasoned with a marinade or basting sauce, on a grill or spit over hot coals.

Batter: Mixture of flour and liquid that can be poured.

Bean curd (tofu): A firm, creamy custard made from soy beans and pressed into squares. See Ingredient Description, pg. 76.

Bind: To equalize, usually by thickening the mixture so it does not separate; as an example, adding rice or flour will bind lentil soup.

Biscuit: A small, round quick bread, made with baking powder.

Blanc: *(Fr.)* White.

Blanch: To precook food by suddenly immersing it into fast boiling water or steam for a few minutes.

Blend: To mix two or more ingredients together well.

Bloom: The act of yeast forming a thick curd in soak water.

Bocuse, Paul: The most well-known contemporary French chef (who has said among other notable things that he will not cook with electricity for he feels that the "life" of the flame is an important ingredient in cooking).

Bouillabaisse: A fish soup or stew made with five or six different fish or shellfish, flavored with white wine and saffron, and served on toast or in a soup dish.

Bouillion: A clear liquid stock, rich in flavor.

Bouquet garni: *(Fr.)* A small bunch of herbs wrapped in cheesecloth and used to flavor soups or stews. See Herbs and Spices, pg.● ●.

Braise: To cook food slowly in a covered pan with a small amount of water; it may or may not have been browned first in a small amount of oil.

Brillat-Savarin: (1755–1826) A famous French writer on food and a gourmet of high repute.

Broil: To cook over or under direct heat, such as grilling.

Broth: A liquid in which food has been simmered; same as stock.

Brown: To cook in a little oil at a high heat until brown, sealing in the juices and forming a tasty crust.

Brown Betty: Apple pudding; often with a crispy top, served with vanilla or lemon sauce.

Bruise: To gently crush the leaves of fresh herbs to release their inner essence.

Brunoise: *(Fr.)* Finely chopped or grated celery, carrots, and onions or other vegetables, sauteed and used to flavor soups, stews, or sauces.

Buffet (smorgasbord): A display of ready-to-eat cold or hot foods that are self-service.

Calorie: A unit of measuring the heat/energy producing value of food when burned by the body. The energy supplied by the combustion of protein and carbohydrates is 4 calories per gram.

Cake rack: A slightly elevated wire rack on which cake, bread, or cookies are placed to cool, when fresh out of the oven.

Canape: A small piece of crustless, fancy-cut bread, toast, or sauteed bread spread with a highly seasoned food and garnished.

Cancer: A general term for a malignant cellular tumor that tends to invade surrounding tissues and/or spreads to other parts of the body; many cancers have been linked with improper diet and ingestion of preservatives, pesticides, additives, etc.

Capillaries: Very small (microscopic) blood vessels between arteries and veins that distribute blood to the body's tissues.

Carbohydrate: A nutrient that supplies energy.

Carob (St. John's Bread): From the pods of the carob tree; is rich in sugar and protein and used as a chocolate substitute.

Casserole: A stew pot or Dutch oven in which dishes of meat, vegetables, pasta, beans, or grains, or any combination thereof, are cooked slowly in a thin sauce over direct heat or in an oven.

Champignon: *(Fr.)* Mushroom.

Chapon: *(Fr.)* A slice of French or Italian bread rubbed with garlic, oil and vinegar, then added to salad greens to impart flavor and to be discharged before serving.

Chef: *(Fr., meaning chief or head)* Title earned in preparing food, managing a staff, planning and executing production. A person in charge of the kitchen or a department of the kitchen. A person who likes to cook for guests at home; sometimes referred to as amateur chef. One who is seriously committed to transferring the life forces and natural integrity of the food to the consumer.

Chemise, en: *(Fr.)* A term used to describe vegetables served with their skins on or pieces of food wrapped in a thin layer of dough and baked.

Chiffonade: *(Fr.)* Shredded plants, fresh herbs, lettuce, even onions or beets, used as a garnish for soups or in salads.

Chilis: Peppers, ranging from hot to sweet, used mostly in the Southwest United States, South America, and in Oriental dishes.

Cholesterol: A fat-like substance found in

animal tissue; present only in foods from animal sources such as whole milk dairy products, meat, fish, poultry, animal fats, and egg yolks.

Chop: To cut into irregular pieces.

Chutney: A highly seasoned, preserved relish made from fruits and vegetables and served traditionally with curry.

Coat: To cover the surface of one food with another food.

Cobbler: A deep-dish baked pie, usually made of fruit.

Coddle: To simmer food just below the boiling point for a short time.

Combine: To mix two or more ingredients.

Comcassar: To chop coarsely.

Compote: Fruit or fruits stewed in a syrup.

Condiment: A highly seasoned ingredient or combination of ingredients, used to enhance, compliment, or alter the flavor of the food to which it is added or with which it is eaten.

Condition: A person's recent and present state of health, as opposed to the inherited state of health.

Connoisseur: A critic trained to make a competent judgment in the matter of art and taste.

Constitution: A person's state of health and vitality, determined before birth by parents, grandparents, great-grandparents, and other ancestors.

Coronary artery disease: Conditions that cause narrowing of the coronary arteries so that blood flow to the heart muscle is reduced.

Coronary heart disease: The most common form of adult heart disease, in which the main arteries of the heart have atherosclerotic deposits, and the normal blood flow of the heart is impaired.

Couscous: *(Fr.)* North African or Arabian version of crushed millet or other grains.

Cream soup: A soup that is thickened with tofu, grain milk, or roux.

Cresson: *(Fr.)* Watercress.

Crisp: To make food firm and brittle by letting it stand in ice water or by heating in an oven.

Croutons: Small cubes of bread browned to a golden color in an oven or by frying, served with soups or salads.

Croquette: A ground food made into a ball and deep fried.

Cruciferae (kroo-sif-e-rye): A large family of plants with numerous small four-petaled flowers. The petals are arranged in the form of a cross, hence the name of the family. Cruciferae include some common vegetables, such as cabbage, cauliflower, kale, brussels sprouts, broccoli, kohlrabi, turnip, black mustard (the chief source of commercial mustard), and watercress. Cruciferae may be recommended to reduce the risks of certain types of cancer.

Crudites: *(Fr.)* Crisp, raw vegetables usually served with a dip.

Cube: Tout into dice shapes.

Cuisine: The art of cooking.

Cuisine Minceur: *(Fr.)* A new approach to cooking to reduce calories by reducing sugar and fats.

Culinary Institute of America: A private, non-profit culinary arts school that offers a 21-month associate's degree program, continuing education courses, and video training tapes. Situated on an 83-acre riverside campus in New York state, the school has an enrollment of 1,850 students and a network of over 19,000 alumni in key industry positions who have helped to earn the Institute its reputation as America's center for culinary education.

Cure: Preserve by pickling or salting.

Cut in: One ingredient blended into another or others.

Daikon: A radish from Japan, North America, and the British Isles (where it is known as *mooli*). Often served with oily or fatty foods to assure the burning of fat around the organs as well as the body. May be served grated or as a vegetable, cooked or uncooked.

Deep fry: To fry submersed in oil.

Degenerative disease: Caused when organs and bodily systems become weak and non- or partially functioning, as by negative outside influences (primarily ingested by eating); degenerative effects or infectious bacteria become dominant over a healthy body.

Demi: *(Fr.)* Half.

Dietary fiber: Plant cells providing bulk to the intestine and necessary for cleaning the walls of the intestine. Dietary fiber is found in all whole grains, legumes, fruits, and vegetables.

Discharge: Term used to describe the results of a cleansing process of the body; most commonly seen as pimples, boils, rashes, sweats, phlegm, and sniffles.

Dissolve: A dry substance absorbed into a liquid to become a fluid.

Dice: To cut into small cubes.

Dot: To place small particles on the surface of another item.

Drain: To strain liquid from solid food.

Dredge: To coat or cover food with a dry ingredient such as flour or corn meal, etc.

Dress: Term used with poultry and fish, meaning to trim and clean.

Drizzle: To sprinkle a liquid mixture.

Duchesse: *(Fr.)* A style of pressing through a pastry tube mashed potatoes, carrots, sweet potatoes, etc.

Du jour: *(Fr.)* Of the day.

Dust: To sprinkle food with a dry ingredient such as flour.

Dutch oven: A heavy stew pot with a tight-fitting lid for soups, stews, or braising.

En chemise: *(Fr.)* See Chemise, en.

Emincer: To cut into very fine slices.

Entree: *(Fr.)* The main course of an informal meal or a subordinate dish served between main courses.

Entremets: *(Fr.)* Usually a side dish or to be served between courses or as a dessert.

Enzyme: A protein that acts as a catalyst in the digestion of food by breaking foods down into their basic elements.

Epicure: A gourmet who is a connoisseur of food and wine.

Escarole: A variety of salad greens with dark green leaves, used with other greens.

Escoffier, Georges-Auguste: (1846–1935) A famous French chef and author of cookbooks.

Essence: An oily or volatile liquid extracted by distilling vegetables, fruits, fresh herbs, etc., such as rose or orange water.

Extracts: Essential flavoring oils of products dissolved or pressed in alcohol.

Fat-controlled diet: A cholesterol-lowering diet, in which saturated fat is reduced or eliminated. Polyunsaturated fat is substituted for saturated fat, and total fat and cholesterol are reduced or eliminated; the dishes may be referred to as "low-" or "no-fat."

Fava: *(Ital.)* Large white beans.

Fermentation: Decomposition (as opposed to digestion) of sugar and starch, and their conversion to carbon dioxide, alcohol, acetic acid, and lactic acid.

Finish: The final garnishing of a dish before it goes to the table.

Five basic tastes: Sweet, sour, pungent, salty, bitter.

Five-spice powder: *(Chin.)* A blend of anise, star anise, cinnamon bark, fennel, and clove.

Flavor: The overall impression formed by the combination of taste, smell, temperature, and thought impressions.

Floret: A small flower, one of a large cluster as in broccoli or cauliflower.

French Cut: To cut vegetables on a 30° to 45° angle.

Fry: To cook in oil.

Garam Massala: Ground equal parts of cardamom seed, cinnamon stick, whole cumin, whole cloves, whole black pepper.

Garnish: To decorate a dish by adding small amounts of food or herbs for color and/or flavor. See Garnish Chart, pg. 53.

Glace: *(Fr.)* Certain iced, glazed, or frozen foods; to cover with a glossy coating.

Glaze: To cover with a glossy coating.

Gluten: An albuminous substance found in flour that is activated by a liquid, such as in bread dough. The smooth and elastic properties of gluten are activated in bread dough by kneading.

Gould, Blake: Founder and Director of North Star—Health Care for the Whole Person, in Hyde Park, Vermont; leading authority in natural healing and the medicinal use of food, both for individuals and institutions.

Goulash: A rich, savory brown stew; the primary flavor is paprika.

Gourmet: A lover of fine foods.

Guerrard, Michel: *(Fr.)* Credited with the creation of "cuisine minceur."

Gumbo: A rich, thick, spicy Cajun-style soup served over rice; made with a little meat or fish or seafood, or combination thereof, including a few vegetables. Heavily spiced to have three tastes: one when you first put it in your mouth, one just before you swallow it, and one after you have swallowed it.

Hasenpfeffer: *(Ger.)* A dish made with rabbit and pepper; rabbit meat is high in nutrition, low in fat.

Heart attack: Death of, or damage to, part of the heart muscle due to an insufficient blood supply.

Hoisin sauce: *(Chin.)* A thick, dark sauce made of soybeans, chili, spices, and garlic.

Honey: Consists mostly of fructose and glucose with a few minerals and fewer vitamins and additives, from the digestive system of the bee.

Hydrate: Food from which water content has been removed.

Infusion: The material, flavor, or odor that results from steeping material in boiling water or oil, such as tea or garlic.

Insalivation: The process of secretion of saliva that helps moisten food to initiate digestion.

Jambalaya: (Cajun/Creole) Traditional dish combining meat, fish, shellfish, rice, and vegetables (predominantly greens).

Jardiniere *(Fr.)* To cut $1/4" \times 1/4" \times 1"$; or prepared or garnished with vegetables.

Julienne: To cut into thin strips about $1/8" \times 1/8"$ to $2^1/2"$.

Kushi, Michio: Leading macrobiotic and natural lifestyle educator whose principles of balanced, natural whole foods are followed by millions of people worldwide. The principles are based on whole cereal grains, beans, vegetables, sea vegetables, non-fatty animal foods, and seasonal fruits, and encompass the spirit of respecting nature and traditions.

La nouvelle cuisine: *(Fr.)* A new way of French cooking that minimizes fats, starches, and sugar; developed by Paul Bocuse at his restaurant in Cologne, near Lyon, France.

Leek: Plant of the onion family; has little or no bulb; broad, unique, mild flavor. Green stems or white section used for flavoring in soups, stews, or with other vegetables.

Legumes: Edible seeds such as beans, peas, or lentils. See Legumes, pp. 183–196.

Lukewarm: Temperature of about 95°, neither hot nor cold when dripped on the wrist.

Lyonnaise: *(Fr.)* To prepare or serve with onions.

Maitre d'hotel: Head of dining room service.

Marinade: A seasoned non-liquid or liquid mixture often containing an acid such as wine or vinegar in which food is soaked to gain extra flavor or to be tenderized.

Marinate: To cover or soak an item in a marinade.

Marmite: Earthenware pot in which soup is heated and served.

Mask: To cover completely, usually with a sauce or jelly.

Matchsticks: See Julienne, above.

Mince: To chop into very fine pieces.

Minestrone: *(Ital.)* Thick vegetable soup of dried legumes and pasta.

Mirepoix: *(Fr.)* Diced carrots, 25%; onions, 50%; celery 25%; often sauteed in oil with or without other herbs to add flavor to soups or sauces. Leeks or mushrooms may be added.

Mix: To merge two or more ingredients into one mass.

Mocha: A coffee/chocolate flavoring.

Mold: Metal or glass form in which foods are shaped.

MSG: Monosodium Glutsmate; a bity-tasting taste enhancer and preservative, used to restore the fresh taste of food. It is extracted from wheat gluten and sugar beets. Kombu has the highest source of natural glutamic acid. The synthetic, commonly used MSG can have harmful health effects, including chest pain and headaches. The naturally-occurring glutamic acid in kombu has no harmful effects.

Mousse: A soft, creamy food, either sweet or savory.

New England Culinary Institute: The New England Culinary Institute is in Montpelier, Vermont, and features a rigorous two-year hands-on training program in working food service operations. This program features a 7:1 student-teacher ratio, teaching both through classes and professionally supervised work. Periodic courses and workshops on natural whole foods are presented for professionals and non-professionals throughout the year. They maintan five kitchens serving the public. Skills are tested and refined in paid internship programs all over the United States.

Nightshade family: See Healthy and Unhealthy Foods; Nightshade Family, pg. 11.

North Star, Health Care for the Whole Person: In Hyde Park, Vermont, founded and directed by Blake and Lora Gould; a leading center for the teaching and practice of natural foods cooking and nutrition, with expert instruction in all aspects of these cooking arts, for individuals and institutions.

Nutrition: The sum total of all processes that interact to supply nutritive needs.

Obesity: An increase in body weight beyond physical and skeletal requirements due to an accumulation of excess fat. It is usually applied to a condition of 20% or more over ideal body weight. Obesity puts a strain on the heart and can increase the chances of developing high blood pressure and diabetes.

Olives: The hard-stoned fruit of the olive tree, preserved for eating or pressed to make olive oil.

•*Black olives:* picked ripe, boiled in salt water or oil.

•*Green olives:* green fruit of the olive tree, treated in a hot, weak, alkali solution and then pickled in brine.

•*Kalmata olives:* large oval Greek olives with a smooth purple skin.

•*Spanish olives:* green olives stuffed with pimiento; an appetizer.

•*Queen olives:* grown strictly for eating.

Oxidation (of oils): Caused primarily by air, light, and overheating, excess of which causes a flavor change followed by rancidity.

Paella: *(Span.)* A classic, traditional rice-based dish with vegetables, seafoods, chicken, herbs, seasonings, and spices; one of the main ingredients is saffron.

Pan fry: To fry in a pan with a small amount of oil or water.

Panache: A term meaning "of mixed colors," of two or more items.

Parboil: To boil until partially cooked.

Parcook: To complete cooking to the point where the ingredient is almost but not completely cooked.

Pasta: *(Ital. for paste)* A wheat-floured product coming in many shapes and sizes; basically made from white flour or whole wheat flour; macaroni, spaghetti, noodles, etc. In Oriental cuisine, there are also pastas made of buckwheat, rice, or mung beans.

Pastry bag: A cone-shaped bag used to pipe by squeezing soft mixtures in their final form for serving, such as pastry dough, icing, mashed carrots, or sweet potatoes.

Pesto: *(Ital.)* A thin paste made from crumbled basil leaves, garlic, olive oil, and pine nuts or walnuts, and served over pasta.

Pilaf or Pilau: A rice dish popular in Greece, the Middle East, and Asia; flavored with saffron or turmeric; sometimes containing meat, poultry, or fish.

Pinch: An amount less than $1/8$ teaspoon.

Pipe: To decorate with a mixture forced through the nozzle of a pastry tube.

Poach: To simmer a liquid just below the boiling point at 205° to 210°.

Polyunsaturated fats: Are recommended to reduce fats and are usually liquid oils of vegetable origin. Oils such as corn, cottonseed, safflower, sesame seed, and sunflower are high in polyunsaturated fat and tend to lower the level of cholesterol in the blood. (See pp. 77–79.)

Polenta: A staple of northern Italy, made of thick, well-cooked corn meal.

Portion: The size of one serving.

Pot roasting: A method of slow cooking by steam in a covered pot.

Potage: *(Fr.)* A thick soup.

Printaniere: *(Fr.)* Served with three or four small-cut spring vegetables.

Proof: To let yeast dough rise at 85° in a warm moist place out of a draft.

Protein: The prime nutrient for the maintaining and building of body cells and tissue.

Puree: To press food through a fine sieve or food mill or to make soft in a blender or food processor.

Putrefaction: Decomposition of proteins and their conversion to poisonous substances.

Ragout: A thick, savory brown stew of meat, vegetables, and potatoes.

Reconstitute: To add water to concentrated food to return it to its natural form.

Reduce: To boil down a liquid, reducing it in quantity and concentrating its flavor.

Refresh: To pour cold water over previously blanched or drained food.

Restaurant: *(Fr.)* From Latin "restaurare," to rebuild, repair, renew.

Rhizome: In botany, horizontal, underground plant stem capable of producing the shoot and root systems of a new plant. This capability allows the parent plant to propagate vegetatively (asexually) and also enables a plant to perennate (survive an annual unfavorable season) underground. In some plants, ginger root, water lilies, and many ferns.

Rice balls: Brown rice rolled into a small ball and covered with toasted nori sheets or rolled in gomasio. Can be made with other ingredients incorporated in it or on the outside; good for snacks, buffets, lunches, or traveling.

Rice vinegar: A rice vinegar used in Chinese cooking; made from brown rice.

Roast: To heat in an oven on all sides.

Roux: *(Fr.)* A cooked paste of flour and corn oil, used as the thickening base for sauces and gravies; based on French classical method of using butter or potato flour.

St. Germain: Containing a puree of peas, as in split pea soup.

Sake: *(Jap.)* A fermented rice wine, usually served warm.

Sachet: A mixture of herbs and spices tied in a cheesecloth bag, used for flavoring soups, stews, sauces.

Saturated fats: Tend to raise the level of cholesterol in the blood and are therefore restricted in a low-fat diet, and are characterized by hardening at cool room temperature. Saturated animal fats are found in beef, lamb, pork, poultry, butter, cream, cheese, milk, ice cream, etc. Saturated vegetable fats are found in some vegetables, shortenings, spreads, coconut oil, cocoa butter, palm oil, non-dairy milk, cream substitutes, whipped toppings, etc.

Sauce: A liquid, thick or thin, accompanying a food to enhance, season, or alter its flavor.

Saute: *(Fr.)* To cook in a small amount of oil or water.

Sautoir: Heavy, flat, copper sauce pan.

Scoop: A hand dipping device used for dipping ice cream or portion control for serving food. Scoops are identified by a number that represents the number of scoops of a food in a one-quart container. A #8 scoop will get 8 scoops out of a one-quart container; a #20 scoop will get 20 scoops out of a one-quart container.

Score: To mark the surface of a food with shallow slits.

Sear: To dry and seal the surface, usually of meat.

Semolina: A high-gluten pasta made from durum wheat.

Serrate: To cut a decorative, notched border in vegetables or pastries.

Set: Firm enough to hold its shape, as applied to jellied dishes.

Setting time: When food is removed from cooking and is allowed to stand, as in bread or cookies.

Shiitake: *(Oriental)* A mushroom with a delicate, noticeable flavor; comes dry or fresh; originated in China and Japan and is now grown in the West.

Shocking: A process of adding cold water to boiling noodles or beans to improve taste or texture.

Shortening: Oil used to tenderize flour products.

Shred: To cut into thin strips with coarse blade or grater.

Shrimp: (Also called prawn, squill fish, scampi, Norway lobster, and camaron.) A clawless crustacean; hundreds of species grow worldwide. Comes in five categories depending on how many per pound: 10–12, 20–25, 25–35, 35–45, 75–100.

Simmer: To cook a liquid at below the boiling point (about 185°F.) The liquid should do no more than move gently, with bub-

bles forming below the surface.

Six basic flavor components: Taste, smell, touch, temperature, sight, and thought (which includes social acceptance).

Skillet: Commonly referred to as a *griswald* or a heavy cast iron frying pan. A *satuce* with vertical sides or a *satwa* with sloping sides are also considered a skillet.

Skim: To remove undesirable residue from the surface of a liquid, as in soup, sauce, or from cooking some grains, legumes, and vegetables.

Slurry: Made by adding and mixing liquid to dissolve or make thinner a solid powder or paste into a durable mixture.

Smoke point: The point at which oil begins to smoke.

Smorgasbord: *(Scand.)* A meal featuring a varied number of hot and cold dishes served buffet style, on a walk-around table in the center of the room. *(Swed.)* A self-service appetizer buffet, or the first course.

Snack: *(Dutch)* From "snacken," meaning to bite.

Snip: With scissors, to cut into fine pieces, such as chives.

Soak: To let food sit in water until thoroughly moistened or swollen to rehydrate, such as legumes.

Sous-chef: Second in command of a kitchen.

Soy (soya) sauce: Any of various soy bean–based sauces. Traditionally-made shoyu or tamari sauces from Japan are the best quality. Modern sauces, made in either the East or the West, are often used as substitutes for shoyu or tamari. These are mostly unfermented, often containing hydrolyzed vegetable protein (HVP), corn syrup, monosodium glutamate (MSG); not recommended.

Spatula: A flat blade, usually of metal, used to remove food from cooking surface to which it may stick if left to cool. A rubber spatula may be used to remove the last of the food from a bowl or to spread as desired.

Spinach: High in oxalic acid, which weakens the liver and kidneys and hinders utilization of calcium.

Stability: The rancidity-resisting characteristic of oil.

Standardized recipes: A set of instructions describing the way to prepare a specific dish.

Standing time: The time cooked food should stand or "rest" before the next step in preparation or being served.

Starch: A thickening agent, as found in rice or wheat flour or arrowroot.

Steam: To par-cook, cook, or reheat in a closed container a food that is totally immersed in steam, with or without pressure.

Steel: A tool to sharpen knives.

Steep: To soak in a very hot liquid to extract the flavor or color, as in tea.

Sterilize: To destroy bacteria and microorganisms by boiling in water, heat, or steam.

Stew: To boil or simmer; to make a thick liquid in which grains, legumes, or vegetables have been cooked.

Stir fry: *(Oriental)* A term for the cooking and preparation of food native to the Orient by cooking in a wok, usually with peanut or sesame oil, often flavored with grated ginger root; initially cooking the food at a very high heat for the first three minutes, and then at a low heat for two minutes, and adding rice flour to make a gravy or glaze to encase the vegetables and maintain their color, texture, and flavor.

Stir: To mix food in a circular motion.

Stock: A liquid in which grains, beans, or vegetables have been cooked; a liquid containing nutrients and flavor that has been extracted from food, usually by slow cooking.

Strain: To drain liquid from a solid food.

Stuff: To fill food with another food.

Stuffing: A seasoned filling.

Succotash: A mixture of equal amounts of corn cut from the cob and fresh lima beans; a native dish of the Algonquin Indians.

Suribachi: An earthenware bowl with serrated interior, used to grind food with a pestle.

Sushi: *(Jap.)* Boiled rice and raw fish or vegetables, often wrapped in nori sheets. Prepared either in a roll or cut in half lengthwise; the roll is sometimes sliced in 1" slices or made into one or two bite-sized balls. Used as a snack, appetizer, or side dish. If umbushi plum or paste is used as part of the stuffing, it is good for travel food without refrigeration for some days.

Swirl: To rotate a liquid in a pan to semi-mix ingredients or to remove clinging particles of food from the sides of the pan.

Tabouli: See recipe, pg. 240.

Tapioca: A powdered starch of the cassava plant used in desserts and in some soups. Fine-grained tapioca is called *pearled*.

Tart: A small shell (often referred to as Pate Brisee tart shells), filled with fruit, legumes, or vegetables.

Tartlet: An approximately 1" shell (often referred to as Pate Brisee tartlet shell), filled with fruit, legumes, or vegetables.

Tea: See Infusion, above, and Beverages, pp. 102–107.

Tempura: *(Jap.)* A specially flavored, batter-dipped, deep-fried seafood or vegetable.

Terrine: *(Fr.)* An earthenware bowl from which soups or stews are served.

Thicken: To add flour, kuzu, arrowroot, corn starch, or other thickening agent to a liquid mixture.

Thin: To dilute with a liquid.

Tortilla: *(Mex.)* A flat, unleavened bread made of specially ground yellow corn or white flour; originated with the Aztecs and used as a staple today in Mexico and Central America. Served as:

• A bread without butter, as is;

• Corn chips;

• Tacos, either fried or shaped in a U-form and rolled with a stuffing;

• Enchiladas, rolled with a stuffing, covered with a sauce, and baked;

• Burritos, rolled with a stuffing.

Toss: To mix with light vertical and diagonal strokes with a fork or spoon, lifting and flipping into the air, as in salads.

Trim: To shape and cut away unwanted portions of food, before or after cooking.

Tureen: A decorative large, deep bowl used to serve soups and stews.

Turn: To flip over or reverse food during or after the cooking process; to trim or shape vegetables for cooking or garnish.

Vanilla: Comes two ways:

•*Vanilla bean,* used mostly in cooking liquid desserts and for making vanilla extract. 734 metric tons of vanilla bean were imported into the United States in 1985.

•*Vanilla extract,* has alcohol as a medium and is dark brown; is made from the vanilla bean and held in a soluble solution of 35% alcohol, which will evaporate in cooking. Brought to Europe by the Spanish from Mexico. Vanilla clippings from the orchid plant originated in Mexico. The word "vanilla" comes from the Spanish for "little sheath" (from the Latin *vagina*), which accounts for its reputation as an aphrodesiac.

Vermicelli: A very thin thread of pasta made from grains or beans; sometimes clear in color, delicate in flavor.

Vert: *(Fr.)* Green.

Vinegar: An impure dilute solution of acetic acid, obtained from the fermentation of wine or cider beyond the alcoholic stage; used as a condiment, for flavoring, or as a preservative.

Vinaigrette: A sauce or dressing made from vinegar, oil, onions, parsley, and herbs.

Volatile: Easily dispersible with low heat.

Whisk: Often referred to as a whip; a tool used to beat or whip.

Whip: To very completely mix food so as to cause it to contain air.

Wok: *(Chin.)* A metal cooking pot shaped like a salad bowl; used for stir frying.

Yeast: A microscopic fungus that reproduces by blooming or budding and causes fermentation and the giving off of carbon dioxide. The ancient Egyptians used yeast by making half-baked bread of wheat and barley and soaking it in water (a form of barley malt), and allowing it to ferment; many types of beer with a high alcoholic content are made with yeast.

Yogurt: *(Turk.)* A semi-solid creamy culture with a sour taste; used in cooking or eaten by itself, with or without fruit, sweetener, or granola. Made from milk and bacteria coming from other yogurt; a native of the Middle East. (See recipe, pg. 210.)

Zest: The thin layer of the oily outer skin of an orange or lemon without the white, pulpy part of the skin.

Zester: A small triangular tool mounted on a wooden or plastic handle with a row of four or five holes that takes the zest off fruit and not the bitter white pulp.

"The discovery of a new dish does more for the happiness of mankind than the discovery of a star."
Brillat-Savarin

9. FLAVOR

FLAVOR

Flavor is an overall sensory impression perceived when food is eaten: taste, smell, and mouth feel—components of flavor—are the results of minerals and oils. Flavor is a measurable thing (in that what causes flavor can be measured), attained by a pragmatic and intuitive approach to food preparation; flavor can broken down and seen as the separate components that go into it.

The primary goal in the preparation of natural whole foods is to maintain the integrity of the uncooked food from the kitchen to the table. Preparing food in such a way as to enhance, maintain, preserve, and elevate the essential character by adding herbs, spices, or combining other selected foods is referred to as flavoring. Flavoring is a preconceived notion that is most personal and individual.

Major Influences on Flavor:
- Smell
- Taste
- Temperature
- Touch

Minor Influences on Flavor:
- Sight
- Thought
- Music
- Sound
- Health of the customer

Major Influences

Smell is the stimulation of olfactory nerves, and occurs by three different methods:

- Coming through the nose directly from the foods;
- When chewing releases volatized oils that are exhaled through the mouth and rise up into the nose;
- When volatized oils go back into the throat and into the nasal passage. The release of smells is partially dependent on temperature (see below).

Taste is activated by about 10,000 taste buds in the mouth, mostly concentrated on the tongue. Young people usually have more active and healthier taste buds, allowing them to find more sensory satisfaction from simple, fresh foods and to appreciate their natural flavors. In youth, every day the taste buds regenerate; this slows down with age. The deterioration of taste buds can explain why adults prefer spicier foods. If the taste buds have been desensitized by a continuous bombardment of salt and sugar, natural foods will come to seem bland initially. With the cultivation of new values, the essential taste characteristics of natural whole food will rise above the artificially-processed and -flavored foods so common today.

Living in an overstimulated society—in which we are pelted with the products of taste and flavoring laboratories—is fostering a lack of sensitivity and appreciation of the subtleties of real food.

Half of what we perceive as taste is actually smell, and that is proven when you have a cold. All foods tend to taste the same when you have a cold, but it is not the taste buds that are affected, it is the sense of smell. With blocked nasal passages or sinuses, people say that food does not taste good, when actually what they mean is that the flavor of the food is being perceived differently. This is because they have temporarily eliminated the most acute, most important, and most sensitive of the flavor senses—smell.

Temperature is a subcategory of touch, is tactile, and in some ways affects the nerves and mouth feel. The release of natural whole food smells is dependent, to some degree, on the food being served very warm, usually between 80° and 110°. The use of temperature alters flavor. When we eat foods that are very hot, we don't appreciate their tastes as much. Eating food that is very cold usually desensitizes most of our taste buds, and we discern only a very few flavors, usually to a minimum degree.

Temperatures of certain foods are most important when being eaten. Fresh fruit or vegetables are on the tasteless side when eaten at 40°, but we realize the full flavor range at a warmer temperature. Hot coffee will mask taste elements, many of which are not pleasant at room temperature, yet our favorite soft drink served hot will have an altogether different taste than when it is served cold. Even the highest-quality ice cream, left to sit a number of hours at room temperature, will taste unbearably sweet.

Smell is affected by temperature. In order for food to smell, oils must be volatized by increasing temperature. There are a number of dishes that taste good served hot, where fewer dishes taste good at room temperature.

Touch is the stimulation of nerve fibers with touch, making them astringent (puckering or drying sense), as with the tartness of an acid or alkaline food. A concentration of hot spices from peppers is not taste, but a stimulation of the nerves.

Minor Influences

Sight of food can relate to the old axiom that you eat with your eyes. The well-garnished platter will draw acceptance and desire as will skillfully selected color combinations of foods. Consideration should be given in selecting the plate color, shape, and size. The finished plate that has been carefully prepared, taking into account size, layout, shape, and color, will make all the difference in the world in creating a craving for it, even before it is smelled. Food that looks and gives the impression that it is bad, probably won't be eaten, even if it tastes good. But, if it looks good, even though the quality is not the best, customers or guests will probably taste it.

Thought is closely related to sight. If it looks good, you think it will probably have a good flavor. If people constantly tell you that something is good, then, often, you will believe it. On the other hand, if people you consider knowledgeable and trustworthy tell you that something is bad tasting, you will often begin to perceive it to taste the way they suggest.

A good example is canned soup. We have been conditioned to accept the metallic, salt taste of canned soup for so long that we think that is the way soup is supposed to taste. As one chef I know said, "It may be a good idea, after this book is written, to package and market that metallic chemical tang so that natural whole food soups will be more acceptable to the public."

Music and sound are managed in the dining room. If someone's combined impression of these components of flavor is that of being good, then they will like the food. Consumer flavor perceptions are as numerous and unique as fingerprints, and the competent chef must successfully meet the consumer's flavor expectations.

The **health** of the customer relates to the flavor of the food, in that if the customer is healthy, energetic, feeling well, and probably hungry, the food tends to taste better. If the customer is not well, or his or her health is in a state of degeneration, the same food will tend to taste worse.

The demands upon the chef to meet his consumers' approval in selecting what dishes to serve, how to prepare them, and making them taste good as well as being nutritious, can be mind-boggling.

"You don't have to be a magician; it's a matter of using the ingredients correctly."
Victor Gielisse, D.E.C.
National Culinary Review, November 1988

MAKING TASTE

To have even the shallowest idea of the flavor qualities of foods and how they blend and become more pleasing to others, the cook must experience the food. If you are not willing to look at, smell, taste and feel your food, and then evaluate the impression, correct the deficiencies, and experience it again, you will never become much of a chef. You must experience the food and understand how each product relates to the others. It takes a lot of experimentation and exposure before you can even begin to control the flavor.

Students of the world of cookery, both professional and non-professional, must put aside their learned prejudices and be prepared to look at, smell, taste, and evaluate the impression again and again. Seasoning means to enhance the natural flavor of the food. If in doubt as to what to add, make a practice of cross-checking the smell of what you are cooking and the flavor you anticipate adding. You must be

sure to give the seasoning enough time to be absorbed into the food, yet to not cook it so long that the flavors evaporate or become over-concentrated, keeping in mind that many elements of seasonings are highly volatile and therefore easily destroyed.

All potential chefs must learn to evaluate and continually correct throughout the cooking process. The ability to evaluate and correct improves only through the continuous experience and careful attention to detail of flavor, and the manner in which you use them, trying again and again.

A young chef, when I asked him how he knew what seasonings to put into food replied, "I just smell the food and then smell the seasoning and after cross-checking, use what is complementary." A few years later the subject came up again and I reviewed his method of a few years before. His reply now was, "All that is not necessary, since a chef knows what seasonings smell like and he knows what will go with what." It seems the experience, the maturing process, had been developing.

"The greatest of all professions...the chef or cook...holds in the palm of the hand the quality, happiness and future of today's and coming generations."
Unknown

NOTES

Foreword

1. "Heart Facts," a pamphlet distributed by the American Heart Association, 1988.

Introduction

1. Quoted by permission from *Reversing Heart Disease*, Julian M. Whitaker, M.D., © 1985, Warner Books, Inc.
2. The Associated Press, *Burlington Free Press*, Sunday, March 13, 1988.
3. National Restaurant Association, *Washington Weekly*, June 15, 1987.

Chapter 1: Healthy and Unhealthy Foods

1. Reprinted with permission from *The McDougall Plan*, John A. and Mary A. McDougal, ©1983, New Century Publishers, Piscataway, N.J.
2. Reprinted with permission from *Nutrition Action Healthletter*, Na-E-61, ©1988, Center for Science in the Public Interest.

3. Murray, K. B. "Hazard of Microwave Ovens to Transdermal Delivery Systems," *New England Journal of Medicine*, 310:721.
4. NIN of India Study, pp. 138–141.

Chapter 5: Philosophy, Practice, Tradition

1. Reprinted by permission from *Diet and Nutrition*, Rudolph Balentine, M.D., ©1978, Himalayan International Institute of Yoga Science and Philosophy.

Chapter 7: Ingredient Description

1. *Cooking With Sea Vegetables*, Peter and Montie Bradford, Inner Trad, 1985.

2. Ibid.

SUGGESTED READING

1. Bradford, Peter and Montse, *Cooking with Sea Vegetables*, Inner Trad, 1985.

2. *East–West Journal.*

3. Berger, Stuart M. , M.D., *Immune Power Diet*, NAL, 1985.

4. Farah, Madelian, *Lebanese Cuisine*, 1979.

5. Kushi, Aveline, *Macrobiotic Cooking*, Japan Pubns. USA, 1985.

6. Metcalf de Plata, Edith, *Mexican Vegetarian Cooking*, Inner Trad, 1984.

7. Estella, Mary, *Natural Foods cookbook*, Japan Pubns. USA, 1985.

8. Whitacar, Julian M., M.D., *Reversing Heart Disease*, Warner Books, 1989.

10. Trevanian, *Shibumi*, Ballantine, 1983.

11. Seamens, Dan, and Wollner, David, *Shopper's Guide*.

12. Hurd, Frank J. and Rosalind, *Ten Talents*, Ten Talents, 1985.

13. Veith, Ilza, trans., *The Yellow Emperor's Classic of Internal Medicine*, U. of Cal. Press, 1966.

14. McClane, A. J., *The Encyclopaedia of Fish Cookery*, H. Holt & Co., 1977.

15. Colbin, Anne Marie, *The Book of Whole Meals*, Ballantine, 1986.

16. Kushi, Michio, *The Book of Macrobiotics*, Japan Pubns. USA, 1977.

17. McDougall, John A. and Mary A., *The McDougall Plan*, New Century Publishers, 1983.

18. Chisti, Hakim G. M., M.D., *The Traditional Healer*, Inner Trad, 1988.

19. Miller, Gloria Bley, *The Thousand Recipe Chinese Cookbook*, Simon & Schuster, 1984.

20. Robertson, Laurel, Carol Flinders, and Brian Ruppenthal, *The New Laurel's Kitchen*, Ten Speed Press, 1986.

PART II.
Recipes

GUIDELINES FOR PREPARING FOOD

General

•Judgment must be an ingredient in each recipe.

•Cooking harbors no flavor mysteries.

•Many have started to learn about cooking by washing dishes, pots and pans, and not stopped learning even after retirement as a chef; one can never know too much.

•Flavor and nutritional value are retained and enhanced by traditional and technical methods, based on and coupled with the intelligence and intuition of the chef.

•Simplicity does not rule out beauty and technical knowledge.

•Intuition, experience, and necessity foster the development of new recipes and techniques.

•Humility, patience, memory, and a sense of humor (and more patience) are inherent in the successful chef.

•If major ingredients are missing, don't make the recipe. If minor ingredients are missing, either leave them out or carefully substitute.

Purpose of Recipes

•To provide consistency for:

–customer preference;

–cost control.

•To duplicate a desired dish.

•To control a cooking process.

•To bring certain ingredients together by selected procedures.

•To obtain desired flavor, *from:*

–major ingredients;

–interchanging more than one ingredient.

By:

–method of heating (first step in digestion);

–length of cooking individual ingredients and intensity of heat.

•To maintain:

–nutritive value;

–texture.

Recipe Limitations

•Variation of ingredients.

•Variation of equipment.

•Vagueness of instructions:

–How thick is "thick"?

–What is "medium" heat?

–What does "desired" mean?

–When is cooking "complete"?

–What actually is "parcooked" or "al dente"?

•Inappropriate heat application.

•Different measuring tools (cups and spoons) of the same size varying in the quantity they actually hold.

The basic rules of cookery must be absorbed into the cooking process. The first-time cook will tend to need help or supervision to understand the recipes.

GUIDELINES FOR RECIPE USE

The memorization of hundreds of recipes is no substitute for the individual development of:

•Experience

•Intuition

•Knowledge

Feel what you are cooking, experience what you are cooking—see it, smell it, taste it. Feel how you are changing the food, feel how your knowledge, intuition, and experience are being transferred from you to the food to the consumer.

You must also have an understanding of cooking principles with various basic techniques that are used in the recipes.

In addition to managerial skills, development of ingredients, and procedure, judgment is essential for the growth and evolution of a chef. This includes:

•Establishing what is wrong with a poorly written recipe before using it;

•Familiarity with the use of different cooking equipment or cooking processes;

•Knowledge of the substitution of ingredients;

•Achieving variations for slightly different results.

THE RECIPE FORM

These natural whole food recipes have been tested and used by various professional chefs and kitchens to promote a healthy, balanced diet, based on grains, fresh fruits and vegetables, and legumes.

The recipes are designed to maintain the natural integrity of the major ingredients of a dish, with complementary flavorings of minor ingredients. Minor flavorings that tend to smother or mask the dish have been purposely avoided. The recipes are simple, clear, and easy to follow, showing step-by-step ingredients and procedures. Be sure to read, learn, and incorporate into each recipe, as applicable, *The Important Guidelines for Cookery* that appear at the beginning of each section. This form of presentation is intended to reduce long-winded repetition in the procedures described in the recipes.

Recipes are listed in alphabetical order by general heading (Beverages, Breads, etc.), and again in alphabetical order within each group of recipes (Barley Tea, Carrot Drink, etc.).

Read through and understand each recipe before starting to make it.

Pan Size, Cooking Time, Oven Temp.

Oven temperature should be checked with an oven thermometer, and the oven adjusted if necessary. Cooking time may vary from the approximate time given, due to the quality or temperature of ingredients at the beginning of cooking. Learning to test for doneness and judging for proper consistency, taste, temperature, and texture are also part of cooking.

Ingredients and Procedures

These standard components show the basic concept of the recipe, and list them in the order of their use and application. Often key ingredients are repeated from recipe to recipe, thus saving in ordering, stocking, and in storage space.

Procedures that are continuously repeated and are therefore not described in detail in each recipe are as follows:

•*Simmer* point is reached by turning heat up to high, and upon boiling, immediately turning it down to low; remove foam that forms in the first 5 minutes of simmering; then cover to simmer.

•*Saute garlic* until garlic flavor is infused into oil and garlic begins to turn dark tan; remove garlic from oil.

•*Tofu, cooked,* refers to precooking tofu by placing tofu in boiling salted water for 5 minutes, and cooling before using it in a recipe that calls for no cooking. Do not eat or serve raw tofu.

•*Thickener* refers to arrowroot slurry (using arrowroot, kuzu, flour, or cornstarch)—mix and dissolve in equal amounts of water and then slowly add to the boiling liquid to be thickened. Care should be taken that the thickener not gel in undissolved lumps when heat is applied, but is quickly and evenly distributed through the boiling liquid.

•*Tofu, dried, before marinating*: slice $1/2$" (+/- as needed) and place on dry towel; cover with towel, press lightly so towel will absorb water. Repeat this process one or two more times, but after pressing let tofu rest 10–15 minutes before pressing again on new dry towel or before using.

•*Quick-cool:* to immerse the outside of the hot cooking pot in a sink of cold water immediately after removing from heat, and stirring the contents to distribute the cooled food.

•*Adjust* refers to flavor, consistency, and/or thickness. If using agar-agar, it means to spoon-test it (see pg. 80) for gel quality.

•*Mise en Place* means, *before beginning the recipe:*

—Tools and equipment should be stored at the work station within one-step reach when needed.

—Herbs and spices should be within one-step reach of work place; other dry ingredients should be assembled by weight or volume.

—Collecting, washing, trimming, and cutting raw ingredients according to procedures.

—Assembling (preferably stored at work station) and preparing equipment, such as preheating oven and oiling pans.

•*Puree* refers to liquid mixtures, such as sauces, and is usually done in a blender. Mixtures of a thicker nature, such as dips, are done in a food processor.

•*Storing* prepared food (although it is preferable to serve it immediately): cool to room temperature, cover, refrigerate.

Yield–Serves–Portion Column

Generally, all recipes serve 10, with noted "yield," "serves," and "portion" amounts, shown in the left half of the center column of each recipe. Larger yields often can be calculated easily by multiplying each ingredient of the recipe by the increase of yield desired.

For home use, the recipes can be easily adjusted by dividing. *Use the blank right column to note your adjustments.*

Below that, also in the left half of the center column, the quantities of each ingredient are listed, occasionally by pounds, but mostly by cups, tablespoons, teaspoons, etc.

Make adjustments in yield and/or in quantities as desired.

The right half of the center column is designed for home use or for the house standardized recipe for:

•Yield, number served;

•Extension of ingredient quantities;

•Alteration of ingredients with quantities.

Most recipes are for round-figure yield, serves, and portion amounts, which the chef may adjust to fit the house needs.

Yield Increase

As the yield is increased, subtle adjustments may need to be made. If in-creasing 10 portions to 300 portions, the adjustments become far less subtle, such as with:

•Evaporation rates;

•Handling of ingredients;

•Thickening agents (may fluctuate up or down);

•Seasonings (may have to be reduced).

Yields, depending on the ingredients and procedures, may have to be prepared in more than one batch.

Recalled experience is the greatest factor for these judgments. All the new calculations can be recorded in the blank column provided.

Abbreviations

tsp.	=	teaspoon
Tbs.	=	tablespoon
lb.	=	pound
oz.	=	ounce
pt.	=	pint
qt.	=	quart
"	=	inches
sq. in.	=	square inches
doz.	=	dozen
min(s).	=	minute(s)
hr(s).	=	hour(s)

All measurements are to the top of the measuring container except as noted.

Variations

The ingredients or notes in the "variations" box at the bottom of each recipe include compatible flavorings or methods changing the *minor* characteristics of the dish.

Instructions regarding the "variations" items are purposely vague, to encourage experimentation and putting to use your own experience and knowledge; we do not want to limit you by exact instructions.

NOTE: In some recipe sections, a blank recipe form has been provided for your use.

BEVERAGES

BARLEY (roasted) TEA	Yield: 10 cups	Yield:	Pan size:
	Serves: 10	Serves:	Cooking time: 15–30 mins.
	Portion: 1 cup	Portion:	Oven temp.: 400°
Barley (or brown rice)	1½ cups		Place in pan. Roast at 400°. Stir and shake every 5 mins. until dark brown. (Be careful not to burn grains while roasting. The darker they are, the stronger the tea.)
Water	11 cups		Add to barley in pan. Simmer 15 mins.
			Strain; serve hot or at room temp.

Variations: Substitute 50% of grains with sweet brown rice. Barley can be roasted and stored in tightly lidded container, or roast a single layer of barley in the oven at 300° for 15 mins., or until dark brown.

CARROT DRINK	Yield: 6 cups	Yield:	Pan size: 4 qt.
	Serves: 6	Serves:	Cooking time: 25 mins.
	Portion: 1 cup	Portion:	Oven temp.:
Carrots, whole	1½ lb.		Trim. Place in pan.
Water, to cover			Add. Simmer 25 mins. or until cooked *al dente.*
Carrots, cooked (above)			Place in blender.
Cook water	6½ cups		Add, blend well.
Salt	1 tsp.		Add; adjust.
			Serve hot.

Variations: Add 1 Tbs. of white or green onion.
Add 2 Tbs. tahini.

CIDER, SPICED

Pan size:	1 qt.	Yield:	10 cups	Yield:	
Cooking time:	5 mins.	Serves:	10	Serves:	
Oven temp.:		Portion:	1 cup	Portion:	

Apple cider	10 cups		Place in pan.
Nutmeg	1/4 tsp.		Add.
Clove	1/4 tsp.		Add.
Cinnamon	1/4 tsp.		Add.
			Bring slowly to simmer (to prevent separation) for 5 mins., covered.
			Rest 10 mins. covered. Serve.

Variations: Add orange peel before cooking.

CRANBERRY TEA

[Adapted from *Complete Cooks Guide*, printed in 1683.]

Pan size:	4 qt.	Yield:	10 cups	Yield:	
Cooking time:	20 mins.	Serves:	10	Serves:	
Oven temp.:		Portion:	1 cup	Portion:	

Cranberries	1 cup		Place in pan; mash.
Water	10 cups		Add.
Oats, rolled	2 Tbs.+		Add, simmer 15 mins.
Barley malt	2 Tbs.+		Add, mix, simmer 5 mins.
			Rest 10 mins. Stir rapidly.
			Serve hot.

Variations: Add 1 Tbs. fennel seed; 1 tsp. vanilla; or cinnamon, nutmeg, cloves, allspice, and ginger in equal amounts.
Whir oats in blender.

FENNEL TEA

	Yield:	10 cups	Yield:		Pan size:	1 qt.
	Serves:	10	Serves:		Cooking time:	5 mins.
	Portion:	1 cup	Portion:		Oven temp.:	

Water	10 cups	Place in pot.
Fennel seed	4 Tbs.	Add, bring to boil.
		Simmer 4 mins. covered.
		Steep 5 mins. covered.
		Strain, serve.
		[NOTE: A traditional Egyptian social and medicinal tea for the digestion and the kidneys.]

Variations:

GRAPE COOLER

	Yield:	10 cups	Yield:		Pan size:	
	Serves:	10	Serves:		Cooking time:	
	Portion:	1 cup	Portion:		Oven temp.:	

Grape juice	5 cups	Place in glass or china container.
Water	5 cups	Add.
Lemon juice	1 tsp.	Add, mix, serve.

Variations: Substitute apple juice or seltzer water for water.

Pan size:	Yield:	10 cups	Yield:		**JASMINE TEA**
Cooking time:	Serves:	10	Serves:		
Oven temp.:	Portion:	1 cup	Portion:		

Water	10 cups		Place in pot. Bring to rolling boil. Turn heat off immediately.
Jasmine tea	1 Tbs.		Add, mix only to immerse leaves; cover. Steep 10 mins.
			Strain; serve hot.
			[NOTE: Traditionally served with no condiments.]

Variations:

Pan size:	Yield:	10 cups	Yield:		**KUKICHA (twig) TEA**
Cooking time:	Serves:	10	Serves:		
Oven temp.:	Portion:	1 cup	Portion:		

Water	10 cups		Place in pot.
Kukicha (twigs)	3 Tbs.		Add, bring to boil.
			Simmer 10 mins. covered. Steep 10 mins. covered.
			Strain; serve.

Variations: **For an extra rich flavor, roast twigs in skillet, stirring for a few minutes over medium-high heat.**

LICORICE–CINNAMON TEA

	Yield:	10 cups	Yield:		Pan size:
	Serves:	10	Serves:		Cooking time:
	Portion:	1 cup	Portion:		Oven temp.:

Water	10 cups		Place in pot.
Licorice root, dry	1/4 cup		Add.
Cinnamon stick, knife-crushed	2		Add; simmer 10 mins. covered. Steep 10 mins. covered.
			Strain; serve.
			[NOTE: According to Oriental medicine, licorice aids digestion, neutralizes toxins, and strengthens the stomach. Cinnamon warms the body, expels toxins, heightens the vitality of kidneys and reproductive organs, and the whole body.]

Variations: Steep longer if stronger tea desired.
Reuse licorice and cinnamon a second time or simmer 30 mins. for 20 cups of water.

PEACH COOLER

	Yield:	10 cups	Yield:		Pan size:
	Serves:	10	Serves:		Cooking time:
	Portion:	1 cup	Portion:		Oven temp.:

Water, iced	5 cups		Place in blender.
Peaches, skinned and diced	4 cups		Add.
Tofu, cooked	1/2 lb.		Add.
Almond extract	1/4 tsp.		Add.
Mint leaves	5		Add, blend.
			Serve.

Variations: Add 1/2 tsp. mace, ginger, or cinnamon.

WATERMELON BEVERAGE

Pan size:	Yield:	10 cups	Yield:	
Cooking time:	Serves:	10	Serves:	
Oven temp.:	Portion:	1 cup	Portion:	

Watermelon	10 cups		Place in blender.
Water	5 cups		Add, blend.
			Serve cold.

Variations: Garnish with mint or lemon.

YOGURT COOLER

Pan size:	Yield:	10 cups	Yield:	
Cooking time:	Serves:	10	Serves:	
Oven temp.:	Portion:	1 cup	Portion:	

Yogurt	1 lb.		Place in blender.
Mint, fresh leaves	5		Add, blend.
Cucumber, peeled, quartered	1 lb.		Add, blend smooth.
Water	7 cups		Add.
Salt	pinch		Add, blend smooth.
			Serve.

Variations: Add 2 Tbs. fresh lemon juice, 2 tsp. finely chopped parsley, or 2 tsp. ginger. Use fruit to replace cucumber.

BREADS

THREE BASIC BREADS:

•Yeast bread using yeast for fermentation;

•Quick bread, using baking powder and/or baking soda;

•Sourdough, using natural bacteria for fermentation.

IMPORTANT GUIDELINES FOR BREAD BAKING

•Avoid wheat that has been bleached, enriched, fortified, restored, and wheat that is not organic.

•Store flour in a cool place and use at room temperature.

•For bread, use hard red spring wheat.

•Use house-grown high-gluten whole grain flour or stone-ground flour less than 2 months old.

•Mix all ingredients at room temperature.

•Old wheat or flour insures an undesirable product.

•Sift all dry ingredients that will go through a sifter.

•Always oil baking pans before baking, shake on or dust with a fine layer of flour, or cut parchment paper into pan bottom.

•Preheat oven to 400° and turn to desired temperature when starting to bake.

•If yeast doesn't bloom, use yeast from another batch or from another source.

•If you have started to make bread and yeast doesn't bloom, add 1 Tbs. baking powder to about 5 cups of flour and unbloomed yeast.

•Different types of yeasts, conditions of storage, and batches, have different results.

•Use less flour in dry weather and more flour in humid weather.

•2 Tbs. oil per loaf will help rising.

•As dough rises, keep surface from drying out with oil or a damp cloth cover.

•Slower-rising dough at 65–70° will aid in better taste and nutritional value.

•Knead from the abdomen, not from your arms.

•5 cups of ingredients will fill 12 2½" muffin forms or about one-third full 9 × 13" pan.

•Baking weight loss is about 11%.

•Bread sticks are just small yeasted bread loaves that have been dried at 190° for an hour or so, depending on size, before baking at 350° for 35 minutes.

•Use muffin cups (liners) to prevent breakage and make easier pan cleaning, using a paper or paper-lined aluminum foil (not aluminum alone).

•Ripe dough (ready for baking) is elastic—a bit dry and not sticky.

•"Finger test" oven-ready dough by gently pushing into risen dough.

–If hole refills itself completely or immediately, it's not ready; let it keep rising.

–If hole remains and only partially (50%) refills itself, it's ready for baking.

•*Bread doneness test:* Remove a loaf from the pan. If bottom is brown, tap it and listen for a hollow sound or slice a corner off. Finger-press interior crumb (inner dough), which should spring back to touch.

•Uneven color of inner bread indicates that dough was too wet.

•As bread goes into the oven, cut top with razor blade, allowing oven spring, and creating an attractive surface.

•Indications of quick bread (not yeast) completion:

–Toothpick or knife comes out clean from center of quick bread.

–Sides of bread pull away from pan and/or turn slightly tan/brown.

–Bread will spring back at quick, light finger-touch to center.

CORN BREAD
(or muffins)

Pan size:	9 × 13"*	Yield:	9 × 13"*	Yield:	
Cooking time:	22 mins.+	Serves:	12	Serves:	
Oven temp.:	375°	Portion:	3 × 4"	Portion:	

Tofu	½ lb.		Place in blender.
Water	¾ cup		Add, blend.
Maple syrup	¾ cup		Add.
Oil	¾ cup		Add, blend.
Corn meal	2 cups		Place in bowl.
Whole wheat pastry flour	1 cup		Add.
Unbleached white flour	1 cup		Add.
Salt	1 tsp.		Add, mix *very well.* Add liquid, mix. Pour into oiled 9 × 13" pan or 12 2¼" muffin forms.*
			Bake 22 mins. at 375° or until done. Cut and serve from pan.

Variations: Add 2 tsp. rice vinegar to liquids for more rise.

CORN BREAD,
SWEET RICE
[Basic recipe by Chuck Conway, O Bakery, Shelburne, Vt.]

Pan size:	9 × 13"	Yield:	9 × 13"	Yield:	
Cooking time:	55 mins.	Serves:	12	Serves:	
Oven temp.:	350°	Portion:	3 × 4⅓"	Portion:	

Brown rice, sweet	1½ cups		Place in pan.
Water	3¾ cups		Add. Simmer 40 mins. Rest and cool for 30 mins.
Water	3 cups		Place in bowl.
Salt	2 tsp.		Add.
Currants	9 oz.		Add.
Corn oil	⅓ cup		Add.
Corn meal	4 cups		Add.
Whole wheat pastry flour	1 cup		Add, mix, adjust water.
Blueberries	1 cup		Add and fold in.
			Pour into oiled 9 × 13" pan. Bake 55+/- mins. at 350° until sides pull away from pan and top cracks. Cool 10 mins. in pan. Cut and serve from pan.

Variations: Instead of fruit add diced onion, carrot.

GINGER BREAD

	Yield: 9 × 13"	Yield:	Pan size: 9 × 13"
	Serves: 12	Serves:	Cooking time: 25 mins.
	Portion: 3 × 4⅓"	Portion:	Oven temp.: 350°

Whole wheat flour	2 cups		Place in bowl.
Whole wheat pastry flour	1 cup		Add.
Corn meal	½ cup		Add.
Baking powder	2 Tbs.		Add.
Salt	½ tsp.		Add.
Ginger, ground	4 tsp.		Add.
Cinnamon	1 tsp.		Add.
Mustard, ground	½ tsp.		Add, mix. Reserve.
Tofu	¼ lb.		Place in blender.
Apple cider	2¼ cups		Add; blend smooth.
Corn oil	½ cup		Add.
Barley Malt	½ cup		Add.
Ginger, grated	⅓ cup		Add, blend smooth. Adjust flavors.
Lemon zest	1 Tbs.		Add, mix with spoon. Add to flour, mix.
			Pour into oiled 9 × 13" pan. Bake 25 mins. at 350° or until done.
			Rest 10 mins. in pan. Place on cake rack.

Variations:

RICE KAYU BREAD (Japanese)

[Recipe from Pine Grove Bakery, Thetford, Vt.]

		Pan size: 4 × 8"	Cooking time: 1¼ hrs.	Oven temp.: 350°

Yield: 4 loaves Serves: Portion:

Yield: Serves: Portion:

Brown rice, short grain, organic	½ cup		Place in pot.
Water	6 cups		Add, simmer, tightly covered, for 3–4 hrs. until rice is glutinous (sticky). Cool to 80°.
Whole wheat flour	4 cups		Add.
Sea salt	4 tsp.		Add, mix by hand 3 mins.
Safflower oil, expeller pressed	⅓ cup		Add, mix by hand.
Whole wheat flour	1 cup +/-		Add and adjust until dough springs back to touch (should be soft, not stiff). Place dough in oiled wood or glass container. Rest in warm place overnight, cloth covered. When dough starts to rise, place in 4 well-oiled loaf pans; cloth cover and let sit in extra warm place until loaf begins to fill pans. Bake at 350° for 1 hour and 15 mins.

Variations:

WHOLE WHEAT BREAD, BASIC

Pan size: 4 × 8"	Cooking time: 50 mins.	Oven temp.: 300°

Yield: 4 loaves Serves: Portion:

Yield: Serves: Portion:

Water, 110°	5 cups		Place in warm bowl.
Barley malt	2 Tbs.		Add; mix.
Yeast	½ oz.		Add, cover, set in warm place until it blooms.
Whole wheat flour	10 cups		Place in bowl.
Salt	2 tsp.		Add; mix.
Yeast water (above)			Add.
Corn oil	¼ cup		Add; mix.
			Knead with dry flour 5 mins. Place dough ball in oiled bowl and oil ball. Cover with cloth. Set aside in warm place.
			Let rise to double size. Punch down. Put in oiled baking pans and bake for 50 mins. at 300°.

Variations:

CAKES

IMPORTANT GUIDELINES FOR CAKE BAKING

•Don't use cake mixes because of chemical content and highly processed ingredients.

•Preheat oven fully for a minimum time to conserve energy.

•Do not place pans touching each other or the edge of the oven.

•Bake at correct temperature (use oven thermometer).

•Don't open and close oven door while cake is rising or is partially browned.

•For pastries, use fine-ground soft winter wheat.

Tests for doneness:

•Insert in center of cake a knife, fork, straw, or toothpick; it will come out clean if ready.

•Cake will pull away from sides of pan and/or become slightly tanned or browned.

•The top of the cake in the center will spring back when touched lightly.

Cooling:

•Cool cakes in pans for 15 minutes.

•Place empty sheet pan on top, bottom- side down.

•Invert quickly.

•Remove baking pan.

•Remove parchment from cake.

Altitude Adjustments: General Formula

Ingredient	2500'	5000'	7500'
Baking powder	−20%	−40%	−60%
Flour		+4%	+9%
Sweetener	−3%	−6%	−9%
Oil			−9%
Liquid	+9%	+15%	+22%

APPLE CAKE

Yield: 9 × 13"	Yield:	Pan size: 9 × 13"
Serves: 12	Serves:	Cooking time: 50 mins.
Portion: 3 × 4$^{1/3}$"	Portion:	Oven temp.: 350°

Apples, peeled, cored, $^{1/4}$"-diced	1 cup		Place in bowl.
Barley malt	$^{1/4}$ cup		Add.
Cinnamon, clove, ginger, allspice	pinch ea.		Add, mix, reserve.
Whole wheat pastry flour	5 cups		Place in bowl.
Baking powder	2 Tbs.		Add.
Salt	$^{1/2}$ tsp.		Add, mix, reserve.
Tofu	$^{1/4}$ lb.		Place in blender.
Apple cider	2$^{1/2}$ cups		Add, pulse, blend smooth.
Barley malt	$^{1/2}$ cup		Add.
Corn oil	$^{1/2}$ cup		Add, pulse, blend smooth. Add to flour mix; combine with apple mix. Pour into 9 × 13" oiled pan. Bake at 350°. Cool, serve.

Variations: Add grated lemon peel.

BROWNIES I

Pan size:	9 × 13"	Yield:	9 × 13"	Yield:	
Cooking time:	30 +/- mins.	Serves:	12	Serves:	
Oven temp.:	350°	Portion:	3 × 4"	Portion:	

Whole wheat pastry flour	2 cups		Place in bowl.
Salt	1 tsp.		Add.
Carob powder	1½ cups		Add.
Walnuts	1½ cups		Add.
Adzuki beans	1 cup		Add, mix, reserve.
Tofu	¼ lb.		Place in blender.
Water	1½ cups		Add.
Barley malt	1½ cups		Add.
Oil	½ cup		Add.
Maple syrup	⅓ cup		Add.
Vanilla extract	1 tsp.		Add.
Adzuki beans	1 cup		Blend smooth. Add to flour mix. Bake for 30–40 mins., depending on desired consistency.

Variations: Add grated lemon peel.

BROWNIES II

Pan size:	9 × 13"	Yield:	9 × 13"	Yield:	
Cooking time:	35 mins.	Serves:	12	Serves:	
Oven temp.:	350°	Portion:	3 × 4"	Portion:	

Carob powder	1 cup		Place in bowl.
Salt	1 tsp.		Add.
Whole wheat pastry flour	2 cups		Add.
Walnuts	1½ cups		Add.
Raisins	½ cup		Add.
Carob chips	½ cup		Add, mix, reserve.
Tofu	½ lb.		Place in blender.
Water, oil	½ cup ea.		Add.
Tahini	¼ cup		Add, blend smooth, stop.
Maple syrup	½ cup		Add.
Barley malt	1½ cups		Add.
Adzuki beans, cooked	2 cups		Add.
Vanilla	1½ tsp.		Add, blend smooth. Add to flour mixture, mix. Place in oiled 9 × 13" pan, caress top with bottom of spoon to develop glaze. Bake; cool & cut in pan. Serve.

Variations:

CHEESECAKE

	Yield:	9" pie	Yield:		Pan size:	9" round
	Serves:	8	Serves:		Cooking time:	22 mins.
	Portion:	1/8	Portion:		Oven temp.:	300°

Tofu, cooked	1 lb.		Place in blender.
Salt	1/2 tsp.		Add.
Lemon juice	1 1/2 Tbs.		Add.
Maple syrup	1/4 cup		Add.
Tahini	2 Tbs.		Add.
Vanilla	1 1/2 tsp.		Add, blend, stop.
Rice vinegar	1/2 tsp.		Add.
Almond extract	2 drops		Add, blend. Adjust flavor. Pour into molds or pre-baked pie crust. Bake 25 mins. at 300°. Turn oven off. Rest in oven 25 mins. Cool, cover, refrigerate.
			Serve. [NOTE: Tastes better served the next day.]

Variations: Top with blueberry, carob, or raspberry topping (see following 3 recipes). A crust made of oat bran and corn oil (not pre-baked) may be used in a spring-form for a more traditional cheesecake look.

BLUEBERRY TOPPING for cheesecake

	Yield:	2 cups	Yield:		Pan size:	
	Serves:	10	Serves:		Cooking time:	
	Portion:	3.2 Tbs.	Portion:		Oven temp.:	

Water	1/2 cup		Place in pan, heat.
Barley malt	1/2 cup		Add, mix, dissolve.
Blueberries	1 cup		Add, simmer 4 mins., mash.
Arrowroot	2 tsp.		Make slurry, add.
Blueberries	1 1/2 cups		Add to pan, parcook. Quick-cool. Pour on cheesecake.

Variations:

Pan size: 1 qt.	Yield: for 2 cakes	Yield:	**CAROB TOPPING**
Cooking time: 10 mins.	Serves:	Serves:	**for cheesecake**
Oven temp.:	Portion:	Portion:	

Water	$^3/_4$ cup		Place in pan.
Agar-agar	1 tsp.		Add, mix, simmer 10 mins., dissolve.
Carob powder	$^1/_4$ cup		Add, mix, dissolve.
Carob chips	1 cup		Place in blender, coarsely chop. Add to water mixture; mix. Pour on cheesecake.
			Cool, serve.

Variations:

Pan size: 1 qt.	Yield: for 9" cake	Yield:	**RASPBERRY TOPPING**
Cooking time: 16 mins.	Serves:	Serves:	
Oven temp.:	Portion:	Portion:	**for cheesecake**

Water	$^1/_3$ cup		Place in pan.
Agar-agar	1 tsp.		Add, mix, simmer 10 mins., dissolve.
Raspberries	$^1/_2$ cup		Add, simmer 5 mins. Mix and mash.
Raspberries	$^1/_2$ cup		Add, simmer 1 min. Do not mash berries.
			Semi-cool.
			Pour on cheesecake.
			Cool, serve.

Variations:

COUSCOUS CAKE

	Yield:	9 × 13"	Yield:		Pan size:	9 × 13"
	Serves:	12	Serves:		Cooking time:	
	Portion:	3 × 4.3"	Portion:		Oven temp.:	

Apple–raspberry juice	8 cups		Place in pan.
Couscous	3 cups		Add, stir, bring to boil; simmer until expanded, still soft, not dry.
			Pour into lightly oiled pan. Cool till solid; cut and serve.

Variations: Cover with Raisin–Nut Dip (pg. 146) cooked with arrowroot or Tofu Icing (pg. 179).
Use apple cider instead of apple–raspberry juice.
Put berries in cake.
Use strawberry or fruit topping with arrowroot.

SPICE CAKE

	Yield:	9 × 13"	Yield:		Pan size:	9 × 13"
	Serves:	12	Serves:		Cooking time:	40 mins.
	Portion:	3 × 4¼"	Portion:		Oven temp.:	370°

Whole wheat flour	3 cups		Place in bowl.
Unbleached flour	2 cups		Add.
Salt	1 tsp.		Add.
Baking powder	4 tsp.		Add.
Allspice, cinnamon, clove, giner, nutmeg	½ tsp. ea.		Add, mix, reserve.
Maple syrup	1½ cups		Place in bowl.
Corn oil	1½ cups		Add.
Water	1 cup		Add.
Vanilla extract	2 tsp.		Add, mix. Add to flour (above). Mix.
			Place in oiled pan. Bake, cool 10 mins. Remove from pan to cake rack, cool, serve.

Variations: Add raisins, coriander, grated apples, or anise. Add 1 cup chopped walnuts.
Sprinkle top with ½ cup coarsely chopped walnuts before baking.
Use 2½ cups barley malt instead of 1½ cups maple syrup, and heat the water.

SPRING CAKE

Pan size: 9 × 13"	Yield: 9 × 13"	Yield: ___
Cooking time: 30–35 mins.	Serves: 12	Serves: ___
Oven temp.: 325°	Portion: 3 × 4¼"	Portion: ___

Unbleached flour	5 cups		Place in bowl.
Baking powder	4 tsp.		Add.
Salt	½ tsp.		Add.
Cinnamon	¼ tsp.		Add, mix, set aside.
Apple juice	1¾ cups		Place in bowl.
Corn oil	½ cup		Add.
Maple syrup	½ cup		Add.
Anise seed, crushed	½ tsp.		Add, mix.
			Add to flour (above). Bake, cool 10 mins.
			Place on cake rack, serve.

Variations: Instead of unbleached flour, use whole wheat pastry flour.
Instead of apple juice, use apple–raspberry juice.
Add poppy seeds.

Pan size:	Yield: ___	Yield: ___
Cooking time:	Serves: ___	Serves: ___
Oven temp.:	Portion: ___	Portion: ___

Variations:

CONDIMENTS

CARROT WITH SWEET RICE WINE (Sweet)	*Yield:* ³/₄ cup	*Yield:*	*Pan size:*
	Serves: 10	*Serves:*	*Cooking time:*
	Portion: 1 Tbs.	*Portion:*	*Oven temp.:*
Carrots, finely grated	³/₄ cup		Place in bowl.
Sweet rice wine	3 Tbs.		Add, mix, cover.
			Refrigerate, serve.

Variations:

CARROT–WALNUT PATE (Pungent-Sweet)	*Yield:* 4 cups	*Yield:*	*Pan size:* 2 qt.
	Serves: 10	*Serves:*	*Cooking time:* 40 mins.+/-
	Portion: .4 cup	*Portion:*	*Oven temp.:*
Walnuts, roasted	¹/₄ lb.		Reserve.
Carrots, whole	1 lb.		Place in pan.
Celery seed	¹/₂ tsp.		Add.
Water			Add to cover; cover pan; cook *al dente*.
			Place carrots in blender. Blend, adjusting cook water.
Walnuts, above			Add a handful at a time, blend. Adjust water.
			Pulse repeatedly (a pate, not a sauce).
			Serve.

Variations:

[This recipe tested and approved by Chris Quilty, Chef Instructor at New England Culinary Institute.]

Pan size:	Yield:	4 cups	Yield:		**CHUTNEY, CRANBERRY (Pungent)**
Cooking time:	Serves:	10	Serves:		
Oven temp.:	Portion:	.4 cup	Portion:		

Cranberries, uncooked	3 cups	Place in blender.
Orange, quartered, de-seeded	1	Add.
Ginger (fresh), chopped	2 Tbs.	Add.
Water	1/2 cup	Add.
Raisins, soft	1/4 cup	Add.
Barley malt	1/4 cup	Add.
Salt	1/2 tsp.	Add.
Red pepper	1/4 tsp.	Add, blend smooth, adjust.
		Serve.

Variations:

Pan size:	Yield:	2 cups	Yield:		**CHUTNEY, RAISIN (Pungent)**
Cooking time:	Serves:	10	Serves:		[from Edward Kentish, Chef, East Calais, Vermont]
Oven temp.:	Portion:	3.2 Tbs.	Portion:		

Raisins, soft	2 cups	Place in blender.
Ginger (fresh), chopped	2 Tbs.	Add.
Cayenne	1/2 tsp.	Add.
Salt	1 tsp.	Add.
Water	1/4 cup	Add.
Lemon juice (fresh)	2 Tbs.	Add, pulse, blend.
		Adjust water if necessary.
		Serve.

Variations: Use white raisins for different flavor and character; add 1/4 tsp. cayenne for sharper taste.

DAIKON, GRATED (Pungent)

	Yield: 10 Tbs.	Yield:	Pan size:
	Serves: 10	Serves:	Cooking time:
	Portion: 1 Tbs.	Portion:	Oven temp.:
Daikon	½ lb.		Finely grate, cover. Refrigerate. Serve cold.

Variations: Add 10% fresh grated ginger or carrots; add 2 Tbs. tamari; add 2 Tbs. rice vinegar; or add 2 Tbs. finely diced green onions.

GOMASIO (Bitter-Salty)

	Yield: 1 cup	Yield:	Pan size: 10" skillet
	Serves: 10	Serves:	Cooking time: 15+/- mins.
	Portion: 1.6 Tsp.	Portion:	Oven temp.:
Sesame seeds	1 cup		Place in dry skillet.
Salt	2 tsp.		Add, mix, cook at medium heat. Shake pan to spread. Stir often with wooden spoon. When seeds have expanded, begin to pop, and have a nutty flavor and odor, they are finished cooking.
			Place in blender. Pulse to coarse consistency. Serve fresh.

Variations:

Pan size:	Yield:	3⅓ Tbs.	Yield:		**GINGER PICKLES**
Cooking time:	Serves:	10	Serves:		**(Pungent)**
Oven temp.:	Portion:	1 tsp.	Portion:		

Ginger root (fresh)	3⅓ Tbs.		Remove skin. Finely slice against the grain. Cut pieces that are smaller than a dime on a diagonal.
			Place in jar.
Brown rice vinegar	2 Tbs.		Add, cover, shake. Settle ginger pieces well.
			Refrigerate, serve.

Variations:

Pan size:	Yield:	1½ cups	Yield:		**MISO RELISH**
Cooking time:	Serves:	10	Serves:		**(Salty)**
Oven temp.:	Portion:	2 Tbs.	Portion:		

Ginger (fresh)	1 Tbs.		Remove skin. Place in blender.
Carrot, ½"-chopped	1 cup		Add.
Water	¼ cup		Add.
Barley miso	5 tsp.		Add, blend, reserve.
Daikon, finely grated	¼ cup		Place in bowl.
			Add pureed ginger.
			Mix, serve.

Variations:

Pan size:	Yield:	3 sheets	Yield:		**NORI STRIPS**
Cooking time:	Serves:	10	Serves:		**(Bitter)**
Oven temp.:	Portion:	⅓ sheet	Portion:		

Nori sheet	3 pieces		Roast each sheet separately by drawing over medium burner flame until the dark purple sheet turns to dark fluorescent green.
			With scissors, cut into ½"-wide strips or desired shapes.
			Serve fresh.

Variations: Crush to a coarse powder instead of cutting.

PARSLEY LEAVES, DRIED (Bitter)

	Yield: 10 tsp.	Yield:	Pan size:
	Serves: 10	Serves:	Cooking time:
	Portion: 1 tsp.	Portion:	Oven temp.:

Fresh parsley	2+/- bunches		Wash, water dry.
			Remove leaves from large stems. Chop to desired size.
			Sprinkle on baking pan. Set in warm, well-ventilated place until dry.
			Serve.
			[NOTE: Should be stored to allow air circulation (e.g., plastic-covered, with holes punched in it).]

Variations:

SCALLIONS, CHOPPED (Pungent)

	Yield: 10 Tbs.	Yield:	Pan size:
	Serves: 10	Serves:	Cooking time:
	Portion: 1 Tbs.	Portion:	Oven temp.:

Scallions or green onions	2 bunches		Slice very fine; do not crush.
			Place in bowl, cover.
			Refrigerate, serve fresh.
			[NOTE: For same-day use only.]

Variations: Use dry for cooking. French cut instead of finely slicing.

SCALLIONS, MISO (Pungent)

Pan size:	Yield:	10 tsp.	Yield:	
Cooking time:	Serves:	10	Serves:	
Oven temp.:	Portion:	1 tsp.	Portion:	

Miso, light	5 tsp.		Place in bowl.
Water	4 Tbs.		Add, mix and mash smooth.
Green onion, sliced very fine	1½ bunches		Add, mix but don't mash.
			Serve.

Variations: Add grated ginger or lemon juice.

SUNFLOWER SEEDS, TAMARI–GARLIC (Pungent)

Pan size:	10" skillet	Yield:	¾ cup	Yield:	
Cooking time:	10+/- mins.	Serves:	10	Serves:	
Oven temp.:		Portion:	1.2 Tbs.	Portion:	

Tamari	2 Tbs.		Place in skillet.
Water	2 Tbs.		Add.
Garlic, finely chopped	1 Tbs.		Add.
Sunflower seeds	¾ cup		Add, mix. Cook at medium heat. Tamari will form a scum on the pan; don't scrape burnt tamari loose.
			Stir until all liquid evaporates and seeds become dry and brown.
			Cool; serve.
			Keep in airtight container.

Variations: Use pumpkin seeds.
Delete garlic.

SWEET POTATO PUREE, SPICED (Sweet)

		Yield: 1¾ cup	Yield:	Pan size:
		Serves: 10	Serves:	Cooking time:
		Portion: 2.8 Tbs.	Portion:	Oven temp.:

Sweet potato, baked, peeled hot	1 lb.		Place in bowl.
Barley malt	1 Tbs.		Add.
Ginger, cinnamon, clove, nutmeg, allspice	pinch ea.		Add, mix, mash, adjust flavor.
			Serve.
			[NOTE: May be served hot or cold.]

Variations: Apply to plate with pastry bag; adjust thickness with hot water or apple cider.

TOFU, MARINATED (Bitter-Salty)

		Yield: ½ lb.	Yield:	Pan size:
		Serves: 10	Serves:	Cooking time:
		Portion: 3 pieces	Portion:	Oven temp.:

Tofu, cooked	½ lb.		Cut into ½" slices. Place on double thickness towel. cover with towel, press gently.
			Rest 10 mins. to draw out water. Repeat two more times on dry towel.
			Cut each piece into sixths. Reserve.
Tamari	3 Tbs.		Place in sterilized glass jar.
Rice vinegar	3 Tbs.		Add.
Sesame oil	1 tsp.		Add.
Sesame seeds	1 tsp.		Add, mix. Place tofu in liquid, cover, roll to distribute liquid. Rest on side of jar; gently roll a few times. Refrigerate.
			Serve from 2 hours to 1 week.

Variations: Serve in or on salads, as a side dish, or with grains.

COOKIES

IMPORTANT GUIDELINES FOR BAKING COOKIES

Basic Qualities
Chewiness:

- Chewy cookies are soft (but not necessarily chewy).
- Have low oil content.
- Have higher liquid and sweetener content.
- Can be achieved with blended tofu.

Crispness:

- Low liquid content (stiff dough).
- Higher fat content.
- Higher sweetener content.
- Long-cooking or higher temperatures tend to evaporate moisture.
- Small cookies tend to lose moisture faster than large cookies.
- Crisp cookies can absorb moisture in improper storage containers.

Softness:

- Higher liquid content.
- Lower oil content.
- Lower sweetener.
- Underbaking.
- Larger cookie size.
- Store in airtight container.

Spread:

- Higher sweetener.
- Higher leavening.
- Higher liquid content.
- Incorporate unbleached flour with whole wheat pastry flour.
- Heavily oiled baking pan.
- Lower baking temperatures.

Cookie Types
Bar:

- Press dough with pastry bag directly on cookie sheet to size and shape desired. Weigh dough into 1–1$\frac{3}{4}$-lb. equal units. Shape evenly by hand, each unit the length or width of pan. Place on pan with maximum space between units of dough. Flatten with fingers about 3$\frac{1}{2}$" wide and $\frac{1}{4}$" thick. Glaze if desired.
- Immediately after baking, while still hot, cut to size desired with spatula.

Dropped:

(Made of soft batter or dough.)

1. Use two spoons to portion dough to pan—one spoon to gather dough from mixing bowl, and one spoon to help place dough in baking pan.
2. Use scoop:
   - For small, use #60 scoop
   - For medium, use #40 scoop
   - For large, use #30 scoop
   - For extra large, use #20 scoop

Place scoop of dough on oiled baking pan, allowing for spread. Pat down with wet fork if neccessary.

Ice Box:

- Roll dough by hand into cylinder shapes. Control dough cylinder yields by standardizing diameter and length of rolls.
  - Large cookies: 3-lb. units of dough
  - Small cookies: 1$\frac{1}{2}$-lb. units of dough
- Wrap cylinders in moisture-proof wrapping. Place in refrigerator overnight.
- When ready to use, unwrap dough. Slice with constant thickness to allow for even baking. (Slice plain dough on machine; but slice dough with nuts, seeds, or fruits by hand.)
- Bake with 2" between cookies.

Sheet:

•Spread soft dough on well-oiled sheet pan (with paper baking sheet) by hand. Roll to even thickness.

•After baking, cut with spatula or pizza cutter to desired size immediately on removal from oven.

General

Baking:

•Usually bake at high temperatures for short time: lower temperatures tend to increase spread, increase evaporation, and make a hard cookie.

•High temperature tends to decrease spreading, and overcook or burn bottoms and edges.

•It is difficult to pinpoint exact baking time when seconds count.

To Cool Cookies:

•Remove from pan with spatula as soon as they are firm enough to move. Will vary in time from type to type.

•Place on cake rack to cool, out of drafts.

•Completely cool before storing in airtight containers.

•Maintain moistness by putting wedge of apple or potato in container.

CAROB COOKIES

Yield: 22 pcs.	*Yield:* _____	*Pan size:*	
Serves: 10	*Serves:* _____	*Cooking time:* 30 mins.	
Portion: 2.2 pcs.	*Portion:* _____	*Oven temp.:* 350°	

Oil, warm	¼ cup		Place in blender.
Raisins	¾ cup		Add.
Tofu	¾ lb.		Add.
Barley malt, warm	1 cup		Add.
Adzuki beans, cooked (hot)	1 cup		Add.
Maple syrup	¼ cup		Add.
Hot Water	½ cup		Add, blend smooth, reserve.
Carob powder	¾ cup		Place in bowl.
Whole wheat pastry flour	1 cup		Add.
Salt	½ tsp.		Add.
Baking powder	1 tsp.		Add.
Carob chips	½ cup		Add, mix. Add liquid, mix. Place walnut-sized portions on well-oiled baking pan.
			Bake 30–40 mins. depending on desired result. Cool on cake rack.

Variations:

Pan size:	Yield:	24	Yield:		**MAPLE–NUT**
Cooking time: 14+/- mins.	Serves:	10	Serves:		**COOKIES**
Oven temp.: 360°	Portion:	2.4	Portion:		

Whole wheat pastry flour	$1^1/_4$ cups		Place in bowl.
Oat flakes	1 cup		Add.
Walnuts, roasted	$^3/_4$ cup		Add.
Salt	$^1/_4$ tsp.		Add, mix.
Apple juice	$^1/_2$ cup		Add.
Corn oil	$^1/_4$ cup		Add.
Vanilla extract	1 tsp.		Add.
Maple syrup	$^1/_3$ cup		Add, mix. Rest 10 mins. Mix.
			Place walnut-sized portions on well-oiled baking pan. Flatten with wet fork to $2^3/_4$" diam.
			Bake until done.

Variations: Use $^2/_3$ cup barley malt instead of maple syrup.
Add sunflower seeds; or add sesame seeds in or on top.
Chopped, unsalted peanuts may be substituted.

Pan size:	Yield:	36	Yield:		**OATMEAL**
Cooking time: 14–18 mins.	Serves:	36	Serves:		**COOKIES**
Oven temp.: 400°	Portion:	1	Portion:		

Oat flakes	8 cups		Place in bowl.
Whole wheat pastry flour	2 cups		Add.
Cinnamon	$1^1/_2$ tsp.		Add.
Baking powder	3 Tbs.		Add, mix, reserve.
Maple syrup	$1^1/_2$ cups		Place in bowl.
Water	3 cups		Add.
Oil	$1^1/_2$ cups		Add.
Walnuts, $^1/_4$"-chopped	2 cups		Add.
Raisins	$^3/_4$ cup		Add to flour; mix. Place on oiled baking pan. Mash with wet fork. Bake until edges turn brown.
			Cool on cake rack. Serve.

Variations:

PEANUT BUTTER COOKIES

	Yield:	24	Yield:		Pan size:
	Serves:	10	Serves:		Cooking time: 15 mins.
	Portion:	2.4	Portion:		Oven temp.: 350°

Water, hot	$^1/_4$ cup		Place in warm bowl.
Barley malt	$^3/_4$ cup		Add.
Peanut butter	$^3/_4$ cup		Add.
Vanilla extract	$^1/_2$ tsp.		Add, mix smooth.
Whole wheat pastry flour	1 cup		Add, mix smooth.
Raisins	$^1/_2$ cup		Add.
			Place walnut-sized portions of dough on well-oiled pan. Flatten with wet fork. Bake until done.
			Cool on rack. Serve.

Variations: Use crunchy peanut butter and 2 Tbs. more water.

TAHINI–NUT COOKIES

	Yield:	24	Yield:		Pan size:
	Serves:	10	Serves:		Cooking time: 14+/- mins.
	Portion:	2.4	Portion:		Oven temp.: 350°

Barley malt	$^1/_2$ cup		Place in bowl.
Water	$^1/_4$ cup		Add.
Oil (corn or sesame)	2 Tsp.		Add.
Tahini	$^1/_2$ cup		Add.
Cinnamon	$^1/_4$ tsp.		Add.
Vanilla extract	$^1/_2$ tsp.		Add, mix.
Nuts	$^1/_2$ cup		Add.
Whole wheat pastry flour	$^1/_2$ cup		Add.
Oat flakes	$1^1/_4$ cups		Add, mix. Rest 4 mins., mix. Rest another 4 mins., mix.
			Place walnut-sized portions on oiled pan. Partially flatten. Bake until done. Cool and serve.

Variations: Substitute $^1/_2$ cup raisins for $^1/_2$ cup nuts.

[This recipe tested and approved by Chris Quilty, Chef Instructor at New England Culinary Institute.]

DESSERTS

BASIC TYPES OF DESSERTS

[NOTE: Selection of dessert is usually based on the type of meal and the season.]

FRUIT

• Check sour and sweet characteristics and add sweetener accordingly.

• Preparation alternatives:

–Baked whole, halved, or diced in Bettys, or topped with topping or granola.

–Raw, sliced, diced, sweetened, or spiced.

GRAIN

• Simmered, thickened, spiced, or sweetened.

JELLIED

• Jellied with:

–agar-agar;

–one juice or a combination;

–5–15% millet or quinoa.

• Cooked with sliced or small bite-sized fruit.

• Topped with kanten of a different color or fruit puree.

[NOTE: Texture of ingredients and/or degree of gel affects flavor. Generally, the softer the dessert, the more flavor it has.]

PUDDINGS

• Tofu-based, baked and cooled.

• Grain-milk–based with agar-agar and/or thickener, cooked and cooled.

Pan size:	Yield:	10 cups	Yield:		**AMBROSIA**
Cooking time:	Serves:	10	Serves:		
Oven temp.:	Portion:	1 cup	Portion:		
Apples, 1/2"-diced		2 cups		Place in bowl.	
Peaches, 1/2"-diced		2 cups		Add.	
Honeydew, 1/2"-diced		1 cup		Add.	
Watermelon, 1/2"-diced		2 cups		Add.	
Cantaloupe, 1/2"-diced		1 cup		Add.	
Strawberries, sliced in half		1 cup		Add.	
Blueberries, whole		1 cup		Add, save as much juice as possible.	
Coconut (unsweetened), grated		2 Tbs.		Add, gently mix. Place in serving bowl. Cover; refrigerate.	
Coconut (unsweetened), grated		1 Tbs.		Sprinkle evenly on top just before serving.	
				Serve.	

Variations:

APPLE, BAKED

	Yield:	10 apples	Yield:		Pan size:	
	Serves:	10	Serves:		Cooking time: 45 mins.	
	Portion:	1 apple	Portion:		Oven temp.: 375°	
Raisins	1 cup			Place in bowl.
Walnuts, finely chopped	1 cup			Add.
Barley malt	1/2 cup			Add.
Cinnamon	1/4 tsp.			Add.
Salt	1/4 tsp.			Add.
Lemon rind, grated	2 tsp.			Add, mix, reserve.
Apples, cored 90% from top	10			Remove skin from top 10% of apples. Place in baking pan, tops up. Stuff with filling.
Water	1/2"			Add to bottom of pan. Bake, basting every 10 mins. Continue baking uncovered for 15 mins.
				Serve hot, room temp., or cold.

Variations: Delete ground cinnamon and insert 1 cinnamon stick halfway into apple. Add tahini.

APPLE CRISP

	Yield:	9 × 13"	Yield:		Pan size: 9 × 13"	
	Serves:	12	Serves:		Cooking time: 25 mins.	
	Portion:	3 × 4"	Portion:		Oven temp.: 375°	
Apples, cored, quartered, sliced	6 lg.			Place in oiled 9 × 13" pan.
Whole wheat pastry flour	2 Tbs.			Sprinkle on top.
Raisins	3/4 cup			Sprinkle on top.
Cinnamon	1 tsp.			Sprinkle on top.
Lemon juice (fresh)	2 Tbs.			Sprinkle on top.
Water	1/4 cup			Sprinkle on top.
Topping, below				Cover apples evenly and press into apples. Bake until apples are soft. Serve.
Topping:				
Barley malt	1 cup			Place in bowl.
Corn oil	1/2 cup			Add, warm and mix.
Cinnamon	2 tsp.			Add.
Salt	1/2 tsp.			Add.
Oat flakes	1 cup			Add.
Walnuts, chopped very fine	1/2 cup			Add.
Whole wheat pastry flour	1/2 cup			Add, mix, reserve.

Variations: Add peaches and/or pears to apples; use just peaches and/or pears; add cranberries or raisins.

APPLE–RASPBERRY PARFAIT

Pan size: 4 qt.	Yield: 10 cups	Yield:
Cooking time: 10 mins.	Serves: 10	Serves:
Oven temp.:	Portion: 1 cup	Portion:

Tofu	1 lb.		Place in blender.
Apple–raspberry juice	2 cups		Add, pulse, blend smooth. Reserve.
Apple–raspberry juice	6 cups		Place in pan.
Agar-agar powder	2 Tbs.		Add, simmer 10 mins., stir often to dissolve.
Arrowroot	5 tsp.		Make slurry. Add to juice, stirring to desired consistency. Turn off heat, cool until it begins to gel.
Tofu, above			Add, mix well. Make spoon test. Cool, refrigerate.
			Blend smooth. Pour into mold. Refrigerate; serve. If too solid a gel, re-blend and re-refrigerate.

Variations: Cook with fresh fruit; garnish with fruit puree, Tofu Supreme Icing (pg. 179), and/or roasted, chopped, or whole nuts.

APPLE SAUCE

Pan size: 4 qt.	Yield: 10 cups	Yield:
Cooking time: 20+/- mins.	Serves: 10	Serves:
Oven temp.:	Portion: 1 cup	Portion:

Apples, peeled, cored, quartered	3 lbs.		1/2"-chop, place in pan.
Water	1 cup		Add.
Salt	1/2 tsp.		Add.
Barley malt	1/4 cup		Add, simmer 20 mins. or until apples are soft. Stir, mash smooth.
			Serve.

Variations: Add cinnamon, anise, or lemon.
Serve with Tofu Supreme Icing (pg. 179) and chopped, roasted nuts.

APPLES, STEWED

	Yield: 10 cups	Yield:	Pan size: 4 qt.
	Serves: 10	Serves:	Cooking time: 12+/- mins.
	Portion: 1 cup	Portion:	Oven temp.:

Apples, peeled, cored, quartered	2 lbs.		Cut into eighths, place in pot.
Water	1 cup		Add.
Salt	1/4 tsp.		Add.
Lemon juice (fresh)	3 Tbs.		Add.
Barley malt	2 Tbs.		Add, simmer until apples are tender.
Arrowroot	3 Tbs.		Make slurry, add.
Raisins	3/4 cup		Add. Adjust.
			Serve.

Variations: Garnish: Tofu Supreme Icing (pg. 179) and/or roasted filberts or walnuts; or pour on pancakes.

BEAN PUDDING

	Yield: 8 cups	Yield:	Pan size:
	Serves: 10	Serves:	Cooking time:
	Portion: .8 cups	Portion:	Oven temp.:

Garbanzo beans, cooked, hot; no water	4 cups		Place in blender.
Rice syrup	2 cups		Add.
Tofu	1 lb.		Add.
Almond extract	1 tsp.		Add.
Tahini	2 Tbs.		Add, blend smooth. Reserve.
Water, cold	2 cups		Place in pan.
Raisins	1 cup		Add.
Agar-agar powder	1 Tbs.		Add, dissolve, simmer 10 mins.
Walnuts, roasted	1 cup		Add, blend smooth, spoon test.
			Cool, refrigerate; serve.

Variations:

Pan size: 9 × 13"	Yield: 12	Yield:	**BREAD PUDDING**
Cooking time: 30 mins.	Serves: 12	Serves:	
Oven temp.: 350°	Portion: 3 × 4.3"	Portion:	

Bread, stale	21 pieces		Place slices in 4 layers in pan.
Raisins	3/4 cup		Spread between layers and on top.
			Press down very hard with both hands. Reserve.
Tofu	1/2 lb.		Place in blender.
Water	2 cups		Add.
Vanilla extract	2 Tbs.		Add.
Cinnamon	1 1/2 tsp.		Add.
Maple syrup	1/4 cup		Add.
Tahini	1 Tbs.		Add; blend until smooth. Adjust. Pour over bread. Rest 1 hr. Bake covered for 30 mins. Remove cover; bake for desired crust.
			Serve.

Variations:

[This recipe tested and approved by Chris Quilty, Chef Instructor at New England Culinary Institute.]

Pan size: 3 qt.	Yield: 10 cups	Yield:	**FLAN**
Cooking time: 10 mins.	Serves: 10	Serves:	
Oven temp.:	Portion: 1 cup	Portion:	

Water	6 cups		Place in pan, simmer.
Agar-agar	1 2/3 Tbs.		Add, mix, dissolve. Simmer 10 mins. Mix often.
Vanilla extract	1 1/2 tsp.		Add.
Almond extract	3/4 tsp.		Add.
Rice syrup	1 cup		Add, mix, dissolve.
Barley malt	1/2 cup		Add.
Turmeric	pinch		Add. Remove from heat. Reserve.
Tofu	1 lb.		Place in blender.
Water, above			Add, blend smooth; spoon test.
			Pour into mold. Cool, refrigerate. Serve.

Variations: Serve with Mock Caramel Sauce (pg. 255) and/or roasted chopped hazelnuts.

INDIAN PUDDING

	Yield: 10 cups	Yield:	Pan size: 4 qt.
	Serves: 10	Serves:	Cooking time: 25 mins.
	Portion: 1 cup	Portion:	Oven temp.:

Water	6 cups		Place in pot.
Corn meal	3 cups		Add, mix, break up lumps.
Oat milk	6 cups		Add.
Salt	1 tsp.		Add.
Barley malt	1 cup		Add, mix, bring to boil. Simmer, cover. Stir often. Cook 15 mins.
Raisins	1/2 cup		Add.
Walnuts	1/2 cup		Add.
Cinnamon, ginger, nutmeg	1/4 tsp. ea.		Add. Cook 10 mins. Stir often, adjust.
Corn oil	1/4 cup		Add, mix.
			Keep hot; serve hot.

Variations: Pour hot into mold or bread pans; slice and serve or saute in corn oil and a little salt; use barley milk instead of oat milk.

KANTEN, APPLE

	Yield: 10 cups	Yield:	Pan size: 2 qt.
	Serves: 10	Serves:	Cooking time: 10 mins.
	Portion: 1 cup	Portion:	Oven temp.:

Apple cider	10 cups		Place in pot, heat.
Salt	1/8 tsp.		Add.
Agar-agar powder	2 1/2 Tbs.		Add, mix, simmer 10 mins. to dissolve. Spoon test for gel quality.
			Pour into mold, cool, refrigerate.
			Serve.

Variations: Cook 1/2 cup millet in 3 cups apple cider (adding 7 more cups when millet is cooked); add and cook berries or sliced fruit; garnish with Tofu Supreme Icing (pg.179); add 1/4 cup mint, finely diced; use combination of juices.

Pan size: 3 qt.	Yield: 10 cups	Yield:	**KANTEN,**
Cooking time: 20 mins.	Serves: 10	Serves:	**CRANBERRY**
Oven temp.:	Portion: 1 cup	Portion:	

Apple cider	8½ cups		Place in pan.
Agar-agar	2 Tbs.		Add, mix, dissolve, simmer 10 mins. Mix often.
Almond extract	½ tsp.		Add.
Barley malt	1 cup		Add, mix, dissolve.
Cranberries	12 oz.		Add, simmer 10 mins. Adjust.
			Cool, pour into mold.
			Serve.

Variations:

Pan size: 3 qt.	Yield: 10 cups	Yield:	**NEW YEAR'S**
Cooking time: 5 mins.	Serves: 10	Serves:	**PUDDING**
Oven temp.:	Portion: 1 cup	Portion:	

Barley, well cooked	1 cup		Place in blender.
Water	2 cups		Add, blend smooth.
Water	8 cups		Add.
Maple syrup	⅔ cup		Add.
Almond extract	1 tsp.		Add.
Vanilla extract	1 tsp.		Add.
Tahini	1 Tbs.		Add.
Salt	½ tsp.		Add, blend smooth. Place in pan.
Agar-agar powder	1 Tbs.		Add, dissolve, simmer. Stir often.
Arrowroot	3 Tbs.		Make slurry, add. Simmer 5 mins, mixing often. Pour in mold. Cool, refrigerate. Serve.
			[NOTE: Taken from a Lebanese recipe.]

Variations: Garnish with hazelnuts, roasted and finely chopped.

PEACHES, SLICED

	Yield: 10 cups	Yield:	Pan size: 4 qt.
	Serves: 10	Serves:	Cooking time: 10 mins.
	Portion: 1 cup	Portion:	Oven temp.:
Nutmeg, grated	1 tsp.		Place in pan.
Cinnamon	1/4 tsp.		Add.
Peaches, skinned and stoned	5 lbs.		Quarter. Add peaches to pan. Shake to settle.
Cloves, whole	2 tsp.		Put 3 in each peach quarter.
Water	2 cups		Add.
Rice syrup (opt.)	1/2 cup		Add, bring to boil; simmer until peaches are cooked. Adjust.
			Serve.

Variations: Mash, pour on pancakes.

PEACHES, STEWED

	Yield: 10 cups	Yield:	Pan size: 3 qt.
	Serves: 10	Serves:	Cooking time: 10 mins.
	Portion: 1 cup	Portion:	Oven temp.:
Peaches, skinned and stoned	5 lbs.		Quarter. Slice each quarter into 3. Place in pan. Shake to settle.
Water	1 cup		Add, bring to boil; simmer.
Cinnamon	1/4 tsp.		Add.
Vanilla extract	1/2 tsp.		Add.
Salt	1/4 tsp.		Add.
Arrowroot	1/2 tsp.		Make slurry, add. Gently stir until thickened. Adjust.
			Place pot in cold water to stop cooking.
			Serve room temp. or cold.

Variations: Cook with raisins; garnish with roasted nuts; pour over pancakes, waffles, or couscous.

PEARS, BAKED

Pan size: 9 × 13"	*Yield:* 10 halves	*Yield:*	
Cooking time: 25 mins.	*Serves:* 10	*Serves:*	
Oven temp.: 400°	*Portion:* 1 half	*Portion:*	

Apple cider	1½ cups		Place in pot.
Cinnamon	¾ tsp.		Add.
Maple syrup	¼ cup		Add.
Raisins	¼ cup		Add.
Salt	¼ tsp.		Add, mix, simmer.
Arrowroot	2 Tbs.		Make slurry, add, mix to thicken. Reserve.
Pears, stemmed	5		Halve, scoop out core with spoon. Place in 9 × 13" pan cut-side down.
Whole cloves	50		Place 5 in each pear half.
Walnuts	½ cup		Add, distribute evenly. Bake, basting every 10 mins.
			Serve.

Variations:

RICE PUDDING

Pan size: 8 qt.	*Yield:* 16 cups	*Yield:*	
Cooking time: 55 mins.	*Serves:* 16	*Serves:*	
Oven temp.:	*Portion:* 1 cup	*Portion:*	

Water	18 cups		Place in pan, boil.
Brown rice	4 cups		Add.
Salt	1 tsp.		Add, simmer 45 mins.
Maple syrup	1½ cups		Add.
Nutmeg	2 tsp.		Add.
Vanilla extract	2 Tbs.		Add.
Tahini	¼ cup		Add.
Raisins	1 cup		Add, mix, simmer 10 mins. Stir often, adjust.
			Serve.

Variations: Add more vanilla and nutmeg to suit.
Garnish with roasted, chopped hazelnuts.

[This recipe tested and approved by Chris Quilty, Chef Instructor at New England Culinary Institute.]

STRAWBERRY CUSTARD

	Yield:	10 cups	Yield:		Pan size:	2 qt.
	Serves:	10	Serves:		Cooking time:	10 mins.
	Portion:	1 cup	Portion:		Oven temp.:	

Apple cider	8 cups		Simmer.
Agar-agar powder	2 Tbs.		Add, mix, simmer to dissolve. Cool to warm. Put in blender.
Tahini	3 Tbs.		Add.
Tofu	1/2 lb.		Add.
Salt	1/2 tsp.		Add.
Maple syrup	1/2 cup		Add.
Strawberries, stemmed	4 cups		Add, blend, adjust. Pour into mold or cups. Cool, refrigerate.
			Serve.

Variations: Garnish with fresh, whole strawberries.

WONDERFUL WHEAT

	Yield:	10 cups	Yield:		Pan size:	4 qt.
	Serves:	10	Serves:		Cooking time:	23 mins.
	Portion:	1 cup	Portion:		Oven temp.:	

Water	8 cups		Place in pan.
Bulgur, coarse	3 cups		Add.
Salt	1/2 tsp.		Add, mix, simmer 20 mins. or until bulgur done.
Barley malt	1/2 cup		Add.
Raisins	1/2 cup		Add.
Walnuts, roasted	1/2 cup		Add.
Cinnamon	1/2 tsp.		Add, mix, simmer 3 mins. Adjust. Rest 10 mins., covered.
			Serve with sauce.

Variations: Add diced apple or peach; make wet and add arrowroot; bake with crumb topping; serve with apple, peach, or cranberries.

[This recipe tested and approved by Chris Quilty, Chef Instructor at New England Culinary Institute.]

DIPS

Pan size:	Yield:	2 cups	Yield:		**APPLE BUTTER**
Cooking time: 1½ hrs.	Serves:	10	Serves:		
Oven temp.:	Portion:	3.2 Tbs.	Portion:		

Apples, cored and diced	4 lbs.		Place in blender.
Apple juice	1½ cups		Add, blend smooth. Place in pot, simmer covered for 1½ hours. Stir occasionally.
			Cool, reblend.
Cinnamon	2 tsp.		Add.
Nutmeg	1 tsp.		Add.
Clove	½ tsp.		Add, blend, cool, serve.

Variations: Add ginger, salt, cayenne, or lemon.

Pan size: 2 qt.	Yield:	19 oz.	Yield:		**CAULIFLOWER, TAHINI**
Cooking time: 15 mins.	Serves:	10	Serves:		
Oven temp.:	Portion:	3.2 Tbs.	Portion:		

Cauliflower head	2 lbs.		Trim; place in pan.
Water	½"		Add.
Celery seed	½ tsp.		Add to water. Cover; boil under tender.
			Reserve water. Place cauliflower in bowl. Remove core.
Tahini	½ cup		Add.
Salt	½ tsp.		Add, mix, mash well. Adjust; cool.
			Serve.

Variations: Add 2 Tbs. lemon juice.
Add olive oil with sauteed onion and garlic.
Garnish with parsley or green onion.

CRANBERRY DIP, CHINESE

	Yield: 3 1/2 cups	Yield:	Pan size:
	Serves: 10	Serves:	Cooking time: 10 mins.
	Portion: 5.6 Tbs.	Portion:	Oven temp.:

Mustard, ground	3 Tbs.		Place in bowl.
Vinegar	1 1/2 tsp.		Add, mix.
Water	1/2 cup		Add, mix smooth. Rest 10 mins.
Water	3/4 cup		Place in pan.
Barley malt	1 cup		Add.
Cranberries	12 oz.		Add, simmer 10 mins., mix.
			Place in blender. Blend smooth with minimum cook water. Add to mustard mix.
Lemon juice (fresh)	1 tsp.		Add, mix.
			Serve.

Variations: Thicken with arrowroot before blending.

CRANBERRY– ORANGE RELISH

	Yield: 3 cups	Yield:	Pan size: 2 qt.
	Serves: 10	Serves:	Cooking time: 5+/- mins.
	Portion: 4.8 Tbs.	Portion:	Oven temp.:

Water, hot	1 cup		Place in blender.
Barley malt	1/2 cup		Add.
Orange, seeded	1		Cut into eighths. Add.
Cranberries	3 cups		Add, blend to coarse. Place in pan; simmer.
Arrowroot	2 Tbs.		Make slurry. Add, mix, adjust; cool, serve.

Variations: Blend very fine. Add 1 1/2 cups water and substitute agar-agar for arrowroot; spoon test for gel quality; pour into mold, cool, and serve.

CURRY DIP

Pan size:	Yield:	1½ cups	Yield:	
Cooking time:	Serves:	10	Serves:	
Oven temp.:	Portion:	2.4 Tbs.	Portion:	

Tofu (cooked), mashed	½ lb.		Place in food processor.
Rice vinegar	1 tsp.		Add.
Barley malt	1 Tbs.		Add.
Curry powder	2 tsp.		Add.
Mustard powder	1 tsp.		Add.
Salt	½ tsp.		Add.
Water	½ cup		Add, blend, adjust for thickness and consistency. Cover, refrigerate.
			Serve cold.

Variations: Other possible bases for a curry dip are beans, flour, blended vegetables.

GINGER DIP

Pan size:	Yield:	2 cups	Yield:	
Cooking time:	Serves:	10	Serves:	
Oven temp.:	Portion:	3.2 Tbs.	Portion:	

Tofu, cooked	½ lb.		Place in blender.
Green onions, diced	4 Tbs.		Add.
Lemon juice	2 Tbs.		Add.
Ginger, grated	2 Tbs.		Add.
Barley malt	1 Tbs.		Add.
Walnuts	¼ cup		Add.
Water	¼ cup		Add, blend, adjust, serve.

Variations: Chop walnuts and add after blending. Omit green onions.

LABNI DIP
(Lebanese)

	Yield: 1¼ cups	Yield:	Pan size:
	Serves: 10	Serves:	Cooking time:
	Portion: 2 Tbs.	Portion:	Oven temp.:
Yogurt	2 cups		Place in cheesecloth bag. Hang from sink faucet overnight.
			Cover and refrigerate. Place in serving dish; smooth out.
Olive oil	2 Tbs.		Add.
			Serve.

Variations: Garnish with a little oregano. Before refrigerating, mix or garnish with basil, dill, thyme, parsley, garlic, chives, scallions, curry, cumin, or turmeric.

LENTIL PATE

	Yield: 6 cups	Yield:	Pan size: 4 qt.
	Serves: 10	Serves:	Cooking time: 1¼ hrs.
	Portion: .6 cups	Portion:	Oven temp.:
Water, cold	12 cups		Place in pan.
Bay leaf	1		Add.
Split peas	2 cups		Add.
Kelp or kombu, 1"-chopped	24 sq.in.		Add, simmer 30 mins.
Lentils	4 cups		Add, simmer 45 mins. Place solids in blender.
Cumin	1 tsp.		Add.
Tamari	2 Tbs.		Add.
Garlic	1 Tbs.		Add.
Cilantro leaves, finely chopped	½ cup		Add, mix.
			Serve.
			[NOTE: Best when made one day ahead.]

Variations:

Pan size:	Yield:	3 cups	Yield:		**MISO–WALNUT DIP**
Cooking time:	Serves:	10	Serves:		
Oven temp.:	Portion:	4.8 Tbs.	Portion:		

Miso, chick pea (light color)	½ cup		Place in bowl.
Walnuts, roasted and blended	2 cups		Add, mix, serve.
Water, boiling	½ cup		Add, mix, mash to smooth consistency.
			Serve.

Variations: Add 2 Tbs. tahini.

Pan size:	Yield:	2 cups	Yield:		**MUSHROOM DIP**
Cooking time:	Serves:	10	Serves:		
Oven temp.:	Portion:	3.2 Tbs.	Portion:		

Corn oil	⅛ cup		Place in skillet.
Salt	½ tsp.		Add.
Mushrooms, diced	3 cups		Saute until mushrooms change color. Cool.
Tofu, cooked	½ lb.		Place in blender.
Water	½ cup		Add, blend smooth.
Mushrooms, above			Add, blend smooth.
			Serve.

Variations:

MUSHROOM PATE

		Yield:		Pan size:
	Yield: 3 cups	Serves:		Cooking time:
	Serves: 10	Portion:		Oven temp.:
	Portion: 4.8 Tbs.			
Mushrooms	1 lb.		Slice thin; reserve.	
Soy oil	¼ cup		Place in skillet, medium high heat.	
Green onion, lg. whites diced	3		Add, saute.	
Mushrooms, above			Add, saute 5 mins.	
Dry white wine	½ cup		Add, stir often; reduce 95%. Place in blender.	
Tofu, cooked	½ lb.		Add, pulse, blend. Add saute oil if necessary. Adjust with water. Blend smooth.	
			Serve.	

Variations:

ORIENTAL DIP, BASIC

		Yield:		Pan size:
	Yield: 1 cup	Serves:		Cooking time:
	Serves: 10	Portion:		Oven temp.:
	Portion: 1.6 Tbs.			
Water	¾ cup		Place in bowl.	
Brown rice vinegar	1 Tbs.		Add.	
Rice wine	1 Tbs.		Add.	
Tamari	1 Tbs.		Add.	
Sesame oil, dark	1 tsp.		Add.	
Sesame seeds	2 tsp.		Add, mix; serve.	

Variations: Omit dark sesame oil.

Pan size:	Yield:	1¼ cups	Yield:		**ORIENTAL DIP,**
Cooking time:	Serves:	10	Serves:		**SWEET & SOUR**
Oven temp.:	Portion:	2 Tbs.	Portion:		

Oriental Dip, Basic (pg. 144)	1 cup		Place in blender.
Ginger (fresh), skinned, minced	1 tsp.		Add.
Lemon juice	1 Tbs.		Add.
Barley malt	3 Tbs.		Add, blend.
			Serve; *or*
			Place in pan, simmer.
Arrowroot	1 Tbs.		Add slurry, mix to desired consistency. Serve.

Variations:

Pan size:	Yield:	1 cup+	Yield:		**ORIENTAL DIP,**
Cooking time:	Serves:	10	Serves:		**TAMARI–GINGER**
Oven temp.:	Portion:	1.6 Tbs.+	Portion:		

Tamari	¼ cup		Place in bowl.
Water	¾ cup		Add.
Ginger (fresh), skinned, grated	3 Tbs.		Add, mix, cover.
			Rest overnight. Serve.

Variations: Add 1 Tbs. roasted sesame seeds, 1 Tbs. chopped green onion, 1 Tbs. chopped scallions. Or fry tempeh or tofu in it.

RAISIN–NUT DIP

	Yield: 3 cups	Yield:	Pan size: 1 qt.
	Serves: 10	Serves:	Cooking time: 10 mins.
	Portion: 5 Tbs.	Portion:	Oven temp.:

Ginger (fresh)	1 Tbs.		Place in blender.
Raisins	2 cups		Add. Cover with water. Simmer 10 mins. Rest to cool.
			Place in blender. Reserve water for thinning.
Walnuts	1 cup		Add.
Lemon rind	1 Tbs.		Add, blend.
Cook water			Adjust water for desired consistency. Adjust flavor.
			Serve.

Variations: Add ½ cup tahini. Substitute hazelnuts. Add 1 tsp. orange zest.

TAHINI DIP, BASIC

	Yield: 1 cup	Yield:	Pan size:
	Serves: 10	Serves:	Cooking time:
	Portion: 1.6 Tbs.	Portion:	Oven temp.:

Tahini	½ cup		Place in bowl.
Water (room temp.)	½ cup		Add, mix until creamy.
			Adjust; serve.

Variations: Blending: add garlic, lemon juice, and salt. Add cumin and fresh parsley, cilantro, dill, or thyme. Add tofu. Substitute tamari for salt. Garnish: roasted sesame seeds, or finely diced green onion.

Pan size:	Yield:	1 cup	Yield:		**TOFU DIP,**
Cooking time:	Serves:	10	Serves:		**BASIC**
Oven temp.:	Portion:	1.6 Tbs.	Portion:		

Miso	1 Tbs.		Place in blender.
Tahini	2 Tbs.		Add.
Water	2 Tbs.		Add.
Tofu	1/2 lb.		Add.
Green onion	1/4 cup		Add. Blend; adjust.
			Serve.

Variations: Use in sandwiches.
Add tamari.

Pan size:	Yield:	1¼ cups	Yield:		**TOFU DIP,**
Cooking time:	Serves:	10	Serves:		**TARRAGON**
Oven temp.:	Portion:	2 Tbs.	Portion:		

Water	1/4 cup		Bring to boil.
Tarragon	2 Tbs.		Add, mix.
			Steep 10 mins. Put in blender.
Tofu	1/2 lb.		Add, blend with repeated off-on.
			Serve.

Variations: Add to blend: 1 Tbs. safflower oil, 1 Tbs. sesame oil, 1 Tbs. rice vinegar, 1 Tbs. tamari, 1 tsp. garlic, fresh dill, thyme, or basil.

FISH

IMPORTANT GUIDELINES FOR FISH COOKERY

• It is preferable to use fresh whole fish, house cut.

• Fish cooks quickly at medium heat.

• Fish is naturally tender.

• Handle fish carefully, or it will fall apart.

• Fish is easily overcooked.

• *Doneness* characteristics:

—Flesh separates or flakes.

—Flesh separates from bones.

—Flesh turns from translucent to white.

• Lean fish, usually white-fleshed, are most commonly poached, sauteed, or fried. Bake in a small amount of oil or baste with oil or lemon juice to prevent drying.

• It's better to have on hand only as much as you need for one day; order daily.

• Store on ice in a pan with drain, not in water.

FISH AND SHELLFISH				
FISH	**SIZE IN LBS.**	**FLAVOR**	**TEXTURE WHEN COOKED**	**COOKING METHOD**
Black Sea Bass	2–5	Delicate	Firm	Steam, fry, broil
Carp	2–10	Mild	Firm	Fry, broil
Flounder	1–7	Delicate	Firm	Bake, saute, fry, poach
Halibut	10–75	Mild	Tender	Bake, poach, saute
Rock Fish (Striped Bass)	2–5	Mild	Very tender	Saute, poach, broil
Cod	3–20	Delicate	Very Soft	Poach, broil
Sole	1–7	Delicate	Firm	Bake, saute
Sturgeon	15–300	Mild	Firm, compact	Bake
Smelt	1–2 oz.	Mild	Firm	Fry
SHELLFISH				
Clams		Definite	Chewy	Water simmer, fry
Crabs		Mild	Tender	Water simmer
Lobster		Mild	Firm	Water simmer, boil
Oysters		Definite	Soft	Simmer, bake, saute
Scallops		Mild	Firm	Saute, fry, bake
Shrimp		Mild	Firm	Boil, saute
Mussels		Mild	Chewy	Bake, simmer, steam

FISH AND SHELLFISH FLAVORINGS
Commonly Used Seasonings

- Olive, sesame, or peanut oil
- Black pepper
- Garlic
- Lemon
- White wine (Chablis preferable)
- Oregano
- Green onion, finely chopped

- Onion
- Sake
- Rice vinegar
- Lime
- Green pepper, diced
- Paprika
- Fresh dill, minced

				CAJUN JAMBALAYA
Pan size: 8 qt.	*Yield:* 20 cups	*Yield:*		
Cooking time: 40 mins.	*Serves:* 10	*Serves:*		
Oven temp.:	*Portion:* 2 cups	*Portion:*		

Oil, soy	1 cup		Place in pan.
Onions, 1/2"-chopped	2 cups		Add. Saute until dark brown.
Water, hot	12 cups		Add.
Bell pepper, 1/2"-chopped	1 cup		Add.
Bay leaves	2		Add.
Parsley leaves, 1/2"-chopped	2 cups		Add.
Green onion, 1/2"-chopped	1 cup		Add.
Celery, 1/2"-chopped	3 cups		Add.
Salt	2 tsp.		Add. Mix, bring to boil.
Brown rice	4 cups		Add, simmer 20 mins.
Garlic, minced	2 Tbs.		Add.
Fish, 1"-diced	1 lb.		Add. Cook until done.
Shrimp	1 lb.		Add. Mix. Rest covered.
			Adjust (it should be thick and stew-like). Serve.

Variations: White meat of chicken may be substituted for all or some of the fish.

[This recipe tested and approved by Chris Quilty, Chef Instructor at New England Culinary Institute.]

FLOUNDER, MANDARIN

[From Chef Huang, Suzhou Hotel Restaurant, Canton, China]

	Yield: 2 lbs.	Yield:	Pan size: wok
	Serves: 7	Serves:	Cooking time: 18 mins.
	Portion: 4.5 oz.	Portion:	Oven temp.:

Flounder, whole, cleaned; score 4 times each side $1/4$" deep, head and tail on	$1^1/_2$ lbs.		Place in pan.
Mirin	2 Tbs.		Add.
Salt	1 tsp.		Add, mix, marinate 20 mins.
Green beans, $1/2$" chopped	$1/_4$ cup		Place in bowl.
Mushrooms, $1/4$" chopped	$1/_4$ cup		Add.
Bamboo shoots (fresh)	$1/_2$ cup		Add, mix, reserve.
Corn oil	$1/_2$ cup		Place in wok with high flame.
Shrimp, fresh-water, 1"	1 cup		Add, saute $1^1/_2$ mins. Remove, reserve.
Herring, above			Add to high-flamed wok.
Mirin	4 tsp.		Add.
Sugar	1 Tbs.		Add.
Salt	$1/_4$ tsp.		Add, mix, cook 5 mins. covered. Turn fish over. Turn down flame; cook 7 mins. Remove; reserve.
Oil	2 Tbs.		Add to high flame.
Beans, mushrooms, bamboo shoots, above			Add, stir fry 2 mins. Turn flame down.
Kuzu	1 Tbs.		Place in bowl.
Water	$1/_2$ cup		Add, make slurry, add to stir fry, mix.
Shrimp, above			Add, stir fry 2 mins. Pour over fish.
			Serve.

Variations:

Pan size: lg. skillet	Yield: 3 lbs.	Yield:	**HALIBUT, ORIENTAL**
Cooking time: 4 mins.+/-	Serves: 10	Serves:	
Oven temp.:	Portion: 5 oz.	Portion:	

Tamari	¼ cup		Place in pan.
Ginger (fresh), peeled, grated	2 tsp.		Add.
Sesame oil, dark	1 tsp.		Add.
Sesame seeds, roasted	1 tsp.		Add, mix, reserve.
Halibut filets, skinless	3 lbs.		Cut on bias into 1-oz. slices. Marinate 3 mins. in above mixture.
			Heat skillet. Add fish, cook 30 seconds on each side or until done.
Marinade, above			Add, simmer 3 mins.
			Serve 5 medallions per person with marinade drizzled over.

Variations: Garnish with roasted sesame seeds, lemon juice, lemon wheels.

Pan size:	Yield: 3 lbs.	Yield:	**SMELTS, FRIED**
Cooking time: 10 mins.	Serves: 10	Serves:	
Oven temp.:	Portion: 4.2 oz.	Portion:	

Smelts	3 lbs.		Clean, wash, drain.
			Either: Remove backbone and flatten or leave round; or leave backbone and leave round.
Unbleached flour	2 cups		Place in bowl.
Salt	1 Tbs.		Add, mix.
Smelts, above			Dredge and set aside.
Olive oil	1 cup		Place in skillet at medium heat.
Smelts, above			Add and saute until golden brown.
Lemon, rolled and halved	2		Squeeze juice on smelts.
			Serve hot.

Variations:

SOLE, BAKED

	Yield: 4 lbs.	Yield:	Pan size:
	Serves: 10	Serves:	Cooking time: 4 mins.
	Portion: 4½ oz.+/-	Portion:	Oven temp.: 400°
Oil, peanut	⅓ cup		Place in bowl.
Ginger (fresh), grated	4 Tbs.		Add.
Onion, finely diced	½ cup		Add.
Pepper, white	½ tsp.		Add, mix. Hand-rub onto fish.
Sole filets, each 6 oz.+	4 lbs.		Dredge in oil. Lay out so they are not touching.
			Bake until flaky.

Variations: Add dark sesame oil to peanut oil.

	Yield:	Yield:	Pan size:
	Serves:	Serves:	Cooking time:
	Portion:	Portion:	Oven temp.:

Variations:

GLAZES

Glazes can be made from fruit juices or water from cooked fruit, depending on the flavor and color desired, such as blueberries, cranberries, peaches, or raspberries.

See also ICING recipes, pg. 179.

APPLE–MINT GLAZE

Pan size: ½ qt.	Yield: 1 cup	Yield:
Cooking time: 3 mins.	Serves: 10	Serves:
Oven temp.:	Portion: 1.6 Tbs.	Portion:

Mint, finely chopped	1 Tbs.		Reserve.
Apple juice	1 cup		Place in pan; simmer.
Arrowroot	1 Tbs.		Make into sauce. Add to pan and adjust.
			Mix until jellied. Adjust immediately. Turn heat off.
Mint, above			Immediately add mint; mix. Cover; rest 15 mins.
			Use or serve.
			[NOTE: Do not cook mint.]

Variations: Use on light-flavored pastry or as a sauce on carrots, millet, or quinoa. Use other juices and omit mint.

MAPLE–MINT GLAZE

Pan size: ½ qt.	Yield: 1 cup	Yield:
Cooking time: 3 mins.	Serves: 10	Serves:
Oven temp.:	Portion: 1.6 Tbs.	Portion:

Mint, finely chopped	3 Tbs.		Set aside.
Water	¾ cup		Place in pan.
Maple syrup	¼ cup		Add, boil.
Arrowroot	1 Tbs.		Make sauce. Pour slowly into maple syrup, stirring to desired consistency. Adjust. Turn off heat.
Mint, above			Add, mix, cover. Rest 15 mins.
			Use or serve.

Variations: Substitute equal amounts of water for maple syrup.

MAPLE–MUSTARD GLAZE

[From Lyndon Vickler, Head Chef, Sam Rupert's Restaurant, Warren, Vt.]

	Yield: 1 cup	Yield:	Pan size: 1/2 qt.
	Serves: 10	Serves:	Cooking time: 5 mins.
	Portion: 1.6 Tbs.	Portion:	Oven temp.:
Maple syrup	1/2 cup		Place in pan, heat.
Dijon mustard	1/2 cup		Add.
Pommery mustard	1/2 cup		Add, mix, simmer 5 mins.
			Use or serve.

Variations: Glaze chicken, sweet potatoes, carrots, squash, or turnips; or use as a dip.

MAPLE–TAHINI GLAZE

	Yield: 2 1/4 cups	Yield:	Pan size: 1/2 qt.
	Serves: 10	Serves:	Cooking time: 3 mins.
	Portion: 4 Tbs.	Portion:	Oven temp.:
Maple syrup	1 cup		Place in bowl.
Tahini	1/2 cup		Add.
Salt	1/2 tsp.		Add.
Clove, ground	1/4 tsp.		Add, mix well, adjust, use.

Variations: Substitute barley malt for maple syrup. Or thin maple syrup with water to make it less sweet.

SIMPLE SPICE GLAZE

Pan size:	½ qt.	Yield:	1 cup	Yield:	
Cooking time:	5 mins.	Serves:	10	Serves:	
Oven temp.:		Portion:	1.6 Tbs.	Portion:	

Water	1 cup	Place in pan; heat.
Cinnamon	½ tsp.	Add; simmer 5 mins. Steep 5 mins. simmer.
Arrowroot	1 Tbs.	Make sauce with 1 Tbs. water. Add slowly to stirring water. Mix and adjust consistency.
Maple syrup or barley malt	2 Tbs.	Add, mix.
		Use or serve.

Variations: Use apple juice instead of water. Use other or additional spices. Add 1+ Tbs. fresh grated ginger to boiling water and simmer 5 mins.

TAMARI–GINGER GLAZE

Pan size:	½ qt.	Yield:	1 cup	Yield:	
Cooking time:	5 mins.	Serves:	10	Serves:	
Oven temp.:		Portion:	1.6 Tbs.	Portion:	

Tamari	¼ cup	Place in pan.
Water	¾ cup	Add.
Ginger (fresh), grated	3 Tbs.	Add, bring to boil.
Arrowroot	1 Tbs.	Make sauce; slowly add to water while stirring to desired thickness.Adjust.
		Use or serve.
		[NOTE: This is a traditional Chinese recipe.]

Variations:

GRAINS

"Rice is a necessary and appropriate food for the virtuous and graceful life."

Confucius

BUGS IN YOUR CUPBOARD

Microscopic weevil eggs and mealy moths are sometimes found in grains, and they need the right conditions to grow—namely, time and high room temperature. Even the federal government has allowable quantities of animal protein in refined grains and flours. In the not too distant future, the time may come when you will have no choice but to learn how to save food whenever possible.

The high food value of grains far overshadows the slight inconvenience this problem may cause, and if your grains have not been chemically treated, you may get a few of them in your supply. One reason so many cigarette shops don't carry many brands of foreign cigarettes is that they have not been chemically treated, while our American cigarettes will keep for years with no bugs. Be assured that if you do have any bugs, it is because you have a good product, and one that has not been chemically treated after harvesting.

If it is offensive to think of preparing food with animal life in it, simply throw it out and be convinced that you need to store it under better conditions. The alternative is to cope with the problem and save it. If weevils are in your grain, they themselves are living on an excellent diet, and no doubt are healthy.

Three things to do:

• Sift them out and sort over the grain, removing them.

• Freeze the grain for 72 hours to kill the eggs.

• Put the grain in water; remove them when they float to the top.

If mealy moths (about a ½" wingspread), show up in your grains, simply freeze them and stop their growing cycle; then remove them from the grain. These creatures have been with grains throughout the history of the world, and they have enough sense to go where there is good eating.

WHOLE GRAINS

Grains have three main parts:

• *Bran,* the tough outer layer of fiber, removed by milling;

• *Endosperm,* the largest structure of the grain where the rich nutrients, starch, and most of the protein is stored—he more the milling, the less the nutrient value;

• *Embryo (germ),* which makes up about 2% of the whole.

Bran usually contains most of the fiber, oil, B Vitamins, and 25% of the protein.

Minimally milled grain is preferable because it is higher in nutritive value, although it requires a little longer cooking time.

GENERAL RULES FOR COOKING GRAINS

• Approximate volume water quantities are shown for full rehydration.

• Add a pinch of salt per cup of grains to water at start of cooking. Bring to boil, then simmer.

• Place grains in unheated water to cook (except millet, bulgur, and kasha, which are placed in boiling water).

• If cooking 5 lbs. (appx. 10 cups) or more of grains, they should be added to boiling water and immediately stirred for heat distribution.

• Simmer first 5 minutes uncovered, skim excess darker foam if any; then cover.

• When using less grain, use more water; for more, use less water, because of evaporation.

• Add herbs and spices 15 minutes before cooking ends.

•If using oil, add at end of cooking process.

•Protect stored grains from bug infestation in sealed bags or containers.

•Allow steam shafts to form while cooking, releasing the maximum water vapor to leave the grain. Remove or tilt lid at this point, depending on cooking development.

•Do not stir after water leaves the surface to maintain steam shafts.

•At end of cooking, remove grains from pot and fluff or toss while putting them into serving containers.

•For higher nutrition, fuller flavor, and a more glutinous texture, use a pressure cooker.

•For fluffy brown rice, add two cups of water per cup of rice with salt, cover, simmer fifteen minutes, and place in a 300° oven for 45 minutes or until done.

•Presoak grains to reduce cooking time.

•Grains requiring short cooking times are buckwheat, quinoa, and bulgur.

•Adjust water as needed.

•Use more water for softer grains.

•If grain is presoaked, use less cooking water and cooking time.

•Garnish with chopped parsley, green onions, cilantro, gomasio.

•Remove from cooking pot with a fluffing action to allow moisture to leave grains, reducing sogginess.

DESCRIPTION OF WHOLE GRAINS

Barley, hulled or whole (with the outer layer removed leaving all or most of the endosperm): × 2½–3 water; chewy, delicate flavor; stimulates the liver, accelerating discharge of poisonous wastes. Barley is not extensively milled. It is nourishing and easily digestible. Hulled barley was used in ancient Egypt, Greece, Rome, and Tibet. Caesar's armies brought it to most of Europe and the British Isles. Hippocrates prescribed barley soup for the sick to restore health and vitality, and adjusted its strength to the type of illness. In England, water in which barley has been cooked has been considered a cure-all, and barley gruel was traditionally served to invalids or as a remedy for a hangover.

Barley, pearled: more highly processed, easy to digest, most vitamins and minerals have been removed.

Buckwheat (Cossack food): an excellent food for fall or winter, it can be mixed with other grains or vegetables. Grown in the northern regions of Europe, Russia, and Asia. Buckwheat is associated with Russian cooking, where it is mainly used as a porridge. Buckwheat is a member of the rhubarb family, and no relation to wheat. If a wheat-free diet is desired, this may be substituted.

There are two kinds (very quick cooking):

•*buckwheat groats,* × 3–4 water depending on consistency desired. Add to boiling water; cooks like noodles, with a similar texture. When adding more water, cooks into a porridge. For extra rich tasting "gourmet" buckwheat, stir-toast buckwheat groats in a heavy skillet before cooking in the usual manner.

•*buckwheat (kasha),* × 3 water, has a distinctive flavor. Expensive but very nutritious.

Bulgur (Burghul) Wheat: × 2 water, has a rich, nutty flavor, and comes two ways:

•*fine-grain:* pour boiling water evenly over it and cover, rest for ten minutes, toss, and adjust boiling water.

•*coarse-grain:* quick cooking, very expanding in appearance; a cracked wheat made by first boiling, then drying and grinding.

Corn Meal: × 4 water, offers a pleasant, unique, corny flavor; fine grains, easy to adjust water and flavor. Simmer 10–15 minutes; stir often. Serve as a porridge or poured into a bread pan, refrigerated, sliced and sauteed, to be served with a sweetener. Not highly nutritious. Fossilized corn is believed to be from 60,000 to 80,000 years old, and was found in archaeological diggings in Mexico City.

Couscous (KusKus): × 2½ water, has a

delicate flavor. Highly processed, cracked, semolina flour or refined wheat; minimally nutritious. Pour boiling water evenly over it, cover, rest five minutes, toss, adjust water. There are a maximum number of flavoring alternatives. Couscous is not a grain, but since it is served like one, it is mentioned here.

Millet: × 2¹/₂ water, has a slight, distinctive flavor, served as a main dish with a condiment or sauce or in soups, stews or desserts. Traditionally considered to be strengthening to the urinary tract; used as a staple in the British Isles during the Middle Ages. Easily digested and very nutritious.

Oats: easily assimilated and come in five ways:

•*Hulled:* × 6 water, are tasty; some of the bran has been removed. They are high in amino acid balance and are a good source of Vitamin E and thiamine. Oats were another grain brought by the Roman legions to Europe and the British Isles.

•*Steel cut:* × 3 water, are hulled, steamed, and coarsely cut; tend to boil over.

•*Rolled:* × 2¹/₂ water; known as "old-fashioned oatmeal," is more highly processed, rolled, and flattened into flakes.

•*Quick:* × 3 water, quick-cooking version of "old-fashioned oatmeal," are the most processed and least nutritious.

Oat Flour: is sweet and excellent for baking, easily assimilated. It offers a longer shelf life than whole wheat flour. Used mostly in baking.

Quinoa (keen-wa): × 2 water; gives a delicate, unique, sweetish flavor. It is light, easy to digest, and tosses easily. It requires 15 minutes cooking time, and is often over 20% protein, high in calcium, fiber, phosphorus, iron, lysine, and amino acids, and is a complete protein. It is good in soups, salads, desserts, as a grain, or a breakfast cereal. The National Academy of Science calls it "one of the best sources of protein in the vegetable kingdom." Quinoa is especially good for the old, sick, and infirm. It originated in the Andes with the Incas.

Rice, Brown: × 2 water; tends to be sweet and robust. Requires longer cooking time

than white rice, is unpolished, usually cream-colored, gold, reddish, or greenish in color. Brown rice is very high in nutritive value, with the best balance of minerals, carbohydrates, and protein.

It comes as three kinds:

•*Short-grain:* less than five millimeters long, for winter use.

•*Medium-grain:* between five and six millimeters long, for use in spring and fall.

•*Long-grain:* over six millimeters long, for summer use.

Rice, Sweet Brown: × 2 water; offers sweeter flavor, is more easily digested than most grains, and is very nutritious. Very glutinous. Often mixed with other grains.

Rice, White: is highly refined; most of the food value has been removed in processing; it is quick cooking and easy to chew. White rice is often treated with asbestos to prevent insect infestation that cannot be completely removed by washing.

Rice, Enriched: has had most of the white nutrients removed in processing and is coated with a small selection of chemical vitamins to partially compensate for the removal of a wide variety and large quantity of natural nutrients.

Rice, Instant: highly processed by pre-cooking and drying; has lost its natural integrity, does not hold well, losing its shape and turning easily to mush.

Rice, Parboiled or Converted: processed by partial cooking with steam and drying, followed by milling or polishing; natural flavor, texture, and nutrients have been substantially compromised.

Rye, Whole: × 1¹/₂ water; has a rich, pleasant flavor, alone or mixed with other grains. High in acid lysine, low in gluten. Soak the night before cooking for softer grains. Rye flour is preferable for unleavened bread, or mixed with whole wheat flour if leavening is used.

Wheat, Whole: × 3 water; gives a distinctive sweet but nutty taste. Serve mixed with other grains, beans, alone, or with complementary flavoring vegetables, salads, or breakfast. Serve as a hot cereal for breakfast, with beans or vegetables, or in salads. Roasting before cooking brings out a strong, sweet, nutty flavor. Whole wheat often contains 14% protein and is high in nutritive value.

Whole wheat flour should be stone ground. The quality of gluten in wheat flour directly relates to the quality of protein, therefore high-gluten flours are preferable. Fresher flour tastes better; it is best to grind and bake whole wheat on site, for maximum nutrition and flavor.

Whole Wheat Flour (Bread Flour): is usually high in gluten and is made from hard winter wheat.

Whole Wheat Pastry Flour: intended for pastries, pie crusts, or crackers. It is made from spring soft wheat and tends to rise better than bread flour.

White Flour: contains low quantities of gluten and protein and tends to be more highly processed. It is denuded of most nutrients and is less desirable to the digestive system. It is often used as a wallpaper paste.

Whole Wheat Elbow Macaroni: × 3 water. Add pasta to boiling water. Noodles have a distinctive flavor and can be cooked with tamari and shiitake mushrooms and garnished with diced green onions.

GRAINS COOKED–YIELD CHART

GRAINS	UNCOOKED		COOKED		RATIO OF UNCOOKED TO COOKED, IN CUPS
	LBS.	CUPS	LBS.	CUPS	
Barley, Hulled	1	$2^1/2$	$8^1/2$	2	1:2
Barley, Pearled	1	$2^1/4$	3	8	1:3.5
Buckwheat	1	$2^1/2$	$6^1/4$	10	1:4
Bulgur	1	$2^3/4$	$3^1/4$	$7^1/2$	1:2.7
Corn Meal	1	3	4	10	1:3.3
Couscous	1	$2^3/4$	2.4	8	1:2.9
Millet	1	$2^1/2$	$3^1/4$	8	1:3.4
Noodles, Buckwheat	1	NA	$3^1/2$	12	NA
Noodles, Whole Wheat Elbow	1	$4^3/4$	$2^2/3$	$8^1/4$	1:1.74
Oats, Hulled	1	3	$5^1/4$	11	1:3.6
Oats, Rolled	1	$5^3/4$	$5^1/2$	11	1:2.5
Oats, Steel Cut	1	3	$5^1/4$	$8^1/2$	1:2.8
Quinoa	1	$3^1/3$	$2^1/2$	10	1:3
Rye Berries	1	$2^1/2$	$3^1/2$	$7^1/2$	1:3
Wheat Berries	1	$2^3/4$	4	6	1:2.2
Wheat, Cracked	1	$2^3/4$	$4^1/3$	8	1:2.9
Rice, Basmati	1	$2^1/2$	$3^1/2$	9	1:3.6
Rice, Long-grain	1	$2^1/2$	3	$8^1/4$	1:3.3
Rice, Short-grain	1	$2^1/2$	$3^1/2$	6	1:2.4
Rice, Sweet	1	$2^1/3$	$2^1/2$	5	1:2

NA = Not applicable.

GRAIN FLAVORING CHART

	Barley	Buckwheat	Bulgur	Corn Meal	Couscous	Millet	Oats	Quinoa	Rice, Brown	Rice, Basmati	Rye	Wheat
Allspice	●											
Anise	●				●			●				
Basil				●								
Bay Leaf		●	●	●		●			●	●	●	
Caraway		●					●					
Cardamom	●						●					
Cayenne												
Celery Seed				●			●					
Chervil												
Chili Pepper										●		
Chives				●						●	●	●
Cilantro			●				●				●	●
Cinnamon	●						●		●			
Clove	●				●		●					
Coriander				●						●		
Currants	●						●			●		
Curry							●			●	●	
Dill Seed				●								
Dill Weed				●								
Fennel							●	●				
Garlic		●	●			●		●	●	●		●
Ginger	●						●					
Mace	●						●	●				
Marjoram				●								
Mint	●											
Mustard												
Nutmeg	●						●	●				
Onion		●		●	●	●		●	●	●		●
Oregano				●								
Paprika										●		
Parsley		●	●	●	●	●	●	●	●	●	●	●
Pepper, black				●								
Pepper, white												
Poppy Seed		●	●	●	●	●	●	●	●	●	●	●
Rosemary				●								
Saffron					●				●	●		
Sage									●	●		
Savory												
Sesame Seed		●	●	●	●	●	●	●	●	●	●	●
Tarragon			●	●				●				
Thyme				●					●			
Turmeric					●			●		●		
Barley Malt				●			●					●
Maple Syrup				●								●
Sweet Rice Wine								●	●			●
Miso		●					●					●
Rice Vinegar			●	●	●	●		●	●	●	●	●
Tahini		●	●	●	●	●	●	●	●	●	●	●
Tamari		●	●	●	●	●	●	●	●	●	●	●
Lemon	●			●								

BARLEY

Pan size:	6 qt.	Yield:	10 cups	Yield:	
Cooking time	1½ hrs.	Serves:	10	Serves:	
Oven temp.:		Portion:	1 cup	Portion:	

Water	15 cups		Place in pot, heat.
Salt	1 tsp.		Add.
Barley	5 cups		Add, bring to boil; simmer covered.
			Serve when cooked.

Variations: Cook with 10 sq. in. kelp or kombu.
Cook with carrots or mushrooms.
For breakfast, cook with raisins and garnish with barley malt and seeds.

BREAKFAST PORRIDGE

SUGGESTIONS
(cook and serve soft)

Winter

Grains	**Condiment Alternatives**
Buckwheat	Fruit, sliced or diced
Corn Meal	Ginger, pickled
Millet	Nuts and seeds, roasted with or without tamari
Oats, rolled	Raisins
Oats, steel cut	Tahini
Rice, brown, short-grain	Yogurt
Rice, brown, sweet	Barley, Almond, or Oat milk (see pp. 197–198)

Summer

Barley	Apple butter, fruit jam
Bulgur	Fruit, sliced or diced
Rice, Brown, long grain	Raisins
Corn Meal	Seeds, roasted
	Watercress sprigs or any winter garnish

Variations: Serve after Miso Soup.

BUCKWHEAT

	Yield: 10 cups	Yield:	Pan size: 4 qt.
	Serves: 10	Serves:	Cooking time: 20+ mins.
	Portion: 1 cup	Portion:	Oven temp.:
Water	8 cups		Place in pot, boil.
Salt	1 tsp.		Add.
Buckwheat, groats	2½ cups		Add, simmer covered. Cook until grains are soft.
			Serve.

Variations: Cook with tamari instead of salt.
Pre-parcook onions before adding buckwheat.
Add 3 Tbs. olive oil at end of cooking.

BUCKWHEAT AND ONIONS

	Yield: 10 cups	Yield:	Pan size: 4 qt.
	Serves: 10	Serves:	Cooking time: 20+ mins.
	Portion: 1 cup	Portion:	Oven temp.:
Olive oil	¼ cup		Place in pan.
Onions	2 cups		Add, saute until clear.
Water, boiling	6 cups		Add.
Salt	½ tsp.		Add.
Buckwheat	2¼ cups		Add, simmer 20 mins. or cook until done.
Tamari	1 Tbs.		Add, mix, adjust.
			Serve.

Variations: Cook with 1"-diced potato and add 1 Tbs. olive oil at the end of cooking.

Pan size: 4 qt.	Yield: 10 cups	Yield:	**BULGUR**
Cooking time: 10 mins.	Serves: 10	Serves:	
Oven temp.:	Portion: 1 cup	Portion:	

Water	8 cups		Place in pan.
Salt	1/2 tsp.		Add, bring to boil.
Bulgur (coarse)	3.6 cups		Add, bring to boil. Cover, simmer 10 mins.
			Turn off heat. Rest 30 mins.
			Serve.

Variations: Add 1 Tbs. tahini.
Cook with diced onion.
Saute onions and garlic in olive oil; add water and proceed with recipe.

Pan size: 4 qt.	Yield: 10 cups	Yield:	**BULGUR AND LENTILS**
Cooking time: 50 mins.	Serves: 10	Serves:	
Oven temp.:	Portion: 1 cup	Portion:	

Water	10 cups		Place in pot.
Lentils	2/3 cup		Add, simmer 25 mins.
Bulgur (coarse)	3 cups		Add, simmer.
Onions, 1/2"-diced	2 cups		Add.
Tamari	2 Tbs.		Add, simmer 10 mins.
Zucchini, sliced	3 cups		Add.
Thyme	1 tsp.		Add.
Basil	1 tsp.		Add.
Olive oil	1/4 cup		Add, simmer until zucchini is cooked or parcooked; adjust.
			Serve.

Variations:

BULGUR, TARRAGON

	Yield: 10 cups	Yield:	Pan size: 4 qt.
	Serves: 10	Serves:	Cooking time: 25 mins.
	Portion: 1 cup	Portion:	Oven temp.:

Olive oil	¼ cup		Place in pan.
Salt	½ tsp.		Add.
Onions, ¼"-diced	2 cups		Add, saute until clear.
Water, boiling	6 cups		Add, boil.
Bulgur	3¼ cups		Add, simmer 15 mins.
Tarragon	1 tsp.		Add, simmer 10 mins. to completion.
			Adjust; serve.

Variations:

CORN, BAKED

	Yield: 10 ears	Yield:	Pan size:
	Serves: 10	Serves:	Cooking time: 30 mins.
	Portion: 1 ear	Portion:	Oven temp.: 400°

Corn with husks	10 ears		Place in oven not touching each other.
			Bake 20–30 mins. until done.
			Remove husks and silk. Serve immediately.
			[NOTE: Cooking time depends on temperature of corn, diameter of ear, and age of corn.]

Variations:

CORN, STEAMED

Pan size:	12 qt.	Yield:	10 ears	Yield:	
Cooking time:	10–15 mins.	Serves:	10	Serves:	
Oven temp.:		Portion:	1 ear	Portion:	

Corn with husks, silk removed	10 ears		Place in steamer.
			Steam until cooked.
			Serve immediately.
			[NOTE: Cooking time depends on temperature of corn, diameter of ear, and age of corn.]

Variations:

CORN MEAL MUSH

Pan size:	4 qt.	Yield:	10 cups	Yield:	
Cooking time:	30 mins.	Serves:	10	Serves:	
Oven temp.:		Portion:	1 cup	Portion:	

Water, room temp.	20 cups		Place in pot.
Salt	1 tsp.		Add.
Corn meal	5 cups		Add, mix to remove all lumps. Bring to boil, simmer.
			Cover, cook 30 mins. *Stir often.*
			Serve.
			[NOTE: Mush hardens when cool.]

Variations: Garnish with raisins, nuts, seeds, barley malt, granola.
Fried corn meal mush: Pour into 9 × 5" pan, refrigerate, slice, and saute until dark brown crisp is formed on both sides; serve with barley malt.

CORN MEAL, POLENTA (Italian)

	Yield: 10 cups	Yield:	Pan size: 4 qt.
	Serves: 10	Serves:	Cooking time: 30 mins.
	Portion: 1 cup	Portion:	Oven temp.:
Water	12 cups		Place in pot.
Salt	1 Tbs.		Add.
Corn meal	3 cups		Add; boil 15 mins.
Basil	$^3/_4$ tsp.		Add.
Oregano	1 tsp.		Add.
Celery seed	$^3/_4$ tsp.		Add.
Thyme	1 tsp.		Add, mix, bring to boil; simmer 15 mins. covered. Stir often to prevent sticking to bottom.
			Adjust flavor and serve.

Variations: Serve 1" cubes in fish soup.
Can be served fried, as with Corn Meal Mush (see previous pg.).

COUSCOUS

	Yield: 10 cups	Yield:	Pan size: 4–6 qt.
	Serves: 10	Serves:	Cooking time: 1 min.
	Portion: 1 cup	Portion:	Oven temp.:
Water	$3^1/_2$ cups		Bring to hard boil.
Salt	1 tsp.		Add, mix.
Couscous	$3^1/_2$ cups		Add, evenly level couscous. Turn off heat, cover. Rest 3 mins., then fluff up.
			Leave cover off.

Variations: Add to cooked kasha, colored vegetable, or diced tofu.

COUSCOUS AND BUCKWHEAT

Pan size: 4 qt.	*Yield:* 10 cups	*Yield:*
Cooking time: 20 mins.	*Serves:* 10	*Serves:*
Oven temp.:	*Portion:* 1 cup	*Portion:*

Water	8 cups		Place in pan.
Salt	1/2 tsp.		Add.
Buckwheat	1³/₄ cups		Add, simmer 20 mins. or until done.
			Bring to boil.
Couscous	1 cup		Add, mix, turn off. Cover. Rest 5 mins.
			Adjust; serve.

Variations:

MILLET

Pan size: 4 qt.	*Yield:* 10 cups	*Yield:*
Cooking time: 30 mins.	*Serves:* 10	*Serves:*
Oven temp.:	*Portion:* 1 cup	*Portion:*

Water	8 cups		Place in pot.
Salt	1/2 tsp.		Add, bring to boil.
Millet	3 cups		Add, simmer 30 mins. or until done.
			Serve.

Variations: Add water to onions and garlic sauteed in olive oil and proceed with recipe.
Add 2 tsp. caraway seed 10 mins. before completion of cooking.
Garnish with a sauce.

MILLET, MASHED

	Yield:	10 cups	Yield:		Pan size:	4 qt.
	Serves:	10	Serves:		Cooking time:	40+ mins.
	Portion:	1 cup	Portion:		Oven temp.:	

Water	9 cups		Place in pot.
Salt	½ tsp.		Add, simmer.
Millet	3 cups		Add, cook until soft. Mash.
Currants	½ cup		Add.
Walnuts, chopped	½ cup		Add, mix; adjust.
			Serve.
			[NOTE: Cooks softer if started in cold water.]

Variations: Add 2 tsp. caraway seeds 10 mins. after adding millet.
Add soft cooked cauliflower before mashing.
Garnish: sauce and/or diced greens.

MILLET WITH SQUASH

	Yield:	10 cups	Yield:		Pan size:	4 qt.
	Serves:	10	Serves:		Cooking time:	40+ mins.
	Portion:	1	Portion:		Oven temp.:	

Water	9 cups		Place in pot.
Salt	½ tsp.		Add.
Millet	2½ cups		Add.
Winter squash, 1"-diced	3 cups		Add, simmer, cover until well-cooked and soft. Turn off heat. Adjust hot water.
			Serve.

Variations: Garnish: chopped greens and/or sauce.
Add ⅓ cup tahini and mix.

[This recipe tested and approved by Chris Quilty, Chef Instructor at New England Culinary Institute.]

OATS, HULLED

Pan size:	4 qt.	Yield:	10 cups	Yield:	
Cooking time:	6–10 hrs.	Serves:	10	Serves:	
Oven temp.:	175°	Portion:	1 cup	Portion:	

Water	18 cups		Place in pan.
Kelp	4"		Add.
Salt	½ tsp.		Add.
Oats, hulled	3 cups		Add, bring to hard boil for 2 mins. Stir, cover.
			Place in oven. Bake 6–10 hrs.
			Stir; serve.
			[NOTE: Traditional winter dish cooked on woodstove with the fire going out overnight.]

Variations: Instead, simmer 20 mins., rest 8 hrs. without heat, simmer another 20 mins. Good for breakfast and lunch.

[This recipe tested and approved by Chris Quilty, Chef Instructor at New England Culinary Institute.]

OATS, ROLLED

Pan size:	4 qt.	Yield:	10 cups	Yield:	
Cooking time:	10–12 mins.	Serves:	10	Serves:	
Oven temp.:		Portion:	1 cup	Portion:	

Water	12½ cups		Bring to boil.
Salt	1 tsp.		Add.
Oat flakes	5 cups		Add, mix, simmer 10–12 mins. until done.
			Serve.

Variations: Cook with raisins, diced apples, cinnamon, or barley malt. Garnish: gomasio, nuts, seeds, raisins, diced fresh fruit, applesauce.

OATS, STEEL CUT

	Yield: 10 cups	Yield:	Pan size: 6 qt.
	Serves: 10	Serves:	Cooking time: 2+/- hrs.
	Portion: 1 cup	Portion:	Oven temp.:
Water	10 cups		Place in pot.
Salt	1 tsp.		Add.
Oats, steel cut	3³/4 cups		Add, simmer, cover.
			Adjust water; cook until done.
			Serve.

Variations: Cook with 5" kelp.

QUINOA (keen-wa)

	Yield: 10 cups	Yield:	Pan size: 4 qt.
	Serves: 10	Serves:	Cooking time: 15+/- mins.
	Portion: 1 cup	Portion:	Oven temp.:
Water	6.6 cups		Place in pot.
Salt	1 tsp.		Add.
Quinoa	3.3 cups		Rinse in strainer. Add. Slow simmer, covered, for 15 mins.
			Cook until it becomes translucent and germ ring becomes visible.
			Serve.

Variations: Garnish for breakfast: raisins, nuts and seeds, gomasio, diced or stewed fruit.
Garnish for lunch or dinner: gomasio, sauce, diced parsley, cilantro, green onion.
Cook with saffron.

QUINOA, ITALIAN

Pan size:	4 qt.	Yield:	10 cups	Yield:	
Cooking time:	15+/- mins.	Serves:	10	Serves:	
Oven temp.:		Portion:	1 cup	Portion:	

Olive oil	1/2 cup	Place in pan.
Onions, 1/2"-diced	2 cups	Add.
Garlic, finely diced	2 Tbs.	Add, saute until clear.
Zucchini, 1/4" slices	4 cups	Add, mix.
Water	4 cups	Add.
Tamari	1/4 cup	Add.
Basil leaves	1 tsp.	Add.
Oregano	2 tsp.	Add, mix.
Quinoa	2 cups	Add, mix; simmer, covered, 15 mins. until quinoa is cooked.
		Serve.

Variations:

RICE BALLS

Pan size:		Yield:	10 cups	Yield:	
Cooking time:		Serves:	10	Serves:	
Oven temp.:		Portion:	2 balls	Portion:	

Brown rice, cooked	9 cups	Place in bowl.
Tahini	1/2 cup	Add.
Adzuki, lentil, or other small bean, cooked	1 cup	Add.
Parsley, finely diced	1/4 cup	Add, mix by hand. Divide into 20 equal amounts.
Gomasio or salted sesame seeds (adjust salt in seeds as needed)	4 cups	Spread a thin layer on immediate area. Roll and shape 1 ball in hands. Roll and press in gomasio to coat evenly. Set aside.
		Make and coat all balls.
		Serve.

Variations: Use any small bean or diced vegetable, or diced green onions. Wrap in roasted nori sheets or use miso and chopped walnuts instead of gomasio or sesame seeds.

[This recipe tested and approved by Chris Quilty, Chef Instructor at New England Culinary Institute.]

RICE BALLS, FRIED

Yield:	10 cups	Yield:	Pan size:
Serves:	10	Serves:	Cooking time:
Portion:	1 cup	Portion:	Oven temp.:

Oil, light sesame or safflower	1/4 cup		Place in pan. Apply medium heat.
Rice balls, unbaked (see pg. 171)	10 cups		Cut in half with wet knife. Place in skillet. Saute until slight crust develops.
Tamari	2 Tbs.		Add by drizzling on oil. Saute 3 mins. Place on drying towels.
			Serve.

Variations:

RICE, BASMATI (White)

Yield:	10 cups	Yield:	Pan size:	4 qt.
Serves:	10	Serves:	Cooking time:	20 mins.
Portion:	1 cup	Portion:	Oven temp.:	

Water	13 cups		Place in pot.
Salt	1 tsp.		Add.
Basmati rice	2³/4 cups		Add, simmer intil cooked.

Variations: Garnish with sliced toasted almonds.

Pan size: 4 qt.	Yield: 10 cups	Yield:	**RICE, BROWN (Boiled)**
Cooking time: 1 hr.	Serves: 10	Serves:	
Oven temp.:	Portion: 1 cup	Portion:	
Water	6.6 cups		Place in pot.
Salt	1 tsp.		Add.
Brown rice	3.3 cups		Add, simmer, cover. Cook 45+/- mins. Remove or crack lid as needed.
			Cook until done.
			Serve.
			For fluffy brown rice, add 2 cups water per cup of rice with salt, cover, simmer 15 mins., and place in a 300° oven covered for 45 mins. or until done. Adjust; serve.

Variations: Cook with sea vegetables, turmeric, saffron, other herbs or with sweet brown rice. Garnish: gomasio, diced parsley, cilantro, or green onions; or sauce, seeds. Add 25% whole wheat berries.

Pan size:	Yield: 10 cups	Yield:	**RICE, BROWN (Pressure Cooked)**
Cooking time: 50 mins.	Serves: 10	Serves:	
Oven temp.:	Portion: 1 cup	Portion:	
Water	5 cups		Place in pressure cooker.
Salt	1 tsp.		Add.
Brown rice	3.3 cups		Add, cover and seal. Bring to pressure. Reduce heat and cook 45 mins.
			Turn off heat. Rest, sealed, for 15 mins.
			Immediately remove from pressure cooker to plates or holding pan with fluffing motions, allowing air to circulate and reducing possibility of soggy rice.

Variations: Cook with tamari instead of salt. Garnish as with Boiled Brown Rice, above.

RICE, BROWN, AND RED LENTILS

	Yield:	10 cups	Yield:		Pan size:	4–6 qt.
	Serves:	10	Serves:		Cooking time: 1 hr.	
	Portion:	1 cup	Portion:		Oven temp.:	

Water	6.6 cups		Place in pot, heat.
Salt	1 tsp.		Add.
Brown rice	3 cups		Add.
Red lentils	1/2 cup		Add, simmer, cover.
			Cook until done, adjust.
			Serve.

Variations: Cook with finely chopped parsley or cilantro stems added 15 mins. before completion.
Sautee onion and garlic in olive oil, add tamari, and mix with rice.
Garnish: minimum.

RICE, SUSHI–VEGETABLE (NORI)

	Yield:	10 cups	Yield:		Pan size:	
	Serves:	10	Serves:		Cooking time:	
	Portion:	1 cup	Portion:		Oven temp.:	

Brown rice, cooked	10 cups		Cool, but still warm; reserve.
Nori sheets	4		Roast, reserve.
Filling:			
Carrots, julienned	2 cups		Reserve.
Parsley, cilantro, or gr. onion	2 cups		Dice; reserve.
Cucumber, julienned	2 cups		Reserve.
Ginger, grated fine	1/8 cup		Reserve.

Put bamboo mat on work space. Place nori sheets on bamboo mat. Place 1–2 cups rice on one edge of nori about 3" wide from side to side. Use wet fingers. Make a V-groove down the center of rice from end to end. Place filling in and on V. Roll mat so rice will cover filling, then roll nori by hand. Dampen nori with water on fingers if it doesn't adhere. Roll so filling is in the center, rice surrounds filling, nori surrounds rice, about 2" diam. Cover and refrigerate until cool. Slice 3/4–1" thick, round slices.

Variations: Serve with Oriental Dip, Basic (pg. 144).

Serve or wrap in plastic until ready to cut.

RICE, SWEET

Pan size:	4 qt.	Yield:	10 cups	Yield:	
Cooking time:	50–60 mins.	Serves:	10	Serves:	
Oven temp.:		Portion:	1 cup	Portion:	

Water	10 cups		Place in pot, heat.
Salt	1 tsp.		Add.
Rice, sweet	5 cups		Add, simmer, cover. Cook 50–60 minutes or until done.
			Serve.

Variations: Cook combined with other rice; or cook with adzuki beans.
Garnish: chopped parsley, green onion, cilantro, or roasted nuts.
Use 1 Tbs. tamari instead of salt.

RICE AND WHEAT

Pan size:	4 qt.	Yield:	10 cups	Yield:	
Cooking time:	1+ hr.	Serves:	10	Serves:	
Oven temp.:		Portion:	1 cup	Portion:	

Water	11 cups		Place in pan.
Salt	1/4 tsp.		Add, boil.
Wheat	1 cup		Add.
Brown rice	2³/₄ cups		Add, simmer 1 hr. or until done.
			Adjust; serve.

Variations:

RYE, WHOLE

	Yield:	10 cups	Yield:		Pan size:	4 qt.
	Serves:	10	Serves:		Cooking time:	1½ hrs.
	Portion:	1 cup	Portion:		Oven temp.:	

Water	5 cups		Place in pot; heat.	
Salt	1 tsp.		Add.	
Whole rye, soaked previous night	3.3 cups		Add, simmer, cover.	
			Cook until grains have opened and are soft.	
			Serve.	

Variations: Cook with other grains.
Garnish for breakfast: raisins or seeds.
Garnish for lunch: diced parsley, sauce.

WHEAT BERRIES (Soft Spring)

	Yield:	10 cups	Yield:		Pan size:	3 qt.
	Serves:	10	Serves:		Cooking time:	1½ hrs.
	Portion:	1 cup	Portion:		Oven temp.:	

Water	7 cups		Place in pot, heat.	
Salt	½ tsp.		Add.	
Wheat berries (soft spring), soaked 4 hrs. and drained.	4½ cups		Add, simmer, cover.	
			Cook until berries have burst.	
			Serve.	

Variations: Cook with other grains or barley malt, mace and nutmeg, saffron.
Garnish: thick sauce, Tahini Sauce, Basic (pg. 264), diced parsley.
Add diced cooked vegetables.

Pan size:	4 qt.	Yield:	10 cups	Yield:		WHEAT BERRIES "FRUMENTY"
Cooking time:	30 mins.	Serves:	10	Serves:		
Oven temp.:		Portion:	1 cup	Portion:		

Water	7 cups		Place in pan.
Salt	$\frac{1}{2}$ tsp.		Add.
Wheat berries (soft spring)	5 cups		Add, soak 1 hr., boil 20 mins.
			Place in oven. Rest 8 hrs.
			Boil 10 mins.
			Serve.
			[NOTE: Popular in medieval Europe and British Isles.]

Variations: Garnish: raisins, barley malt or maple syrup, chopped parsley, green onion, gomasio.

WHOLE WHEAT SEITAN

	Yield:	3.3 lbs.	Yield:	Pan size:
	Serves:	10	Serves:	Cooking time:
	Portion:	5.3 oz.	Portion:	Oven temp.:

Whole wheat flour, high gluten (not coarse-ground bread flour)	18 cups		Place in bowl.
Water, 120°	29 cups		Add, mix. Knead for 20 minutes until stringy stretch marks develop. Cover with cold water. Set aside for 45 mins. to overnight.
Water	21 cups		Place in tall, thin pot.
Tamari	1 cup		Add.
Onions	6 cups		Add.
Kelp, rinsed	50 sq.in.		Add.
Celery seed	1 Tbs.		Add.
Sage	1½ tsp.		Add.
Bay leaf	3		Add, simmer 5 mins. Reserve.
Whole wheat flour, above			The longer it rests, the easier it is to wash out bran.
			Place in large pot. Add cold water to cover. Knead: wash bran and starch into the water. Gluten will remain.
			Reserve first rinse water. Alternate cold and 110°+/- water for rinsing. Last rinsing in cold water.
			Divide into 4–6" diam. pieces or balls. Put in boiling seasoned water. Water should more than cover gluten balls because they will expand.
			Simmer 1 hr. covered. Remove seitan balls (gently stir sticking balls off pan bottom) and use or serve.

Variations: Cook water is an excellent stock for soups or sauces; use rinse water as you would an arrowroot thickener in soups, stews, sauces, or for starting sourdough bread.
Serve seitan as you would meat. Make gravy with cook water and rinse water.
Cook thick-sliced or quartered mushrooms with sliced seitan as in beef tips, mushrooms, and gravy.
Dice seitan and serve with sauce.
Saute and serve for breakfast, lunch, or supper.
Use in sandwiches or cut burger size.
Use in spaghetti sauce; add to soups, stews, or salads.
Serve with sweet and sour sauce; or as kabobs.

ICINGS

See Glazes, pp.153–155

Pan size: for 9 × 13"	Yield: 1.2 cups	Yield:	**APPLE–TAHINI ICING**
Cooking time:	Serves: 10	Serves:	
Oven temp.:	Portion: 1.9 Tbs.	Portion:	
Apple cider	1 cup		Place in pan.
Tahini	3 Tbs.		Add, mix well. Simmer 1 min.
Arrowroot	2 Tbs.		Make slurry. Add to pan to make icing desired consistency.
			Cool, use.

Variations: Add lemon zest, glazed ginger.
Add roasted nuts diced *very* fine.

Pan size: See Note*	Yield: 2$\frac{1}{2}$ cups	Yield:	**TOFU SUPREME ICING**
Cooking time:	Serves: 10	Serves:	
Oven temp.:	Portion: 4.4 Tbs.	Portion:	
Maple syrup	$\frac{1}{2}$ cup		Place in blender.
Tahini	2 Tbs.		Add.
Tofu	1 lb.		Add.
Vanilla extract	1 tsp.		Add.
Salt	$\frac{1}{4}$ tsp.		Add.
Almond extract	3 drops		Add.
Nutmeg	$\frac{1}{8}$ tsp.		Add, pulse–blend. When off, move mixture with spoon, then pulse. Adjust flavor. Do not add more liquid. Blend until smooth.
			[*NOTE: Will ice double 9 × 13" cakes or 322 sq. in.]

Variations:

[This recipe tested and approved by Chris Quilty, Chef Instructor at New England Culinary Institute.]

JAMS

APPLE–RAISIN JAM

		Yield:	3 cups	Yield:		Pan size:	2 qt.
		Serves:	10	Serves:		Cooking time:	40+/- mins.
		Portion:	4.8 Tbs.	Portion:		Oven temp.:	

Apples	1 lb.	Quarter, core, 1/8"-slice. Place in pot, shake to settle.
Water	2 cups	Add, simmer, cover. Cook 20 mins.
Barley malt	1/4 cup	Add, mix.
		Blend 1 cup apples, using cook water. Return to pot.
Lemon rind, grated	1/4 tsp.	Add.
Salt	pinch	Add.
Raisins	1/4 cup	Add, mix, cook 20 mins.
Cinnamon	1/4 tsp.	Add.
Arrowroot	2 Tbs.	Make slurry. Add slowly while stirring.
		Cover, cool, serve.

Variations: Use apple or grape juice instead of water.
Use cardamom instead of cinnamon.
Use grated ginger with or without lemon.

APRICOT JAM, COOKED

		Yield:	2³/₄ lbs.	Yield:		Pan size:	1 qt.
		Serves:	10	Serves:		Cooking time:	15 mins.
		Portion:	4.5 oz.	Portion:		Oven temp.:	

Apricots, dried, unsulphured	1 lb.	Place in pan.
Anise seed	1/4 tsp.	Add.
Water	2 cups	Add, soak overnight.
		Simmer 15 mins. Set aside, cool. Place in blender.
Salt	pinch	Add. Blend to almost smooth.
Apple cider	1 cup	Place in pan; simmer.
Apricots, above		Add, bring to boil.
Arrowroot	2 Tbs.	Make slurry; add while stirring apricots. Adjust to desired thickness.
		Refrigerate; serve.

Variations: Use another juice instead of apple cider.
Add roasted nuts on completion.

Pan size:	2 qt.	Yield:	3¼ cups	Yield:		**APRICOT JAM, UNCOOKED**
Cooking time:		Serves:	10	Serves:		
Oven temp.:		Portion:	5.2 Tbs.	Portion:		

Apricots, dried, unsulphured	1 lb.		Place in bowl. cover; soak overnight.
Water	2¼ cups		Place in blender.
Barley malt	¼ cup		Add.
			Slow-pulse; do not blend smooth. Use minimum soak water.
			Serve.

Variations: Add pinch of salt.
Use apple cider instead of water.
Add lemon zest or juice.

Pan size:	1 qt.	Yield:	2 cups	Yield:		**PEACH JAM**
Cooking time:	10 mins.	Serves:	10	Serves:		
Oven temp.:		Portion:	3.2 Tbs.	Portion:		

Peaches, skinned, stoned	3 lbs.		½" dice; save juice and add. Place in pan.
Water	2 cups		Add; simmer low, covered, for 10 mins.
Salt	¼ tsp.		Add.
Cinnamon	pinch		Add.
Vanilla extract	6 drops		Add, mix. Adjust water; simmer for 10 mins. covered.
Arrowroot	2 tsp.		Add arrowroot slurry.
			Cool, serve.

Variations: Use pears instead of peaches; or use apple cider instead of water.
For extra rich jam, refrigerate overnight, simmer 5 mins., cool and serve.
Cook with grated ginger.

RAISIN JAM

	Yield: 4½ cups	Yield:	Pan size: 1 qt.
	Serves: 10	Serves:	Cooking time: 15 mins.
	Portion: 7.2 Tbs.	Portion:	Oven temp.:

Raisins	2 cups		Place in pot.
Apple cider	1½ cups		Add, simmer, cover, cook 15 mins. Set aside to cool.
			Place in blender. Reserve some cook water. Pulse, blend, adjust cook water.
Apple cider	1 cup		Place in pan.
Lemon rind, grated	½ tsp.		Add. Simmer.
Arrowroot	2 Tbs.		Make slurry. Add while stirring cider to desired consistency.
Raisins, above			Add, mix.
			Refrigerate; serve.

Variations: Add ½ cup chopped roasted nuts.
Use grape juice instead of apple cider.
Use prunes instead of raisins.

RAISIN–TAHINI JAM

	Yield: 2½ cups	Yield:	Pan size: 1 qt.
	Serves: 10	Serves:	Cooking time: 5 mins.
	Portion: 2 Tbs.	Portion:	Oven temp.:

Water	1 cup		Place in pan; heat.
Raisins	2 cups		Add, simmer 5 mins., mix. Rest, cool. Place in blender.
Tahini	½ cup		Add to blender. Blend to desired consistency.
			Adjust; serve.

Variations: Use 50% grape juice instead of water.
Add fresh lemon juice; add roasted nuts or roasted sesame seeds when blending.

LEGUMES

IMPORTANT GUIDELINES FOR COOKING LEGUMES

(Hydrates are foods to which water must be added.)

• Cook beans with about 2" of rinsed kombu or kelp per cup of beans, to reduce amount of added salt, and to soften the beans, which makes them more digestible, adds flavor, and reduces flatulence.

• Cooking time and quantity of water used will depend on age of hydrates, humidity of storage conditions, and degree of evaporation while cooking.

• Leftover beans can make an excellent base for dips, sauces, or salad dressings.

• 5 lbs. (10 cups) or more of beans added to boiling water allows for more heat distribution.

• When using fewer beans, use more water because of evaporation rate; with more beans, use less water.

• Add salt, herbs, and spices 15 minutes before cooking ends.

• Add oil at end of cooking.

• Approximate volume water quantities are shown for full rehydration.

• Presoak beans overnight, drain, cook in fresh water with kombu or kelp. Water in which beans are soaked overnight often will naturally become a sauce.

• In the case of an emergency (didn't soak the beans the night before) place beans in cold water, bring to hard boil for three minutes, cover tightly, turn off heat, rest for one hour, then simmer until done. (These will taste slightly different.)

Buying:

• Avoid purchasing old beans—they take longer to cook.

• Buy where turnover is high—ethnic stores, Chinese, Hispanic, Indian, or a known supplier.

Storing:

• Store in a cool, dry place.

• Store in sealed containers, if available.

VARIETIES OF LEGUMES

Adzuki (Aduki) Beans: small, reddish, unique taste; not necessary to presoak, but it is desirable to do so to improve digestion. Has a very high nutritive value, low in fat, therefore very easy to digest; Japanese origin.

Black-Eyed Peas: a small white bean with a little black eye; traditional in the southern U.S.

Black Beans: traditionally cooked with spices and garlic and served with rice or corn. A staple of South America and some parts of Mexico.

Garbanzo Beans (Chick Peas): a tan bean, unlike other beans; use the soaking water to cook with. Very high in nutritive value. Northern and Eastern Mediterranean origins; was found to have been used in Turkey 7,500 years ago.*

Great Northern Beans: a medium-sized white bean with a mellow flavor and good in baked beans or soups; good nutritive value.

Kidney (Red) Beans: a large bean, high in fat, native to America. Used in chilis, casseroles, soups, and stews.

Lentils: brown or green in color, small and flat; used in soups, pate, or served as a bean. No presoaking required, very high in nutritive value.

"Archaeologists found the oldest remains of lentils from about 8000 B.C., while lentil paste was discovered in Egyptian tombs of Thebes that date from about 2300 B.C." *

Lentils, Red: no presoaking required; excellent as a soup base or added to grains.

*Aramco World, May-June, 1988.

Lima Beans: come in three sizes—baby, large, and flat (the largest). Absorb flavor well.

Mung Beans: a small green pea, served mostly in India as *dahl*, a thick, highly-spiced pate. Often sprouted and served in salads or stir fries.

Navy Beans: commonly served as baked beans. Leeks and carrots are complementary. Served aboard ships during the 1800s.

Pinto Beans: a rose-colored American bean that can easily be substituted for kidney beans; often used for refried beans.

Soy Beans: a small, yellow bean with unique flavor. Very high in oil and protein, other high nutritive values; hard to digest. Most digestible when served as tofu, tempeh, tamari, or as miso.

Soldier Beans: a white bean with a large reddish design on one side.

Split Pea, Green: mostly used as a soup base; no need to presoak.

Split Pea, Yellow and Orange: mostly used as a soup or pate base; no need to presoak.

Yellow-Eyed Bean: a white bean with a small yellow eye on one side; bland berry flavor.

BEAN SPROUTS

Bean sprouts grown in the dark are light white-tan in color and have a delicate flavor. Grown near sunlight, they are greener. Eaten as a vegetable they have a rich, nutty, fresh flavor.

•They are crisp, crunchy, used in salads, soups, stews, sandwiches, and blended beverages.

•Select organic adzuki, garbanzo, lentils, mung beans.

•Different legumes make different quantities of sprouts.

•2–3 Tbs. makes 1½ cups, or 6–8 oz. sprouts. 1½ cups of beans yields about 20 cups.

General suggestions for growing bean sprouts:

•Type of bean and temperature affect length of sprout and shape, rapidity of growth, and flavor; the newer the bean, the better the sprout.

•Remove discolored beans.

•Soak overnight in lukewarm water.

•Drain and soak beans in lukewarm water.

•Avoid tap water; spring or distilled water is preferable.

•Place 5–6 layers of cheesecloth, or clean well-rinsed towel, on bottom of clay, china, or glass baking dish or container to keep them damp and out of the water.

•Avoid iron, aluminum, copper sprouting containers.

•Place beans on cheesecloth or towel.

•Tie a double layer of cheesecloth over container.

•Every 10–12 hours (twice a day), drain water well and replace with fresh lukewarm water.

•Fourth day: remove unsprouted beans.

•Fifth day: rinse sprouts, remove loose skins or beans from sprouts.

•Refrigerate; serving the same day as harvested preferable.

•Adzukis sprout in 4+/- days, tastes like fresh garden peas.

•Garbanzos sprout in 2 days; full, nut-like flavor.

•Lentils sprout in 4- days; have a lentil flavor; easiest to work with.

•Mung beans sprout in 4+/- days; full-bodied, sweet, tender, and crunchy; found in many Chinese restaurants.

"Happiness, for me, is largely a matter of digestion."
Lin Yutang

LEGUMES COOKED–YIELD CHART					
LEGUMES	**UNCOOKED**		**COOKED**		**RATIO OF UNCOOKED TO COOKED, IN CUPS**
	LBS.	CUPS	LBS.	CUPS	
Adzuki	1	$2^{1}/_{3}$	$3^{1}/_{2}$	7	1:3
Black Bean	1	$2^{1}/_{3}$	$3^{1}/_{2}$	6	1:25
Black-eyed Pea	1	$2^{1}/_{2}$	$3^{2}/_{4}$	7	1:28
Garbanzo	1	$2^{1}/_{2}$	$3^{1}/_{2}$	7	1:2.8
Great Northern	1	$2^{1}/_{3}$	$3^{1}/_{3}$	$6^{1}/_{4}$	1:2.7
Kidney	1	$2^{1}/_{3}$	3	$6^{3}/_{4}$	1:2.9
Lentil	1	$2^{1}/_{3}$	$4^{7}/_{8}$	$7^{3}/_{4}$	1:3.3
Lentil, red	1	$2^{1}/_{2}$	$4^{7}/_{8}$	$7^{3}/_{4}$	1:2.3
Lima	1	$2^{1}/_{3}$	$4^{1}/_{2}$	6	1:2.8
Mung	1	$2^{1}/_{3}$	$4^{1}/_{4}$	8	1:3.4
Navy	1	$2^{1}/_{4}$	$3^{1}/_{8}$	$6^{1}/_{2}$	1:2.9
Pinto	1	$2^{1}/_{3}$	$3^{1}/_{2}$	$6^{1}/_{4}$	1:2.7
Soldier	1	$2^{1}/_{3}$	3	$6^{1}/_{2}$	1:2.8
Soy	1	$2^{1}/_{2}$	3	$6^{1}/_{2}$	1:2.6
Split Pea, green	1	$2^{1}/_{2}$	$3^{1}/_{3}$	6	1:2.4
Split Pea, yellow	1	$2^{1}/_{2}$	$3^{1}/_{3}$	6	1:2.4
Yellow-eyed Bean	1	$2^{1}/_{3}$	$3^{1}/_{2}$	6	1:2.5

LEGUME FLAVORING CHART

	Adzuki	Black Bean	Black-Eyed Pea	Garbanzo	Great Northern	Kidney	Lentil	Mung	Lima	Navy	Pinto	Soldier	Soy	Split Pea	Yellow-Eye
Allspice	•	•		•	•		•	•	•	•		•	•	•	•
Anise															
Basil	•	•		•	•		•	•	•	•		•	•	•	•
Bay Leaf	•	•	•	•	•	•	•	•	•	•	•	•	•	•	•
Caraway			•	•	•	•					•	•			•
Cardamom		•									•				
Cayenne							•								
Celery Seed		•					•								
Chervil		•	•								•				•
Chili Pepper															
Chives	•	•		•	•		•	•	•	•	•	•	•	•	•
Cilantro	•	•	•	•	•	•	•	•	•	•	•	•	•		
Cinnamon			•			•					•				
Clove															
Coriander				•			•								
Currants				•			•	•		•			•		•
Curry	•						•	•					•		
Dill Seed															
Dill Weed															
Fennel		•													
Garlic	•	•		•	•		•	•	•	•		•	•	•	•
Ginger	•	•	•	•	•	•	•	•	•	•	•	•	•	•	•
Mace			•			•			•		•				
Marjoram															
Mint	•	•		•	•		•	•	•	•		•	•	•	•
Mustard	•	•	•	•	•		•	•	•	•	•	•	•	•	•
Nutmeg			•			•					•				
Onion	•	•		•	•		•	•	•	•		•	•	•	•
Oregano	•	•	•	•	•	•	•	•	•	•	•	•	•	•	•
Paprika			•			•					•				
Parsley	•	•		•	•		•	•	•	•		•	•	•	•
Pepper, black			•			•					•				
Pepper, white															
Poppy Seed	•	•		•	•		•					•	•		
Rosemary	•	•	•	•	•	•	•	•	•	•	•	•	•	•	•
Saffron			•	•		•					•				
Sage	•	•		•	•		•	•	•	•		•	•	•	•
Savory			•			•	•				•				
Sesame Seed															
Tarragon							•								
Thyme	•	•		•	•		•	•	•	•		•	•	•	•
Turmeric			•			•					•				
Barley Malt															
Maple Syrup															
Sweet Rice Wine															
Miso	•	•		•	•		•	•	•	•		•	•	•	•
Rice vinegar			•			•					•				
Tahini															
Tamari	•	•		•	•		•	•	•	•		•	•	•	•
Lemon		•	•			•					•				

ADZUKI BEANS

Pan size: 3 qt.	Yield: 10 cups	Yield:
Cooking time: 1 hr.	Serves: 10	Serves:
Oven temp.:	Portion: 1 cup	Portion:

Water	6 cups		Place in pot.
Kelp or kombu (rinsed)	10"		Add.
Adzuki beans	3⅓ cups		Add, simmer.
			Adjust water to keep beans covered.
Salt	1 tsp.		When 90% cooked, add; cook to completion, serve.

Variations: Add 3 cups buttercup squash for sweetness.
Add 2 Tbs. barley malt.
Presoak beans to reduce cooking time.

BLACK BEANS

Pan size: 4 qt.	Yield: 10 cups	Yield:
Cooking time: 1½ hrs.	Serves: 10	Serves:
Oven temp.:	Portion: 1 cup	Portion:

Black beans	4 cups		Place in pot.
Water	8 cups		Add.
Kelp or kombu	8"		Add. Bring to boil, fast simmer, cover. When 80% cooked, adjust water.
Salt	1 tsp.		Add.
Celery seed	1 tsp.		Add.
Fennel seed	1 tsp.		Add. Mix, cook to completion, serve.

Variations: Add ½"-diced celery.
Add ¼ cup fresh lemon juice and ½ cup olive oil on completion.
Garnish: chopped celery leaves, green onion, or cilantro.

BLACK-EYED PEAS (Texan)

	Yield: 10 cups	Yield:	Pan size: 4 qt.
	Serves: 10	Serves:	Cooking time: 50–60 mins.
	Portion: 1 cup	Portion:	Oven temp.:
Black-eyed peas	3 cups		Place in pot.
Water	8 cups		Add.
Kelp or kombu	8"		Add, bring to boil, simmer covered. Cook 80%. Adjust water.
Salt	1 tsp.		Add.
Celery, diced	2 cups		Add.
Onion, diced	1 cup		Add, mix, cook until done.

Variations: Garnish: chopped parsley, a few tomatoes for color, thyme, or a bay leaf.

FUL MEDAMIS (Arabic)

	Yield: 10 cups	Yield:	Pan size: 4 qt.
	Serves: 10	Serves:	Cooking time: 5–6 hrs.
	Portion: 1 cup	Portion:	Oven temp.:
Ful or fava beans, soaked overnight	3½ cups		Place in pan.
Water	7 cups		Add.
Onions, ½"-diced	1 cup		Add.
Red lentils	⅓ cup		Add.
Tomato, quartered	½ cup		Add, slow simmer, tightly covered, for 5–6 hrs. Adjust water.
Salt	1 tsp.		Add.
Cumin	½ tsp.		Add.
Garlic, finely diced	1 Tbs.		Add, mix, low simmer, covered, for 15 mins. Serve.

Variations: Garnish: olive oil, lemon juice, finely chopped parsley, mint, cardamom, cumin, or mint.

Pan size:	4 qt.	Yield:	10 cups	Yield:		**GARBANZO**
Cooking time:	2–2¹/₂ hrs.	Serves:	10	Serves:		**BEANS**
Oven temp.:		Portion:	1 cup	Portion:		

Garbanzo beans	3 cups		Place in pot.
Water	8 cups		Add.
Kelp or kombu	8"		Add. Bring to boil, simmer, cover. When 80% cooked, adjust water.
Onions, diced	3 cups		Add.
Carrots	1 cup		Add.
Salt	1 tsp.		Add, mix, cook to completion, serve.
			[NOTE: Mixture may be pureed to make a dip or spread.]

Variations: At end of cooking, add 1 Tbs. light sesame oil or 1 tsp. dark sesame oil.

Pan size:	4 qt.	Yield:	10 cups	Yield:		**GARBANZOS &**
Cooking time:	2–2¹/₂ hrs.	Serves:	10	Serves:		**GREENS**
Oven temp.:		Portion:	1 cup	Portion:		**(Armenian)**

Kelp or kombu	8"		Place in pot.
Garbanzo beans	3 cups		Add.
Water	8 cups		Add, bring to boil, simmer, cover. When 80% cooked, adjust water. Simmer, covered.
Onion, ¹/₂"-diced	2 cups		Place in skillet.
Olive oil	¹/₂ cup		Add; low heat.
Garlic, finely diced	1¹/₂ Tbs.		Add.
Salt	1¹/₂ tsp.		Add.
Pepper, black	1 tsp.		Add, mix, sautee; reserve.
Kale greens, 2" cut	1 lb.		Add to beans when cooked. Parcook greens. Pour off most of bean water. Add olive oil, mix. Serve hot, cold, or room temp.

Variations: Use Chinese cabbage.

[NOTE: This dish is best served the next day.]

GARBANZO (Hummus)

		Yield: 7 cups	Yield:	Pan size: 4 qt.
		Serves: 10	Serves:	Cooking time: 2–2½ hrs.
		Portion: .7 cup	Portion:	Oven temp.:

Kelp or kombu	8"		Place in pot.
Garbanzo beans and soak water	2 cups		Add, bring to boil, simmer, cover. When 90% cooked, adjust water.
Salt	2 tsp.		Add, mix, complete cooking.
			Cool bean pot in cold water. Reserve 12 selected whole beans for garnish. Place rest in blender.
Lemon juice (fresh)	1 cup		Add.
Tahini	⅔ cup		Add.
Garlic clove	2 lg.		Add.
Salt	1 tsp.		Add, blend until smooth. Adjust 4 flavorings so they taste equal and have a slightly acidic taste.

Variations: Add tamari instead of salt when blending.
Garnish: olive oil, paprika, chopped parsley.

GREAT NORTHERN BEANS (Italian)

		Yield: 10 cups	Yield:	Pan size: 4 qt.
		Serves: 10	Serves:	Cooking time: 1 hr.
		Portion: 1 cup	Portion:	Oven temp.:

Kelp or kombu	8"		Place in pot.
Great northern beans	3 cups		Add.
Water	9 cups		Add, bring to boil, simmer, cover. When 90% cooked, adjust water.
Onions, ½"-diced	3 cups		Add.
Celery with leaves, ½"-diced	2 cups		Add.
Cilantro or parsley stems, finely diced	1 cup		Add.
Garlic, finely diced	1 Tbs.		Add.
Tamari	2 Tbs.		Add, mix, cook to completion.
			Serve.

Variations: Garnish: chopped cilantro or green onion.
Add sliced zucchini 10 mins. before cooking ends.
Add ½ cup olive oil at end of cooking and mix.

Pan size: 4 qt.	Yield: 10 cups	Yield:	**KIDNEY BEANS,**
Cooking time: 1 hr.	Serves: 10	Serves:	**CURRIED**
Oven temp.:	Portion: 1 cup	Portion:	

Kelp or kombu	8"		Place in pot.
Kidney beans	3^1/$_2$ cups		Add.
Water	9 cups		Add, bring to boil, simmer, cover. Cook 90%, adjust water.
Onions, ^{1}/$_2$"-diced	2 cups		Add.
Garlic, finely diced	1 tsp.		Add.
Curry powder	1 Tbs.		Add.
Bay leaf, large	1		Add, mix, cook to completion; adjust curry.
			Serve.

Variations: Garnish with green onion.

Pan size: 4 qt.	Yield: 10 cups	Yield:	**KIDNEY BEANS**
Cooking time: 1 hr.	Serves: 10	Serves:	**("Red Beans &**
Oven temp.:	Portion: 1 cup	Portion:	**Rice," Cajun)**

Kelp or kombu	8"		Place in pot.
Kidney beans	3^1/$_2$ cups		Add.
Water	9 cups		Add.
Onions, ^{1}/$_2$"-diced	2 cups		Add, bring to boil, simmer, cover. Cook 90%; adjust water.
Onions, ^{1}/$_4$"-diced	3 cups		Add.
Garlic	1 Tbs.		Add.
Green pepper, ^{1}/$_4$"-diced	^{1}/$_2$ cup		Add.
Pepper, black and white	^{1}/$_4$ tsp. ea.		Add.
Pepper, cayenne	^{1}/$_8$ tsp.		Add.
Salt	1 tsp.		Add, mix, simmer to completion.
Rice flour			Adjust 80% water to a gravy.
			Serve in bowl over brown rice.

Variations: Garnish with green onion or cilantro.

LENTILS (BROWN OR GREEN)

		Yield:		Pan size: 4 qt.
	Yield: 10 cups	Serves:		Cooking time: 35–40 mins.
	Serves: 10	Portion:		Oven temp.:
	Portion: 1 cup			
Kelp or kombu	8"		Place in pot.	
Lentils (brown or green)	3½ cups		Add.	
Water	9 cups		Add, bring to boil, simmer, cover. Cook 90%; adjust water.	
Celery seed	2 tsp.		Add.	
Onions, ½"-diced	2 cups		Add.	
Carrots, ¼"-diced	1 cup		Add.	
Parsley stems, finely chopped	1 Tbs.		Add.	
Tamari	1½ Tbs.		Add, mix, cook to completion.	
			Serve.	

Variations: Garnish with chopped mint.
Use miso instead of tamari.

LENTIL STEW

		Yield:		Pan size: 4 qt.
	Yield: 10 cups	Serves:		Cooking time: 30–40 mins.
	Serves: 10	Portion:		Oven temp.:
	Portion: 1 cup			
Water	8 cups		Place in pan.	
Kelp, ¼"-chopped	6 sq. in.		Add.	
Lentils	2 cups		Add.	
Brown rice	1 cup		Add.	
Onions, ¼"-diced	1 cup		Add.	
Carrots, ¼"-diced	1 cup		Add, simmer 20 mins.	
Bay leaf	1		Add.	
Tarragon	½ tsp.		Add.	
Basil	¾ tsp.		Add.	
Lemon juice (fresh)	2 Tbs.		Add.	
Barley malt	2 Tbs.		Add.	
Rice vinegar	1 Tbs.		Add.	
Tamari	2 Tbs.		Add, mix, simmer 10 mins. Adjust; serve.	

Variations: Add olive oil.

LIMA BEANS (Dry)

Pan size:	4 qt.	Yield:	10 cups	Yield:	
Cooking time: 1½ hrs.		Serves:	10	Serves:	
Oven temp.:		Portion:	1 cup	Portion:	

Kelp or kombu	8"		Place in pot.
Lima beans	4 cups		Add.
Water	10 cups		Add, bring to boil, simmer, cover.
			Cook 90%; adjust water.
Onions, ½"-diced	2 cups		Add.
Tamari	2 Tbs.		Add.
Cumin, ground	2 Tbs.		Add.
Caraway seed	1 Tbs.		Add, mix, cook to completion.
			Serve.

Variations: Garnish with cilantro leaves.

MUNG BEANS ("Dahl," Indian)

Pan size:	4 qt.	Yield:	10 cups	Yield:	
Cooking time: 50–60 mins.		Serves:	10	Serves:	
Oven temp.:		Portion:	1 cup	Portion:	

Kelp or kombu	8"		Place in pot.
Mung beans	3 cups		Add.
Water	9 cups		Add, bring to boil, simmer, cover. Cook 90%; adjust water.
Salt	1 tsp.		Add.
Turmeric	1½ tsp.		Add.
Ginger, grated	1 tsp.		Add.
Lemon juice	4 tsp.		Add.
Cardamom, ground	1 tsp.		Add.
Coriander	2 Tbs.		Add, mix, cook to completion.
Corn oil	½ cup		Place in pan.
Onions, ¼"-diced	3 cups		Add.
Cumin seed	2 Tbs.		Add, saute until golden. When beans are cooked, add oil and onions. Serve.

Variations:

NAVY BEANS (Baked Beans)

	Yield: 10 cups	Yield:	Pan size: 4 qt.
	Serves: 10	Serves:	Cooking time: 2 hrs.
	Portion: 1 cup	Portion:	Oven temp.: 325°
Kelp	8"		Place in pot.
Navy beans	4 cups		Add.
Water	10 cups		Add, bring to boil, then simmer, covered, until cooked (about 1 hr.).
			Adjust water; remove from heat.
Corn oil	1/4 cup		Place in pan.
Onions, 1/2"-diced	2 cups		Add, saute until clear.
Barley malt	1 cup		Add.
Tamari	3 Tbs.		Add.
Mustard, prepared	3 Tbs.		Add, mix, saute 2 mins. Add to beans, mix, cover.
			Bake at 325° for 1 hour.
			Serve.

Variations: Use miso instead of tamari.

PINTO BEANS

	Yield: 10 cups	Yield:	Pan size: 4 qt.
	Serves: 10	Serves:	Cooking time: 1–1 1/2 hrs.
	Portion: 1 cup	Portion:	Oven temp.:
Kelp or kombu	8"		Place in pot.
Pinto beans	3 3/4 cups		Add.
Water	9 cups		Add, bring to boil, simmer, cover. When 90% cooked, adjust water.
Celery seed	1 1/2 tsp.		Add.
Tamari	3 Tbs.		Add.
Cardamom	1 Tbs.		Add.
Caraway seed	1 Tbs.		Add, mix, cook to completion.
			Serve.

Variations: Add 2 Tbs. finely cut cilantro stems with tamari.
Mix onions and garlic sauteed in olive oil in the last minute of cooking.
Add coriander or cumin with tamari.
Mash and fry in soy oil for refried beans.

Pan size: 4 qt.	Yield: 10 cups	Yield:	**SOLDIER BEANS**
Cooking time: 1½ hrs.	Serves: 10	Serves:	
Oven temp.:	Portion: 1 cup	Portion:	
Kelp or kombu	8"		Place in pot.
Soldier beans	3½ cups		Add.
Water	9 cups		Add, bring to boil, simmer, cover.
			Cook 90%; adjust water.
Bay leaf	1 lg.		Add.
Tamari	3 Tbs.		Add.
Caraway	2 tsp.		Add, mix, cook to completion.
			Serve.

Variations: Garnish with chopped green onion or parsley.

Pan size: 4 qt.	Yield: 10 cups	Yield:	**SOY BEANS**
Cooking time: 3–4 hrs.	Serves: 10	Serves:	
Oven temp.:	Portion: 1 cup	Portion:	
Kelp or kombu	12"		Place in pot.
Water	16 cups		Bring to rolling boil.
Soy beans	4 cups		Add so that water does not stop boiling.
			When 95% cooked, adjust water.
Onions, ½"-chopped	2 cups		Add.
Red lentils	½ cup		Add, cook 30 mins.
Celery seed	1 tsp.		Add.
Tarragon	1 tsp.		Add.
Fennel	1 tsp.		Add.
Barley malt	½ cup		Add.
Salt	1 tsp.		Add, mix, cook 10 mins. Serve.

Variations: Add 2 cups bite-sized carrots, near end of cooking.
Add ½ cup barley malt.
Thicken water with whole wheat flour slurry.
It is preferable to pressure cook soy beans for 55 mins.

VEGETARIAN CHILI

	Yield: 10 cups	Yield:	Pan size: 4 qt.
	Serves: 10	Serves:	Cooking time: 1¼ hrs.
	Portion: 1 cup	Portion:	Oven temp.:

Beans, pinto or kidney	2½ cups		Rinse, soak overnight. Rinse, place in pan.
Kelp, rinsed, ½"-chopped	6 sq. in.		Add.
Water	10 cups		Add, simmer, covered, until 80% cooked.
Carrots, ¼"-diced	1 cup		Add.
Bell pepper, red, ¼"-diced	½ cup		Add.
Bell pepper, green, ¼"-diced	½ cup		Add.
Onions, ¼"-diced	2 cups		Add.
Garlic, minced	2 Tbs.		Add.
Cumin, cayenne pepper	¼ tsp. ea.		Add.
Coriander	¼ tsp.		Add.
Salt	1 tsp.		Add.
Parsley leaves, ¼"-chopped	½ cup		Add, mix, adjust. Cook to completion. Serve.

Variations:

[This recipe tested and approved by Chris Quilty, Chef Instructor at New England Culinary Institute.]

YELLOW-EYED BEANS

	Yield: 10 cups	Yield:	Pan size: 4 qt.
	Serves: 10	Serves:	Cooking time: 30–50 mins.
	Portion: 1 cup	Portion:	Oven temp.:

Kelp or kombu	8"		Place in pot.
Yellow-eyed beans	4 cups		Add.
Water	9 cups		Add, bring to boil, cover, simmer. When 90% cooked, adjust water.
Mace	1 tsp.		Add.
Marjoram	1 tsp.		Add.
Salt	1 tsp.		Add, mix, complete cooking.
			Serve.

Variations:

MILK

Pan size: Cooking time: Oven temp.:	Yield: 10 cups Serves: 10 Portion: 1 cup	Yield: _____ Serves: _____ Portion: _____	**ALMOND MILK**
Almonds	1 cup		Place in blender. Blend to powder.
Water	1 cup		Add, blend 1 min., adjust. Stop.
Rice (cooked)	1 cup		Add, blend 1 min., stop.
Water	1 cup		Add, blend 1 min., stop.
Salt	1/4 tsp.		Add.
Water	6 cups		Add.
Barley malt	1 Tbs.		Add.
Vanilla extract	3/4 tsp.		Add, blend 1 min. Adjust. Serve.

Variations: Strain in cheesecloth.

Pan size: Cooking time: Oven temp.:	Yield: 10 cups Serves: 10 Portion: 1 cup	Yield: _____ Serves: _____ Portion: _____	**BARLEY MILK**
Barley or whole oats (hot, well cooked, not dry)	1 cup		Place in blender.
Water, hot	1 cup		Add, pulse, blend 1 min., stop.
Water	8 cups		Add.
Salt	1/2 tsp.		Add, blend. Serve. [NOTE: Use in place of liquid in many soups.]

Variations: Deluxe: blend 1/4 cup walnuts, 1/4 cup raisins or prunes, 2 Tbs. rice syrup, and pinch of salt with barley malt. Use for cereal cream.
Cook fennel seed with oats to increase lactation.

[This recipe tested and approved by Chris Quilty, Chef Instructor at New England Culinary Institute.]

ROLLED OATS MILK

	Yield: 5 cups	Yield:	Pan size:
	Serves: 10	Serves:	Cooking time:
	Portion: 1/2 cup	Portion:	Oven temp.:
Rolled oats, cooked	1 cup		Place in blender.
Water	1 cup		Add, blend at high speed 1 min. Stop.
Water	3 cups		Add, blend. Adjust.
			Serve.

Variations: Thicken for use on cereal.
Thin more for drinking milk.
Add roasted nuts and/or raisins for first blend.
Cook fennel seed with oats to increase lactation.

TOFU MILK (for cooking)

	Yield: 4 cups	Yield:	Pan size:
	Serves:	Serves:	Cooking time:
	Portion:	Portion:	Oven temp.:
Tofu	1/2 lb.		Break up, place in blender.
Water	1 cup		Add, blend smooth.
Water	2 cups		Add, blend smooth.
			Use.
			[NOTE: Less water will give a cream-like consistency.]

Variations:

MISCELLANEOUS

Pan size:	4 qt.	Yield:	10 cups	Yield:		**BURGERS, RICE**
Cooking time:	75 mins.	Serves:	10	Serves:		
Oven temp.:	550°	Portion:	6 balls	Portion:		

Brown rice	1 cup		Place in pan.
Lentils	1 cup		Add.
Water	7 cups		Add, cook 40 mins.
Onions, 1/2"-diced	2 cups		Add.
Tamari	3 Tbs.		Add.
Thyme	1 tsp.		Add.
Sage	1 1/4 tsp.		Add.
Celery seed	1 1/4 tsp.		Add, mix, simmer 15 mins.
Whole wheat pastry flour	3 Tbs.		Add, turn off heat. Drain and reduce excess water.
Rolled oat flakes	2 cups		Place in bowl.
			Add rice, etc., above.
			Mix, mash, and squeeze by hand.
			Rest 20 mins. and mix by hand every 5 mins. for correct consistency.
			Using salted corn oil, place and shape patties about 1/2" thick with oiled fingers on well-oiled pan.
			Pat top with coat of oil.
			Bake 10 mins. on each side until browned.

Variations: Add chopped parsley or cilantro at end of cooking.
Make 3/4" to 1" balls.

CHINESE EGG ROLLS

Yield: 96 egg rolls	*Yield:* _____	*Pan size:*
Serves: _____	*Serves:* _____	*Cooking time:*
Portion:	*Portion:*	*Oven temp.:*

Onions, coarsely grated	9 cups		Place in bowl.
Celery, coarsely grated	9 cups		Add, blanch, place in colander to dry; reserve.
Cabbage, coarsely grated	18 cups		Add, blanch, place in colander to dry; reserve.
Carrot, finely grated	2 cups		Add to onions.
Garlic powder	2 Tbs.		Add.
Ginger, ground	$1\frac{1}{2}$ Tbs.		Add.
Five Spices	$1\frac{1}{2}$ Tbs.		Add.
Sea salt	$1\frac{1}{2}$ Tbs.		Add, mix.
Egg roll wrappers	96		Place on table with one corner toward you.
			Add $\frac{1}{3}$ cup mix to near center. Fold right and left corners together, leaving desired length on table. Lift near corner over mix and roll to far corner.
Eggs, beaten	2		Cover last 3" of wrapper with egg inside and complete roll. Reserve.
Peanut oil, new	1 gal.		Deep fry, hand turning until dark gold; remove to cake rack.
			Drain and serve.

Variations:

CRUMB TOPPING

Yield: 5 cups	*Yield:* _____	*Pan size:*
Serves: _____	*Serves:* _____	*Cooking time:*
Portion:	*Portion:*	*Oven temp.:*

Whole wheat pastry flour	4 cups		Place in bowl.
Salt	$\frac{3}{4}$ tsp.		Add.
Cinnamon	$\frac{1}{4}$ tsp.		Add.
Clove	$\frac{1}{4}$ tsp.		Add.
Nutmeg	$\frac{1}{4}$ tsp.		Add.
Walnuts, $\frac{1}{8}$"-chopped	$\frac{1}{2}$ cup		Add, mix.
Oil, safflower	$\frac{1}{2}$ cup		Add.
Barley malt	$\frac{3}{4}$ cup		Add, mix by hand until mixture feels gritty and crumbly. Spread evenly. Pat lightly and bake.

Variations: Use as a top crust on fruit or winter squash pie.

Pan size:	Yield:	6 cups	Yield:		**FRENCH TOAST, EGGLESS DIP**
Cooking time:	Serves:	10	Serves:		
Oven temp.:	Portion:	.6 cup	Portion:		[from Lora Gould, Chef, Stowe, Vt.].
Tofu, cooked		1 lb.			Place in blender.
Water		4 cups			Add.
Turmeric		1/2 tsp.			Add.
Rice syrup		1 cup			Add.
Salt		1/2 tsp.			Add, blend smooth, adjust. Use (for 10 pieces of bread).

Variations: Add barley malt or cinnamon.

Pan size:	Yield:	9 cups	Yield:		**GRANOLA**
Cooking time: 8 mins.	Serves:	10	Serves:		
Oven temp.: 350°	Portion:	.9 cups	Portion:		
Barley malt		1/2 cup			Place in bowl.
Water, hot		1/4 cup			Add, mix.
Salt		1 1/2 tsp.			Add.
Vanilla extract		2 tsp.			Add.
Corn oil		1/2 cup			Add, mix, reserve.
Walnuts, chopped		1/2 cup			Place in bowl.
Sunflower seeds		1 cup			Add.
Rolled oats		6 cups			Add.
Liquid, above					Add, mix, spread 1/2" thick on baking pan. Bake about 8 mins. Turn twice with spatula until light golden brown. Cool completely.
Raisins		1 cup			Add, mix; store in airtight container.

Variations:

GRANOLA SUPREME

	Yield: 4 cups	Yield:	Pan size: 9½ × 13"
	Serves:	Serves:	Cooking time: 12 mins.
	Portion:	Portion:	Oven temp.: 350°

Rolled oats	1½ cups		Place in bowl.
Whole wheat pastry bran flour	⅓ cup		Add.
Sunflower seeds	¼ cup		Add.
Sesame seeds	¼ cup		Add.
Walnuts	¼ cup		Add, mix, reserve.
Oil (corn, soy)	⅓ cup		Place in pan, heat; don't boil.
Maple syrup	⅓ cup		Add.
Vanilla extract	1 Tbs.		Add.
Salt	⅛ tsp.		Add.
Cinnamon	½ tsp.		Add.
Dry ingredients, above			Add, mix. Place in oven. Bake about 12 mins. Turn twice with spatula until light golden brown. Cool completely.
Raisins	1 cup		Add, mix, serve. Store in airtight container.

Variations: Substitute or add diced filberts.
Substitute ½ cup barley malt for maple syrup.
Substitute or add spices, caraway seeds, anise.

Pan size:	Yield:	10 pancakes	Yield:		**PANCAKES**
Cooking time:	Serves:	5	Serves:		
Oven temp.:	Portion:	2 pancakes	Portion:		

Tofu	¹/₂ lb.		Place in blender.
Water	¹/₂ cup		Add; blend until smooth; stop.
Corn oil	¹/₄ cup		Add.
Barley malt	¹/₂ cup		Add.
Salt	¹/₂ tsp.		Add; blend until smooth; stop.
Rice vinegar	1 tsp.		Add.
Water	2¹/₄ cups		Add.
Whole wheat pastry flour	3 cups		Add.
Baking powder	1 Tbs.		Add; blend until smooth.
			Pour ¹/₂-cup portions of batter in a circular fashion on hot oiled grill or skillet to make 7" diam. pancakes; adjust heat.
			When color turns from batter to wet, darker tan and gets air holes, flip over.
			Punch air holes in bubbles.
			Punch 8 holes over surface of pancake.
			When it stops steaming, flip again if necessary.
			[NOTE: Flip pancakes on the brink of burning.]

Variations: Add fresh berries or sliced seasonal fruit to batter.
Substitute 1 cup oat bran for 1 cup flour.

[This recipe tested and approved by Chris Quilty, Chef Instructor at New England Culinary Institute.]

PIZZA CRUST

		Yield:	Pan size: 2 9 × 13"
Yield: 2 9 × 13"		Serves:	Cooking time: 30 mins.
Serves: 24		Portion:	Oven temp.: 375°
Portion: 3 × 4¹/₄"			

Whole wheat pastry flour	1¹/₂ cups		Place in bowl.
Unbleached flour	1 cup		Add.
Salt	³/₄ tsp.		Add, mix.
Water	1 cup		Add.
Sesame oil, dark	1 Tbs.		Add, mix by hand.
			Knead until smooth.
			Place in oiled pan; cover, rest 30 mins.
			Divide in half by weight. Roll or hand roll into oiled and corn meal floured baking pans.
			Bake 30 mins. at 375°.

Variations: Sprinkle and pat sesame seeds on edge of crust before baking.

PIZZA FILLING

		Yield:	Pan size:
Yield: 2 9 × 13"		Serves:	Cooking time: 25 mins.
Serves: 24		Portion:	Oven temp.: 375°
Portion: 3 × 4¹/₄"			

Tofu	¹/₂ lb.		Place in blender.
Water	¹/₂ cup		Add.
Sesame oil, dark	¹/₄ cup		Add; blend until smooth.
Onions, thinly sliced	¹/₂ cup		Add.
Celery, diced	1 cup		Add; blend until smooth.
Parsnips, diced	1 cup		Add.
Salt	¹/₄ tsp.		Add.
Green pepper	¹/₄ cup		Add; blend.
			Place in pot; simmer 15 mins. Stop cooking.
Green onion, diced	¹/₂ cup		Add.
Green pepper, diced	¹/₄ cup		Add.
Black olives, diced	¹/₄ cup		Add, mix, pour onto crust. Bake 10 mins. at 375°.

Variations:

Pan size:	Yield:	1 cup	Yield:		**SOUR CREAM, TOFU**
Cooking time:	Serves:	10	Serves:		
Oven temp.:	Portion:	.6 Tbs.	Portion:		

Tofu	$^1/_2$ lb.		Place in blender or food processor.
Lemon juice (fresh)	3 Tbs.		Add.
Salt	$^3/_4$ tsp.		Add.
Water	$^1/_4$ cup		Add, pulse, blend until smooth.
			Adjust: add hot water or more salt to neutralize lemon.
			Cover, refrigerate; serve.

Variations:

Pan size:	Yield:	1$^3/_4$ cups	Yield:		**SUNFLOWER BUTTER**
Cooking time:	Serves:	10	Serves:		
Oven temp.:	Portion:	2.8 Tbs.	Portion:		

Water	1 cup		Place in blender.
Tamari	1 Tbs.		Add.
Corn oil	1 Tbs.		Add.
Sunflower seeds	1 cup		Add, blend until smooth.
			Adjust; serve.

Variations: Roast sunflower seeds first.

TEMPEH BACON

Yield:	1 lb.	Yield:		Pan size:
Serves:	10	Serves:		Cooking time: 8 mins.
Portion:	1.6 oz.	Portion:		Oven temp.:

Oil (safflower, sesame, or corn)	½ cup		Place in pan.
Salt	½ tsp.		Add, mix.
Tempeh, cut ⅛–³/₁₆"	1 lb.		Saute on medium heat until golden tan on both sides.
			Drain twice on towels.
			Serve.

Variations: Garnish with Oriental Dip, Basic (pg. 144).

TEMPEH, BAKED

Yield:	2 lbs.	Yield:		Pan size:
Serves:	10	Serves:		Cooking time: 20+/- mins.
Portion:	3.2 oz.	Portion:		Oven temp.: 400°

Water	1 cup		Place in bowl.
Tamari	½ cup		Add.
Tempeh, ½"-sliced	2 lbs.		Ad, rest 30 mins. Place on oiled baking pan. Bake 10 mins., turn. Bake until almost crisp.
			Serve immediately.

Variations: Add grated ginger to tamari.

Pan size:	Yield: 1 lb.	Yield:	**TOFU, BAKED**
Cooking time: 15 mins.	Serves: 10	Serves:	**("Oriental**
Oven temp.: 300°	Portion: 1.6 oz.	Portion:	**Delight")**

Tofu	1 lb.		Cut in half; make ¹/₂" slices. Lay on dry towel; cover and pat. Repeat on dry towel 2 times. Rest in towel for 10 mins.
Miso	¹/₄ cup		Place in bowl.
Tahini	¹/₄ cup		Add.
Water	¹/₄ cup		Add.
Sesame seeds, roasted	¹/₄ cup		Add, mix and mash. Adjust water for thin, spreadable paste.
			Spread on half of tofu slices. Cover spread with unspread slices.
Nori sheet	1		Cut in ¹/₂" strips. Wrap one strip around each miso sandwich with ends on bottom.
			Bake; serve.

Variations:

Pan size:	Yield: 1 lb.	Yield:	**TOFU, BROILED,**
Cooking time: varies	Serves: 10	Serves:	**SPICED**
Oven temp.: broiler, near high	Portion: 1.6 oz.	Portion:	

Tamari	¹/₃ cup		Place in blender.
Garlic, finely diced	1 Tbs.		Add.
Mustard powder	1 tsp.		Add.
Curry powder	1 tsp.		Add.
Tahini	¹/₄ cup		Add; blend until smooth. Place in bowl. Reserve.
Tofu, dried	1 lb.		Cut in half. Make ¹/₄–³/₈" slices.
			Dip in tamari mixture. Place on oiled baking pan. Broil each side until a little crispy.
			Serve.

Variations: Cut slices on diagonal.

TOFU MARINADE I (Oriental)

		Yield:		Pan size:
Yield: 1 lb.		Yield:		Pan size:
Serves: 10		Serves:		Cooking time:
Portion: 1.6 oz.		Portion:		Oven temp.:

Oriental Dip, Basic (pg. 144)	1 batch		Place in jar.
Tofu, towel dried, 3/4"-diced	1 lb.		Add; seal lid. Roll jar to distribute contents.
			Refrigerate 24 hrs.
			Roll every 6–8 hrs.
			Serve.

Variations:

TOFU MARINADE II (Lebanese)

		Yield:		Pan size:
Yield: 1 lb.		Yield:		Pan size:
Serves: 10		Serves:		Cooking time:
Portion: 1.6 oz.		Portion:		Oven temp.:

Lebanese Dressing (pg. 245)	1 batch		Place in jar.
Tofu, towel dried, 3/4"-diced	1 lb.		Add; seal lid.
			Roll jar to distribute contents.
			Refrigerate 24 hrs.
			Roll every 6 hours.
			Drain and serve.

Variations:

TOFU, SCRAMBLED

Pan size:	Yield:	3 lbs.	Yield:	
Cooking time:	Serves:	10	Serves:	
Oven temp.:	Portion:	4.8 oz.	Portion:	

Oil (light safflower or sesame)	¹/₄ cup	Place in skillet, heat.
Onions, finely diced	2 cups	Add.
Celery, very finely diced	2 cups	Add.
Carrot, finely grated	¹/₂ cup	Add; saute. Turn heat higher.
Tofu, hand crumbled	3 lbs.	Add, mash, mix.
Water	2 Tbs.	Add, mix, cover and steam.
Turmeric	2–3 tsp.	Add; mix to obtain desired color.
		Serve.

Variations: Saute garlic, green pepper.
Add ¹/₄ cup Tofu Mayonnaise (pg. 245) for creaminess.
Add and adjust herbs and spices; and/or add tamari.
Use as sandwich spread.

TOFU POUCHES

Pan size:	Yield:	1 lb.	Yield:	
Cooking time:	Serves:	10	Serves:	
Oven temp.:	Portion:	1.6 oz.	Portion:	

Tofu	1 lb.	Squeeze out excess water without cracking tofu.
		Slice ⁵/₁₆" thick.
		Lay on dry cloth and cover with another dry cloth. Hand pat and let sit 20 mins. Repeat with new dry cloths.
Oil (safflower or sesame)	2 cups	Deep-fry tofu in oil at 350°until golden brown. Remove; place on cake rack.
		Heat oil to 450°. Deep fry for 2 mins. Remove to flat surface. Gently roll with rolling pin. Cut in half. Gently open pouch by pulling 2 crusts apart and stuff with desired stuffing.

Variations: Use 5%+/- dark sesame oil for a nut-like flavor.

QUICHE, VEGETABLE

	Yield:	9" pie	Yield:		Pan size:	9" pie
	Serves:	6	Serves:		Cooking time:	20+/- mins.
	Portion:		Portion:		Oven temp.:	350°

Prebaked pie crust, pp. 223–224			Reserve.
Olive oil	3 Tbs.		Place in skillet.
Carrots, 1/4"-diced	2 Tbs.		Add, saute 5 mins.
Onion, 1/2"-diced	1/4 cup		Add; saute to 50% clear.
Garlic, minced	1 tsp.		Add.
Mushrooms, thinly sliced	1/2 cup		Add, mix, saute 3 mins.
Broccoli, small florets	1/2 cup		Add.
Celery seed	1/4 tsp.		Add, mix, saute until all is par-cooked.
Tofu	1/2 lb.		Place in blender.
Salt	1/2 tsp.		Add.
Turmeric	pinch		Add.
Nutmeg	pinch		Add.
Water	1 3/4 cups		Add, blend smooth.
Vegetables, above			Place in pie shell, distribute evenly.
Tofu mixture, above			Add.
Variations:			Bake, turn off heat. Rest in oven 15 mins.; serve.

YOGURT

	Yield:	10 cups	Yield:		Pan size:	
	Serves:	10	Serves:		Cooking time:	
	Portion:	1 cup	Portion:		Oven temp.:	

Milk	10 cups		Place in pot with heavy bottom. Slowly bring to boil. Immediately remove from heat; rest.
Yogurt, commercial	3 Tbs.		Place in 3 paper towels in soup bowl to remove excess liquid. Remove towels, stir until smooth.
			Place scum from heated milk and 1 Tbs. milk on starter and mix.
			When milk is 115°, add starter to milk and mix. Place in warm oven overnight.
			Refrigerate; serve.
Variations:			

MUFFINS

Pan size: 2¼" muf.	Yield: 10⅓ cups	Yield:	**ALL-AROUND**
Cooking time: 20 mins.	Serves: 10	Serves:	**MUFFINS**
Oven temp.: 375°	Portion: 2¼" muf.	Portion:	

Whole wheat pastry flour	2½ cups		Place in bowl.
Corn meal	1 cup		Add.
Baking powder	4 tsp.		Add.
Salt	¼ tsp.		Add, mix, reserve.
Raisins	1 cup		Place in blender.
Water	1¼ cups		Add, pulse, blend smooth.
Tofu	¼ lb.		Add; blend smooth.
Corn oil	½ cup		Add; blend smooth.
			Add to flour mixture. Place ⅓ (scant) cup batter in oiled muffin forms. Bake 20 mins. at 375°. Rest in pan 5 mins. to cool.
			Place on side or on cake rack.
			Serve.

Variations: Add singly or in combination, making 1 cup: blueberries, cranberries, nuts, raisins, seeds; and/or add vanilla or almond extract.
Instead of corn meal, use unbleached whole wheat flour, rolled oats, or bran.
Use apple cider instead of water.

Pan size: 2¼" muf.	Yield: 12	Yield:	**BRAN MUFFINS**
Cooking time: 30 mins.	Serves: 12	Serves:	
Oven temp.: 325°	Portion: 1	Portion:	

Whole wheat bread flour	3 cups		Place in bowl.
Bran	2 cups		Add.
Baking powder	1 Tbs.		Add.
Salt	½ tsp.		Add, mix, reserve.
Raisins	¼ cup		Place in bowl.
Water	2 cups		Add.
Oil	¼ cup		Add.
Maple syrup	⅓ cup		Add, mix, add to flour mixture. Spoon into muffin pan. Bake until done; rest in pan 10 mins.
			Remove to cake rack; serve.

Variations: Add ¼ cup sunflower seeds; and/or lemon zest, walnuts, hazelnuts, other seeds.
Substitute apple juice for water; or barley malt for maple syrup.
Add vanilla or almond extract, tahini, raisins. Or use onion and oregano.

CAMPER'S MUFFINS

Yield: 12	Yield:	Pan size: 2½" muf.	
Serves: 12	Serves:	Cooking time: 27 mins.	
Portion: 1	Portion:	Oven temp.: 375°	

Whole wheat bread flour	2 cups		Place in bowl.
Whole wheat pastry flour	1 cup		Add.
Corn meal	½ cup		Add.
Rolled oats, uncooked	¾ cup		Add.
Baking powder	1 Tbs.		Add.
Anise seed	½ tsp.		Add.
Salt	½ tsp.		Add.
Five Spices	½ tsp.		Add, mix; reserve.
Oil	½ cup		Place in bowl.
Tahini	¼ cup		Add.
Maple syrup	½ cup		Add.
Water	1½ cups		Add.
Vanilla extract	1 Tbs.		Add, mix; reserve.
Walnuts, roasted	1 cup		Place in bowl.
Raisins	⅓ cup		Add.
Sesame seeds, roasted	¼ cup		Add.
Sunflower seeds, roasted	¼ cup		Add.
Pumpkin seeds, roasted	¼ cup		Add; mix. Pour liquids on flour; add nuts; mix.
			Place in oiled baking tins. Bake 27 mins. at 375°.
			Cook on cake rack; serve.

Variations:

Pan size: 2½" muf.	Yield: 72 muffins	Yield: _____	**CARROT MUFFINS**
Cooking time: 28 mins.	Serves: 72	Serves: _____	[from Vermont Natural Foods, Marshfield, Vt.]
Oven temp.: 325°	Portion: 1	Portion: _____	

Whole wheat flour	8 cups		Place in bowl.
Unbleached flour	5 cups		Add.
Corn meal	1 cup		Add.
Pecan meal	1 cup		Add.
Cashew meal	1 cup		Add.
Coconut	2 cups		Add.
Baking powder	6 Tbs.		Add.
Sesame seeds	1 cup		Add.
Salt	4 tsp.		Add.
Allspice, cinnamon, cloves, ginger, nutmeg	1 tsp. ea.		Add, mix; reserve.
Water, hot	4 cups		Place in bowl.
Barley malt	3 cups		Add, mix.
Vanilla extract	½ cup		Add.
Tahini	1 cup		Add.
Maple syrup	3 cups		Add.
Oil	2 cups		Add.
Carrots, grated	6 cups		Add.
Orange peel, grated	3 Tbs.		Add, mix; reserve.
Walnuts, whole	6 cups		Place in bowl.
Dates, flour-covered or ¼"-chopped	2 cups		Add.
Figs, ¼"-chopped	1 cup		Add.
Raisins	4 cups		Add.
Sunflower seeds	2 cups		Add, mix. Add to liquid, mix. Add to flour, mix.
			Place in muffin pans with liner.
			Bake 28 mins. at 325°.
			Cool, serve.
			[NOTE: Refrigerator shelf life in airtight container is 3 weeks.]

Variations: Bake with 3–4" batter in loaf pan at lower temp. for a longer time.

OATMEAL RAISIN NUT MUFFINS	Yield:	12 muffins	Yield:		Pan size:	2½" muf.
	Serves:	12	Serves:		Cooking time:	25 mins.
	Portion:	1 muffin	Portion:		Oven temp.:	375°
Whole wheat bread flour	3 cups			Place in bowl.		
Rolled oats, uncooked	1 cup			Add.		
Salt	½ tsp.			Add.		
Baking powder	2 tsp.			Add.		
Cinnamon	½ tsp.			Add; reserve.		
Tofu	½ lb.			Place in blender.		
Apple juice	1½ cups			Add.		
Vanilla extract	4 tsp.			Add.		
Tahini	¼ cup			Add.		
Oil	½ cup			Add.		
Walnuts	½ cup			Add.		
Raisins	¼ cup			Add, mix, place in oiled muffin pans.		
				Bake; cool; serve.		

Variations: Add ¼ cup sesame seeds and ¼ sunflower seeds, instead of nuts.
Use maple syrup instead of juice.

	Yield:		Yield:		Pan size:	
	Serves:		Serves:		Cooking time:	
	Portion:		Portion:		Oven temp.:	

Variations:

NUTS AND SEEDS

ROASTING NUTS

Cold ingredients and/or thick roasting pan will increase roasting time. After removing from oven, spread on cool pan.

Room Temperature	Thin Baking Pan	Room Temperature	Thin Baking Pan
Nuts:		*Seeds:*	
Almonds	7 mins. at 350°	Pumpkin	7 mins. at 350°
Filberts	7 mins. at 350°	Sesame	9 mins. at 350°
Pecans	4 mins. at 350°	Sunflower	12 mins. at 350°
Walnuts	7 mins. at 350°		

NUTS, SPICED

Pan size:
Cooking time: 9 mins.
Oven temp.: 350°

Yield: 1 cups
Serves: 10
Portion: 1.6 Tbs.

Yield:
Serves:
Portion:

Whole wheat pastry flour	2 Tbs.		Place in bowl.
Cinnamon	¼ tsp.		Add.
Allspice	pinch		Add.
Ginger, ground	pinch		Add.
Nutmeg	pinch		Add.
Cloves	pinch		Add, mix.
Maple syrup	2 Tbs.		Add, mix.
Nuts (almonds, filberts, walnuts)	1 cup		Add, mix.

Spread on oiled baking pan so that nuts are not touching each other.

Bake 5 mins.; turn. Bake another 4 mins.; turn.

Cool; serve.

Variations: Use warm barley malt instead of maple syrup.
Substitute nuts and seeds according to roasting time (see chart above).
Add salt.

PASTA

GENERAL DESCRIPTION

A general guideline for good uncooked pasta is that it should be gray, tan, or yellow in color; make a sharp, clean break; and be very hard, brittle, and springy/flexible.

When cooked, it should be firm, and able to hold its shape well.

There are many shapes of pasta, the more common of which are *elbow macaroni, fettuccine, lasagna, spaghetti,* and *vermicelli* (many are made of beans or rice from the Orient, and sometimes are translucent).

IMPORTANT GUIDELINES FOR PASTA COOKERY

Cooking:

• Add pasta to rolling boil; do not disrupt rolling boil and cook uncovered *al dente* (for serving).

• Parcook for casseroles that will be baked for 30+/- mins.

• At the end of cooking process, pour off cook water and do one of the following:

  —*Serve immediately:* coat pasta with olive oil and serve.

  —*Serve hot:* quick-rinse in hot water and return to pot.

  —*Serve cold or reserve for later use:* rinse in hot water to remove the starch that makes pasta stick together, and then rinse in cold water to cool it.

• When cooking large quantities, cool in cold water to stop cooking.

• If pasta sticks together, place in simmering water and it will separate.

• To cook, add pasta to 4 times (in volume) rolling boiling water; cover and simmer until done.

• Gently stir a few times to keep from sticking to each other and the bottom of the pan.

Serving:

• Serve freshly cooked.

• Pasta does not hold well when hot; it tends to stick.

• Add a little oil or sauce immediately after cooking to prevent sticking.

NOTE: the common practice of adding oil at the beginning of cooking is nutritionally less desirable than the methods mentioned above, which provide for minimum cooking time for the oil.

Compatible Sauces for Pasta

(These can be found under Dips, pp. 139–147; Sauces, pp. 252–267.)

Bitter:

Parsley–Tofu Sauce; Verte Sauce.

Pungent:

Spaghetti Sauce, Broccoli; Curry Sauce; Garlic–Parsley Sauce; Ginger–Tamari Sauce; Hollandaise, Mock.

Salty:

Brown Rice Sauce; Seitan Sauce; Miso–Tahini Sauce, Basic; Onion–Tamari Sauce; Tofu–Miso Sauce.

Rich Natural Flavor:

Cauliflower, Tahini Dip; Mushroom Dip; Tofu Salad, re-mashed and thinned.

Garnish Alternatives

Broccoli, fine florets

Carrots, finely diced, parcooked

Celery, finely diced

Cilantro, finely diced

Green onion, finely diced

Olives, chopped or sliced

Onions, finely diced

Sesame seeds, roasted

Tempeh bacon, 1/2"-chopped

Tofu, marinated

Thyme, fresh; finely diced

Pan size:	6 qt.	Yield:	10 cups	Yield:		**NOODLES, WHOLE WHEAT**
Cooking time:	15 mins.	Serves:	10	Serves:		
Oven temp.:		Portion:	1 cup	Portion:		

Water ×3.5	21 cups		Place in pot; warm.
Salt	1 Tbs.		Add, bring to rolling boil.
Whole wheat elbow noodles (1.3 lbs.)	6 cups		Add; cook *al dente*.
			Pour off cook water; rinse.
			To reheat, steam until hot.
			Serve or use.

Variations: Garnish: thick sauce, diced parsley.

Pan size:	lg.skillet	Yield:	10 cups	Yield:		**PASTA FAGIOLI WITH TEMPEH**
Cooking time:	15 mins.	Serves:	10	Serves:		
Oven temp.:		Portion:	1 cup	Portion:		

Tempeh	1 lb.		1/4"-dice, reserve.
Whole wheat linguini, cooked (1.1 lbs. dry)	8 cups		Reserve.
Olive oil	1/2 cup		Place in skillet.
Tempeh, above			Add, saute until golden.
Onions, finely diced	1 1/2 cups		Add, saute until clear.
Garlic, finely chopped	2 Tbs.		Add, saute.
Tamari	2 Tbs.		Add.
Linguini, above			Add, toss until hot.
Parsley, chopped	1/2 cup		Garnish with liberal amounts.
			Serve.

Variations: Add mushrooms or fresh basil.

Pan size: 5 qt.	Yield: 10 cups	Yield:	**PASTA, NORI**
Cooking time: 10 mins.	Serves: 10	Serves:	
Oven temp.:	Portion: 1 cup	Portion:	

Sesame oil, light	$1/4$ cup		Place in skillet.
Mushrooms, finely sliced	2 cups		Add.
Water	$1/4$ cup		Add.
Tamari	$1/4$ cup		Add.
Nori sheets, roasted, $1/4$" broken	2		Add, mix, lightly saute, quick-cool; reserve.
Water	12 cups		Place in pan.
Salt	1 Tbs.		Add.
Whole wheat elbow macaroni	$4^{1}/2$ cups		Cook *al dente*, drain, rinse in colander under cold water. Drain; reserve.
Mushrooms, above			Place in pan; heat. Add mushrooms, mix, adjust.
			Serve garnished with crushed nori.

Variations: Use 1.2 lbs. spaghetti instead of elbows.
Saute chopped onions and/or garlic with mushrooms.

Pan size: 2 qt./6 qt.	Yield: 10 cups	Yield:	**SPAGHETTI ROMA**
Cooking time: 25 mins.	Serves: 10	Serves:	
Oven temp.:	Portion: 1 cup	Portion:	

Olive oil	$1/2$ cup		Place in skillet; heat at med. high.
Onions, $1/2$"-diced	2 cups		Add, mix.
Garlic, minced	2 Tbs.		Add, mix, saute until onions are clear.
Brown Rice Flour Sauce (pg.253)	2 cups		Add.
Salt	$1/2$ tsp.		Add.
Basil	1 tsp.		Add.
Oregano	$1/2$ tsp.		Add.
Thyme	$1/4$ tsp.		Add, mix, simmer 10 mins.
Mushrooms, thinly sliced	1 cup		Add, mix, simmer 2 mins. Adjust; reserve.
Water	12 cups		Place in pan.
Salt	1 tsp.		Add.
Pasta	$5^{1}/2$ cups		Add, cook *al dente*. Serve with sauce.

Variations: Add steamed green peas.
Add $1/4$"-diced carrots.

SPAGHETTI SAUCE, BROCCOLI

	Yield: 10 cups	Yield:	Pan size: 4 qt.
	Serves: 10	Serves:	Cooking time: 20 mins.
	Portion: 1 cup	Portion:	Oven temp.:

Water	6 cups		Place in pan; heat.
Broccoli stems, large ones skinned, small ones diced	4 lbs.		Add. Reserve florets.
Celery seed	1 tsp.		Add, simmer to parcooked.
			Place in blender; pulse to coarse-blend. Return to pan.
Onions, $1/2$"-diced	2 cups		Add.
Oregano	$1/2$ tsp.		Add.
Basil	$1/2$ tsp.		Add.
Sage	$1/4$ tsp.		Add.
Garlic, finely diced	1 Tbs.		Add, mix, simmer 15 mins.
Broccoli florets (above), $1/2$"-chopped			Add.
Mushrooms, quartered	1 cup		Add; simmer 5 mins.
Arrowroot	3 Tbs.		Make sauce, add while stirring broccoli.

Variations: Substitute beets and carrots for broccoli.

PICKLES

Pickles form an important and often neglected part of our diet, not only for flavor and texture, but also to aid in digestion. Naturally fermented pickles help to set up a positive bacterial action in the intestines.

PICKLES, BASIC BRINE

	Yield:	1 gal.	Yield:		Pan size:	1 gal.
	Serves:		Serves:		Cooking time:	5 mins.
	Portion:		Portion:		Oven temp.:	

Water	10 cups		Place in pan.
Pickling salt	1/3 cup		Add, boil 5 mins.
			Stir, cool.
Cucumber, onions, carrots, turnips, broccoli, cauliflower, or any combination	14 cups		Fill sterilized jar.
			Cover vegetables with cool salt water. Cover jar with cheesecloth. Put in cool dark place for 3 days.
			Skim off floating sediment.
			Put on lid and refrigerate.

Variations:

GINGER PICKLES

	Yield:	1/2 cup	Yield:		Pan size:	
	Serves:	8	Serves:		Cooking time:	
	Portion:	1 Tbs.	Portion:		Oven temp.:	

Ginger (fresh), peel removed, finely sliced or diced	1/2 cup		Place in glass jar with lid.
Rice vinegar	1/4 cup		Add, tighten lid.
			Roll to mix 6 times in 24 hrs.
			Refrigerate.

Variations:

PICKLING SOLUTION

Pan size:	2 qt.	Yield:	5 cups	Yield:	
Cooking time:	5 mins.	Serves:		Serves:	
Oven temp.:		Portion:		Portion:	

Water	2 cups	Place in pan.
Salt	½ cup	Add, mix, boil 5 mins. Turn off heat.
Vinegar	2½ cups	Add, mix, reserve.
Vegetables, such as cauliflower florets, 1"-diced or larger, or julienned beets, cabbage, carrots, celery, parsnips, or turnips		Place in sterilized jar.
Pickling solution, above		Add, seal airtight. Set aside for 10 days.
		Serve.

Variations:

PRESSED SALT PICKLES

Pan size:		Yield:	5 cups	Yield:	
Cooking time:		Serves:	10	Serves:	
Oven temp.:		Portion:	½ cups	Portion:	

Cabbage, thinly sliced	6 cups	Place in bowl.
Parsley (fresh leaves)	½ cup	Add.
Green onion, diced	½ cup	Add, mix.
Salt	½ cup	Sprinkle half over cabbage, mix well. Sprinkle other half, mix well.
		Place plate that covers cabbage and does not touch bowl on cabbage.
		Put 4+/- lb. weight on plate. Rest 4 hrs.
		Rinse off undesired salt.
		Mix, serve.

Variations: Use tamari instead of salt.
Substitute other crisp, green vegetables.
Add finely sliced root vegetables.

TAMARI PICKLES

	Yield: 1 gal.	Yield:	Pan size: 1 gal.
	Serves:	Serves:	Cooking time: 5 mins.
	Portion:	Portion:	Oven temp.:

Water	10 cups		Boil 5 mins.
Tamari	5 cups		Add, stir, cool.
Cucumber, onions, carrots, turnips, broccoli, cauliflower, or any combination			Fill sterilized jar.
			Cover with cool tamari water. Cover with cheesecloth. Put in cool dark place for 4 hrs. to overnight.
			Skim off floating sediment. Put on lid and refrigerate up to 30 days.
			Add tamari each time a new batch is made.

Variations:

	Yield:	Yield:	Pan size:
	Serves:	Serves:	Cooking time:
	Portion:	Portion:	Oven temp.:

Variations:

PIES

Pan size: 9" pie	Yield: 9" pie	Yield:	**CRUST, NUT, PRE-BAKED**
Cooking time: 16 mins.	Serves: 6	Serves:	
Oven temp.: 400°	Portion: ¹/₆ pie	Portion:	

Walnuts, roasted	1 cup		Place in blender. Blend until finely chopped. Place in bowl.
Whole wheat pastry flour	1¹/₄ cups		Add.
Salt	¹/₂ tsp.		Add, mix, indent center.
Maple syrup	3 Tbs.		Add.
Oil	4 Tbs.		Add.
Water, cold	2 Tbs.		Add.
Vanilla extract	2 tsp.		Add, mix. Form ball. Squeeze and mix for 30 seconds.
			Press evenly in oiled 9" pan. Fork-hole the bottom to prevent air bubbles.
			Bake 16 mins. or until done.
			Cool.

Variations: Use other nuts (do not use almonds).

[This recipe tested and approved by Chris Quilty, Chef Instructor at New England Culinary Institute.]

Pan size: 9" pie	Yield: 2 crusts	Yield:	**PIE CRUST, TOP AND BOTTOM**
Cooking time: 10 mins.	Serves: 8	Serves:	[from Chuck Conway, Baker, O Bread Bakery, Shelburne, Vt.]
Oven temp.: 400°	Portion: ¹/₈ pie	Portion:	

Whole wheat pastry flour	2¹/₄ cups		Place in bowl.
Salt	¹/₂ tsp.		Add, mix.
Corn oil	¹/₃ cup		Add.
Water, cold	¹/₄ cup + 1 Tbs.		Add, cut in with spatula edge for about 1 min. until it forms a ball.
			Roll on pastry cloth with covered rolling pin.
			Place on lightly oiled 9" pie pan and form.
			Add pie filling, place and seal top crust to bottom crust.

Variations: Use apple juice instead of water.

OAT CRUST, HAND-PRESSED

	Yield:	9" shell	Yield:		Pan size:	9" pie
	Serves:	8	Serves:		Cooking time:	10 mins.
	Portion:	1/8 pie	Portion:		Oven temp.:	350°

Oats, rolled	1/3 cup		Place in bowl.
Whole wheat pastry flour	1 cup		Add, mix.
Salt	1/4 tsp.		Add, mix.
Water	1/3 cup + 3 Tbs.		Add, mix.
			Press on slightly oiled 9" pie pan, 1/4" thick. Patch thin spots; press thick spots.
			Fork-hole top edge.
			Pre-bake 10 mins. at 350°. Cool in pan.

Variations: Add 1/4 tsp. spices to dry mix.
Use vanilla or almond extract with water.
Substitute oat bran for rolled oats.

PIE SHELL, ROLLED

	Yield:	2 crusts	Yield:		Pan size:	9"
	Serves:	8	Serves:		Cooking time:	10 mins.
	Portion:	1/8 pie	Portion:		Oven temp.:	400°

Whole wheat pastry flour	1 1/2 cups		Place in bowl.
Unbleached flour	1 1/2 cups		Add.
Salt	1/2 tsp.		Add, mix well, finger-sift and fluff.
Corn oil	1/2 cup		Add; mix until many small balls form.
Water, very cold	1/2 cup		Dribble water over balls slowly, mixing. Form a mass of dough. Divide in half; cover, refrigerate.
			Roll between waxed paper 2" larger than pan.
			Pre-bake bottom crust 10 mins.
			Fit or mold top crust to bottom with a little water and pressure.

Variations:

Pan size:	9" pie	Yield:	9" pie	Yield:		**APPLE PIE**
Cooking time:	45 mins.	Serves:	8	Serves:		
Oven temp.:	425°	Portion:	1/8 pie	Portion:		

Apples,* blended	1/2 cup		Place in bowl.
Cinnamon	pinch		Add.
Salt	1/4 tsp.		Add.
Lemon rind, grated	1 tsp.		Add.
Whole wheat pastry flour	2 tsp.		Add, mix.
Apples,* cored, sliced	6 cups		Add.
Raisins	1/3 cup		Add, mix. Adjust.
			Place in half-baked pie shell. Bake 15 mins. at 425°, then 30 mins. at 350°.
			Serve warm or cool.
*See *Apple Chart*, pg. 60.			

Variations: Use crumb topping or rolled dough crust.
Use other in-season fruits (see *Fruit Shipping Chart*, pg. 69).
Use pecans instead of raisins; or add ginger.

Pan size:	9" pie	Yield:	9" pie	Yield:		**CARROT PIE**
Cooking time:	45 mins.	Serves:	8	Serves:		
Oven temp.:	350°	Portion:	1/8 pie	Portion:		

Carrots, sliced	2 1/2 cups		Cook, drain. Place in blender.
Barley malt	1/4 cup		Add.
Tofu	1/2 cup		Add.
Orange zest	1 tsp.		Add.
Nutmeg, cinnamon, clove, ginger, allspice	1/4 tsp. ea.		Add, pulse, blend. Adjust cook water to puree. Place in pan; boil.
Arrowroot	3 Tbs.		Make sauce, add, mix to desired consistency. Adjust.
			Place in half-baked pie shell. Bake 45 mins. or until done.
			Cool, refrigerate overnight.
			Serve.

Variations: Garnish with toasted almond slivers.

MINCEMEAT PIE

	Yield: 2 crusts	Yield:	Pan size: 9" pie
	Serves: 8	Serves:	Cooking time: 45 mins.
	Portion: 1/8 pie	Portion:	Oven temp.: 425°

Currants	1 cup		Place in pan.
Raisins	1 cup		Place in pan.
Apples, 1/4"-diced	2 cups		Add.
Orange rind	3 Tbs.		Add.
Apple juice	3 cups		Add.
Salt	1 tsp.		Add.
Cinnamon, clove, nutmeg	1/2 tsp. ea.		Add, mix, boil.
Arrowroot	5 Tbs.		Make sauce, add while stirring filling to desired thickness.
Walnuts, 1/8"-chopped	2 cups		Add, adjust. Place in half-baked pie shell.
			Bake 15 mins. at 425°, then 30 mins. at 350° to desired firmness.
			Refrigerate. Serve.

Variations:

PECAN PIE

	Yield: 9" pie	Yield:	Pan size: 9" pie
	Serves: 8	Serves:	Cooking time: 20 mins.
	Portion: 1/8 pie	Portion:	Oven temp.:

Apple cider	2 1/4 cups		Place in pan.
Agar-agar flakes	2 Tbs.		Add, mix.
Raisins	3/4 cup		Add.
Salt	pinch		Add, simmer 20 mins., covered.
Arrowroot	2 Tbs.		Make into sauce with 1/4 cup water. Add, mix.
Vanilla extract	1 tsp.		Add, mix. Remove raisins.
			Blend until smooth. Add puree to liquid mix. Adjust.
Pecans, roasted, chopped	1 1/2 cups		Add, mix, place in baked pie shell.
Pecans, roasted halves	1/2 cup		When filling partially solidifies, place on top of pie.
			Refrigerate, serve.

Variations: Use walnuts instead of pecans.

PUMPKIN PIE

Pan size:	9" pie	Yield:	9" pie	Yield:	
Cooking time:	1 hr.	Serves:	8	Serves:	
Oven temp.:	325°	Portion:	1/8 pie	Portion:	

Pumpkin puree	1 1/2 cups		Place in blender.
Tofu	1/2 lb.		Add.
Water	1 cup		Add.
Barley malt	1/2 cup		Add.
Maple syrup	2 Tbs.		Add.
Cinnamon	1 tsp.		Add.
Nutmeg	1/2 tsp.		Add.
Ginger	1/4 tsp.		Add.
Vanilla extract	3/4 tsp.		Add, pulse, blend smooth. Adjust. Place in half-baked pie shell. Bake 1 hr. or until done.

Variations: Instead of pumpkin, use carrots or butternut squash.

SQUASH, BUTTERNUT, PIE

Pan size:	9" pie	Yield:	9" pie	Yield:	
Cooking time:	50–60 mins.	Serves:	6	Serves:	
Oven temp.:	350°	Portion:	1/6 pie	Portion:	

Butternut squash	3 lbs.		Steam and remove skin; reserve.
Barley malt	1/2 cup		Place in bowl.
Cinnamon	1/2 tsp.		Add.
Ginger, ground	1 tsp.		Add, mash; reserve.
Barley milk	1/2 cup		Place in pan.
Arrowroot	2 Tbs.		Add, mix, simmer, stir.
			Add to squash, mix. Adjust.
			Add to half-baked pie shell. Bake 50–60 mins.
			Cool, refrigerate, serve.

Variations: Add tofu or soy milk instead of barley milk.

POULTRY

IMPORTANT GUIDELINES FOR POULTRY COOKERY

• Avoid birds with off color and off odor, discoloration, or blemishes.

• Skin color varies from white to yellow depending on the bird's diet and geographical origin.

• Remove skin and fat before coooking.

• Use only organic, free-range, hand-cleaned poultry when possible.

• Age of poultry at time of killing will partially determine cooking method:

  Older poultry (needs more moist heat). Cook:

  –in covered baking pan with liquid;

  –by pressure cooking;

  –in baking bag.

  Younger poultry. Cook by:

  –broiling;

  –frying;

  –roasting.

• Poultry meat comes in two colors—

  Light, from the breast and wings:

  –cooks faster than dark meat;

  –has less fat.

  Dark, from the legs and thighs:

  –takes longer to cook;

  –has more fat.

• Fresh poultry is extremely perishable.

• Keep cooked poultry covered and moist to prevent drying out.

• Chicken must be well cooked to be considered safe food. Partially cooked chicken has a 33% chance of causing salmonellosis.

Storage Recommendations

• Should be delivered and stored, packed in ice in a self-draining pan.

• Poultry is best if used within 24 hours, but if the ice is changed daily it may retain freshness for up to 5 days.

• Changing ice removes impurities and prevents water-logging or weight damage, as old ice compacts.

• Thoroughly wash poultry before cooking.

NOTE: In 1988, the USDA announced that one out of three USDA approved chickens is contaminated with salmonella bacteria. Approved mechanical processing of chickens at a speed of 70 to 120 birds a minute causes the puncturing of the intestines, allowing fecal matter to lodge in chicken tissues, mostly in empty feather folicles created by freshly pulled feathers.

Keeping the Kitchen Sanitary

Because of early cross-contamination of kitchen equipment from raw and cooked chicken, thorough sanitization is necessary for:

• holding containers

• cutting boards

• knives

• pans

• sink where chicken is washed

• hands, before handling other foods

Pan size:	Yield:	2 lbs.	Yield:		**CHICKEN AND**
Cooking time:	Serves:	10	Serves:		**NATURAL GRAVY**
Oven temp.:	Portion:	3 oz.	Portion:		

Chicken breasts, skinned, boned, 3/4"-diced	2 lbs.		Reserve.
Olive oil	1/2 cup		Place in skillet at medium-high heat.
Chicken, above			Add, saute until lightly golden brown.
Carrots, 1/4"-diced	1/2 cup		Add, saute until 50% cooked.
Onions, finely diced	1 cup		Add, saute. Adjust oil.
Mushrooms, thinly sliced	1 cup		Add, saute until cooked; reserve.
Whole wheat pastry flour	3 Tbs.		Add, mix.
Water	2 cups		Add.
Allspice	1/4 tsp.		Add.
Tamari	1 Tbs.		Add.
Lemon juice (fresh)	2 Tbs.		Add, mix, adjust; serve.

Variations:

Pan size:	Yield:	3 lbs.	Yield:		**CHICKEN DE**
Cooking time: 40 mins.	Serves:	10	Serves:		**LIBAN (Lebanese)**
Oven temp.: 300°	Portion:	5 oz.	Portion:		

Garlic, finely diced	3 Tbs.		Place in bowl.
Onion, finely diced	5 Tbs.		Add, mash.
Olive oil	1 cup		Add.
Salt	1/2 tsp.		Add.
Black pepper	1/4 tsp.		Add.
Mint (fresh)	1 Tbs.		Add.
Cinnamon	1/4 Tbs.		Add, mix.
Chicken, 10 pieces	3 lbs.		Add, mix, cover, refrigerate 4 hrs. Remix every 2 hrs.
			Drain. Bake in covered pan 40 mins. or until done.
			(Remove white meat first; reserve.)
			Serve.

Variations:

CHICKEN TARRAGON

	Yield: 10 pieces	Yield:	Pan size: skillet
	Serves: 10	Serves:	Cooking time: 40+/- mins.
	Portion: 1 piece	Portion:	Oven temp.:

Unbleached flour	2 cups		Place in bowl.
Chicken, cut up into 10 pieces	3 lbs.+/-		Dredge in flour.
Safflower oil	1/2 cup		Place in skillet.
Chicken, above			Add, quick-saute at high heat until golden, about 2 mins. each side.
Dry white wine	1/2 cup		Add to chicken.
Tarragon (dry leaves)	2 Tbs.		Add, mix, reduce 50%. Reduce heat.
Unbleached flour	2 Tbs.		Add slowly; make gravy.
Salt	to suit		Add. Cook until done.
			Serve.

Variations:

CHICKEN, STEWED

	Yield: 10 cups	Yield:	Pan size: 4 qt.
	Serves: 10	Serves:	Cooking time: 1+/- hr.
	Portion: 1 cup	Portion:	Oven temp.:

Water	7 cups		Place in pan.
Chicken bones	1 lb.		Add.
Mirepoix (pg. 87)	5 cups		Add.
Salt	1 tsp.		Add.
Bay leaf	1		Add.
Thyme	1 tsp.		Add. Simmer 45 mins.
Chicken, white meat, 1/2"-diced	2 lbs.		Add. Parcook.
Whole wheat flour	1/2 cup		Make slurry. Add for desired thickness. Stir very gently.
			Serve.

Variations: Add cinnamon or nutmeg.
Add mushrooms.

ROLLS

Pan size:	Yield:	10	Yield:		**WHOLE WHEAT**
Cooking time: 20 mins.	Serves:	10	Serves:		**ROLLS**
Oven temp.: 400°	Portion:	1	Portion:		

Water, 110°	2¹/₂ cups		Place in warm bowl.
Yeast	4 oz.		Add, cover, set aside until bloomed.
Whole wheat flour	2¹/₂ cups		Place in bowl.
Unbleached flour	1 cup		Add.
Salt	1 tsp.		Add, mix well; reserve.
Oil	¹/₄ cup		Place in warm bowl.
Barley malt	2 Tbs.		Add, mix to dissolve. Add to flour.
Yeast, above			Add to flour.
			Mix and knead 3 mins. Make 1 ball. Oil, pat, place in warm bowl; cover; let rise.
			When doubled in size, knead 1 min.
			Shape rolls.
			Cover, place in cold oven. Turn on heat.
			Bake 20 mins. after reaching 400° or until done.

Variations: Substitute ¹/₂ cup corn meal for ¹/₂ cup whole wheat flour.
Add finely diced onions, oregano, and thyme.
Add coriander.
Add ¹/₄ cup diced pecans.

SALADS

IMPORTANT GUIDELINES FOR SALAD PREPARATION

Various salads are used for a number of purposes in eating establishments, at home, in cafeterias, institutions, and restaurants of any grade. Each type of salad has separate and similar components. All of them commonly use some or all ingredients consisting of:

•The five basic tastes (bitter, sweet, sour, pungent, salty);

•Dressing, with or without herbs and spices (see pp. 243–250);

•One or more types of lettuce or greens;

•A selection of raw, blanched, or pickled vegetables;

•Pressed salt pickles often used as salad (see pg. 221);

•Fruit;

•Starches and/or protein food;

•Aspic.

Selection of ingredients is based mostly on color, flavor, and the purpose of the salad being served.

Types

Appetizer:

•Stimulates the appetite;

•Small and not filling;

•All or mostly greens and dressing;

•Small amounts of
   –vegetables
   –starches/proteins

Accompaniment:

•Served with the main course;

•Not large—to complement the meal, not compete with it;

•Usually consists of vegetables.

Main Course:

•Large enough for full meal;

•Nutritionally balanced selection of ingredients that could include fruit, starches/proteins, and vegetables;

•Balance of flavors, textures, and colors.

The ideal is to serve salads in the form of an accompaniment year round, or as a main course in the summer.

NOTE: The ancient romans ate green vegetables with salt, called *sal*, thus the creation of the word *salad*.

	Appet.	Accomp.	Main
Blanched Salad		•	
Brown Rice, Basic		•	•
Brown Rice, Curried		•	•
Brown Rice, Italian		•	•
Bulgur		•	•
Bulgur Slaw	•	•	
Carrot		•	
Coleslaw		•	
Cranapple Aspic		•	
Fatoosh	•	•	•
Grated Root	•	•	
Greek	•	•	•
Lebanese	•	•	•
Pasta		•	•
Pickled (see pg. 220)	•	•	
Root Vegetable	•	•	•
Tabouli		•	•
Tofu		•	•
Quinoa Super		•	•
Whole Wheat		•	
Zesty Greens	•	•	•

Pan size: 6 qt.	Yield: 10 cups	Yield:	**BLANCHED**
Cooking time: 3 mins.	Serves: 10	Serves:	**SALAD**
Oven temp.:	Portion: 1 cup	Portion:	

Prepared dressing of choice			Reserve.
Broccoli florets	4 cups		Blanch in boiling water $1/2$ min.
Cauliflower florets	4 cups		Blanch in boiling water $1/2$ min.
Carrots, thinly sliced	2 cups		Blanch in boiling water 2 mins.
			Place in bowl.
			Add dressing.
			Serve.

Variations:

Pan size:	Yield: 10 cups	Yield:	**BROWN RICE**
Cooking time:	Serves: 10	Serves:	**SALAD, BASIC**
Oven temp.:	Portion: 1 cup	Portion:	

Celery, $1/8$"-diced	$1/2$ cup		Place in bowl.
Carrots, $1/8$"-diced	2 Tbs.		Add.
Parsley, $1/8$"-chopped	2 Tbs.		Add.
Sea salt	1 tsp.		Add, mix.
Basic Tofu Dip (pg. 147)	2 cups		Add, mix.
Brown rice, cooked (3 cups uncooked)	9 cups		Add, mix, serve.

Variations: Add diced red or white onion, olive oil, dark sesame oil, brown rice vinegar, lemon juice, chopped green onions, tamari.
Substitute equal amounts of pasta for rice.

BROWN RICE SALAD, CURRIED (Indian)

	Yield: 10 cups	Yield:	Pan size:
	Serves: 10	Serves:	Cooking time:
	Portion: 1 cup	Portion:	Oven temp.:

Brown rice cooked with curry (3 cups uncooked)	9 cups		Reserve.
Tofu Mayonnaise (pg. 245) made with curry to taste	2½ cups		Place in bowl.
Parsley leaves, chopped	2 Tbs.		Add.
Green onion, finely diced	2 Tbs.		Add.
Celery, ¼"-diced	¼ cup		Add.
Carrots, ¼"-diced	2 Tbs.		Add.
Apples, ¼"-diced	2 Tbs.		Add.
Raisins	2 Tbs.		Add.
Salt	1 tsp.		Add, mix, adjust.
			Serve.

Variations: Add sesame seeds, coriander.

BROWN RICE SALAD, ITALIAN

	Yield: 10 cups	Yield:	Pan size:
	Serves: 10	Serves:	Cooking time:
	Portion: 1 cup	Portion:	Oven temp.:

Brown rice, cooked (3 cups uncooked)	9 cups		Place in bowl, fluff, cool; reserve.
Black olives, whole or halved	2 Tbs.		Place in bowl.
Parsley, ½"-chopped	1 Tbs.		Add.
Green onion, finely chopped	1 Tbs.		Add.
Red radish, ¼"-diced	3 Tbs.		Add.
Celery, ¼"-diced	4 Tbs.		Add.
Carrots, ⅛"-diced	2 Tbs.		Add.
Olive oil	1 cup		Add.
Sea salt	1 tsp.		Add, mix.
Brown rice, above			Add, mix.
			Serve.

Variations: Add onion and garlic.

BULGUR SALAD

Pan size:	Yield:	10 cups	Yield:	
Cooking time:	Serves:	10	Serves:	
Oven temp.:	Portion:	1 cup	Portion:	

Bulgur, cooked with bay leaf (pg. 163)	9 cups	Reserve.
Tofu Mayonnaise (pg. 245)	2¹/₂ cups	Add.
Parsley leaves, chopped	¹/₂ cups	Add.
Green onion, finely diced	¹/₂ cup	Add.
Carrots, ¹/₈"-diced	¹/₄ cup	Add.
Salt	¹/₂ tsp.	Add, mix, adjust.
		Serve.

Variations: Use tamari.

BULGUR SLAW

Pan size:	Yield:	10 cups	Yield:	
Cooking time:	Serves:	10	Serves:	
Oven temp.:	Portion:	1 cup	Portion:	

Bulgur or cracked wheat, cooked	2 cups	Reserve.
Tofu Mayonnaise (pg. 245)	2 cups	Place in bowl.
Onion, minced	2 Tbs.	Add.
Carrot, minced	2 Tbs.	Add.
Cilantro (fresh), minced	2 Tbs.	Add.
Green pepper, minced	2 Tbs.	Add.
Caraway seeds	¹/₄ tsp.	Add.
Salt	1 tsp.	Add.
Pepper, black	¹/₄ tsp.	Add, mix.
Cabbage, shredded	7 cups	Add, mix, refrigerate.
		Serve.

Variations:

CARROT SALAD

	Yield: 10 cups	Yield:	Pan size:
	Serves: 10	Serves:	Cooking time:
	Portion: 1 cup	Portion:	Oven temp.:
Carrots, grated	9 cups		Place in bowl.
Raisins, parcooked	1/2 cup		Add.
Walnuts (roasted), diced	1/2 cup		Add, refrigerate.
Tofu Mayonnaise (pg. 245), room temp.	1 cup		Place in blender.
Barley malt, hot	2 Tbs.		Add.
Tahini	2 Tbs.		Add, blend.
			Add to carrots. Adjust; mix. Refrigerate.
			Serve.

Variations: Add diced apples or lemon juice.

COLESLAW

	Yield: 10 cups	Yield:	Pan size:
	Serves: 10	Serves:	Cooking time:
	Portion: 1 cup	Portion:	Oven temp.:
Tofu Mayonnaise (pg. 245)	4 cups		Reserve.
Cabbage, thinly sliced	9 cups		Place in bowl. Add 3 cups mayonnaise, mix. Adjust.
			Serve.

Variations: Add lemon juice, or rice vinegar.
Add chopped cilantro, parsley, or grated carrot.
Add cumin, caraway seeds.

CRANBERRY–APPLE ASPIC

Pan size:	4 qt.	Yield:	10 cups	Yield:	
Cooking time:	25 mins.	Serves:	10	Serves:	
Oven temp.:		Portion:	1 cup	Portion:	

Walnuts (roasted), $1/2$"-chopped	1 cup		Reserve.
Apple juice	6 cups		Place in pan. Heat slowly to simmer.
Barley malt	1 cup		Add, mix, dissolve.
Apples, thinly sliced	2 cups		Add, simmer.
Agar-agar powder	$1^1/2$ Tbs.		Add, mix, dissolve.
Cranberries	12 oz.		Add, simmer 10 mins. Stir gently 3 times. Spoon-test; adjust.
Walnuts, above			Add, mix. Pour into mold.
			Serve.

Variations: Add vanilla, 2 Tbs. grated lemon peel, 1 Tbs. fresh mint when cooking stopped. Garnish: Tofu Supreme Icing (pg. 179).

FATOOSH ("Peasant Salad," Arabic)

Pan size:		Yield:	10 cups	Yield:	
Cooking time:		Serves:	10	Serves:	
Oven temp.:		Portion:	1 cup	Portion:	

Whole wheat pita bread, 9" diam.	$1^1/2$ pcs.		Separate layers. Bake on oven until very crisp. Reserve.
Lebanese Dressing (pg. 245)	$1^1/4$ cups		Place in bowl.
Black pepper (freshly ground)	$1/4$ tsp.		Add, mix; reserve.
Lettuce, torn into bite-size	5 cups		Place in bowl.
Mint, fresh or dried	$1/2$ cup		Add.
Onion, thinly sliced half-moons	1 cup		Add.
Celery, $1/2$"-diced	1 cup		Add.
Green onion	1 cup		Add.
Cucumber, peeled, quartered, $1/2$"-diced	1 cup		Add.
Parsley, finely chopped	$1/2$ cup		Add, mix; refrigerate.
Bread, above			When ready to serve, break into bite-size pieces, add.
Dressing, above			Add, mix, adjust.

Variations: Add $1/4$"-chopped walnuts.   Serve immediately.

GRATED ROOT SALAD

	Yield: 10 cups	Yield:	Pan size:
	Serves: 10	Serves:	Cooking time:
	Portion: 1 cup	Portion:	Oven temp.:
Carrots, grated	3 cups		Place in bowl.
Daikon, grated	3 cups		Add.
Parsnips or turnips, grated	4 cups		Add. Mix with dressing of choice.

Variations: Add grated ginger.

GREEK SALAD

	Yield: 10 cups	Yield:	Pan size:
	Serves: 10	Serves:	Cooking time:
	Portion: 1 cup	Portion:	Oven temp.:
Tomatoes, ripe, wedged	4 cups		Cut to bite-size wedges.
Onions, sweet, half-moons	2 cups		Slice thin and cut in half; add.
Cucumbers, 1"-diced	5 cups		Slice and add.
Greek olives	60		Add.
Feta	1 lb.		Cut thick slices and divide onto plates.
Olive oil	2 cups		Add by drizzling over vegetables.

Variations: Instead of feta, use 3/4"-diced cooked tofu or marinated tofu.

LEBANESE SALAD

Pan size:	Yield:	10 cups	Yield:	
Cooking time:	Serves:	10	Serves:	
Oven temp.:	Portion:	1 cup	Portion:	

Lebanese Dressing (pg. 245)	1¼ cups		Reserve.
Lettuce, torn into bite-size	5+ cups		Place in bowl.
Mint (fresh), chopped	½ cup		Add.
Onion, thinly sliced half-moons	½ cup		Add.
Celery, ¼"-sliced	1 cup		Add.
Cucumber, peeled, quartered, ½"-sliced	1½ cups		Add.
Carrots, very finely sliced	1 cup		Add.
Parsley leaves, coarsely chopped	½ cup		Add, mix.
Lebanese Dressing, above			Add, mix, serve immediately.
			[NOTE: If not serving immediately, refrigerate salad without dressing.]

Variations:

PASTA SALAD

Pan size:	Yield:	10 cups	Yield:	
Cooking time:	Serves:	10	Serves:	
Oven temp.:	Portion:	1 cup	Portion:	

Hollandaise Sauce (pg. 259)	¾ cup		Place in bowl.
Green onion, finely diced	½ cup		Add.
Parsley (fresh), finely diced	½ cup		Add.
Carrots, finely diced	¼ cup		Add.
Cauliflower, fine florets	¼ cup		Add, mix.
Noodles, cooked (4–6 cups uncooked)	8 cups		Add, mix, rest 1 hr.
			Serve.
			[NOTE: For best results use small-shaped pasta, not long noodles.]

Variations:

ROOT VEGETABLES, GRATED

	Yield: 10 cups	Yield:	Pan size:
	Serves: 10	Serves:	Cooking time:
	Portion: 1 cup	Portion:	Oven temp.:
Carrots, finely grated	3 cups		Place in bowl.
Daikon, finely grated	3 cups		Add.
Parsnips, turnips, or rutabaga, finely grated	3 cups		Add.
Tofu Mayonnaise (pg. 245)	2 cups		Add, mix, cover.
			Refrigerate; serve.

Variations: Add 1 Tbs. tamari.

TABOULI

	Yield: 10 cups	Yield:	Pan size: 4 qt.
	Serves: 10	Serves:	Cooking time: 20 mins.
	Portion: 1 cup	Portion:	Oven temp.:
Bulgur wheat	3 cups		Place in bowl.
Salt	1/2 tsp.		Add.
Water	7 cups		Simmer 20 mins. Rest, covered, 1 hr. Drain and squeeze excess water. Place in bowl. Fluff.
Parsley, finely chopped	4 cups		Add.
Green onion, finely chopped	1 cup		Add.
Mint, finely chopped	1/3 cup		Add, fluff mix; reserve.
Lemon juice (fresh)	1 cup		Place in bowl.
Sea salt	2 tsp.		Add.
Nutmeg	1 tsp.		Add, mix, pour on salad, refrigerate.
Olive oil	2/3 cup		Add just before serving.
Tomatoes, 1/2"-diced	2 cups		Add and fluff-mix, serve.

Variations: The Eastern manner of making Tabouli is to be heavy with greens, and the Western way is heavy with grain. This recipe is in the Eastern way.

[NOTE: Tastes excellent the next day.]

TOFU SALAD

[from Pamela Kentish, Chef, East Calais, Vt.]

Pan size:	Yield: 8½ cups	Yield:
Cooking time:	Serves: 10	Serves:
Oven temp.:	Portion: .85 cup	Portion:

Tahini	1 cup + 2 Tbs.		Place in bowl.
Miso, white	¾ cup		Add.
Lemon juice (fresh)	3 Tbs.		Add, mix.
Tofu, cooked	3 lbs.		Add, mix and mash to desired consistency.
Green onion, finely diced	2 cups		Add, mix.
			Serve.

Variations: Add chopped parsley, red onion, scallions, mustard, or curry; thyme, sage, rosemary, basil, oregano, and/or prepared mustard.
Thin with water for pasta sauce.

QUINOA SALAD, SUPER

Pan size: 4 qt.	Yield: 10 cups	Yield:
Cooking time: 15 mins.	Serves: 10	Serves:
Oven temp.:	Portion: 1 cup	Portion:

Water	4 cups		Place in pot.
Tamari	¼ cup		Add.
Quinoa	2 cups		Rinse in seive under running cold water. Add to pot.
			Cover, simmer 15 mins. until cooked.
Carrots, finely diced	1 cup		Add.
Celery	1 cup		Add.
Sunflower seeds, roasted	1 cup		Add.
Parsley	1 cup		Add.
Garlic, very finely diced	1 Tbs.		Add.
Olive oil	⅓ cup		Add.
Lemon juice (fresh)	⅔ cup		Add, mix, adjust, refrigerate.
			Serve.

Variations: Garnish with diced or whole black olives.

WHEAT BERRY SALAD

	Yield: 10 cups	Yield:	Pan size: 3 qt.
	Serves: 10	Serves:	Cooking time: 1½ hrs.
	Portion: 1 cup	Portion:	Oven temp.:

Water	6 cups		Place in pot; heat.
Salt	½ tsp.		Add.
Wheat berries (soft spring, soaked overnight)	3.6 cups		Add, simmer, cover; cook 80%.
Celery, finely diced	½ cup		Add. Cook wheat 90%.
Corn, cooked	½ cup		Add. Complete cooking, turn off heat.
Parsley, diced	½ cup		Add.
Green onions	½ cup		Add.
Red pepper, finely diced	¼ cup		Add, mix, cool.
			Serve.

Variations: Before serving, add diced, steamed vegetables.

ZESTY GREENS

	Yield: 10 cups	Yield:	Pan size:
	Serves: 10	Serves:	Cooking time:
	Portion: 1 cup	Portion:	Oven temp.:

Lettuce, torn to bite-size pcs. (remove tender leaves)	4 cups		Place in bowl.
Escarole, bite-size	2 cups		Add.
Romaine, bite-size	2 cups		Add.
Watercress, bite-size	2 cups		Add, mix, serve with preferred dressing.

Variations:

SALAD DRESSINGS

GUIDELINES FOR SALAD DRESSING PREPARATION

[NOTE: Salad dressing should be applied to dry salad so that the dressing will adhere to it.]

Salad dressings are a liquid or liquid-like sauce used to enhance, moisten, and complement the salad. They may contain any one or a combination of the five basic flavors, or include predominant flavors of:

- fruit
- herbs and spices
- oil
- tahini
- tofu

Pan size:	Yield:	2 cups	Yield:		**FRENCH**
Cooking time:	Serves:	20	Serves:		**DRESSING**
Oven temp.:	Portion:	3.2 Tbs.	Portion:		
Soy oil		$1^{1}/_{4}$ cups		Place in jar.	
Lemon juice (fresh)		$^{2}/_{3}$ cup		Add.	
Parsley (fresh), finely diced		1 Tbs.		Add.	
Green onion, finely diced		$^{1}/_{4}$ cup		Add.	
Basil		$^{1}/_{2}$ tsp.		Add.	
Salt		$^{1}/_{2}$ tsp.		Add.	
Rosemary		$^{1}/_{8}$ tsp.		Add.	
Oregano		$^{1}/_{8}$ tsp.		Add.	
Celery seed (ground)		$^{1}/_{2}$ tsp.		Add.	
Dill		$^{1}/_{2}$ tsp.		Add, cover, shake well, adjust.	
				Refrigerate 24 hrs.; adjust.	
				Serve.	

Variations:

GREEN GODDESS DRESSING

		Yield: 1¾ cups	Yield:	Pan size:
		Serves: 10	Serves:	Cooking time:
		Portion: 2.8 Tbs.	Portion:	Oven temp.:
Tofu, cooked	½ lb.			Place in blender.
Water	¼ cup			Add.
Rice vinegar	¼ cup			Add, pulse, blend. Stop.
Parsley leaves (fresh)	½ cup			Add, blend smooth. Adjust.
Green onions, finely chopped	½ cup			Add, mix by hand.
				Serve.

Variations:

ITALIAN DRESSING

		Yield: ¾ cup	Yield:	Pan size:
		Serves: 10	Serves:	Cooking time:
		Portion: 1.2 Tbs.	Portion:	Oven temp.:
Olive oil	½ cup			Place in jar.
Lemon juice (fresh)	¼ cup			Add.
Salt	¼ tsp.			Add.
Onion, finely diced	1 tsp.			Add.
Garlic, finely diced	1 tsp.			Add, shake, rest 1 hr.; adjust.
				Serve.

Variations: Add oregano, sage, thyme.

LEBANESE DRESSING

Pan size:	Yield:	1¼ cups	Yield:	
Cooking time:	Serves:	10	Serves:	
Oven temp.:	Portion:	2 Tbs.	Portion:	

Garlic, finely diced	1 Tbs.		Place in bowl; mash.
Olive oil	¾ cup		Add.
Lemon juice (fresh)	½ cup		Add.
Salt	½ tsp.		Add.
Pepper, black	⅛ tsp.		Add, whip, adjust. Rest 1–2 hrs.
			Serve.
			[NOTE: Adjust for designed representation of all flavors.]

Variations:

MAYONNAISE, TOFU

Pan size:	Yield:	2½ cups	Yield:	
Cooking time:	Serves:	10	Serves:	
Oven temp.:	Portion:	4 Tbs.	Portion:	

Tofu, cooked	1 lb.		Place in blender.
Oil (safflower or soy)	¼ cup		Add.
Rice vinegar	2 Tbs.		Add.
Mustard	½ tsp.		Add.
Barley malt	1 Tbs.		Add.
Salt	½ tsp.		Add.
Lemon juice	1 Tbs.		Add, blend, adjust, refrigerate.
			Serve.
			[NOTE: For a low-oil version, leave out oil.]

Variations: Add basil, dill, rosemary, etc.
Garnish: paprika, roasted sesame seeds.

MISO DRESSING, WHITE

	Yield: 1 cup	Yield:	Pan size:
	Serves: 10	Serves:	Cooking time:
	Portion: 1.6 Tbs.	Portion:	Oven temp.:
Miso, white	1/2 cup		Place in warm bowl.
Water, boiling	1/2 cup		Add, whip, cool, refrigerate.
			Serve.

Variations: Add very finely sliced green onion.

OLIVE OIL AND LEMON DRESSING

	Yield: 1 cup	Yield:	Pan size:
	Serves: 10	Serves:	Cooking time:
	Portion: 1.6 Tbs.	Portion:	Oven temp.:
Lemon juice	1/2 cup		Place in jar.
Salt	1/2 tsp.		Add.
Olive oil	1/2 cup		Add, shake, adjust.
			Serve.

Variations: Add fennel or oregano.
Omit salt.

Pan size:	Yield:	1 cup	Yield:		OLIVE OIL AND
Cooking time:	Serves:	10	Serves:		VINEGAR
Oven temp.:	Portion:	1.6 Tbs.	Portion:		DRESSING

Olive oil		²/₃ cup		Place in jar.
Vinegar		¹/₃ cup		Add.
Salt		¹/₂ tsp.		Add, shake, adjust.
				Serve.

Variations: Add basil and thyme; dill and dried mustard; tarragon and marjoram; prepared mustard; pepper.

Pan size:	Yield:	³/₄ cup	Yield:		ORIENTAL
Cooking time:	Serves:	10	Serves:		DRESSING
Oven temp.:	Portion:	1.2 Tbs.	Portion:		

Water		¹/₂ cup		Place in bowl.
Vinegar, brown rice		2 Tbs.		Add.
Barley malt		2 Tbs.		Add.
Tamari		1 Tbs.		Add.
Sesame oil, dark		¹/₈ tsp.		Add.
Sesame seed		1 tsp.		Add, whip, adjust.
				Serve.

Variations: Sesame oil, light.

POLYNESIAN DRESSING

	Yield: 1¼ cups	Yield:	Pan size:
	Serves: 10	Serves:	Cooking time:
	Portion: 2 Tbs.	Portion:	Oven temp.:
Sesame oil, light	¼ cup		Place in bowl.
Orange juice	1 cup		Add.
Orange zest	1 Tbs.		Add.
Lemon zest	1 tsp.		Add, mix, adjust.
			Serve.

Variations: Add ¼–½ tsp. dark sesame oil.
Add brown rice vinegar.
Add 1 tsp. ground mustard and 1 Tbs. dry dill weed.

TAHINI DRESSING

	Yield: 1½ cups	Yield:	Pan size:
	Serves: 10	Serves:	Cooking time:
	Portion: 2.4 Tbs.	Portion:	Oven temp.:
Olive oil	½ cup		Place in blender.
Green onion, minced	2 Tbs.		Add.
Tahini	½ cup		Add, blend smooth, stop.
Water	1 Tbs.		Add.
Tamari	2 Tbs.		Add.
Lemon juice	¼ cup		Add, blend smooth, adjust.
			Serve.

Variations: Add garlic, herbs.

TAHINI–TOFU DRESSING

Pan size:	Yield:	1¼ cups	Yield:		
Cooking time:	Serves:	10	Serves:		
Oven temp.:	Portion:	2.2 Tbs.	Portion:		

Tofu, cooked	½ lb.		Place in blender.
Water	½ cup		Add, pulse.
Tahini	¼ cup		Add, blend, adjust.
			Serve.

Variations: Add salt, seasonings, miso, green onion, and/or lemon juice.

TAHINI YOGURT DRESSING

Pan size:	Yield:	4 cups	Yield:		
Cooking time:	Serves:	10	Serves:		
Oven temp.:	Portion:	6.4 Tbs.	Portion:		

Water, warm	½ cup		Place in blender.
Garlic	2 tsp.		Add.
Tahini	1 cup		Add, blend smooth; stop.
Yogurt	¼ cup		Add.
Lemon juice (fresh)	¼ cup		Add.
Salt	½ tsp.		Add, blend smooth.
			Serve.

Variations: Use selected herbs instead of salt.

THOUSAND ISLAND DRESSING

		Yield:	3 cups	Yield:		Pan size:
Serves:	10	Serves:		Cooking time:
Portion:	4.8 Tbs.	Portion:		Oven temp.:

Mayonnaise	2½ cups	Place in bowl.
Parsley (fresh), finely chopped	2 Tbs.	Add.
Olives, finely diced	¼ cup	Add.
Green onion, finely chopped	¼ cup	Add.
Salt	¼ tsp.	Add.
Celery, very finely chopped	2 Tbs.	Add.
Dill seed	⅛ tsp.	Add, mix, refrigerate 2 hrs.
		Adjust; serve.

Variations:

VERTE DRESSING

		Yield:	2 cups	Yield:		Pan size:
Serves:	10	Serves:		Cooking time:
Portion:	3.2 Tbs.	Portion:		Oven temp.:

Tofu, cooked	½ lb.	Place in blender.
Water	½ cup	Add.
Parsley, chopped	½ cup	Add.
Green onion, chopped	½ cup	Add.
Watercress	1 cup	Add.
Salt	1 tsp.	Add, blend smooth.
		Serve.

Variations: Add vinegar, lemon juice, or tahini.

SANDWICHES

ABOUT SANDWICHES

Sandwiches are to be used as a quick snack, and are not considered a substitute for a meal.

Three parts of a sandwich:

• Bread: whole wheat, rye, pumpernickel, French, or Italian, etc.

• Spread: placed on bread to regulate moisture and add a specific flavor, such as mustard, tarragon, cilantro, watercress, curry, tahini, etc.

• Filling: establishes the type of sandwich and major component of flavor.

SANDWICH IDEAS

Use Tofu Dip, Basic (pg. 147) or Tofu Mayonnaise (pg. 245) with the following, except for with those that are asterisked. Italicized items can be found in the Recipes section of this book.

• Apples (thinly sliced) and Peanut Butter (or chopped walnuts)*

• Bean Dip and/or Lettuce or Sprouts

• Chutney and/or *Carrot–Walnut Pate*

• Cucumber (with *Sunflower Butter*)

• *Hummus*

• Kelp, sauteed

• Seitan with Lettuce and Pickles

• *Sunflower Butter* and Jam*

• Tahini and Jam*

• Tahini, Raisins, and Sesame Seeds

• *Tempeh Bacon*, Lettuce, Mustard

• Tofu Salad and Lettuce or Sprouts

• Watercress, Walnut, and *Sour Cream, Tofu*.

SAUCES

IMPORTANT GUIDELINES FOR SAUCE COOKERY

Following are simple, quick-to-make sauces for complementing and enhancing a dish or meal, based on the five basic flavors. Sauce should be part of the original conception of the dish. It should add a positive element to flavor; if it does not, the sauce should not be used.

Basic Ingredients

Liquid:

- fruit juices
- liquid sweetener
- oil–vinegar
- vegetable or bean water
- water
- beans, blended

Major ingredients affecting color:

- curry
- fruit
- mustard
- tahini
- tamari
- tofu

Appearance:

- finely diced raw vegetables or fruit—raw, blanched, or cooked—each of various sizes and shapes.

Thickeners:

- arrowroot, kuzu, etc. (see pg. 74)
- tofu
- tahini
- pureed vegetables
- brown rice flour
- roux
- beans

Flavor developed from:

- five basic flavors
- full, rich, natural flavor of
  - beans
  - fruit
  - garlic
  - ginger, fresh
  - herbs, preferably fresh
  - nuts & seeds
  - oils
  - root vegetables
  - tahini
  - tamari
  - vegetables

Pan size:	1 qt.	Yield:	1 cup	Yield:		**BROWN RICE**
Cooking time:	10 mins.	Serves:	10	Serves:		**FLOUR SAUCE,**
Oven temp.:		Portion:	1.6 Tbs.	Portion:		**BASIC**

Brown rice flour	3 Tbs.		Place in pan.
Water	1 cup		Add, mix, dissolve lumps.
			Simmer 10 mins, covered; stir often.
			Rest 5 mins. Adjust.
			Serve hot.

Variations: Add tamari and miso.

Pan size:	1 qt.	Yield:	1¼ cups	Yield:		**BROWN RICE**
Cooking time:	20 mins.	Serves:	10	Serves:		**FLOUR SAUCE**
Oven temp.:		Portion:	2 Tbs.	Portion:		**(Sweet)**

Brown rice flour	3 Tbs.		Place in pan.
Water	1 cup		Add, mix, dissolve lumps. Simmer 5 mins, covered. Mix often.
Barley malt	¼ cup		Add, mix, simmer another 5 mins. Mix often.
			Rest 10 mins., covered. Adjust.
			Use or serve hot.

Variations: Use maple syrup instead of barley malt.

BROWN RICE FLOUR SAUCE (Salty)

		Yield: 1 cup	Yield:	Pan size: 1 qt.
		Serves: 10	Serves:	Cooking time: 20 mins.
		Portion: 1.6 Tbs.	Portion:	Oven temp.:

Brown rice flour	3 Tbs.	Place in pan.
Water	1 cup	Add, mix, dissolve lumps. Simmer 10 mins. covered, mix often.
Tamari	1 Tbs.	Add, mix. Rest, covered, 10 mins.; adjust.
		Serve hot.

Variations:

BROWN SAUCE, BASIC (Salty)

		Yield: 3¹/₄+ cups	Yield:	Pan size: 2 qt.
		Serves: 10	Serves:	Cooking time: 10 mins.
		Portion: 5.2+ Tbs.	Portion:	Oven temp.:

Corn oil	¹/₄ cup	Place in skillet.
Sesame oil, dark	¹/₂ tsp.	Add, mix.
Whole wheat pastry flour	¹/₈ cup	Add, mix, simmer 10 mins. Stir often. Adjust oil.
Salt	¹/₂ tsp.	Add.
Water	2¹/₂ cups	Add slowly while stirring.
Celery seed	³/₄ tsp.	Add, rest 15 mins.
		Serve.

Variations: Add finely chopped greens.
Serve with grains, pasts, vegetables.

Pan size: 1 qt.	Yield: 1 cup	Yield:	CARAMEL SAUCE,
Cooking time: 5 mins.	Serves: 10	Serves:	MOCK (Sweet)
Oven temp.:	Portion: 1.6 Tbs.	Portion:	

Water	1/2 cup		Place in pan; boil. Turn heat off.
Barley malt	1/2 cup		Add.
Vanilla	1 Tbs.		Add.
Salt	pinch		Add, mix until smooth. Adjust. Refrigerate.
			Use or serve.

Variations: Add spices.
Garnish: finely chopped baked nuts or seeds.
Serve with puddings, root vegetables.

Pan size: 1 qt.	Yield: 1 1/4 cups	Yield:	CINNAMON
Cooking time: 5 mins.	Serves: 10	Serves:	SAUCE (Sweet)
Oven temp.:	Portion: 2 Tbs.	Portion:	

Cinnamon	1/2 tsp.		Place in pan.
Water	1 cup		Add, whip, dissolve lumps.
Barley malt	1/4 cup		Add, mix, simmer 5 mins.
Arrowroot	1 tsp.		Make slurry, add, mix. Simmer 2 mins. Adjust, cover.
			Rest 15 mins.
			Serve.

Variations: Add blended roasted nuts or seeds before serving.
Use clove instead of cinnamon.

CRANBERRY SAUCE (Sour)

	Yield: 3 cups	Yield:	Pan size: 1 qt.
	Serves: 10	Serves:	Cooking time: 10 mins.
	Portion: 4.8 Tbs.	Portion:	Oven temp.:
Water	¾ cup		Place in pan; heat.
Barley malt	1 cup		Add, dissolve, boil.
Cranberries	12 oz.		Add, simmer 8 mins.
Arrowroot	1 Tbs.		Make slurry, add.
			Simmer 2 mins.
			Cool, serve.

Variations: Add 1 Tbs. lemon rind, grated; or 1 tsp. vanilla extract.
Add ½ cup roasted walnuts, finely chopped.
Delete arrowroot and blend with tofu.

CRANBERRY–ALMOND SAUCE (Sour)

	Yield: 3¼ cups	Yield:	Pan size:
	Serves: 10	Serves:	Cooking time: 10 mins.
	Portion: 5.2 Tbs.	Portion:	Oven temp.:
Almonds, roasted	1 cup		Reserve.
Apple juice	1 cup		Place in pan.
Barley malt	1 cup		Add, mix, simmer, dissolve.
Cranberries	12 oz.		Add, simmer 10 mins., turn heat off.
Almond extract	¾ tsp.		Add, mix.
Almonds, above			Blend fine. Add, mix, serve.

Variations: Substitute water for apple juice.

Pan size:	Yield: 3½ cups	Yield:	**CREAM SAUCE**
Cooking time:	Serves: 10	Serves:	**(Sweet)**
Oven temp.:	Portion: 5.6 Tbs.	Portion:	

Barley (well cooked, not dry)	½ cup		Place in blender.
Water	½ cup		Add.
Walnuts, roasted	¼ cup		Add.
Walnuts, roasted	¼ cup		Add.
Prunes or raisins, soft	¼ cup		Add.
Rice syrup or barley malt	2 Tbs.		Add, pulse, blend 30 seconds. Stop.
Water	2½ cups		Add, blend smooth. Adjust.
			Serve.

Variations: Add ¼ tsp. vanilla or almond extract; pinch nutmeg.
Use roasted hazelnuts instead of walnuts; or cooked oats instead of barley.
Add nuts and/or soft raisins at the first blend.
Serve with desserts, berries.

Pan size: 2 qt.	Yield: 1½ cups	Yield:	**CURRY SAUCE**
Cooking time: 15 mins.	Serves: 10	Serves:	**(Pungent)**
Oven temp.:	Portion: 2.4 Tbs.	Portion:	

White beans, cooked	1 cup		Place in blender.
Water	½ cup		Add, blend smooth. Place in pan.
Salt	½ tsp.		Add.
Curry powder	1 tsp.		Add. Make slurry, add, mix with beans.
			Place in pan, bring to low boil.
			Simmer 15 mins., stirring.
			Adjust flavor and consistency.
			Serve.

Variations: Adjust consistency with whole wheat pastry flour.
Serve with grains, pasta, vegetables.
Add miso.

GARLIC–PARSLEY SAUCE (Pungent)

| | Yield: 1¼ cups | Yield: | Pan size: |
| | Serves: 10 | Serves: | Cooking time: |
	Portion: 2+ Tbs.	Portion:	Oven temp.:
Garlic, finely chopped	2 Tbs.		Place in bowl; mash.
Parsley, finely chopped	3 Tbs.		Add.
Olive oil	1 cup		Add.
Salt	½ tsp.		Add, mix, cover, reserve.

Variations: Add or substitute basil for parsley.
Serve with pasta.

GINGER–TAMARI SAUCE (Pungent)

| | Yield: 1¼ cups | Yield: | Pan size: 1 qt. |
| | Serves: 10 | Serves: | Cooking time: 10 mins. |
	Portion: 2 Tbs.	Portion:	Oven temp.:
Tamari	2 Tbs.		Place in bowl.
Water	1 cup		Add.
Ginger (fresh), finely grated	2 Tbs.		Add, mix, simmer 10 mins. Rest 1 hr. Serve.

Variations: The fresher the ginger, the juicier and stronger the taste.
Serve with pasta and vegetables.

Pan size:	Yield:	$^3/_4$ cup	Yield:		HOLLANDAISE, MOCK (Pungent)
Cooking time:	Serves:	10	Serves:		
Oven temp.:	Portion:	1.2 Tbs.	Portion:		

Tofu, cooked	$^1/_2$ lb.		Place in blender.
Tahini	1 Tbs.		Add.
Salt	$^1/_2$ tsp.		Add.
Lemon juice	3 Tbs.		Add.
Water	$^1/_4$ cup		Add, blend, adjust.
			Serve.
			[NOTE: Add 1 tsp. turmeric for deeper color.]

Variations: Serve with grains, pasta, vegetables.

[This recipe tested and approved by Chris Quilty, Chef Instructor at New England Culinary Institute.]

Pan size:	Yield:	1 cup	Yield:		MISO–TAHINI SAUCE, BASIC (Salty)
Cooking time:	Serves:	10	Serves:		
Oven temp.:	Portion:	1.6 Tbs.	Portion:		

Miso, dark	3 Tbs.		Place in bowl.
Tahini	$^1/_4$ cup		Add.
Water	$^1/_4$ cup		Add, mix and mash until smooth. Adjust flavor and consistency.
			Serve.

Variations: Add chopped parsley, green onions.
Serve with grains, pasta, vegetables.
Using less water, spread on $^1/_4$"-sliced tofu and bake.

MUSHROOM SAUCE, BASIC

		Yield:	1½ cups	Yield:		Pan size:	
		Serves:	10	Serves:		Cooking time:	
		Portion:	2.4 Tbs.	Portion:		Oven temp.:	
Oil (safflower or soy)		⅛ cup				Place in skillet.	
Salt		½ tsp.				Add.	
Mushrooms, finely sliced		3 cups				Add, saute until par-cooked.	
Water		½ cup				Add, boil.	
Arrowroot		1 Tbs.				Make slurry. Add slowly; stir to desired consistency.	
						Adjust; serve.	

Variations: Saute ½ tsp. finely diced green onions first.
Use tamari instead of salt.
Serve with grains, pasta, vegetables.

MUSTARD–TAHINI SAUCE (Pungent)

		Yield:	¾+ cup	Yield:		Pan size:	1 qt.
		Serves:	10	Serves:		Cooking time:	10 mins.
		Portion:	1.2+ Tbs.	Portion:		Oven temp.:	
Tahini		½ cup				Place in bowl.	
Water		⅓ cup				Add, mix until smooth.	
Mustard, ground		1 tsp.				Add, mix, simmer 10 mins. Rest 1 hr.	
						Serve.	

Variations: Use salt.
Use 1 Tbs. prepared mustard in place of 1 tsp. ground mustard.
Serve with grains, pasta, vegetables.

Pan size: 1 qt.	Yield: 1 cup, 2 Tbs.	Yield:	ONION–TAMARI
Cooking time: 5 mins.	Serves: 10	Serves:	SAUCE (Salty)
Oven temp.:	Portion: 1.7 Tbs.	Portion:	

Water	1 cup		Place in blender.
Tamari	1 Tbs.		Add.
Onion	1/2 cup		Add.
Whole wheat pastry flour	1/4 cup		Add, blend until smooth. Place in pan. Simmer and stir 5 mins. Adjust.
			Serve.

Variations: Add more water and tahini.
Serve with grains, pasta, vegetables.

Pan size:	Yield: 2 cups	Yield:	PARSLEY–TOFU
Cooking time:	Serves: 10	Serves:	SAUCE (Bitter)
Oven temp.:	Portion: 3.2 Tbs.	Portion:	

Tofu, cooked	1/2 lb.		Place in blender.
Water	1/2 cup		Add.
Parsley leaves (fresh)	1 cup		Add.
Salt	pinch		Add, pulse, blend smooth. Adjust.
			Use or serve.

Variations: Use on grains, pasta, or vegetables.

PARSLEY, GREENS, AND VINEGAR SAUCE (Bitter)

	Yield: 3 cups	Yield:	Pan size:
	Serves: 10	Serves:	Cooking time:
	Portion: 4.8 Tbs.	Portion:	Oven temp.:
Vinegar	1 cup		Place in blender.
Parsley leaves (fresh)	1 cup		Add.
Greens	1 cup		Add, pulse, blend, adjust.
			Serve.

Variations: Use on grains, pasta, vegetables.

PEACH SAUCE (Sweet)

	Yield: 2 cups	Yield:	Pan size:
	Serves: 10	Serves:	Cooking time:
	Portion: 3.2 Tbs.	Portion:	Oven temp.:
Peaches, peeled, pitted, chopped	3 cups		Place in blender.
Nutmeg	1 Tbs.		Add.
Apple juice	1 cup		Add, blend. Place in pot, simmer.
Arrowroot dissolved in water	2 Tbs.		Add, mix until done.
			Serve hot or cold.

Variations: Add cinnamon.
Serve with desserts.

Pan size:	Yield:	1¼ cups	Yield:		RAISIN–APPLE
Cooking time:	Serves:	10	Serves:		CIDER SAUCE
Oven temp.:	Portion:	2 Tbs.	Portion:		(Sweet)

Raisins	½ cup		Place in blender.	
Apple cider	¾ cups		Add. Blend until smooth. Adjust.	
			Serve.	

Variations: Add tarragon; roasted, blended nuts or seeds; and/or barley malt.

Pan size: ½ qt.	Yield:	3 cups	Yield:		SAVORY ROOT
Cooking time: 30 mins.	Serves:	10	Serves:		SAUCE
Oven temp.:	Portion:	4.8 Tbs.	Portion:		(Pungent)

Carrots, diced	2 cups		Place in pan.	
Parsnips, diced	1 cup		Add.	
Ginger (fresh), finely chopped	2 Tbs.		Add.	
Salt	½ tsp.		Add.	
Water	2 cups		Add, boil, cover, simmer until parcooked.	
			Place solids in blender; blend. Add cook water as needed.	
			Serve.	

Variations: Serve with grains, pasta, vegetables.
            Add sesame oil, tahini, or brown rice flour.

SEITAN SAUCE (Salty)

	Yield: 1 cup	Yield:	Pan size: 1 qt.
	Serves: 10	Serves:	Cooking time: 30 mins.
	Portion: 1.6 Tbs.	Portion:	Oven temp.:
Tamari	2 Tbs.		Place in pan.
Water	1¹/₂ cups		Add.
Onion, finely chopped	¹/₃ cup		Add.
Kelp, finely chopped	4 sq.in.		Add. Simmer, covered, 15 mins.
Celery seed	¹/₄ tsp.		Add, mix, simmer, covered, 15 mins.
Whole wheat pastry flour	¹/₄ cup		Make sauce; add slowly, stirring to desired consistency.
			Adjust flavor and thickness.
			Simmer 15 mins.
			Serve.

Variations: Serve over seitan with grains, pasta, vegetables.

TAHINI SAUCE, BASIC

	Yield: 2 cups	Yield:	Pan size:
	Serves: 10	Serves:	Cooking time:
	Portion: 3.2 Tbs.	Portion:	Oven temp.:
Tahini	1 cup		Place in bowl.
Water	³/₄ cup		Add slowly while stirring until smooth. Adjust to desired consistency.
			Serve.

Variations: Add crushed, finely diced garlic and lemon juice to suit.
Add salt.
Serve with grains, vegetables.

Pan size:	Yield:	1¼ cups	Yield:		**TOFU–LEMON**
Cooking time:	Serves:	10	Serves:		**SAUCE (Sour)**
Oven temp.:	Portion:	2 Tbs.	Portion:		

Tofu	½ lb.		Place in blender.
Water	¼ cup		Add.
Lemon juice (fresh)	2 Tbs.		Add, pulse.
Salt	pinch		Add, pulse, blend smooth.
			Adjust, serve.

Variations:

Pan size:	Yield:	1½ cups	Yield:		**TOFU–MISO**
Cooking time:	Serves:	10	Serves:		**SAUCE (Salty)**
Oven temp.:	Portion:	2.8 Tbs.	Portion:		

Water	½ cup		Place in blender.
Tofu, cooked	½ cup		Add after cooking.
Miso	1 Tbs.		Add, blend until smooth. Adjust. Rest 30 mins.
			Serve.

Variations: Add or substitute tamari.
Add herbs; add tarragon or salt.
Serve with grains, pasta, vegetables.

TOFU–TAMARI SAUCE (Salty)

	Yield: 1 cup	Yield:	Pan size:
	Serves: 10	Serves:	Cooking time:
	Portion: 1.6 Tbs.	Portion:	Oven temp.:

Water	$^1/_2$ cup		Place in blender.
Tofu, cooked	$^1/_2$ lb.		Add.
Tamari	2 Tbs.		Add, blend, adjust.
			Serve.

Variations: Garnish with chopped greens.

TOFU–VINEGAR SAUCE (Sour)

	Yield: 1$^3/_4$ cups	Yield:	Pan size:
	Serves: 10	Serves:	Cooking time:
	Portion: 2.8 Tbs.	Portion:	Oven temp.:

Tofu, cooked	$^1/_2$ lb.		Place in blender.
Water	$^1/_4$ cup		Add.
Rice vinegar	$^1/_4$ cup		Add, blend until smooth.
			Serve.

Variations:

Pan size:	Yield:	2 cups	Yield:		**VERTE SAUCE**
Cooking time:	Serves:	10	Serves:		**(Bitter)**
Oven temp.:	Portion:	2 Tbs.	Portion:		

Tofu, cooked	$\frac{1}{2}$ lb.		Place in blender.
Olive oil	4 Tbs.		Add.
Parsley, chopped	$\frac{1}{4}$ cup		Add.
Lettuce, chopped	$\frac{1}{4}$ cup		Add.
Watercress, chopped	$\frac{1}{4}$ cup		Add.
Rosemary	1 Tbs.		Add.
Lemon juice	2 Tbs.		Add.
Salt	$\frac{1}{4}$ tsp.		Add.
Vinegar	1 Tbs.		Add.
Water	1 Tbs.		Add, blend smooth, adjust.
			Serve.

Variations: Use on grains, pasta, vegetables.

Pan size:	Yield:	Yield:
Cooking time:	Serves:	Serves:
Oven temp.:	Portion:	Portion:

Variations:

SNACKS

CRACKERS, WHOLE WHEAT

	Yield: 9 × 13"	Yield:	Pan size: 9 × 13"
	Serves: 10	Serves:	Cooking time: 12–13 mins.
	Portion: 2.4 pieces	Portion:	Oven temp.: 400°

Whole wheat pastry flour	1½ cups		Place in bowl.
Salt	½ tsp.		Add.
Sesame seeds	¼ cups		Add.
Baking powder	1 Tbs.		Add, mix.
Oil	2 Tbs.		Add.
Water	¼ cup + 2 Tbs.		Add, mix into thick ball. With wet hands, spread in 9 × 13" pan; roll level. Score cracker size. Bake until starting to brown.
			Recut with spatula. Cool for 5 mins. Break into crackers.
			Cool, serve.

Variations:

CRACKERS, RYE

	Yield: 9 × 13"	Yield:	Pan size: 9 × 13"
	Serves: 12	Serves:	Cooking time: 24 mins.
	Portion: 3 × 4⅓"	Portion:	Oven temp.: 400°

Whole wheat pastry flour	½ cup		Place in bowl.
Rye flour	1 cup		Add.
Caraway seeds	2 tsp.		Add.
Salt	½ tsp.		Add.
Baking powder	1 tsp.		Add, mix well.
Corn oil	¼ cup		Add.
Water, cold	½ cup		Add, mix, place in pan with wet fingers; spread evenly in oiled 9 × 13" pan. Wet-roll for even distribution. Score to cracker size. Bake until done.

Variations:

GRANOLA

Pan size:	Yield:	4 cups	Yield:	
Cooking time: 13 mins.	Serves:	10	Serves:	
Oven temp.: 350°	Portion:	6.4 Tbs.	Portion:	

Walnuts, 1/4"-chopped	1/4 cup	Place on baking pan.
Sunflower seeds	1/2 cup	Add, evenly distribute. Roast 2 mins.
Whole wheat pastry flour	1 Tbs.	Add.
Rolled oats	2 cups	Add, spread evenly. Roast 3 mins.
Barley malt	1/4 cup	Place in bowl, hot.
Cinnamon	1/4 tsp.	Add.
Vanilla extract	1/2 tsp.	Add.
Raisins	1/4 cup	Add, mix, spread evenly on oiled pan.
		Roast 4 mins. Turn, cool.
		Serve. Store in airtight container; refrigerate.

Variations:

RAISIN CRUNCH

Pan size: 2 qt.	Yield:	9 × 13"	Yield:	
Cooking time: 20 mins.	Serves:		Serves:	
Oven temp.: 350°	Portion:		Portion:	

Raisins	3 cups	Place in pan.
Water	1/2 cup	Add, simmer 2 mins., stir often. Drain; place raisins in bowl.
Barley malt	3/4 cup	Add.
Whole wheat pastry flour	1/2 cup	Add.
Vanilla extract	2 tsp.	Add.
Sunflower seeds	4 cups	Add.
Sesame seeds	1/2 cup	Add.
Tahini	1/2 cup	Add, mix.
		Place in oiled 9 × 13" pan. Bake 20 mins. at 350°. Cool, cut into 2 × 2" squares.
		Serve.

Variations: Add 2 Tbs. grated ginger, 1 tsp. vanilla.
Substitute 1/2 cup chopped nuts for sunflower seeds.

PUMPKIN SEEDS, TAMARI-ROASTED	Yield: 1⅓ cups	Yield:	Pan size:
	Serves: 10	Serves:	Cooking time: 10–15 mins.
	Portion: 2.4 Tbs.	Portion:	Oven temp.:
Water	1 Tbs.		Place in skillet.
Tamari	1 Tbs.		Add, mix, boil, low simmer.
Pumpkin seeds	1 cup		Add, mix.
			As liquid evaporates, watch closely and stir often.
			When liquid has turned to a solid, stir often, until seeds puff up and begin to crackle.
			When 60% have turned tan-brown, pour seeds onto a cooling tray.
			Serve.

Variations:

	Yield:	Yield:	Pan size:
	Serves:	Serves:	Cooking time:
	Portion:	Portion:	Oven temp.:

Variations:

SOUPS

An effort has been made with the soup recipes to maintain the natural flavor integrity with enhancing flavors, rather than smothering it with altering flavors, which can be done if the need arises. A good soup depends not only on the selection of complementary ingredients, but on when they are added in the cooking process.

Types of Soup

•**Thin broth** is a clear or semi-clear soup served with or without rice, pasta, sea vegetables, or vegetables. May be seasoned with miso or tamari.

•**Aspic or jellied soup** is served from one mold or from individual molds. Agar-agar is the jelling agent, and is made like thin broth. May be of dramatic presentation.

•**Pot-a-feu** (French), is cooking water from beans, grains, or vegetables that has been strained of solids (which are served with the meal), and combined with other ingredients.

•**Puree** (using blender or precessor) or **creamed soups** are made from one dominant ingredient and complementary seasonings. Creaminess is derived from blended tofu (which separates when boiled, and therefore should be added at end of cooking process) or grain or soy milk.

•**Thick soups, chowders, or stews,** are made with beans, grains, vegetables, or a combination thereof. May be thickened with arrowroot, but usually with the correct ingredients and procedures it is not necessary.

Soup Stock Preparation

•Many cost-effective alternatives exist for making soup stock or adding body to soups, often using items that are clean and wholesome, but commonly thrown away (the soup stock pot is not a garbage container). Such items are:

–asparagus stems (to be removed)

–broccoli stems, skinned

–cabbage hearts and greens

–carrot trimmings

–cauliflower leaves and stems

–celery leaves and hearts

–cilantro stems

–corn cobs, trimmed for sweetness

–mushroom stems

–onion skins

–parsley stems, chopped

–squash cores

–watercress stems, chopped

–odd lots of unused vegetables

•Garnishes made of green leaves, chopped or whole: basil, celery, dill, cilantro/coriander, finely diced green onion, mint, parsley.

•Other suggested garnishes: croutons, tofu sour cream, lemon peel.

IMPORTANT GUIDELINES FOR SOUP COOKERY

•Use vegetable cook water whenever possible.

•Select vegetables that will color complement each other.

•Cut to uniform size.

•Use sea vegetables.

•Add salt near end of cooking process to allow maximum absorption of water, thus less cooking time.

•Instead of all or part of the salt, use tamari or miso, each adding a distinctive, different flavor.

•For long-cooking soups, add most spices and herbs in the last part of cooking so flavors won't cook away.

•Cook with pot covered.

•Parsley and cilantro stems (chopped) bring a strong, distinctive flavor; add 5 mins. before completion.

•Add only boiling water during cooking, never cold water.

BARLEY SOUP (thick)

	Yield: 10 cups	Yield:	Pan size: 6 qt.
	Serves: 10	Serves:	Cooking time: 1½+ hrs.
	Portion: 1 cup	Portion:	Oven temp.:
Water	11 cups		Place in pan.
Barley	1 cup		Add, simmer 1 hr.
Mirepoix (pg. 87)	2 cups		Add, simmer 30 mins.
Mushrooms, ¼"-cut	1 cup		Add.
Tamari	2 Tbs.		Add, mix, simmer 5 mins. Adjust tamari and water.
			Serve.

Variations: Add ¼ cup lentils with barley; add pepper.
Garnish with greens.
Cook barley with finely diced kelp.

BEAN SOUP (thick)

	Yield: 10 cups	Yield:	Pan size: 4 qt.
	Serves: 10	Serves:	Cooking time: 1½ hrs.
	Portion: 1 cup	Portion:	Oven temp.:
Beans (garbanzo, great northern, or navy), soaked	3 cups		Place in pan.
Kelp	6 sq. in.		Add.
Water	10 cups		Add; simmer until 90% cooked.
Mirepoix (pg. 87)	2 cups		Add.
			On completion, blend 40% of beans and return to pan.
			Adjust; serve.

Variations: Adjust with tamari.
Add cardamom, caraway seeds, olive oil and/or lemon juice.
Add cumin and caraway seeds.
Garnish with lemon juice, green onions.

BLACK BEAN SOUP (thick)

Pan size:	4 qt.	Yield:	10 cups	Yield:	
Cooking time:	2 hrs.	Serves:	10	Serves:	
Oven temp.:		Portion:	1 cup	Portion:	

Black beans	2 cups		Soak overnight.
Kelp	6 sq. in.		Rinse; place in pan.
Water	7 cups		Add.
Bay leaf	1		Add.
Carrots, 1/4"-diced	1/2 cup		Add.
Celery, 1/4"-diced	1/2 cup		Add, simmer, cover. Cook until 95% done.
Olive oil	2 Tbs.		Place in skillet at medium-high heat.
Onions, 1/4"-diced	1 cup		Add.
Ginger, finely grated	2 tsp.		Add.
Garlic	1 tsp.		Add, mix, saute until onions are clear.
Salt	1 tsp.		Add to beans; cook to completion.

Variations: Add corn or cumin.
Thicken with thickener and serve over rice.
Puree 20% of beans in blender and return.
Garnish with Tofu Sour Cream (pg. 205).

BORSCHT (thick)

Pan size:	4 qt.	Yield:	10 cups	Yield:	
Cooking time:	40 mins.	Serves:	10	Serves:	
Oven temp.:		Portion:	1 cup	Portion:	

Beets, whole, 2" diam.	2 lbs.		Place in pan.
Turnips, whole	1 lb.		Add.
Salt	1 tsp.		Add.
Rice vinegar	1 tsp.		Add.
Water	7 cups		Add.
Cabbage, coarsely grated	1 cup		Add, cover + 2".
Onions or leeks, 1/2"-diced	1 cup		Add.
Pepper, black	1/2 tsp.		Add, simmer 20 mins. Remove beets and turnips to blender. Blend smooth with cook water. Return to pan.
			Adjust; serve.

Variations:

BROCCOLI SOUP, CREAM OF

	Yield:	10 cups	Yield:		Pan size:	4 qt.
	Serves:	10	Serves:		Cooking time:	30 mins.
	Portion:	1 cup	Portion:		Oven temp.:	

Water	8 cups	Place in pan.
Rolled oats, uncooked, blended	½ cup	Add.
Salt	½ tsp.	Add.
Celery seed	½ tsp.	Add.
Broccoli	3 lbs.	Trim florets from stems and reserve. Trim, skin, and finely dice stems. Add to water. Simmer 30 mins., covered.
		Puree all solids. Return to water.
Broccoli florets, above, finely diced		Add, simmer 2 mins. Do not boil. Adjust (with arrowroot if necessary); serve.

Variations: Use soy milk instead of oats.
Use tamari or miso instead of salt.
Garnish with chopped scallions.
Add cumin.

CABBAGE PUREE

	Yield:	10 cups	Yield:		Pan size:	4 qt.
	Serves:	10	Serves:		Cooking time:	25 mins.
	Portion:	1 cup	Portion:		Oven temp.:	

Water	9 cups	Place in pan.
Salt	½ tsp.	Add.
Cabbage, 1"-chopped	2 lbs.	Add, simmer 15 mins.
Fennel	½ tsp.	Add.
Onion, ¼"-chopped	1 cup	Add, simmer 10 mins.
		Remove to blender and puree. Adjust.
		Return to pan. Heat (do not boil).
		Serve.

Variations:

CABBAGE SOUP (Thin)

Pan size: 4 qt.	Yield: 10 cups	Yield:
Cooking time: 25 mins.	Serves: 10	Serves:
Oven temp.:	Portion: 1 cup	Portion:

Water	9 cups		Place in pan.
Salt	1/2 tsp.		Add.
Cabbage, cut into 1/8" strips	2 lbs.		Add.
Nori, rinsed and diced	6 sq. in.		Add.
Carrots, 1/4"-diced	1 cup		Add.
Caraway seeds	1 tsp.		Add, mix, simmer 15 mins., covered.
Rosemary	1/2 tsp.		Add.
Parsley stems, 1/4"-diced	2 Tbs.		Add, mix, simmer 10 mins.
			Adjust; serve.

Variations: Season with sage, thyme.
Garnish: green onion, cilantro leaves.
Add miso or celery seed.

CARROT ASPIC

Pan size: 4 qt.	Yield: 10 cups	Yield:
Cooking time: 10 mins.	Serves: 10	Serves:
Oven temp.:	Portion: 1 cup	Portion:

Water	8 cups		Place in pan.
Walt	1 tsp.		Add.
Celery seed	1 Tbs.		Add.
Onions, 1/2"-diced	1/2 cup		Add.
Carrots	2 lbs.		Add.
Celery, 1/4"-chopped	4 cups		Add, simmer 22 mins. or until cooked al dente.
			Remove solids to blender, with enough cook water to blend smooth. Return to pot.
Agar-agar powder	2 Tbs.		Add, mix. Bring to simmer and turn off. Mix to dissolve agar-agar. Adjust; spoon test.
			Pour into mold.
			Refrigerate; serve.

Variations:

CARROT PUREE

	Yield:	10 cups	Yield:		Pan size:	4 qt.
	Serves:	10	Serves:		Cooking time:	30 mins.
	Portion:	1 cup	Portion:		Oven temp.:	

Water	6 cups		Place in pan.
Salt	1/2 tsp.		Add.
Onions, finely diced	1 cup		Add.
Carrots, same diameter, trimmed, whole	2 lbs.		Add, simmer 15 mins., covered.
Celery seeds	1 tsp.		Add.
			Cook until carrots are *al dente*. Puree carrots. Return to pan, mix.
			Adjust; serve.

Variations: Add 6 sq. in. nori with onion; or add 1/2 cup winter squash.
Saute leeks 1/4"-diced, and add instead of onion before or after carrots are pureed.
Use cinnamon instead of celery seeds; use cumin seeds instead of celery seeds.

CAULIFLOWER PUREE

	Yield:	10 cups	Yield:		Pan size:	
	Serves:	10	Serves:		Cooking time:	
	Portion:	1 cup	Portion:		Oven temp.:	

Cauliflower	3 lbs.		Trim; place in pan.
Water	4 cups		Add.
Salt	1/2 tsp.		Add to water; boil.
Celery seeds	1/2 tsp.		Add to water, cover, cook until tender.
			Process cauliflower. Add to cook water. Mix, adjust.
			Serve.

Variations: Good over pasta.
Garnish with greens or dash of nutmeg.
Add basil and/or thyme.

CELERY ASPIC

Pan size: 4 qt.	Yield: 10 cups	Yield:
Cooking time: 30 mins.	Serves: 10	Serves:
Oven temp.:	Portion: 1 cup	Portion:

Water	6 cups		Place in pan.
Onion, halved	1 cup		Add.
Celery, 1/2"-chopped	6 cups		Add.
Salt	1 Tbs.		Add, simmer 30 mins.
			Remove all solids to blender and blend with cook water until smooth. Reserve.
Agar-agar powder	1 1/2 Tbs.		Add to cook water; mix until dissolved.
			Return blended celery to pan. Mix, bring to simmer, mix well. Spoon test; adjust. Pour into mold. Refrigerate. Serve.

Variations:

CELERY SOUP, CREAM OF

Pan size: 4 qt.	Yield: 10 cups	Yield:
Cooking time: 30+/- mins.	Serves: 10	Serves:
Oven temp.:	Portion: 1 cup	Portion:

Water	6 cups		Place in pan.
Salt	1/2 tsp.		Add.
Celery, 1/2"-diced	8 cups		Add, cook 30 mins. or until tender. Puree celery.
Tofu	1 lb.		Puree; add to pan.
Caraway seeds	1 tsp.		Add, mix, do not boil.
			Adjust (with arrowroot if necessary); serve.

Variations: Garnish with celery leaves or parsley.
Cream with soy milk instead of tofu, adjusting water as needed.

CORN AND SQUASH SOUP (Thin)

	Yield:	10 cups	Yield:		Pan size:	4 qt.
	Serves:	10	Serves:		Cooking time:	25 mins.
	Portion:	1 cup	Portion:		Oven temp.:	

Corn	5 ears		Place in pan.
Salt	1/2 tsp.		Add.
Water	8 cups		Add, boil, parcook. Remove corn and reserve. Cut corn from cob and reserve.
Onions, finely diced	1 cup		Add to water. Place cobs in water. Simmer 15 mins.
Squash, yellow summer, trimmed, whole	4 lbs.		Add; cook until soft. Remove cobs. Place squash in processor; process.
			Place squash in new pan.
Corn, above			Add. Adjust quantity with cook water; mix.
			Serve.

Variations: Add tamari or miso.
Garnish with chopped parsley.

CORN CHOWDER (Thick)

	Yield:	10 cups	Yield:		Pan size:	4 qt.
	Serves:	10	Serves:		Cooking time:	40+/- mins.
	Portion:	1 cup	Portion:		Oven temp.:	

Corn	10 ears		Cut corn from cob and reserve. Place cobs in pan.
Water	8 cups		Add.
Salt	1/2 tsp.		Add.
Celery, 1/4"-diced	1/2 cup		Add.
Onions, 1/4"-diced	1/4 cup		Add.
Carrots, 1/4"-diced	1/4 cup		Add, mix, simmer covered until 80% cooked.
			Remove cobs.
Celery seeds	1 tsp.		Add.
Rolled oats, blended well	1/4 cup		Add and mix when vegetables 90% cooked.
Corn, above			Add, cook, adjust.
			Serve.

Variations: Add 2 Tbs. white miso.
Add diced green pepper.
Garnish with parsley or diced green onions.

Pan size:	Yield:	10 cups	Yield:		**CUCUMBER SOUP, CREAMED (Chilled)**
Cooking time:	Serves:	10	Serves:		
Oven temp.:	Portion:	1 cup	Portion:		

Garlic, diced	1 tsp.		Place in blender.
Green onion, chopped	4 Tbs.		Add.
Dill (fresh), minced	2 Tbs.		Add.
Water	1 cup		Add, blend smooth, stop.
Water	3 cups		Add.
Cucumber, skinned, diced (seeding optional)	4 cups		Add.
Yogurt	4 cups		Add.
Salt	1$\frac{1}{4}$ tsp.		Add.
Pepper	$\frac{1}{2}$ tsp.		Add, blend smooth.
			Serve chilled.

Variations: Garnish: diced fresh dill or green onion.
Blend cooked tofu with vegetables (don't boil).

Pan size:	4 qt.	Yield:	10 cups	Yield:		**FISH CHOWDER (Thick)**
Cooking time:	37 mins.	Serves:	10	Serves:		
Oven temp.:		Portion:	1 cup	Portion:		

Shiitake mushrooms	3 small		Break, place in bowl.
Water	1 cup		Add, mix, rest.
Water, cold	7 cups		Place in pan.
Rice	$\frac{1}{2}$ cup		Add.
Salt	1 tsp.		Add, simmer 15 mins.
Celery, $\frac{1}{4}$"-diced	2 cups		Add.
Carrots, $\frac{1}{4}$"-diced	1 cup		Add.
White root vegetable, $\frac{1}{4}$"-diced	1 cup		Add, simmer 10 mins.
Sage	$\frac{1}{2}$ tsp.		Add.
Marjoram	$\frac{1}{2}$ tsp.		Add, mix, simmer 10 mins.
Fish (scrod or haddock), boned, 1"-chopped	2 lbs.		Add, mix, simmer 2 mins.
			Adjust; serve.

Variations:

FISH SOUP (Thin)

	Yield:	10 cups	Yield:		Pan size:
	Serves:	10	Serves:		Cooking time:
	Portion:	1 cup	Portion:		Oven temp.:

Water	8 cups	Place in pot. Boil.
Potatoes, whole	3 cups	Add. When well cooked, remove; peel, blend with cook water, return to pot with balance of cook water.
Fish (sole, bass, monk, halibut, grouper, or snapper) cut into bite-size pieces	1 lb.	Add.
Salt	1 tsp.	Add.
Fennel	1/2 tsp.	Add.
Tarragon	1 tsp.	Add.
Thyme	1/2 tsp.	Add.
Leeks, diced	1 cup	Add.
Lemon rind	pinch	Add; simmer 20 mins.
		Adjust and serve.

Variations: Garnish with chopped parsley or green onions.
Use more than one kind of fish, with the total equalling 1 lb.

GREENS SOUP, CREAM OF

	Yield:	10 cups	Yield:		Pan size:	4 qt.
	Serves:	10	Serves:		Cooking time:	10 mins.
	Portion:	1 cup	Portion:		Oven temp.:	

Kale, collards, or mustard greens	2 lbs.	Trim stems. Place in pan.
Water	6 cups	Add. Cover; steam until cooked.
Cook water		Place greens in blender with necessary amount of water. Blend; stop.
Tofu, cooked	1 lb.	Add.
Miso	3 Tbs.	Add, blend; stop.
		Adjust; serve.

Variations:

Pan size: 4 qt.	Yield: 10 cups	Yield:	**LENTIL SOUP,**
Cooking time: 1½ hrs.	Serves: 10	Serves:	**BASIC**
Oven temp.:	Portion: 1 cup	Portion:	**(Thick)**

Water	11 cups		Place in pan. Bring to simmer.
Corn oil	2 Tbs.		Place in skillet, medium high.
Onions, ½"-diced	2 cups		Add, saute until clear. With minimum oil, add to simmering water.
Lentils, brown	3 cups		Add.
Lentils, red	½ cups		Add; simmer 1 hr., 15 mins.
Celery seed	1 tsp		Add; simmer 15 mins.
			Adjust; serve.
			[NOTE: All brown or all red lentils may be used.]

Variations: Serve over rice.
Add cumin and/or caraway; or add cinnamon, ginger, and cloves.
Add coriander.
Garnish with lemon juice, greens.

Pan size: 6 qt.	Yield: 10 cups	Yield:	**LENTIL SOUP,**
Cooking time: 1½ hrs.	Serves: 10	Serves:	**GREEK (Thick)**
Oven temp.:	Portion: 1 cup	Portion:	

Water	10 cups		Place in pan.
Lentils, green	3 cups		Add.
Lentils, red	¼ cup		Add.
Onions, ½"-diced	2 cups		Add, simmer, cover. Cook 1 hr.
Bay leaf	1		Add.
Carrots, ½"-diced	1 cup		Add.
Garlic, minced	2 Tbs.		Add.
Celery, ½"-diced	1 cup		Add, mix, simmer 10 mins., covered. Turn heat off.
Olive oil	2 Tbs.		Add, mix, adjust.
			Serve.

Variations: Garnish with lemon wedges.
Substitute great northern or navy beans for lentils.
Garnish: chopped fresh mint or cilantro.

LENTIL SOUP, RED, Egyptian (Thick)

| | | Yield: 10 cups | Yield: | Pan size: 4 qt. |
| | | Serves: 10 | Serves: | Cooking time: 1½ hrs. |
		Portion: 1 cup	Portion:	Oven temp.:
Water	10 cups			Place in pan.
Lentils, red	3 cups			Add, simmer 1 hr. 15 mins., covered. Stir often to prevent sticking on bottom.
Salt	½ tsp.			Add.
Onions, ¼"-diced	1 cup			Add, mix, simmer 15 mins.
				Adjust; serve.

Variations: Add cumin or coriander or cardamom.
Add carrots or celery.

MISO SOUP (Thin)

| | | Yield: 10 cups | Yield: | Pan size: 3 qt. |
| | | Serves: 10 | Serves: | Cooking time: 35 mins. |
		Portion: 1 cup	Portion:	Oven temp.:
Water	10 cups			Place in pan.
Nori or alaria	12 sq. in.			Rinse until soft, ¼"-chop, add. Simmer 15 mins., covered.
Carrots, finely sliced	1 cup			Add.
Onions, finely sliced, cut to half-moons	2 cups			Add.
Cabbage, finely sliced	1 cup			Add, simmer 15 mins., covered.
Miso	3 Tbs.			Make slurry, add, mix. Poach 5 mins. Do not boil. Adjust.
				Serve immediately.
				[NOTE: Soup should be served immediately and not reheated if nutritional value is to be retained.]

Variations: Cook with fresh greens.
Cook with grated ginger.

Pan size: 4 qt.	Yield: 10 cups	Yield:	MISO SOUP,
Cooking time: 40 mins.	Serves: 10	Serves:	KOREAN
Oven temp.:	Portion: 1 cup	Portion:	(Thin)

Water	8 cups		Place in pot.
Onions, 1"-chopped	1 cup		Add.
Carrots, ³/₄"-chopped	1 cup		Add.
Celery, 1"-chopped	1 cup		Add; parcook.
Chinese cabbage stems, 1"-chopped	1 cup		Add; parcook.
Tofu, ³/₄"-chopped	2 lbs.		Add.
Chinese cabbage greens, 2"-chopped	2 cups		Add.
Barley malt	1 Tbs.		Add.
Sesame oil, dark	1 tsp.		Add.
Miso	3 Tbs.		Make slurry, add, mix, adjust. Poach 5 mins. *Do not boil.*
			Serve.

Variations: Use tempeh instead of tofu.
Garnish: diced green onions or gomasio (pg. 120).

Pan size: 4 qt.	Yield: 10 cups	Yield:	MUSHROOM
Cooking time: 27+/- mins.	Serves: 10	Serves:	SOUP, CREAM OF
Oven temp.:	Portion: 1 cup	Portion:	

Rolled oats	2 cups		Place in blender. Blend to fine flour. Place in pan.
Water	7 cups		Add, mix, simmer 20 mins., stirring. Reserve.
Corn oil	¹/₄ cup		Place in skillet on medium-high heat.
Mushrooms, thinly sliced	2 lbs.		Add, saute until tender.
Water	¹/₂ cup		Add, reduce 50%.
Tamari	1 Tbs.		Add.
			Place half the mushrooms in blender. Blend smooth and pour into oat water.
			Add skillet contents to oat water. Simmer 2 mins.
			Adjust; serve.

Variations: Garnish with green onions and herbed croutons.

NOODLE BROTH (Thin)

	Yield: 10 cups	Yield:	Pan size: 4 qt.
	Serves: 10	Serves:	Cooking time: 30 mins.
	Portion: 1 cup	Portion:	Oven temp.:
Water with tamari or pot-a-feu	9 cups		Place in pan; simmer.
Mirepoix (pg. 86)	3 cups		Add.
Nori, finely diced	6 sq. in.		Add; simmer 15 mins., covered.
Noodles	2 cups		Add, stir occasionally, simmer 15 mins.
Miso	4 Tbs.		Add.
			Serve.

Variations: Add 1 Tbs. grated ginger with noodles.
Garnish with diced cilantro leaves.
Use tamari instead of miso.
Use vegetable cooking water.

NOODLE SQUASH SOUP (Thick)
[from Pamela Kentish, Chef, East Calais, Vt.]

	Yield: 10 cups	Yield:	Pan size: 4 qt.
	Serves: 10	Serves:	Cooking time: 26 mins.
	Portion: 1 cup	Portion:	Oven temp.:
Water	6 cups		Place in pan; simmer.
Corn oil	1 Tbs.		Place in skillet, medium-high heat.
Onions, 1/2"-diced	1 cup		Add, saute until clear.
			Place onions in simmering water with minimum oil.
Salt	1/2 tsp.		Add.
Buttercup squash, stemmed, seeded, 3/4"-chopped	4 cups		Add, mix, simmer 5 mins.
Noodles, whole wheat	2 cups		Add, mix, simmer 15 mins.
			Adjust; serve.

Variations: Use udon or soba noodles.
Garnish with diced parsley or green onions.
Add miso, cinnamon, thyme, rosemary.

Pan size: 4 qt.	Yield: 10 cups	Yield:	**ONION SOUP**
Cooking time: 1+ hr.	Serves: 10	Serves:	**(Thin)**
Oven temp.:	Portion: 1 cup	Portion:	

Oil	¼ cup		Place in pan.
Onions, thinly sliced, cut in half-moons (3 lbs.)	10 cups		Add; saute until almost clear.
Tamari	2 Tbs.		Add, mix, simmer 5 mins.
Water	¼ cup		Add, cover, steam 2 mins.
Water, boiling	12 cups		Add.
Bay leaf	1 large		Add, simmer 40 mins.
Celery seed	1 tsp.		Add, simmer 15 mins.
Miso, dark	2 Tbs.		Add, poach 2 mins.
			Add.

Variations:

Pan size: 4 qt.	Yield: 10 cups	Yield:	**SEITAN SOUP**
Cooking time: 1 hr. 10 mins.	Serves: 10	Serves:	**(Thick)**
Oven temp.:	Portion: 1 cup	Portion:	

Water	10 cups		Place in pan, heat.
Kelp, rinsed, ¼"-chopped	20 sq .in.		Add.
Tamari	½ cup		Add.
Onions, ½"-diced	2 cups		Add, simmer 30 mins.
Sage	½ tsp.		Add.
Celery seed	½ tsp.		Add.
Whole wheat pastry flour	¼ cup		Make slurry; add, mix, simmer 10 mins.
Seitan, ½"-diced	3 cups		Add, adjust.
			Serve.

Variations: Add carrots, celery, green beans, peas, and/or cabbage.
Add whole wheat noodles.

SPLIT PEA SOUP (Thick)

	Yield:	10 cups	Yield:		Pan size:	4 qt.
	Serves:	10	Serves:		Cooking time:	1½ hrs.
	Portion:	1 cup	Portion:		Oven temp.:	

Water	9 cups		Place in pot, simmer.
Split peas, green	2 cups		Add.
Kelp	10 sq .in.		Add, mix, simmer 1 hr. covered.
Carrots, ½"-diced	½ cup		Add.
Celery, ¼"-diced	1 cup		Add.
Onions, ½"-diced	1 cup		Add. Cook until soup is smooth and vegetables are cooked.
Salt	½ tsp.		Add, mix, adjust.
			Immediately before serving, bring soup to boil, turn off.
Mint, finely diced	3 Tbs.		Add, mix, serve immediately.

Variations: Delete mint; add herbs and spices, or miso or tamari.
Substitute carrots, celery, and onion for equal amounts of sauteed leeks and mushrooms.
Serve thick over rice.

SPLIT PEA SOUP, YELLOW (Thick)

[from Richard Sultani, Exec. Chef, Les Champs Restaurant, Washington, D.C.]

	Yield:	10 cups	Yield:		Pan size:	
	Serves:	10	Serves:		Cooking time:	2 hrs.
	Portion:	1 cup	Portion:		Oven temp.:	

Water	10 cups		Place in pot.
Yellow split peas	3 cups		Add, bring to boil, simmer, cover, stir every 10 mins. Cook 1½ hrs. Adjust water.
Onions, chopped	2 cups		Add.
Carrots, diced	½ cup		Add, cook 15 mins.
Celery seed	½ tsp.		Add.
Black pepper	1 tsp.		Add.
Cumin (ground)	1 tsp.		Add.
Lemon juice (fresh)	1 Tbs.		Add, mix, cook 15 mins. Adjust. Turn heat off.
			Serve.

Variations: Garnish: minced parsley; chopped pistachio nuts; lemon wedges.
Add curry powder.
Add ½ cup brown rice when peas have cooked ½ hr.

SQUASH, SUMMER, PUREE

Pan size:	4 qt.	Yield:	10 cups	Yield:	
Cooking time:	15 mins.	Serves:	10	Serves:	
Oven temp.:		Portion:	1 cup	Portion:	

Water	4 cups		Place in pan, simmer.
Yellow squash, whole, or zucchini, trimmed	4 lbs.		Add. Cook squash until tender.
			Puree squash in blender; return to pan. Do not boil. Adjust.
Corn oil	1 Tbs.		Place in skillet at medium-high heat.
Salt	1/2 tsp.		Add.
Onions, 1/4"-diced	1/2 cup		Add, saute until clear.
			Add to soup. Adjust.
			Serve.

Variations: Garnish with grated fresh ginger, parsley, black pepper, or nutmeg.

SQUASH, WINTER, PUREE

Pan size:	4 qt.	Yield:	10 cups	Yield:	
Cooking time:	30+/- mins.	Serves:	10	Serves:	
Oven temp.:		Portion:	1 cup	Portion:	

Squash, hubbard or butternut, seeded, 1"-diced	6 cups		Place in pan.
Salt	1/2 tsp.		Add.
Water	6 cups		Add, heat.
Onions, 1/4"-diced	1 cup		Add, cover, simmer 30+/- mins. until cooked.
			Puree squash in blender. Return to pan. Heat (do not boil).
			Adjust; serve.

Variations: Add nutmeg after blending.
　　　　　　Add curry after blending.

SWEET & SOUR SOUP (Thin)

	Yield:	10 cups	Yield:		Pan size:	4 qt.
	Serves:	10	Serves:		Cooking time:	25+/- mins.
	Portion:	1 cup	Portion:		Oven temp.:	

Corn oil	1 Tbs.	Place in pan.
Salt	1 tsp.	Add.
Onions, $1/2$"-diced	1 cup	Add, saute until clear.
Water, boiling	10 cups	Add, simmer.
Carrots, $1/2$"-diced	$1/2$ cup	Add.
Celery, $1/2$"-diced	$1/2$ cup	Add, simmer 10 mins.
Broccoli stems, skinned, $1/2$"- diced	1 cup	Add.
Celery seed	$1/2$ tsp.	Add.
Barley malt	2 Tbs.	Add.
Rice vinegar	2 Tbs.	Add.
Mustard powder	$1/2$ tsp.	Add, mix, simmer 10 mins.
		Adjust; serve.

Variations: Add cooked beans or other vegetables; or rice or noodles.

VEGETABLE SOUP, BASIC (Thick)

	Yield:	10 cups	Yield:		Pan size:	4 qt.
	Serves:	10	Serves:		Cooking time:	2 hrs.
	Portion:	1 cup	Portion:		Oven temp.:	

Water	8 cups	Place in pan, boil.
Kelp, diced	8"	Add.
Lentils, red	1 cup	Add, simmer $1/2$ hr.; stir.
Cabbage, 3"-diced	1 cup	Add.
Onions, diced	1 cup	Add. Simmer 1 hr., covered.
Barley, hulled	$1/2$ cup	Add.
Salt	1 tsp.	Add.
Bay leaf	1	Add.
Carrots, bite-size diced	1 cup	Add.
Celery seed	1 tsp.	Add.
Celery, bite-size diced	1 cup	Add.
Corn meal	$1/4$ cup	Add, simmer 25 mins., covered.
Green beans or snow peas, whole	$1/2$ cup	Add, simmer 5 mins. Serve.

Variations: Add sea vegetables; or add $1/2$ cup lentils with onion.
    Add cumin and basil.
    Use tamari instead of salt.

			WHITE BEAN
Pan size: 4 qt.	*Yield:* 10 cups	*Yield:*	**SOUP (Thick)**
Cooking time: 1¼+/- hrs.	*Serves:* 10	*Serves:*	
Oven temp.:	*Portion:* 1 cup	*Portion:*	

White beans	2 cups		Soak overnight; rinse.
Kelp, rinsed, ½"-chopped	6 sq. in.		Add.
Water	8 cups		Add, simmer until 80% done.
Carrots, ⅛"-diced	½ cup		Add.
Celery, ⅛"-diced	¼ cup		Add.
Celery seed	½ tsp.		Add.
Bay leaf	1 small		Add, simmer until beans are 95% done.
Olive oil	3 Tbs.		Place in skillet, med-high heat.
Onions, ¼"-diced	2 cups		Add.
Garlic, minced	1 tsp.		Add, mix.
Tamari	2 Tbs.		Add, saute until onions are clear. Add to soup; adjust; complete cooking. Serve.

Variations:

Pan size:	*Yield:*	*Yield:*
Cooking time:	*Serves:*	*Serves:*
Oven temp.:	*Portion:*	*Portion:*

Variations:

VEGETABLES

IMPORTANT GUIDELINES FOR VEGETABLE PREPARATION AND COOKERY

Preparation:

•Wash or rinse in cold water, not bruising the skin.

•Use vegetable brush as necessary and re-rinse in cold water.

•Peel if not organic; otherwise cook with skins.

•Keep minimum time from refrigeration to cooking or serving.

•Make judgmental selection of ingredients that will complement each other if combining:

—Cut vegetables to uniform size and various but uniform shape when possible, adding to the character of soups and salads.

—Use 5 to 6 vegetables.

—Use minimum amount of water.

•Cook whole or in as large a piece as possible to maintain nutrients and flavor.

•Cook as briefly as possible.

—Parcook, if it is going to be held.

—Cook *al dente*, if it is going to be served immediately.

•Cooking time varies depending on temperature of vegetable at time of immersing in boiling water.

•When steaming, use such quantities that will steam evenly.

•Sometimes, to complete stir frying, add water at high heat and cover to steam.

•If water cooking, use as little water as possible.

•If water cooking, upon completion of cooking place pot in a sink of cold water momentarily until cooking process stops.

•Keep minimum time between cooking and serving.

•Don't overcook.

•Though it is preferable to cook and serve immediately, it may be necessary to parcook, refrigerate, and finish the cooking to order by sauteeing and adjusting seasonings or steaming and serving with or without sauce.

•Reserve cooking water for soup.

•People eating natural whole foods tend towards slightly larger portions of vegetables.

Buying:

•Develop a locally-grown, organic produce supplier; it is highly preferable.

•Locally grown, organic produce is highly preferable to that coming from thousands of miles away.

•Locally grown produce often has a different "peak harvesting season" than shown on *Vegetable Shipping Chart* (see pg. 307).

•In-season vegetables have the highest possible nutritive and flavor value, quality, and lowest price.

•Out-of-season vegetables have lowest possible nutritive and flavor value, quality, and highest price.

•Specify and insist on freshness.

•Inspect deliveries; avoid leaky vegetables as seen on boxes.

•Buy vegetables that are not bruised.

•The use of pesticides and/or post-harvesting chemical treatment is an almost foregone conclusion unless certified as organic.

•Third World countries tend towards the indiscriminate use of chemical pesticides and post-harvesting treatments.

Storing:

Refrigerate immediately upon delivery, except as noted.

ARTICHOKES (GLOBE)

Preparing:

Bend back loose leaves and snap off at base.

Trim stem base.

Cut off woody tops.

To prevent discoloration, rub cut areas with lemon juice.

Serving:

Serve whole with dips of melted butter, herbed Tofu Sauce or Oriental Dressing.

Quality:

Buy vegetables that are compact, plump, heavy, and that have a consistent green color.

Avoid vegetables that are wilting, drying, molding, or have hard tips and spreading leaves.

Portions:

100 portions @ 1 medium artichoke: buy 20–25 lbs.

Buying:

Grades: U.S. 1; U.S. 2

Packed: 7" box holding 20–25 lbs. net.

Sold by count: Lg., 28; Med., 36, 48; Sm., 56.

Storing:

Best stored at 36–40° with 90–95% relative humidity (brief holding).

Basis:

Originated in Sicily; popularized by Catherine de Medici's notorious appetite for artichokes; then considered an aphrodesiac.

ASPARAGUS

Preparing:

Trim white end from stalk and reserve, trying to leave stalks the same length.

Loses tenderness quickly before cooking when it dries out and is warm.

Serving:

Use white ends in soups or stews or finely dice for crunchiness in salads.

Use finely diced green in salads.

Place horizontally, tied in bunches, in large pan of boiling water and simmer; remove with large skimmer and lay soldier-style in serving pan.

Place in steamer soldier-style, horizontally, so that steam can get evenly to all pieces.

Serve hot with Tofu Sauce or butter on top.

Cut into 1" pieces, cook and serve au gratin or in casseroles, quiche, or soups.

Serve cold in salads or plain on a bed of lettuce with dressing.

When cooked aprraragus begins to bend when held horizontally by its base, remove from water immediately.

Quality:

Buy with compact, closed tips; fresh looking, straight, firm, and at least two-thirds green. Diameter has no relationship to tenderness.

Avoid opened and spread tips, more than one-third white, crackcd, limp, angular, or flat stalks.

Portions:

100 portions @ 4 medium spears, cooked: buy 30 lbs.

Buying:

Grades: U.S. 1; U.S. 2.

Packed: container holding 26–30 lbs.; pony crate holding 12 lbs.

Storing:

Best stored at 36–40° with 85–90% relative humidity.

Basis:

Native to central Europe, western and central Asia. Was considered a luxury and was highly prized in ancient Greece, Egypt, and Rome.

BEANS, GREEN (SNAP)

Preparing:

Keep minimum time between refrigeration and cooking.

Trim stem end; preferable to cook whole. Cut or French cut as desired.

Use as soon after delivery as possible.

Bring water to a rolling boil and slowly place beans in water, allowing it to remain boiling; parcook or cook *al dente* and remove beans from water or place pot in a sink of cold water to stop the cooking process.

Good for stir fry or steaming.

Cook whole (low labor), cut, or French cut.

Serving:

Serve with Tofu–Lemon Sauce or a mushroom sauce.

Use in soups or stews.

Serve long beans on a bed of lettuce with lemon juice.

Serve hot garnished with roasted slivered almonds or tamari-roasted sunflower seeds.

Mix with grains and a little tamari.

Cook with anise or cinnamon. Complementary vegetables: onions and mushrooms.

Diced and parcooked in salads.

Quality:

Buy beans that are plump, crisp, firm, and that will snap in your fingers.

Avoid beans that appear shrunken, wilted, moldy, or soft.

Portions:

100 portions @ 3 oz. cooked: buy 23 lbs.

Buying:

Grades: U.S. Fancy; U.S. 1; U.S. Combination; U.S. 2.

Packed in containers, 28–30 pounds net.

Storing:

Best stored at 45–50° F. with 85–90% relative humidity.

Basis:

Originated in Mexico and Central America.

BEETS

Preparing:

When cooking, leave whole with skin, root ends, and an inch of stems intact to prevent bleeding.

Skins slip off easily after cooking while trimming root ends and stems.

Leave in cooking liquid until ready to use. Same is applicable for pressure cooking or steaming.

Serving:

Use uncooked in salads, grated.

Can be pickled.

Use in beet borscht, served hot or cold with Tofu Sour Cream.

Cooked, sliced, or diced, with butter or Tofu Sour Cream.

Quality:

Buy medium size, well shaped with smooth, firm flesh that is purple-red.

Avoid those that are soft, flabby, rough, or shriveled.

Very large beets are more likely to be tough or woody than medium or small beets.

Portions:

100 portions @ 3 oz. cooked, sliced, or diced: buy 44 lbs. with tops or 25 lbs. topped.

Buying:

Grades: U.S. 1; U.S. 2.

Packed: wirebound crates 45 lbs., net $^1/_2$ WGA crate, 45 lbs.; 18 bunches, 15 lbs.; topped beets in sacks, 25 and 50 lbs.

Storing:

Best stored at 34–38° with 90–95% relative humidity.

Basis:

Originally cultivated from wild strains in Egypt and Western Europe.

BROCCOLI

Preparing:

Trim off undesirable sections.

To serve raw, trim florets as needed.

Cut as needed for cooking design.

Finely dice stems for soups.

Cut off skin from main stem and dice for soups or stews.

Serving:

Serve raw pieces in salads or for dips.

Make broccoli soup, either pureed or creamed with tofu.

Select stalk size for portion control; cut and steam until parcooked and serve with butter, lemon sauce, garlic sauce, or Oriental Sauce.

$1/4$"-French-cut pieces for stir frying in peanut oil with grated ginger.

Parcook in water and reserve water for soups or stews.

Buying:

Buy compact heads that are lush with their natural color, depending on their variety, such as sage or dark green or slightly purplish.

Look for tender green stems that have not dried out.

Avoid yellow buds or yellow bud stems (over-maturity), dry, woody stems, wrinkled or wilted leaves. Avoid soft, slippery, dark, water-soaked spots; they are signs of deterioration.

Portions:

100 portions @ 3 oz. cooked, cut spears: buy 30 lbs.

Buying:

Grades: U.S. Fancy; U.S. 1; U.S. 2.

Packed: containers of 21 lbs. net; pony crate 40–42 lbs.

Storing:

Best stored at 34–38° with 90–95% relative humidity; keep well ventilated.

Basis:

Originated in the wild form around the Mediterranean.

BRUSSELS SPROUTS

Preparing:

Place in warm water (70–80° F.) for removal of insects.

Rinse in cold water.

Trim stems and remove discolored leaves.

Preferable to parcook in steamer or simmer in pot.

Overcooking tends to change color, make them become mushy, and adds a strong flavor.

Serving:

Serve with butter or a tofu sauce with lemon, garlic, and onion.

Serve with lemon juice.

Sautee garlic in olive oil, cool, add lemon juice, and marinate before steaming.

Sautee small Brussels sprouts, add sliced mushrooms, sautee, serve.

Quality:

Select small firm heads with minimally discolored leaves, or preferably all fresh green leaves that have no blemishes. Inspect inner leaves for freshness and to see that they are compact.

Avoid large, puffy heads, where the leaves have become loose, with many discolored outer leaves.

Portions:

100 portions @ 3 oz. cooked : buy 25 lbs.

Buying:

Grades: U.S. 1; U.S. 2.

Packed: container holding 25 lbs.; bushel container of 35 lbs.

Storing:

Best stored at 36° F. with 90–95% relative humidity.

Basis:

A European native, developed mostly by the French. A crucifer (mustard) family.

CABBAGE

Preparing:

Remove discolored leaves.

Cut for use.

Serving:

Slice thinly for cole slaw, after removing inner core; reserve and chop core for use in soups and stews.

Cut in quarters or eighths, leaving the inner core while cooking, and remove inner core when cooked.

Dice to bite-size pieces for boiling or steaming.

Cook red cabbage separately so as not to discolor white cabbage.

Good for flavoring soups and stews.

Cook or steam with caraway seeds or tahini.

Serve plain with a little Oriental Sauce.

Quality:

Red cabbage: look for deep, rich color.

Bok choy: look for crisp, firm stalks.

Chinese cabbage: look for healthy outer leaves.

Reject cabbage with old-looking leaves, burst heads, or unhealthy discoloration. Accept solid, hard, and heavy heads.

Types:

•*Green:* somewhat round and light green.

•*Red:* somewhat round with a purplish-red color.

•*Bok choy:* very tender, large white stalks with dark green leaves (See pg. 74).

•*Chinese cabbage (napa):* has a natural yellowish-green color crinkly leaves, and is strongly veined.

•*Savoy cabbage:* round with strong-veined leaves.

Portions:

100 portions @ 3 oz. wedge, cooked: buy 24 lbs.

Buying:

Grades: U.S. 1; U.S. Commercial.

Packed: containers of 50 lbs. net; bags of 50–60 lbs.

Storing:

Best stored at 36–40° with 90–95% relative humidity; needs ventilation.

Basis:

Used in prehistoric times, mostly in northern Europe.

CARROTS

Preparing:

Organic carrots: rinse, scrub with brush and rinse.

Non-organic carrots: rinse and scrape outer layer of skin with vegetable scraper. Trim ends removing green.

Since carrot tops tend to live off the root, remove immediately.

Serving:

Raw in sticks; finely diced or thinly sliced in salads.

Cut and shape as garnish, cooked or uncooked.

Simmer or steam, serve plain or with a wide variety of glazes.

Good in soups or stews.

Grate for carrot salad.

Cook and blend for a carrot drink.

Add to green vegetables for color contrast.

Quality:

Buy carrots that are firm, with healthy, natural, deep orange color, and that will snap when broken.

Avoid those that are dry, soft, shriveled, or shrunken.

Portions:

100 portions @ 3 oz., sliced or diced, cooked: buy 25 lbs.

Buying:

Grades: U.S. Extra No. 1; U.S. No. 1; U.S. No. 1 Jumbo; U.S. No. 2.

Packed: containers of 50 lbs.; bags containing 25 or 50 lbs.; cellophane packs of 1,2,3, or 5 lbs.

Storing:

Best stored at 34–50° with 90–95% relative humidity.

Basis:

Originated in Afghanistan where they were cultivated for medicinal purposes; spread west, arriving in England from Holland in the 15th century.

CAULIFLOWER

Preparing:

Remove outer leaves and core and reserve for dicing into soups or stews.

For best flavor, steam whole head until cooked; cut and serve.

Boil or steam according to size.

Serving:

Raw, small florets with dips.

Very small florets, raw in salads.

Serve as cooked vegetable, boiled, steamed, or stir fried. Serve plain or with a sauce, garnish, or condiment.

Serve with greens as a color contrast.

Use in pickling.

Marinate with other color contrasting vegetables and serve raw as a salad.

Quality:

Buy large or small heads with firm green leaves and white granular heads.

Avoid discolored heads with open or dry leaves.

Portions:

100 portions @ 3 oz. cooked each: buy 43 lbs.

Buying:

Grades: U.S. No. 1.

Packed: 21–25 lb. containers (9, 12, or 16 heads each); containers holding 40–60 lbs.

Storing:

Best stored at 36–40° with relative humidity of 85–90% (store tops down).

Basis:

A member of the cabbage group in the mustard family; comes initially from Europe.

CELERY

Preparing:

Remove ribs of celery from cluster and place in cold water; drain water, scrub off dirt with bristle brush, rinse, and trim ends.

Reserve leaves for soups or garnishes.

Slow cooking of large pieces maintains most natural integrity.

Do not steam celery.

Serving:

Dice to bite-size pieces and serve as a vegetable.

Finely dice and add to salads or to sandwiches.

Use in stuffings and soups.

Celery is mostly a summer dish served cooked, blanched, parcooked, or raw.

Quality:

Buy celery that is fresh-looking, has natural color and crisp ribs.

Avoid celery that is old-looking, has loose stalks, discolored stalk or limp celery. Leaves should be healthy-looking (green and fresh).

Portions:

100 portions @ 3 oz. sliced, raw: buy 25 lbs.

Buying:

Grades: U.S. Extra 1; U.S. 1; U.S. 2.

Packed: containers of $1^{1}/_{2}$, 2, $2^{1}/_{2}$, or 3 doz.

Storing:

Best stored at 36° with 90–95% relative humidity (keep moist).

Basis:

Originally ranging from Sweden to ancient Greece, where the winner of an athletic event was given a bunch of celery as a trophy of victory.

CHINESE CABBAGE

Preparing:

Cut to size desired (the larger, the more food value).

Boil or steam.

Stir fry.

Serving:

Serve with other greens; as a side dish; use in salads; serve in soups and stews.

Quality:

Buy fresh, crisp, clean, light green color.

Avoid wilted, soft, or discolored vegetables.

Portions:

100 portions @ 2 oz. raw: buy 15 lbs.

Buying:

There are no grades or federal standards.

Packed: 1.45 bushel container holding 50–55 lbs.; container holding 40 lbs.; sometimes smaller container.

Storing:

Best stored at 34–38° with 95% relative humidity (brief storage).

Basis:

Originated in China. In Chinese, *wong nga bok* or *siu choy*. In Japanese, *hakusai*.

CORN (Sweet)

Preparing:

Remove husks and steam until tender.

Bake with husk at 375° for about 20 minutes or until tender.

Cut kernels from cob and serve plain.

Cooking cobs in soups adds a distinctive but delicate flavor.

Serving:

Raw, cut from cob; reserve kernels and cook whole cobs in soups, adding kernels near the end of cooking process and removing cobs before serving.

Serve with greens, as in succotash.

Serve in salads, raw or parcooked.

Serve whole or half cobs, or cut away kernels and serve.

Quality:

Avoid kernels with dents; flattened, depressed kernels; very mature or large kernels; and dry husks.

Buy corn with full, plump kernels and fresh green husks.

Portions:

100 portions @ 1 ear: buy 100 ears.

Buying:

Grades:

U.S. Fancy—cob not less than 6", free of worms, smut, decay, rust, insect damage, or disease. Has plump, milky kernels and covered with fresh husks.

U.S. 1—cob not less than 5" long, covered with fresh husks. Fairly well filled with plump, milky kernels and free of rust, decay, smut, worms, and insect damage or disease.

U.S. 2—not less than 4" long. Cobs not completely filled with plump, milky kernels, but well covered with husks. No worms, smut, decay, rust, insect damage, or disease.

Many varieties, including a new one called "Ultra Sweet" with a high natural sugar content.

Storing:

Best stored at 34–38° with 85–95% relative humidity. Best used upon delivery.

Basis:

Dietary staple of American Indians, Aztecs and Mayans. The word *corn* meant "That which gives us life."

CUCUMBERS

Preparing:

Wash and remove most or all of the green skin (with wax).

Optional to fork-score, slice, or dice.

Serving:

Raw, sliced, or diced, in or with salads.

Serve chilled cucumber soup with yogurt or blended tofu.

Thinly slice for sandwiches.

Serve in salads with curried tofu sauce or any of a number of others.

Use with fresh fruit.

Slice, with olive oil and a little oregano shaken on top.

Serve hot after being quickly sauteed.

Use as a sauce base blended with tofu or yogurt.

Quality:

Buy bright, well shaped, firm cucumbers with good green color, with whitish-green on ridges and tip.

Avoid cucumbers that are dry, shriveled, withered, yellowish or dull green colored, cracked, mushy, or moldy.

Portions:

100 portions @ 3 oz. sliced, peeled, raw: buy 26 lbs.

Buying;

Grades: U.S. Fancy; U.S. Extra 1; U.S. 1 Small; U.S. 1 Large; U.S. 2 Greenhouse.

Packed: containers of 47–55 lbs.; containers of 20–22 lbs.; $^1/_3$ bushel container, 19 lbs.; container, 14 lbs.; lug, 28–32 lbs.

Storing:

Best stored at 45–50° F. with 85–95% relative humidity.

Basis:

Originated in Asia.

GREENS (Collards, Kale, Mustard Greens, Turnip Tops)

Preparing:

Chop to 3 × 3" pieces.

Boil with a little water.

Steam.

Serving:

Serve with mushrooms.

Cook with tahini.

Serve with beans.

Use in soups and stews.

Quality:

Buy greens that are young, tender, green, and fresh.

Avoid dry, yellowing, insect damaged, or with seed stems with dirt and poor development.

Portions:

100 portions @ 3 oz. cooked, buy:

32 lbs. mustard greens

24 lbs. collards

24 lbs. kale

40 lbs. turnip greens (untrimmed)

Buying:

Grades: U.S. 1.

Packed: container holding 18–25 lbs.; WGA crate holding 45 lbs.

Storing:

Best stored at 32–40° with 90–95% relative humidity (briefly).

Cracked ice helps keep greens fresh.

Basis:

Kale originated in ancient Europe. Dandelions are very good when young and tender. Known as the "Benevolent Weed."

LETTUCE

Preparing:

Use whole heads, not commercially cut and dipped lettuce.

Cut out stem; reserve stem chopped for soups.

Preferable not to cut lettuce, but to tear by hand to size needed for serving. Use only a stainless steel knife.

Keep minimum time between refrigeration and serving.

Serving:

Use whole leaves (flattened) or large pieces as a bed for platters of aspic or pasta or rice salad; as a garnish to be eaten.

Basis for a side dish of many flavor combinations:

Lemon juice	Tofu dressing
Olive oil	Fruit
Garlic	Vinegar
Other vegetables	Herbs
Beans	Oriental tofu

Sliced thin and quick-pickled with other vegetables of other color combinations and types.

Quality:

Buy solid, heavy lettuce (indicates a mature head); the leaves may be hard to separate, yet still of good quality. Soft heads indicate it is less mature, with leaves that are easier to separate from the head. Avoid old-looking lettuce with signs of decay, rusty appearance, ragged brown areas, abnormal swelling at top.

Portions:

100 portions @ 2 oz. raw: buy 17 lbs.

Buying:

Grades: U.S. 1; U.S. 2; U.S. Fancy (greenhouse lettuce).

Packed: containers holding 40–45 lbs.; 1¹/₉ bushel containers, 26 lbs.; 5 and 10 lb. baskets; 10 lb. clear poly bags.

Storing:

Best stored at 34–38° F. with 80–90% relative humidity.

Basis:

Served in 55 B.C. to Persian kings; known then for its medicinal value.

MUSHROOMS

Preparing:

Very delicate and easily absorb water that alters flavor and texture.

To wash, immerse in cold water, agitate for dirt removal, and quickly lift mushrooms out of water, then quickly drain or dry.

Do not soak in water.

Trim stem ends if they are expanded or woody-looking or are waterlogged.

Taste best cooked whole.

Halve, quarter, slice, or dice depending on need.

Cook slowly to maintain maximum flavor.

Mushrooms sautee or stir fry very well; easily steamed.

Serving:

Diced or quartered in salads.

Stuffed with dips.

Served with green vegetables.

Served with a lemon or herb sauce.

Sauteed.

Make a mushroom sauce for grains or greens, either fine-diced or blended.

Quality:

Buy thick, white, firm, fresh, commercially grown mushrooms, having a fresh, clean appearance with closed caps.

Avoid discoloration, pitting, wilting, and open caps.

Portions:

100 portions @ 3 oz.: buy 19 lbs.

Buying:

Grades: U.S. No. 1; U.S. No. 2.

Packed: 8, 12, and 16 oz. containers, 12 to a case; 2 oz. containers, 10 to a case; 10 and 20 lb. plastic lugs and 3 lb. wooden lugs.

Storing:

Best stored at 34–38° F.(9 days); 40° F. (2–5 days); 50° F. (1–3 days).

Basis:

Considered a delicacy by the Pharaohs of Egypt; cultivated in France in the 1700s.

OKRA

Preparing:

Whole or diced.

(Okra is a natural thickening agent when cooked.)

Serving:

In gumbos, soups, stews, or jambalaya.

Serve fried or deep fried.

Serve as a vegetable in Ginger–Tamari Sauce.

Quality:

Buy 2–4" long; should snap easily when broken. Easily punctured, clean, fresh, young, and tender; dark green to whitish, ridged or smooth.

Avoid okra that is dull, dry, shriveled, or discolored.

Portions:

100 portions @ 3 oz. cooked: buy 20 lbs.

Buying:

Grades: U.S. 1.

Packed: ½ bushel container holding 15 lbs.; 1 bushel container holding 30 lbs.

Storing:

Best stored at 50° F. with 85–95% humidity (maximum 2 weeks).

Basis:

Originated in Africa and came west with the slaves. Slaves from Angola called it *ngombo* (the derivative of *gumbo*).

ONIONS (Dry)

Preparing:

Washing not usually necessary.

Trim root and stem end; peel dry outer skin.

Slice, dice, or leave whole.

Trim both ends to desired degree.

There are various methods of effective dicing, the "correctness" of which depends on the chef.

Serving:

Raw, sliced, or diced, in or on salads.

Thinly sliced in sandwiches.

Bake whole; leaving skin on adds sweetness.

Sweet onion pie.

Boil or steam whole, serve with a sauce, garnish, or condiment.

Used as one of the most common flavorings for a primary or secondary effect.

Quality:

Buy onions with dry skins, well shaped, bright, clean, hard.

Avoid onions with seed stems; moisture at the neck may indicate decay; growth at neck saps texture and taste from onion. Avoid off-shape bulbs and splits.

Portions:

100 portions @ 3 oz., small whole or pieces, cooked: buy 25 lbs.

100 portions @ 1 oz. chopped or grated, raw: buy 8 lbs.

Buying:

Grades: U.S. 1; U.S. Commercial; U.S. 1 Boilers; U.S. 1 Picklers; U.S. 2; U.S. Combination.

Packed: Sacks of 25 or 50 lbs.; containers holding 48–50 lbs.

Varieties:

Pearl: usually white, small.

Red: robust taste, deep red or purple; used in salads and garnishes.

Vidalia: sweet.

White: silver-white color, not large; used in soups and stews and side dishes.

Yellow: pungent, general-purpose; round or golden.

Storing:

Best stored at room temperature in dry, dark area. Every 4–5 days, pour from one container into another and sort out bad ones. Alternative: store at 32° F. with 70–75% relative humidity.

Basis:

Believed to have given valor to the troops of Alexander the Great. Latin, *unio*; French, *oignon*; Old English, *unyun*.

ONIONS, GREEN

Preparing:

Whole or diced to various sizes, depending on need.

Serve raw or cooked.

Serving:

Serve raw as an appetizer, in garnishes, or finely diced in salads.

Cooked, diced in stews, soups, or with other vegetables.

Quality:

Buy vegetables with fresh, full color, plump, firm, young, crisp, and tender.

Avoid wilted, soft, or flabby vegetables.

Portions:

100 portions @ 3 oz. raw, partly topped: buy 32 lbs.

Buying:

Grades: U.S. 1; U.S. 2.

Packed: wirebound container, 15–20 lbs.; 16" container, 25–30 lbs.; container 4 doz. bunches, 15–18 lbs.; WGA crate, 60 lbs.

Storing:

Best stored at 34–38°with 90–95% relative humidity.

PARSLEY

Preparing:

Use spring-raw as a garnish or finely chopped stems, with or without leaves, cooked in soups, stews, gumbos.

Serving:

As a garnish; sprigs; cooked in other dishes.

Quality:

Buy parsley that is bright green, fresh and clean.

Avoid yellow leaves and wilted parsley.

Portions:

100 portions @ ¹/₂ cup: buy 3 lbs.

Buying:

Grades: U.S. 1.

Packed: 16" container holding 19 lbs.; wirebound crate, 26 lbs.; 1¹/₉ bushel, wirebound crate, 22–28 lbs.; 16-quart basket, 10–12 lbs.; 8-quart basket, 5–6 lbs.

Storing:

Best stored at 34–38° with high humidity/crushed ice.

Basis:

Originated as a Mediterranean herb.

PEAS, GREEN

Preparing:

Remove peas from pod.

Serving:

Serve with chopped mint condiment.

Serve with sliced mushrooms.

Use in soups and stews for color, added at end of cooking.

Cook with grains for color, added at end of cooking.

Quality:

Buy peas that are young, tender, sweet; pods should be fresh-looking, well developed.

Avoid flat pods, light colored, or swollen pods (peas that are tough or not sweet are over-mature).

Portions:

100 portions @ 3 oz. cooked: buy 53 lbs.

Buying:

Grades: U.S. 1; U.S. Fancy.

Packed: bushel container, 28–30 lbs.;

WGA crate, 55–60 lbs.

Storing:

Best stored (unshelled) at 34–38° with 85–90% relative humidity.

Basis: Originated in the Middle East; Latin, *pisum*.

PARSNIPS

Preparing:

Slice, dice, mash.

Serving:

Use in soups and stews.

Serve as a vegetable, sliced or diced, with chopped parsley condiment or with herbed tofu sauce.

Parboil and sautee.

Quality:

Buy well-shaped parsnips, firm, smooth, small- or medium-sized.

Avoid large, soft, flabby, or discolored parsnips; or dried roots.

Portions:

100 portions @ 3 oz. cooked: buy 2.3 lbs.

Buying:

Grades: U.S. 1; U.S. 2.

Packed: Bushel or half bushel; bushel contains 45–50 lbs.

Storing:

Best stored at 34–38° with 90–95% relative humidity.

Basis:

Developed mostly in Germany.

PEPPERS, SWEET

Preparing:

Used mostly for flavor, garnish, or for stuffing.

Quarter, remove stem and all white pulp.

Slice or dice.

Serving:

Serve raw, finely diced in salads, or sliced as garnish.

Cook diced in soups or stews; or stir fry.

Quality:

Buy peppers that are bright, fresh and firm.

Avoid those that are shriveled, soft, dull looking, or have blemishes.

Portions:

100 portions @ 1/2 cup raw, chopped or diced:buy 21 lbs.

Buying:

Grades: U.S. Fancy; U.S. 1;U.S. 2.

Packed: bushel container or crate, 28–30 lbs.; 1 1/9 bushel container, 28–33 lbs.; container holding 30–34 lbs.; L.A. lug, 18 lbs.; Imported Fancy Holland Peppers in 11-lb. cases.

Storing:

Best stored at 45–50° F. with 85–90% relative humidity.

Basis:

Originated in Central America.

RADISHES

Preparing:

Sliced or diced.

Use "rose cutters" to cut garnish and hold in ice.

Hold in ice water until served.

Serving:

As a garnish.

Serve raw in salads.

Use in soups or stews.

Lightly sautee (stir fry).

Quality:

Buy radishes that are small, medium, or large depending on use; mild flavor, tender, firm, and crisp, fresh, well formed and smooth.

Avoid those that have black spots or pits, or are mushy or soft.

Portions:

100 portions @ 4 small radishes: buy 9 lbs.

100 portions @ 1 oz. sliced raw: buy 10 lbs. untopped, 7 lbs. topped.

Buying:

Grades: U.S. 1; U.S. Commercial.

Packed: 5 doz. bunches per container, 30–40 lbs.; WGA crate, 8–10 doz. bunches, 80–90 lbs.; film bags, 25 lbs. bulk.

Storing:

Best stored at 34–38° with 90–95% relative humidity.

Basis:

Cultivated in ancient Egypt and China.

SQUASH (Summer, Soft Shell)

Preparing:

Slice, dice, or cook whole to retain flavor.

Sautee in olive oil, with or without garlic and onion.

Serving:

Cooked small, whole for maximum flavor.

Sliced and cooked with grains with tamari and seasoning.

Baked.

Quality:

Buy squash that are heavy, crisp, fresh and tender.

Avoid squash with cuts, bruises, and breaks.

Portions:

100 portions @ 3 oz. sliced or diced, cooked: buy 23 lbs.

100 portions @ ½ medium, baked: buy 50 lbs.

100 portions @ 4 oz. cubed, cooked: buy 44 lbs.

Buying:

Grades: U.S. 1; U.S. 2.

Packed: 40–45 lb. containers; ½ bushel or wirebound crate, 21 lbs.; L.A. lug 24–27 lbs.; 50-lb. containers.

Storing:

Best stored at 32–40° F. with 85–95% relative humidity.

Basis:

Originated by the American Indians.

SQUASH (Winter, Hard Shell)

Preparing:

If not organic, peel.

Thick or thin slices, dice, or mash.

Serving:

Serve mashed with barley malt and spices.

Serve large pieces baked with tamari.

Small squash are often baked in the shell.

Quality:

Buy hard; varied natural coloring.

Avoid soft spots.

Portions:

100 portions @ 3 oz. sliced or diced, cooked: buy 23 lbs.

100 portions @ 4 oz. mashed: buy 31 lbs.

100 portions @ ½ medium acorn squash, baked: buy 50 lbs.

100 portions @ 4 oz. cubed, cooked, Hubbard squash: buy 44 lbs.

Buying:

Grades: U.S. 1; U.S. 2.

Packed: 40–45 lb. containers; ½ bushel or wirebound crate, 21 lbs.; L.A. lug 24–27 lbs.; 50 lb. containers.

Some Varieties:

Acorn: heavily ribbed, oval with pointed end; dark green often tinged with orange; golden acorn is golden in color.

Buttercup: dark green, grayish spots; cylindrical, 4–5" long; sweet orange flesh, gray turban-like top.

Butternut: thick-necked, cylindrical

shaped; dark yellow shell, full orange flesh.

Hubbard: 10–16" long, spherical, tapered ends; hard warted shells; dark blue, greenish-gray to orange tinges.

Storing:

Hard shell: best stored at 50–55°F. with 70–75% relative humidity.

Soft shell: 34–40°F. with 85–95% relative humidity.

Basis:

Originated by the American Indians.

SWEET POTATOES

Preparing:

Cook, slice, dice, mash, or leave whole.

Serving:

Candied; baked, steamed, or boiled in skin for best flavor; mashed; used in pies or puddings.

Quality:

Buy sweet potatoes that are smooth, well shaped, clean, firm, and with bright appearance.

Avoid vegetables that are misshapen, bruised, moldy; and those with cracks or worm injury or damp appearance.

Whitish-tan to brownish-red color; soft, moist, and orange-fleshed when cooked.

Yellowish-tan or fawn-colored (usually): firm, dry, somewhat mealy, and light yellow or pale orange when cooked.

Portions:

100 portions @ 1 medium, cooked in skin: buy 50 lbs.

100 portions @ 3 oz. sliced: buy 23 lbs.

100 portions @ 4 oz. mashed: buy 31 lbs.

Buying:

Grades: U.S. Extra 1; U.S. 1; U.S. Commercial; U.S. 2.

Packed: 40- or 50-lb. container.

Storing:

Best stored at room temperature, above 55°; keep in a dark area; do not refrigerate.

TURNIPS—RUTABAGAS

Preparing:

Slice, dice; steam, boil, mash.

Serving:

Use in soups and stews.

Serve as a side dish.

Thinly slice and mix with green vegetables.

Quality:

Buy vegetables that are firm, healthy, top (if any) green, fresh, crisp; small to medium-sized.

Avoid turnips with many roots, shriveled, old-looking, tops (if any) extra large tend to be undesirable.

Portions:

Turnips:

100 portions @ 3 oz. cubed, cooked: buy 26 lbs.

100 portions @ 4 oz. mashed: buy 35 lbs.

Rutabagas:

100 portions @ 3 oz. cubed, cooked: buy 24 lbs.

100 portions @ 4 oz. mashed: buy 33 lbs.

Buying:

Grades: U.S.1; U.S. 2.

Packed: 42-lb. wirebound crate container; 12 WGA crate, 35 lbs.; WGA crate, 65–70 lbs.; 50-lb. mesh sacks; 25-lb. film sacks.

Storing:

Best stored at 34–38° with 90–95% relative humidity.

Basis:

Originated in Europe.

WATERCRESS

Preparing:

Trim to size desired.

Trim leaves.

Add stems to soups and stews.

Serving:

As a garnish; in sandwiches; mixed with other greens; in salads.

Quality:

Buy healthy color, even-colored green, young, crisp, tender.

Avoid old, wilted, soft, spongy stems, multi-colored showing signs of decay.

Portions:

100 portions @ $1/4$ cup: buy 3 lbs.

Buying:

No federal grades.

Packed: containers holding 12–15 bunches.

Storing:

Best stored at 34–38° with high humidity and crushed ice.

Basis:

A member of the Cruciferae (mustard) family.

VEGETABLE SERVING STANDARDS

Appearance on Plate

•Uniform size and cut; or served whole. Dish character will be influenced by the selection of uniform size and uniform cut of vegetables. Example:

—broccoli florets

—root vegetables sticks

—daikon sliced round or half-moon

—onion slices round or half-moon

—young, small-portion-size vegetable may be served; preferable for nutrition and flavor

•Should be well drained.

•Select for compatibility or contrast of:

—Color

—Flavor

—Texture

—Cut and shape

Color

•Each vegetable should have full, bright natural color.

•Have a selection of contrasting colors.

Flavor

•Organic vegetables assure more full, fresh, natural flavors.

•Strong-flavored vegetables should be cooked until mild.

•Light sauces are a good catalyst for adding flavoring.

Texture

• Cook (including manner of holding) to be served *a point* or *al dente.*

•Most should be tender-crisp or firm, such as green beans, broccoli, carrots, etc.

•Some should be soft, such as sweet potato, squash.

•Overcooking causes:

—wrong texture for each vegetable

—woodiness

—mushiness

Combining

•Usually two or more vegetables.

•Cook separately or add to cooking process so they reach *a point* at the same time.

See chart on next page.

Seasonings

•Maintain the prime, innate, fresh flavor of the vegetable.

•Add seasoning to complement and support the natural integrity of the vegetable.

MAINTAINING VEGETABLE COLOR WHILE COOKING

•Cook a minimum time.

•Steaming is preferable.

•When boiling, place in already boiling water.

See chart on next page.

MAINTAINING VEGETABLE COLOR

Vegetable Color	*Procedure*
Green	Acid and long cooking will insure maximum color loss; cook uncovered; cook small quantities of vegetables in large quantities of boiling water to obtain minimum cooking time and maximum natural color; do not overcook; stop cooking process at *a point*; to hold small portions, parcook, cool quickly, refrigerate, saute, or steam finish; best to cook *a point*, stop cooking, serve.
Red	Acidity will help maintain color; use minimum water; red pigment is water soluble; add a little lemon juice to water; cook *a point*, stop cooking, serve.
White	Acidity will help maintain whiteness; add a little lemon juice; use minimum water; cook only to *a point*, stop cooking, serve.
Yellow/Orange	(Including red peppers & tomato). Long cooking may cause dull color; cook only to *a point*, stop cooking, serve.

COMBINING VEGETABLES

Vegetable	*Complementary Foods*
Asparagus	Peas
Beans, green	Carrots, almonds, celery, sesame seed, mushrooms, onions
Beets	Onions
Broccoli	Almonds, carrots
Cabbage	Carrots, corn and carrots, onions, onions and carrots
Carrots	Celery, onions, peas
Cauliflower	Almonds, leeks sauteed with sesame seeds, peas
Celery	Parsley
Corn	Lima beans, fresh peas
Cucumber	Peas
Daikon	Corn and white miso, other root vegetables
Greens	Onions, tamari, sesame seeds
Mushrooms	Green beans, peas
Onions	Peas
Peas	Carrots, turnips, mushrooms, pearl onions, pecans, water chestnuts
Potato, sweet	Almonds, apples, root vegetables
Squash, summer	Carrots, almonds, walnuts

VEGETABLE FLAVORING CHART

	Asparagus	Beans, green	Beets	Bok Choy	Broccoli	Burssels Sprouts	Cabbage	Cabbage, Chinese	Carrots	Cauliflower	Celery	Corn	Cucumbers	Greens	Kale	Lima Beans	Mushrooms	Onions	Parsnips	Peas	Potato, Sweet	Pumpkin	Rutabaga	Squash, Summer	Squash, Winter	Turnip	Zucchini
Allspice							●		●										●	●	●	●		●	●	●	
Anise		●	●				●		●	●											●					●	
Basil		●							●									●		●							●
Bay Leaf		●	●				●				●																
Caraway				●			●	●			●			●	●						●					●	
Cardamom									●												●	●			●		
Cayenne												●						●									
Celery Seed				●			●	●								●											
Chervil																											
Chili Pepper																											
Chives		●					●		●	●							●				●						
Cilantro			●					●	●		●									●	●						●
Cinnamon			●	●				●										●			●	●			●		
Clove			●						●					●	●						●			●	●		
Coriander											●	●															
Currants									●											●							
Curry			●						●									●								●	
Dill Seed		●					●			●																	
Dill Weed	●			●																							
Fennel	●		●				●									●			●		●			●	●		
Garlic	●	●								●									●								●
Ginger			●						●			●								●	●	●	●	●	●	●	
Mace		●							●	●	●	●					●	●	●	●	●	●		●	●	●	
Marjoram		●				●			●									●		●				●			●
Mint							●		●				●							●	●						
Mustard	●	●					●											●			●						
Nutmeg	●	●							●	●	●	●							●	●	●		●				
Onion		●								●									●							●	●
Oregano		●					●				●		●				●	●									●
Paprika	●						●			●									●								
Parsley				●					●								●										
Pepper, black		●										●														●	
Pepper, white		●							●			●							●							●	
Poppy Seed	●	●					●		●	●								●	●					●			
Rosemary	●									●			●				●							●		●	
Saffron																			●								
Sage							●									●		●									
Savory			●				●											●	●					●			
Sesame Seed		●								●													●				
Tarragon	●		●	●			●				●	●	●				●	●						●			
Thyme		●	●		●												●	●	●								
Barley Malt									●														●		●		
Maple Syrup									●														●		●		
Sw. Rice Wine				●					●																●		
Rice Vinegar										●																	
Tahini				●	●	●		●	●	●				●	●			●					●				●
Tamari		●												●				●					●		●		
Lemon	●		●		●																				●		
Orange									●	●				●				●	●				●				

VEGETABLE SHIPPING CHART
(National Distribution in U.S.)

VEGETABLE	JAN	FEB	MAR	APR	MAY	JUN	JUL	AUG	SEP	OCT	NOV	DEC
Artichokes	- - -	- - -	○ ○ ○	● ● ●	● ● ●	- - -	- - -	- - -	- - -	- - -	- - -	○ ○ ○
Asparagus	- - -	- - -	● ● ●	● ● ●	● ● ●	● ● ●	- - -	- - -	- - -	- - -	- - -	- - -
Beans, Green	○ ○ ○	○ ○ ○	○ ○ ○	○ ○ ○	○ ○ ○	● ● ●	● ● ●	● ● ●	● ● ●	○ ○ ○	○ ○ ○	○ ○ ○
Beets	- - -	- - -	- - -	- - -	- - -	● ● ●	● ● ●	● ● ●	● ● ●	○ ○ ○	- - -	- - -
Belg. Endive	○ ○ ○	○ ○ ○	○ ○ ○	○ ○ ○	○ ○ ○	- - -	- - -	- - -	○ ○ ○	○ ○ ○	○ ○ ○	○ ○ ○
Broccoli	○ ○ ○	○ ○ ○	○ ○ ○	○ ○ ○	○ ○ ○	○ ○ ○	○ ○ ○	○ ○ ○	○ ○ ○	○ ○ ○	○ ○ ○	○ ○ ○
Brus. Sprouts	- - -	- - -	○ ○ ○	○ ○ ○	○ ○ ○	- - -	- - -	○ ○ ○	○ ○ ○	● ● ●	● ● ●	● ● ●
Cabbage	○ ○ ○	○ ○ ○	○ ○ ○	○ ○ ○	○ ○ ○	○ ○ ○	○ ○ ○	○ ○ ○	○ ○ ○	○ ○ ○	○ ○ ○	○ ○ ○
Cabbage, Ch.	○ ○ ○	○ ○ ○	○ ○ ○	○ ○ ○	○ ○ ○	○ ○ ○	○ ○ ○	● ● ●	● ● ●	● ● ●	● ● ●	○ ○ ○
Carrots	○ ○ ○	○ ○ ○	- - -	- - -	- - -	- - -	- - -	○ ○ ○	● ● ●	● ● ●	● ● ●	- - -
Cauliflower	○ ○ ○	○ ○ ○	○ ○ ○	○ ○ ○	○ ○ ○	○ ○ ○	○ ○ ○	○ ○ ○	○ ○ ○	○ ○ ○	● ● ●	● ● ●
Celery	○ ○ ○	○ ○ ○	○ ○ ○	- - -	○ ○ ○	○ ○ ○	○ ○ ○	○ ○ ○	○ ○ ○	● ● ●	● ● ●	● ● ●
Corn	- - -	- - -	- - -	- - -	○ ○ ○	○ ○ ○	● ● ●	● ● ●	● ● ●	- - -	- - -	- - -
Cucumbers	○ ○ ○	○ ○ ○	○ ○ ○	○ ○ ○	○ ○ ○	● ● ●	● ● ●	○ ○ ○	○ ○ ○	○ ○ ○	○ ○ ○	○ ○ ○
Eggplant	○ ○ ○	○ ○ ○	○ ○ ○	○ ○ ○	○ ○ ○	○ ○ ○	○ ○ ○	○ ○ ○	○ ○ ○	○ ○ ○	○ ○ ○	○ ○ ○
Greens	● ● ●	● ● ●	● ● ●	● ● ●	○ ○ ○	○ ○ ○	○ ○ ○	○ ○ ○	○ ○ ○	○ ○ ○	○ ○ ○	○ ○ ○
Lettuce	○ ○ ○	○ ○ ○	○ ○ ○	● ● ●	● ● ●	● ● ●	● ● ●	● ● ●	○ ○ ○	○ ○ ○	○ ○ ○	○ ○ ○
Mushrooms	○ ○ ○	○ ○ ○	○ ○ ○	○ ○ ○	○ ○ ○	- - -	- - -	- - -	○ ○ ○	○ ○ ○	● ● ●	● ● ●
Okra	- - -	- - -	- - -	● ● ●	● ● ●	● ● ●	● ● ●	● ● ●	● ● ●	● ● ●	- - -	- - -
Onions	○ ○ ○	- - -	○ ○ ○	○ ○ ○	● ● ●	● ● ●	● ● ●	● ● ●	○ ○ ○	○ ○ ○	○ ○ ○	○ ○ ○
Onions, Green	- - -	- - -	- - -	● ● ●	● ● ●	● ● ●	● ● ●	● ● ●	○ ○ ○	○ ○ ○	○ ○ ○	○ ○ ○
Parsley	○ ○ ○	○ ○ ○	○ ○ ○	○ ○ ○	○ ○ ○	○ ○ ○	○ ○ ○	○ ○ ○	○ ○ ○	○ ○ ○	○ ○ ○	○ ○ ○
Parsnips	○ ○ ○	○ ○ ○	○ ○ ○	- - -	- - -	- - -	- - -	- - -	- - -	○ ○ ○	○ ○ ○	○ ○ ○
Peas	- - -	- - -	- - -	● ● ●	● ● ●	● ● ●	● ● ●	- - -	- - -	- - -	- - -	- - -
Peppers, Bell	- - -	- - -	○ ○ ○	○ ○ ○	○ ○ ○	● ● ●	● ● ●	● ● ●	● ● ●	○ ○ ○	○ ○ ○	○ ○ ○
Potatoes	● ● ●	● ● ●	● ● ●	● ● ●	○ ○ ○	○ ○ ○	○ ○ ○	○ ○ ○	○ ○ ○	○ ○ ○	○ ○ ○	● ● ●
Potatoes, Sw.	- - -	- - -	○ ○ ○	○ ○ ○	● ● ●	● ● ●	● ● ●	○ ○ ○	○ ○ ○	○ ○ ○	○ ○ ○	○ ○ ○
Radishes	○ ○ ○	○ ○ ○	○ ○ ○	● ● ●	● ● ●	○ ○ ○	○ ○ ○	- - -	- - -	- - -	- - -	- - -
Rhubarb	○ ○ ○	○ ○ ○	○ ○ ○	○ ○ ○	○ ○ ○	○ ○ ○	- - -	- - -	○ ○ ○	○ ○ ○	○ ○ ○	○ ○ ○
Spinach	- - -	- - -	○ ○ ○	○ ○ ○	○ ○ ○	○ ○ ○	● ● ●	● ● ●	● ● ●	● ● ●	● ● ●	● ● ●
Squash	○ ○ ○	○ ○ ○	○ ○ ○	○ ○ ○	○ ○ ○	- - -	- - -	● ● ●	● ● ●	● ● ●	● ● ●	● ● ●
Tomatoes	- - -	- - -	○ ○ ○	○ ○ ○	● ● ●	● ● ●	● ● ●	● ● ●	○ ○ ○	○ ○ ○	- - -	- - -
Turnips	● ● ●	● ● ●	● ● ●	○ ○ ○	○ ○ ○	- - -	- - -	- - -	- - -	○ ○ ○	● ● ●	● ● ●
Watercress	- - -	- - -	● ● ●	● ● ●	● ● ●	- - -	- - -	- - -	- - -	- - -	- - -	- - -

Peak harvesting season: ● ● ●   Available in large volume: ○ ○ ○   Low availability: - - -

Peak harvesting seasons of locally-grown vegetables will vary according to temperature and region. Buy locally-grown *organic* vegetables when possible.

VEGETABLE COOKED–YIELD CHART

VEGETABLE	UNPREPARED LBS.	TRIMMED* CUPS	COOKED† LBS.	COOKED† CUPS
Artichokes	$1^1/_3$	$1^1/_8$	1	2
Asparagus	1	$3^1/_2$	1	3
Beans, green	1	$3^1/_2$	14 oz.	3
Beets	1	$3^1/_3$	1	3
Bok choy	1	$3^1/_3$	14 oz.	3
Broccoli	1	4	10 oz.	3
Brussels sprouts	1	$3^1/_2$	1	3
Burdock	1	$3^1/_2$	12 oz.	$2^1/_2$
Cabbage	1	4	1	$3^1/_3$
Cabbage, Chinese	1	5	12 oz.	$2^1/_2$
Carrots	1	$3^1/_3$	1	3
Cauliflower	1	$3^2/_3$	1	$3^1/_3$
Celery	1	$3^3/_4$	1	$3^1/_2$
Corn, fresh	1	12 oz.	8 oz.	1
Daikon	1	$3^2/_3$	1	3
Fiddleheads	1	4	1	3
Kale	1	8	1	4
Leeks	1	4	14 oz.	3
Mushrooms	1	4	1	2
Onions	1	$3^3/_4$	1	2
Parsnips	1	4	1	2
Rutabaga	1	$3^1/_3$	1	3
Snow peas	1	4	1	3
Spinach	1	11	1	3
Squash	1	$3^1/_3$	1	3
Sweet potato	1	3	14 oz.	$2^1/_2$
Turnips	1	$3^1/_3$	1	3
Zucchini	1	$3^1/_3$	1	$2^1/_2$

*All vegetables brushed, not peeled; and cut into $^3/_4$"-square pieces.
†Steamed or cooked with as little water as possible.

Pan size: 12 qt. Cooking time: 8 mins. Oven temp.:	Yield: 50 stalks Serves: 10 Portion: 5 stalks	Yield: _____ Serves: _____ Portion: _____	**ASPARAGUS, BOILED**
Asparagus	3³/₄ lbs.		Place evenly, soldier-style, in salted, rolling boiling water. Cook *al dente*. Remove with skimmer. Serve.

Variations:

Pan size: 6 qt. Cooking time: Oven temp.:	Yield: 50 stalks Serves: 10 Portion: 5 stalks	Yield: _____ Serves: _____ Portion: _____	**ASPARAGUS, STEAMED**
Asparagus	3³/₄ lb.		Trim white from stalk, leaving spears the same length. Place in steamer soldier-style so they will steam-cook evenly. Cook *al dente*. Serve.

Variations: Garnish: green onion, black pepper, chopped parsley, finely diced sauteed mushrooms, Mock Hollandaise Sauce (pg. 259), or other fresh dill complements.

BEANS, GREEN

	Yield: 20 oz.	Yield:	Pan size: 4 qt.
	Serves: 10	Serves:	Cooking time: 10 mins.
	Portion: 2 oz.	Portion:	Oven temp.:

Beans, green	1½ lbs.		Trim stem ends.
			Place gently in ample amount of rolling boiling water so that water does not stop boiling.
			Boil 10 mins. or until parcooked.
			Place pot in cold water to stop cooking. Serve or refrigerate beans.
			Finish portions as needed by resteaming or cook *al dente* and serve.
			[NOTE: If young beans, cook less.]

Variations: Add olive oil and/or a little lemon juice at end of cooking to coat beans.
Cook with finely chopped onions.
Garnish with whole or chopped roasted pecans, sesame seeds, parsley, slivered almonds.

BEANS, GREEN, AND CARROTS

	Yield: 10 cups	Yield:	Pan size: 4 qt.
	Serves: 10	Serves:	Cooking time: 9 mins.
	Portion: 1 cup	Portion:	Oven temp.:

Corn oil	3 Tbs.		Place in skillet, medium-high heat.
Carrots, julienned	3 cups		Add, saute 2 mins.
Green beans, cut ½" long	1½ lbs.		Add, saute 7 mins. Reduce heat.
Lemon juice	1 Tbs.		Add.
Dijon mustard	3 Tbs.		Add.
Salt	1 tsp.		Add.
Pepper	½ tsp.		Add, mix. Coat beans and carrots.
			Serve.

Variations: Boil without oil.

BEANS, GREEN–GINGER

Pan size:	Yield:	20 oz.	Yield:	Serves:
Cooking time: 5 mins.	Serves:	10	Serves:	
Oven temp.:	Portion:	2 oz.	Portion:	

Green beans, parcooked (pg. 310)	20 oz.		Reserve in refrigerator. Remove as portions are needed for finish-cooking.
Soy oil	1/8 cup		Place in skillet. Bring to medium-high heat.
Ginger, finely grated	3 Tbs.		Add, saute 2 mins.
Beans, above			Add, saute 3 mins; cook al dente.
			Serve.

Variations: Substitute olive oil and garlic for oil and ginger.
Add salt to oil.
Or saute with water and no oil.

BEANS, GREEN, AND MUSHROOMS

Pan size:	lg. skillet	Yield:	10+/- cups	Yield:
Cooking time: 20- mins.		Serves:	10	Serves:
Oven temp.:		Portion:	1+/- cup	Portion:

Corn oil	1/4 cup		Place in skillet.
Green onions	1/2 cup		Add.
Mushrooms, thinly sliced	2 cups		Add, saute at medium heat for 5 mins.
Water	1/4 cup		Add.
Paprika	2 tsp.		Add.
Whole wheat pastry flour	2 tsp.		Make sauce, add; simmer and stir 10–15 mins. Adjust.
Green beans, parcooked (pg. 310)	1 lb.		Add, heat, serve.

Variations: Garnish: roasted and chopped filberts.

BEETS

	Yield: 10 cups	Yield:	Pan size: 4 qt.
	Serves: 10	Serves:	Cooking time: 40 mins.
	Portion: 1 cup	Portion:	Oven temp.:
Beets, whole, 2" diam.	5 lbs.		Place in pan.
Water			Add to cover + 2".
Salt	1 tsp.		Add, boil about 40 mins., depending on size.
			Usually when beet skins crack they are finished cooking.
			Drain water, fill pan with cool water and drain. Trim roots and stems. Skin with thumb and a squeeze of the hand.
			Best served whole.

Variations: Add a little vinegar to cook water to heighten flavor.

BEETS, HARVARD

	Yield: 10 cups	Yield:	Pan size: 1 qt.
	Serves: 10	Serves:	Cooking time: 5 mins.
	Portion: 1 cup	Portion:	Oven temp.:
Beets, recipe above	5 lbs.		Cook, reserve.
Cook water	1/2 cup		Place in pan.
Barley malt	3/4 cup		Add.
Pepper, black	1/4 tsp.		Add.
Cloves	1/2 tsp.		Add.
Lemon rind	1 1/2 tsp.		Add.
Rice vinegar	1/4 cup		Add, mix, simmer 5 mins.
Arrowroot	1 Tbs.		Make slurry, add, mix.
			Adjust.
Beets, above, 1/2–3/4"-diced			Add, mix, heat.
			Serve.

Variations:

Pan size: 4 qt.	Yield: 10 cups	Yield:	**BEETS, SWEET & SOUR**
Cooking time: 5 mins.	Serves: 10	Serves:	
Oven temp.:	Portion: 1 cup	Portion:	

Beets (pg. 312)			Reserve.
Water	¼ cup		Place in pan.
Mustard, dry	⅛ tsp.		Add.
Cloves (ground)	⅓ tsp.		Add, mix.
Vinegar	¼ cup		Add.
Barley malt	3 Tbs.		Add.
Tamari	2 Tbs.		Add, mix, simmer 5 mins.
Beets, above, ½"-diced			Add, mix, simmer to heat.
			Adjust.
			Serve.
			[NOTE: Beets may be sliced or julienned.]

Variations:

Pan size: 6 qt.	Yield: 42 oz.	Yield:	**BOK CHOY**
Cooking time: 8 mins.	Serves: 10	Serves:	
Oven temp.:	Portion: 4 oz.	Portion:	

Bok choy	3 lbs.		Trim stems. ¾"-dice stems. Place in salted boiling water; simmer covered for 5 mins.
Water, minimum			Add greens and steam 3 mins. Drain and serve immediately.

Variations: Add tahini sauce. Add ⅛ tsp. nutmeg per lb. with salt. Add caraway seeds or very thinly sliced onion (to flavor) just before adding stems.
Cut stems on diagonal. Add ¼ cup chopped mushrooms per lb. just before adding greens. Use in stir fry.

BROCCOLI

	Yield: 3 lbs.	Yield:	Pan size: 4 qt.
	Serves: 10	Serves:	Cooking time: 4–6 mins.
	Portion: 4 oz.	Portion:	Oven temp.:
Broccoli	3 lbs.		Skin and cut with 2–4" stems. Place in pan.
Salt	1/2 tsp.		Add.
Water			Add 1/2". Steam to par-cooked.
			Serve.

Variations: Marinate first in finely grated ginger water and tamari, or Oriental Dip, Basic (pg. 144).
Garnish: tofu, tahini sauce, tofu-garlic-lemon sauce, roasted and chopped walnuts.

BROCCOLI, SAUTEED

	Yield: 10 cups	Yield:	Pan size: lg. skillet
	Serves: 10	Serves:	Cooking time: 5 mins.
	Portion: 1 cup	Portion:	Oven temp.:
Broccoli	3 lbs.		Trim, skin stems. Slice with French cut. Cut florets into 1" pieces. Reserve.
Carrots, thinly sliced	1 cup		Reserve.
Oil (peanut, sesame, corn, or soy)	1/4 cup		Place in skillet at medium-high.
Ginger, finely grated	2 Tbs.		Add.
Tamari	2 Tbs.		Add.
Carrots, above			Add, saute 2 mins.
Broccoli stems, above			Add, saute 2 mins., steam 2 mins.
Broccoli florets, above			Add, saute 2 mins., mix often.
Water	1/4 cup		Add, cover, cook 1 min. Adjust.
			Stop the cooking process.
			Serve.

Variations: Add mushrooms with carrots, lemon juice, cooking sherry, freshly ground black pepper, nutmeg, and/or thyme.

BRUSSELS SPROUTS

Pan size:	4 qt.	Yield:	10 cups	Yield:	
Cooking time:	10+/- mins.	Serves:	10	Serves:	
Oven temp.:		Portion:	1 cup	Portion:	

Brussels sprouts (small)	2¹/₂ lbs.		Trim. Place in pan.
Water			Add to cover + ¹/₂".
Salt	1 tsp.		Add.
Tarragon leaves	1 Tbs.		Add, simmer.
			Cook *al dente*, no more. Usually when they start to turn from green to light green they are ready.
			Immerse pan in cold water to stop the cooking process. Over-cooking makes them mushy and bitter.
			Serve.

Variations: Serve with carrot chunks; and/or cook with chunks of carrot. Garnish: Tofu–Lemon Sauce (pg. 265), Hollandaise Sauce, Mock (pg. 259).

BRUSSELS SPROUTS, BAKED

Pan size:		Yield:	10 cups	Yield:	
Cooking time:	20 +/- mins.	Serves:	10	Serves:	
Oven temp.:	350°	Portion:	1 cup	Portion:	

Brussels sprouts	2¹/₂ lbs.		Trim. Place in pan.
Water			Add to cover + ¹/₂".
Salt	1 tsp.		Add, simmer until parcooked. Drain water.
Seitan Sauce (pg. 264)	1¹/₂ cups		Add.
Nutmeg	¹/₂ tsp.		Add, gently mix. Pour into baking dish.
Pecans, ¹/₄"-chopped	¹/₂ cup		Sprinkle on top. Bake 10–15 mins. at 350°.
			Serve.

Variations:

CABBAGE, BOILED

		Yield:		Pan size: 4 qt.
Yield: 10 cups				Cooking time: 25 mins.
Serves: 10		Serves:		Oven temp.:
Portion: 1 cup		Portion:		

Cabbage, whole	3 lbs.		Trim, quarter, core. Cut quarters in half crosswise, break leaves apart. Place in pot.
Water			Add to cover + 1".
Salt	1/2 tsp.		Add, cover, simmer until cooked. Cut out heart.
			Serve.

Variations: Cook with caraway seeds.
Garnish: Tahini Sauce, Basic (pg. 264), Maple–Mustard Glaze (pg. 154).

CABBAGE, CHINESE

		Yield:		Pan size: 10 qt.
Yield: 10 cups				Cooking time: 8 mins.
Serves: 10		Serves:		Oven temp.:
Portion: 1 cup		Portion:		

Chinese cabbage, whole	3 lbs.		Trim, 1/4"-slice greens, reserve. 1/4"-slice stem section, reserve.
Oil, sesame	1/4 cup		Place in pan at high heat.
Salt	1 tsp.		Add.
Cabbage stems, above			Add; saute 2 mins.
Cabbage greens, above			Add; saute 2 mins. Stir often.
Water	1/2 cup		Add, cover, steam 4 mins. or until parcooked. Stop cooking process.
			Serve.

Variations: Add 1 tsp. dark sesame oil to oil.
Garnish: gomasio (pg. 120); finely crumbled, roasted nori flakes.

Pan size: 4 qt.	Yield: 10 cups	Yield:	CABBAGE,
Cooking time: 20 mins.	Serves: 10	Serves:	SINGAPORE
Oven temp.:	Portion: 1 cup	Portion:	

Sesame oil, light	$^1/_4$ cup		Place in skillet at medium heat.
Sesame oil, dark	1 tsp.		Add.
Garlic, finely diced	1 Tbs.		Add, saute until tan.
Salt	$^1/_2$ tsp.		Add. Turn off heat immediately.
Parsley, chopped	1 cup		Add.
Green onion, chopped	1 cup		Add.
Mint (fresh), chopped	$^1/_4$ cup		Add.
Cinnamon	$^1/_4$ tsp.		Add, mix.
Cabbage, Boiled (pg. 316)	10 cups		Add, mix, serve.

Variations: Add 1 Tbs. grated ginger with salt.
Add 2 Tbs. roasted sesame seeds with cinnamon.

Pan size: 4 qt.	Yield: 10 cups	Yield:	CABBAGE,
Cooking time:	Serves: 10	Serves:	STEAMED
Oven temp.:	Portion: 1 cup	Portion:	

Cabbage, whole	2$^1/_2$ lbs.		Trim, quarter, core. Cut quarters crosswise. Break apart leaves. Place in steamer.
Caraway seeds	1 Tbs.		Add when half cooked and mix in. Cook to completion.
			Serve.

Variations: Add chili powder and peanut butter.
Add oregano.

CABBAGE, SWEET & SOUR

	Yield:	10 cups	Yield:		Pan size:	4 qt.
	Serves:	10	Serves:		Cooking time:	
	Portion:	1 cup	Portion:		Oven temp.:	

Water	1 cup		Place in pan; heat.
Tamari	2 tsp.		Add.
Barley malt	1/3 cup		Add.
Rice vinegar	2 Tbs.		Add.
Sesame seeds, roasted	2 Tbs.		Add.
Cinnamon	pinch		Add, mix.
Arrowroot	1 Tbs.		Make sauce, add. Simmer, mix to desired consistency. Adjust; reserve.
Cabbage, whole	2 1/2 lbs.		Trim, quarter, core. Cut quarters crosswise. Break apart leaves. Place in steamer. Cook al dente. Place in holding pan.
Sweet and Sour Sauce, above			Add, mix, serve.

Variations:

CABBAGE, CHINESE, AND LENTILS

	Yield:	10 cups	Yield:		Pan size:	4 qt.
	Serves:	10	Serves:		Cooking time:	
	Portion:	1 cup	Portion:		Oven temp.:	

Olive oil	1/3 cup		Place in pan, heat.
Onions, 1/2"-diced	2 cups		Add, saute until clear.
Garlic, finely diced	2 Tbs.		Add, saute.
Chinese cabbage, 1"-diced	2 lbs.		Add, mix, saute 1 min.
Water	1/4 cup		Add.
Cilantro	1/4 cup		Add.
Lentils, cooked, hot (1 cup uncooked)	3 1/3 cups		Add, mix, cover, steam 2 mins. Adjust.
			Serve hot, room temp., or chilled.

Variations:

Pan size:	4 qt.	Yield:	10 cups	Yield:		**CARROTS**
Cooking time:	22 mins.	Serves:	10	Serves:		
Oven temp.:		Portion:	1 cup	Portion:		

Carrots, whole	3½ lbs.		Trim. Place in pan.
Salt	½ tsp.		Add.
Water			Add to cover + 15%. Simmer 22 mins. or until parcooked.
			Serve diced or whole.

Variations: Add thyme, basil, or curry.
Garnish: toasted sesame seeds.

Pan size:	4 qt.	Yield:	10 cups	Yield:		**CARROTS, MINT-GLAZED**
Cooking time:	22 mins.	Serves:	10	Serves:		
Oven temp.:		Portion:	1 cup	Portion:		

Carrots, whole	3½ lbs.		Trim, place in pan.
Salt	½ tsp.		Add.
Water			Add to cover + 15%.
			Simmer 22 mins. or until parcooked. Stop cooking.
While carrots are cooking, make Maple–Mint Glaze (pg. 153)			Add to very hot carrots. Cover, rest 5 mins.
			Serve.

Variations:

CARROTS VICHY

	Yield: 10 cups	Yield:	Pan size: 1 qt./4 qt.
	Serves: 10	Serves:	Cooking time: 30+/- mins.
	Portion: 1 cup	Portion:	Oven temp.:
Water	$^1/_2$ cup		Place in pan.
Corn oil	$^1/_4$ cup		Add.
Maple syrup	$^1/_4$ cup		Add.
Salt	$^1/_4$ tsp.		Add, mix, simmer 1 min. Turn off heat.
Parsley, finely chopped	$^1/_2$ cup		Add, mix, reserve.
Carrots (similar diam., not large)	$2^1/_2$ lbs.		Trim, leave whole. Place in pan.
Salt	$^1/_2$ tsp.		Add.
Water			Add to cover + 15%. Simmer, covered, until parcooked. Drain water.
Glaze, above			Whip, add parsley, mix. Add to carrots.
			Serve.

Variations: To make dish authentic, carrots should be cooked in Vichy water or other bottled mineral water.

CAULIFLOWER

	Yield: 2 lbs. 4 oz.	Yield:	Pan size: 2 qt.
	Serves: 10	Serves:	Cooking time:
	Portion: 3.6 oz.	Portion:	Oven temp.:
Cauliflower	3.3 lbs.		Trim, leave whole. Place in pan.
Water	$^1/_2$"		Add, boil, cover; cook to desired tenderness. Stop cooking.
			Hold in pan if necessary.
			Remove, cut to portions.
			Serve.

Variations: Add salty or rich sauce.
Serve with Curry Sauce (pg. 257), with or without currants.
Serve 1–2"-diced pieces mixed with $^1/_2$ cup tahini, $^1/_4$ cup water, 3 Tbs. lemon juice, $^1/_2$ cup finely chopped parsley.

Pan size:	5 qt.	Yield:	10 cups	Yield:		**CAULIFLOWER &**
Cooking time:	40 mins.	Serves:	10	Serves:		**MILLET, MASHED**
Oven temp.:		Portion:	1 cup	Portion:		

Water	3 cups		Place in pan.
Salt	½ tsp.		Add, boil.
Millet	2 cups		Add, simmer.
Cauliflower, whole	3 lbs.		Trim, add, cover, cook.
			Remove cauliflower when it is tender. Place in bowl; reserve.
			Cook millet 40 mins. until tender. Add to cauliflower. Mix and mash.
Salt	1 tsp.		Add.
			Serve.

Variations: Roast millet first; add tahini; add tamari instead of salt.
Cook onions with millet.
Place in oven, bake at high heat to develop crust.
Garnish: chopped greens and/or sauce.

Pan size:	4 qt.	Yield:	10 cups	Yield:		**CELERY**
Cooking time:	20+/- mins.	Serves:	10	Serves:		
Oven temp.:		Portion:	1 cup	Portion:		

Celery	3.3 lbs.		Trim, ½"-dice. Place in pan.
Salt	½ tsp.		Add.
Water	1 cup		Add, steam until parcooked; stir occasionally.
			Quick-cool to stop cooking.
			Serve.

Variations: Garnish: parsley, Verte Sauce (pg. 267), Hollandaise Sauce, Mock (pg. 259).

CUCUMBERS

| | Yield: 5 cups | Yield: | Pan size: |
| | Serves: 10 | Serves: | Cooking time: |
	Portion: 1/2 cup	Portion:	Oven temp.:
Cucumbers	1.8 lbs.		Trim ends. Cut length in half. Peel in strips. Fork-score peeled strips. Slice or dice. Serve.

Variations: Garnish with olive oil and chopped parsley or a salad dressing.

DAIKON

| | Yield: 30 oz. | Yield: | Pan size: 6 qt. |
| | Serves: 10 | Serves: | Cooking time: 18 mins. |
	Portion: 3 oz.	Portion:	Oven temp.:
Daikon	2 lbs.		Trim, 1/4"-slice. Place in pan.
Salt	1/4 tsp.		Add.
Water			Add to cover + 10%.
			Simmer until *al dente*.
			Serve.

Variations: Garnish: chopped greens and/or Oriental Dip, Tamari–Ginger (pg. 145).

Pan size:	8 qt.	Yield:	10 cups	Yield:		GREENS (KALE), STEAMED
Cooking time:	8–12 mins.	Serves:	10	Serves:		
Oven temp.:		Portion:	1 cup	Portion:		

Kale	1²/₃ lbs.		Trim stems well into leaf. Tear large leaves into pieces. Place in pan.
Water	¹/₂"		Add, cover, turn heat high. Steam 10 mins. until done. Turn once.
			Serve.
			[NOTE: Because stems are very tough, trim completely.]

Variations: Pre-steam with thinly sliced daikon, cauliflower, carrots, or sesame sauce.
Garnish: sesame seeds and/or Tahini Sauce, Basic (pg. 264).
Top with sauces or salad dressings.

Pan size:	lg. skillet	Yield:	10 cups	Yield:		MUSHROOMS
Cooking time:	5 mins.	Serves:	10	Serves:		
Oven temp.:		Portion:	1 cup	Portion:		

Mushrooms, ¹/₂"-sliced	2¹/₂ lbs.		Reserve.
Oil (corn or sesame)	1 cup		Place in pan.
Salt	2 tsp.		Add, distribute. Cook at medium-high heat.
Mushrooms, above			Add, stir often. When color changes completely to gray-tan, remove immediately.
			Serve.

Variations: Add finely diced onions before mushrooms.
Serve plain or combined with a green vegetable.
Cook with a little dark sesame oil.
Add 2 Tbs. Tahini Sauce, Basic (pg. 264) at end of cooking.

MUSHROOMS, STUFFED

Yield: 20	Yield:	Pan size:	
Serves: 10	Serves:	Cooking time: 8+/- mins.	
Portion: 2	Portion:	Oven temp.:	

Mushroom caps, stems removed and reserved	20		Place caps in skillet. Cook as in Mushrooms (pg. 323). Cool, reserve.
Olive oil	1/4 cup		Add to skillet.
Salt	1/2 tsp.		Add.
Onions, finely diced	1/2 cup		Add.
Garlic, finely diced	2 Tbs.		Add.
Mushroom stems, above			Add.
Pepper, black	1/4 tsp.		Add.
Caraway seeds	1 tsp.		Add.
Cinnamon	1/2 tsp.		Add, mix, saute *al dente*.
Beans or rice, well cooked	1 cup		Add, mix, saute until done, adjust. Place in bowl; mix and mash. Fill caps. Serve.

Variations: Add finely diced parsley or cilantro or sesame seeds.
Sprinkle with bread crumbs and roast in oven.

OKRA

Yield: 4 cups	Yield:	Pan size: 4 qt.	
Serves: 10	Serves:	Cooking time: 5+/- mins.	
Portion: .4 cup	Portion:	Oven temp.:	

Corn oil	1/3 cup		Place in skillet.
Onions, 1/4"-diced	2 cups		Add, saute until clear.
Garlic, finely diced	1 Tbs.		Add, saute.
Salt	1 tsp.		Add.
Okra, small	2 1/2 cups		Add; saute until okra slightly changes color (about 5 mins.).
Water	1/2 cup		Add, simmer until tender.
			Serve.

Variations: Add sauteed sliced mushrooms.

ONIONS

Pan size: 4 qt.	Yield: 30 oz.	Yield:
Cooking time: 25 mins.	Serves: 10	Serves:
Oven temp.:	Portion: 3 oz.	Portion:

Onions, 2" diam.	2$^{1}/_{2}$ lbs.		Trim, peel, place whole in pan.
Water			Add to cover + 1". Simmer until cooked. Smaller onions cook faster; larger onions cook more slowly.
			Serve.

Variations: Combine with carrots.
Garnish with Tofu–Tamari Sauce (pg. 266) or Seitan Sauce (pg. 264).

ONIONS, BAKED

Pan size:	Yield: 10 halves	Yield:
Cooking time: 60 mins.	Serves: 10	Serves:
Oven temp.: 325°	Portion: half onion	Portion:

Onions, jumbo	5		Peel, cut in half from top to bottom. Place in baking pan, cut-side up.
Water	1$^{1}/_{2}$ cups		Place in pan.
Tamari	2 tsp.		Add.
Barley malt	$^{1}/_{4}$ cup		Add.
Ginger, finely grated	2 tsp.		Add, mix, simmer 2 mins.
			Pour evenly over each onion half. Cover.
			Bake until tender, about 50 mins.
Walnuts, filberts, or pecans	$^{1}/_{3}$ cup		Chop, place in bowl.
Bread crumbs	$^{1}/_{4}$ cup		Add, mix, reserve.
			Drizzle onions with cooking liquid. Add nut mixture evenly to each onion half.
			Bake at 325° for 10 mins. or until done. Serve.

Variations:

ONIONS, PEARL, GLAZED

	Yield: 6 cups	Yield:	Pan size: 6 qt.
	Serves: 10	Serves:	Cooking time: 20+/- mins.
	Portion: 1/2 cup	Portion:	Oven temp.:
Corn oil	1/4 cup		Place in skillet.
Tamari	2 Tbs.		Add.
Barley malt	1/4 cup		Add, mix. Turn to medium-low heat.
Pearl onions	2 1/2 lbs.		Add, stir gently. Adjust.
			Cover, cook 20+/- mins. until tender.
			Stir gently occasionally. Serve.

Variations: Add grated ginger and/or nutmeg with barley malt.
Bake whole and baste with sauce.

PARSNIPS

	Yield: 30 oz.	Yield:	Pan size: 4 qt.
	Serves: 10	Serves:	Cooking time: 20–25 mins.
	Portion: 3 oz.	Portion:	Oven temp.:
Parsnips	2.3 lbs.		Trim.
Water			Add to cover + 1"; simmer covered until cooked.
			Serve whole, sliced, or diced.

Variations: Add sliced or diced kale.
Cook with lemon juice or finely grated lemon rind.

Pan size: 4 qt.	Yield: 10 cups	Yield:	**PEAS**
Cooking time: 4 mins.	Serves: 10	Serves:	
Oven temp.:	Portion: 1 cup	Portion:	

Mint, finely chopped	¹/₄ cup		Reserve.
Peas	10 cups		Place in pan.
Salt	1 tsp.		Add.
Water			Add to cover, boil 4 mins. until parcooked. Drain water.
Barley malt	2 Tbs.		Add.
Mint, above			Add, mix.
			Serve.

Variations: Add 1 cup shredded lettuce.

Pan size:	Yield: 3¹/₂ lbs.	Yield:	**POTATO, SWEET, BAKED**
Cooking time: 30 mins.	Serves: 10	Serves:	
Oven temp.: 375°	Portion: ¹/₄ lb.	Portion:	

Sweet potatoes	3¹/₂ lbs.		Bake until cooked. Remove skins. Cut to ¹/₄-lb. portions. Serve.

Variations: Add water and mash; adjust water.
Mashed, 1 lb. = 1¹/₂ cups, or *3* ¹/₂-cup portions, or *2* ³/₄-cup portions.

POTATO, SWEET & BAKED CABBAGE

	Yield: 10 cups	Yield:	Pan size:
	Serves: 10	Serves:	Cooking time: 1 hr.
	Portion: 1 cup	Portion:	Oven temp.: 375°

Sweet potatoes, skinned, ¼"-diced	1½ lbs.		Place in pan.
Cabbage, ¾"-diced	1½ lbs.		Add.
Whole wheat pastry flour	2 Tbs.		Add, mix.
Cumin seed	½ tsp.		Add.
Coriander (ground)	½ tsp.		Add, reserve.
Water	1 cup		Place in bowl.
Miso	2 Tbs.		Add, mix, dissolve miso.
			Add to main dish. Mix, cover.
			Bake 1 hr. at 350° or until done.
			Serve.

Variations: ½"-slice and sautee in olive oil and tamari.

POTATO, SWEET, CANDIED

	Yield: 40 oz.	Yield:	Pan size: 1 qt./4 qt.
	Serves: 10	Serves:	Cooking time: 62 mins.
	Portion: 4 oz.	Portion:	Oven temp.: 350°

Sweet potatoes	3½ lbs.		Trim, peel, ¼"-slice; reserve.
Apple cider	1 cup		Place in pan.
Arrowroot	1 tsp.		Add, mix and dissolve.
Barley malt	¼ cup		Add.
Salt	½ tsp.		Add.
Nutmeg	¼ tsp.		Add, mix and dissolve.
Sweet potatoes, above			Place in pan; mix. Shake to settle.
Corn oil	2 Tbs.		Add, sprinkle on top. Cover. Bake 50 mins. or until *al dente*.
Pecans, ½"-diced	1 cup		Uncover dish; sprinkle on top. Bake 12 more mins. uncovered.
			Serve.

Variations:

Pan size:	4 qt.	Yield:	2 3/4 lbs.	Yield:		**RUTABAGA, BOILED**
Cooking time:	20 mins.	Serves:	10	Serves:		
Oven temp.:		Portion:	1/2+ cup	Portion:		

Rutabaga	2 3/4 lbs.		Trim and skin. 3/4"-dice. Place in pan.
Water			Add to cover + 10%. Simmer.
Salt	1/2 tsp.		Add. Cover, simmer 20 mins.

Variations: Add winter squash.
Add cinnamon, cumin, or coriander.
Add vinegar or tamari.

Pan size:	4 qt.	Yield:	10 cups	Yield:		**SQUASH, SUMMER (Yellow)**
Cooking time:	7 mins.	Serves:	10	Serves:		
Oven temp.:		Portion:	1+/- cup	Portion:		

Summer squash, similar size	2.9 lbs.		Trim, 1/4"-slice. Place in pan.
Salt	1/2 tsp.		Add.
Water			Cover. Simmer covered until parcooked.
			Serve.

Variations: Add pepper, celery seed.
Add green beans.
Top with Curry Sauce (pg. 257).

SQUASH, SUMMER (Yellow), SPICED

	Yield: 10 cups	Yield:	Pan size: 4 qt.
	Serves: 10	Serves:	Cooking time: 7 mins.
	Portion: 1 cup	Portion:	Oven temp.:
Water	7 cups		Place in pot.
Bay leaf	2		Add.
Cinnamon	$^1/_2$ tsp.		Add.
Cloves	$^1/_2$ tsp.		Add.
Salt	$^1/_2$ tsp.		Add, mix.
Yellow squash, sliced	11 cups		Add, mix, simmer, covered, until parcooked. Stir occasionally, gently.
			Quick-cool to stop cooking.

Variations: Garnish: chopped parsley.

SQUASH, SUMMER (Yellow or Zucchini)

	Yield: 10 small	Yield:	Pan size: 8 qt.
	Serves: 10	Serves:	Cooking time: 5–10 mins.
	Portion: 1 squash	Portion:	Oven temp.:
Summer squash, whole, small/small-medium	10		Place in pan.
Water	1"		Add; steam.
			Cook *al dente*.
			Serve.

Variations:

Pan size: 4 qt.	Yield: 10 cups	Yield:	**SQUASH, SUMMER**
Cooking time: 4 mins.	Serves: 10	Serves:	**(Zucchini)**
Oven temp.:	Portion: 1 cup	Portion:	

Zucchini	2.9 lbs.		Trim, $1/4$"-slice. Place in pan.
Salt	$1/2$ tsp.		Add.
Water			Add to cover. Simmer covered until parcooked.
			Serve.

Variations: Garnish: basil, thick Cauliflower Puree (pg. 276).

Pan size: 4 qt.	Yield: 10	Yield:	**SQUASH, SUMMER**
Cooking time: 12 mins.	Serves: 10	Serves:	**(Zucchini), ITALIAN**
Oven temp.:	Portion: 1	Portion:	

Olive oil	$1/3$ cup		Place in skillet.
Onions, $1/2$"-diced	1 cup		Add, saute 5 mins.
Garlic, finely diced	1 Tbs.		Add, saute until onions are clear.
Water	4 cups		Add, simmer.
Tamari	2 Tbs.		Add.
Herbs (if any)			Add, simmer 5 mins.
Zucchini, $1/4$"-sliced	$2^1/2$ lbs.		Add, simmer 5 mins. or until parcooked; stir often.
			Stop cooking.
			Serve.

Variations: Add with water: oregano, thyme, sage, and/or tamari.
Saute $1/2$"-sliced mushrooms before onions; reserve. Add more oil and saute onions.

SQUASH, WINTER (Acorn)

	Yield: 5 squash	Yield:	Pan size:
	Serves: 10	Serves:	Cooking time: 1½ hrs.
	Portion: ½ squash	Portion:	Oven temp.: 350°
Squash, acorn	5		Cut in half lengthwise, cut again ¼" parallel to first cut on opposite side. Remove seeds and stringy material. Brush completely with oil. Place in baking dish, cut-side down.
Water	½"		Add. Bake 1 hr. until near tender.
Mushrooms, ¼"-diced	¾ lb.		Place in skillet.
Onions, ¼" diced	2 cups		Add, saute until clear. Turn off heat.
Marjoram, sage, thyme	½+ tsp. ea.		Add.
Tamari	1 Tbs.		Add.
Water	3 Tbs.		Add, mix, simmer 5 mins. Cover; rest 15 mins.
Rice, cooked	8 cups		Add, mix, stuff squash. Bake 15 mins. Serve.

Variations: May be mashed or pureed.

SQUASH, WINTER ("Calbaza"), MEXICAN

	Yield: 10 cups	Yield:	Pan size: 6 qt.
	Serves: 10	Serves:	Cooking time: 20+/- mins.
	Portion: 1 cup	Portion:	Oven temp.:
Squash, winter, peeled, cored	11 cups		1"-dice; place in pan.
Water, hot			Add to half cover.
Anise seed	2 tsp.		Add, mix.
Barley malt	2 Tbs.		Add, mix.
Sea salt	½ tsp.		Add, mix, simmer covered until tender.
			Serve.

Variations:

Pan size:	Yield:	10 halves	Yield:		**SQUASH, WINTER**
Cooking time: 70 mins.	Serves:	10	Serves:		**(Acorn), WITH**
Oven temp.: 350°	Portion:	1 half	Portion:		**CRANAPPLE**

Acorn squash, medium-small	5		Trim. Cut in half lengthwise. Remove seeds.
			Baste inside and out with soy oil. Place cut-side down on oiled baking pan. Bake 40 mins. at 350°.
Cranberries, chopped	2$\frac{1}{2}$ cups		Place in bowl.
Apple, cored, $\frac{1}{4}$"-diced	2$\frac{1}{2}$ cups		Add.
Barley malt	$\frac{3}{4}$ cup		Add.
Oil	3 Tbs.		Add.
Lemon rind, grated	1 Tbs.		Add, mix.
			When squash has baked 40 mins., fill with fruit mixture. Bake 30 mins. until done.
			Serve.

Variations:

Pan size: 4 qt.	Yield:	10 cups	Yield:		**SQUASH, WINTER**
Cooking time: 45 mins.	Serves:	10	Serves:		**(Buttercup)**
Oven temp.: 350°	Portion:	1	Portion:		

Water	1 cup		Place in pan.
Brown rice flour	4 tsp.		Add, mix. Simmer 10 mins. Stir often.
Tamari	1 tsp.		Add, mix, reserve.
Buttercup squash			Peel, core, $\frac{3}{4}$"-dice. Place in pan.
Water			Add to cover. Simmer until cooked; stir. Pour off excess water.
Sauce, above			Add, mix.
			Bake 35 mins. until done. Adjust sauce and tamari.
			Serve.

Variations: Garnish with diced green onions or parsley, Sauce Verte (pg. 267), Raisin–Apple Cider Sauce (pg. 263), or Raisin–Nut Dip (pg. 146).

SQUASH, WINTER (Butternut)

	Yield: 10 cups	Yield:	Pan size:
	Serves: 10	Serves:	Cooking time: 30 mins.
	Portion: 1 cup	Portion:	Oven temp.: 325°
Water	1/4 cup		Place in baking pan.
Tamari	2 Tbs.		Add, mix.
Squash, butternut			Trim, 1"-slice, place in oiled baking pan. Rest 5 mins. Turn over.
			Bake 10 mins. at 325°. Turn squash over; cover.
			Bake another 20 mins. covered.
			Serve.

Variations:

SQUASH, WINTER (Delicota)

	Yield: 10 cups	Yield:	Pan size: 4 qt.
	Serves: 10	Serves:	Cooking time: 15+/- mins.
	Portion: 1 cup	Portion:	Oven temp.:
Squash, delicota	10 cups		Trim, 1/4"-slice, remove seeds and strings. Place in pan.
Salt	1 tsp.		Add.
Water			Add to cover; simmer, covered, 15 mins. or until done (firm but tender).
			Serve.

Variations: Garnish: Seitan Sauce (pg. 264).

STIR FRIES

Pan size:	lg. skillet	Yield:	10 cups	Yield:	
Cooking time: 7 mins.		Serves:	10	Serves:	
Oven temp.:		Portion:	1 cup	Portion:	

Mise en Place:			
Sesame oil	$^1/_2$ cup		Place in skillet, medium-high heat.
Carrots, thinly sliced	1 cup		Add. Saute 1 min.
Onions	2 cups		Add, mix, saute 2 mins.
Broccoli florets	2 cups		Add, mix, saute 2 mins.
Chinese cabbage	7 cups		Add, mix, saute 1 min.
Water	2 Tbs.		Add.
Tamari	2 Tbs.		Add, mix, steam 1 min. Stop cooking.
			Serve.

Variations:

TREASURE OF VEGETABLES

[from Chef Huang, Hotel Suzhou Restaurant, Canton, China]

Pan size:	wok	Yield:	$4^1/_2$ cups	Yield:	
Cooking time: 10 mins.		Serves:	8	Serves:	
Oven temp.:		Portion:	$^1/_2$ cup	Portion:	

Mise en Place:			
Bamboo shoots, $^1/_8$"-sliced	$^3/_4$ cup		Reserve.
Mushrooms, $^1/_8$"-sliced	$^3/_4$ cup		Reserve.
Green beans, 1"-chopped	3 cups		Reserve.
Peanut oil	$^1/_4$ cup		Place in wok, high flame.
Mushrooms and bamboo shoots, above			Add, stir fry 2 mins. Remove mushrooms and bamboo shoots and set aside.
Brown rice flour	2 Tbs.		Add.
Water	$^1/_2$ cup		Add, cook 4 mins.
Green beans, above			Add to wok, high flame, 3 mins.
Mushrooms and bamboo shoots			Add.
Salt	$^1/_2$ tsp.		Add, stir.
Water	$^1/_2$ cup		Add, stir, reduce heat, stir fry 1 min.; serve.

Variations:

TURNIPS, BOILED

	Yield: 30 oz.	Yield:	Pan size: 6 qt.
	Serves: 10	Serves:	Cooking time: 35–40 mins.
	Portion: 3 oz.	Portion:	Oven temp.:

Turnips, whole			Add to pan.
Water			Add to cover + 20%.
Salt	½ tsp.		Add. Simmer 35–40 mins.
			When cooked, drain water, cover with cold water for 1 min., drain; cut and trim, ½" -dice.
			Serve with sauce.

Variations: Serve with Tahini Sauce, Basic (pg. 264), Mushroom Sauce, Basic (pg. 260).

	Yield:	Yield:	Pan size:
	Serves:	Serves:	Cooking time:
	Portion:	Portion:	Oven temp.:

Variations:

RECIPE INDEX BY CATEGORY

ALPHABETICAL RECIPE INDEX

MAIL ORDER NATURAL FOODS

HIGH-QUALITY ☆ HARD-TO-FIND

- Cereal Grains
- Whole Grain Pasta
- Beans and Legumes
- Nuts, Seeds, and Nut Butters
- Oils
- Vinegar
- Sea Vegetables
- Tamari (soy sauce)
- Miso

Send for our catalogue:

**North Star Products
P.O. Box 37, Corner of Main and Commonwealth
Hyde Park, Vermont 05655**

☆ EASY ☆ INTRODUCTORY ☆

KITCHEN SET-UP ORDERS

FAMILY SIZE $49.95		PROFESSIONAL SIZE $199.95
5 lbs.	SHORT-GRAIN BROWN RICE	25 lbs.
1 lb.	ROASTED BUCKWHEAT GROATS	5 lbs.
1 lb.	ORGANIC CHICK PEAS	5 lbs.
8 oz.	WHOLE WHEAT NOODLES	10 lbs.
1 lb.	SUNFLOWER SEEDS	5 lbs.
16 oz.	CORN OIL	1 gallon
16 oz.	TAHINI	3 lbs.
1 pint	BARLEY MALT SYRUP	3 pints
8 oz.	WAKAME SEA VEGETABLES	2.2 lbs.
1 lb.	BARLEY MISO	4 lbs.
16 oz.	TAMARI (SOY SAUCE)	32 oz.

PRICES SUBJECT TO CHANGE WITHOUT NOTICE

ORDER FORMS

Please send me *WORKING CHEF'S COOKBOOK FOR NATURAL WHOLE FOODS.*

_____ copies @ $18.97 each = $_____

Shipping/Handling = $_____

Total = $_____

To: _____
_____
_____
_____

Shipping/Handling Charges
4th Class: $2.00 for the first book; $1.00 for each additional book.

Please make out check and send order to:
Central Vermont Publishers
P.O. Box 700
Morrisville, Vermont 05661

If not fully satisfied with the book, return it for a full refund within 30 days.

- -

Please send me *WORKING CHEF'S COOKBOOK FOR NATURAL WHOLE FOODS.*

_____ copies @ $18.97 each = $_____

Shipping/Handling = $_____

Total = $_____

To: _____
_____
_____
_____

Shipping/Handling Charges
4th Class: $2.00 for the first book; $1.00 for each additional book.

Please make out check and send order to:
Central Vermont Publishers
P.O. Box 700
Morrisville, Vermont 05661

If not fully satisfied with the book, return it for a full refund within 30 days.

- -

Please send me *WORKING CHEF'S COOKBOOK FOR NATURAL WHOLE FOODS.*

_____ copies @ $18.97 each = $_____

Shipping/Handling = $_____

Total = $_____

To: _____
_____
_____
_____

Shipping/Handling Charges
4th Class: $2.00 for the first book; $1.00 for each additional book.

Please make out check and send order to:
Central Vermont Publishers
P.O. Box 700
Morrisville, Vermont 05661

If not fully satisfied with the book, return it for a full refund within 30 days.

GIFT ORDER FORM

A GREAT GIFT IDEA FOR BRIDES ... BIRTHDAYS ...
GRADUATES ... YOUR FAVORITE CHEF OR
RESTAURANT OWNER ...

Mail your order to:
Central Vermont Publishers
P.O. Box 700
Morrisville, Vermont 05661

I would like to order _____ copies of *Working Chef's Cookbook for Natural Whole Foods*, to be sent to the people listed below. I have enclosed $18.97 plus $2.00 shipping/handling for each copy I have ordered.

NAME: _____

ADDRESS: _____

_____

GIFT CARD: _____

NAME: _____

ADDRESS: _____

_____

GIFT CARD: _____

NAME: _____

ADDRESS: _____

_____

GIFT CARD: _____

YOUR NAME: _____

ADDRESS: _____

_____

_____